THE BLUE BANNER

Henry Poole MacKeen, QC (1892–1971), charter trustee of
Saint David's, who successfully argued on behalf of
The Presbyterian Church in Canada the only church union
case to reach the Judicial Committee of the Privy Council.
Reproduced by permission of the portraitist, Brenda Bury
of Toronto; www.brendabury.com

The Blue Banner

The Presbyterian Church
of Saint David
and Presbyterian Witness in Halifax

BARRY CAHILL, LAURENCE DEWOLFE,
MURRAY ALARY, ELIZABETH A. CHARD,
AND LOIS YORKE

Published for the Presbyterian Church of Saint David
by
McGill-Queen's University Press
Montreal & Kingston · London · Ithaca

© McGill-Queen's University Press 2008
ISBN 978-0-7735-3358-5

Legal deposit second quarter 2008
Bibliothèque nationale du Québec

Printed in Canada on acid-free paper.

This book has been published with the help of a grant from
The Presbyterian Church of Saint David, Halifax, Nova Scotia.
www.saintdavids.ca.

McGill-Queen's University Press acknowledges the support of the Canada
Council for the Arts for our publishing program. We also acknowledge
the financial support of the Government of Canada through the Book
Publishing Industry Development Program (BPIDP) for our publishing
activities.

Library and Archives Canada Cataloguing in Publication

The blue banner: the Presbyterian Church of Saint David and
Presbyterian witness in Halifax / Barry Cahill ... [et al.].
Includes bibliographical references and index.

ISBN 978-0-7735-3358-5

1. Presbyterian Church of Saint David (Halifax, N.S.) – History.
2. Presbyterian Church – Nova Scotia – Halifax – History. I. Cahill, Barry
II. Presbyterian Church of Saint David (Halifax, N.S.)

BX9215.H28B59 2008   285'.2716225   C2007-905751-9

Typeset in New Baskerville 10/13
by Infoscan Collette, Quebec City

Contents

Preface

The idea for this book was first articulated at the outset of Saint David's seventy-fifth anniversary year – January 2000 – when the then new minister, Laurence DeWolfe, suggested at a meeting of the Mission and Outreach Committee of the Kirk Session that a history of Saint David's should be written. Everyone concurred, but no one saw how it could be done. The omens were not propitious; there was no one to write such a book, and past experience had taught that it would have to be official and authorized, as well as finished and published.

Nothing could have been done immediately and nothing was. But another important initiative was about to proceed more quickly on a parallel track. The late elder Elizabeth A. Chard, then secretary (afterwards chair) of the Board, became concerned about preservation of the congregation's records, and as a result, Session retained a member who was a professional archivist to investigate and report. In due course, he joined the Board and was appointed congregational archivist; Session and Board set up a joint standing committee on records management; a congregational records management policy was developed and approved; and improvements were made to the church's record-keeping practices. The work plan of the Records Management Committee revived the prospect of a scholarly history of the congregation.

Serious work on the book began in July 2002 and continued through December 2005; research and writing proceeded as time permitted. The church history project's debts are legion, and the committee takes pleasure in acknowledging them with most grateful thanks to all concerned. Dr John Pace, minister emeritus, turned over his nearly complete set of church bulletins from the beginning of his twenty-two-year pastorate, as well as other valuable documents bearing on his ministry. Dr W. James S. Farris wrote an account of his term as interim minister in 1998–99. Dr DeWolfe, minister since September 1999, contributed the section dealing with his own pastorate – a work in progress – as well as the relevant section to the chapter on worship.

The late Ross Nelson (Larry) MacLean, director of music from 1961 through 2006, shared invaluable reminiscences and papers and reviewed the preliminary draft of the chapter on music. The children of Frank Lawson, minister in the years 1945–65, shared reminiscences and papers of their father. Malcolm B. (Mac) Mackay, MNSAA, and Mary (Molly) Harvey, children of Dr Donald B. Mackay, minister from 1966 to 1975, did likewise. Elder Mackay also wrote the biographical part of the section on his father as well as the architectural analysis of the church buildings. Roberta (Shaw) Pocklington wrote an account of her three years as director of Christian Education, 1960–63. The Reverend Amy Campbell wrote of her two years as pastoral assistant, 1980–82; Wendy Booth, then president of the Ladies Guild, wrote a narrative of the Guild; journalist Carol Dobson, editor of the quarterly newsletter, *At Saint David's*, transcribed all the inscriptions on memorial gifts, plaques, and windows; and Donald F. Maclean, a long-time member, provided much valuable information through correspondence and conversation. Elders Melvin and Patricia Calkin, both retired professors at Dalhousie University, wrote about their discovery of Saint David's, and Patricia critically reviewed the entire manuscript. Judith Moreira (née MacKeen), daughter of a "father of the church" and, as first woman chair of the Board, a historical figure in her own right, graciously shared many valuable reminiscences. Retired elder George Miller, a former chair of the Board, shared written recollections of his years as convener of property.

Dr John R. Cameron, moderator of the 117th (1991) General Assembly of The Presbyterian Church in Canada, graciously responded to many queries and facilitated access to the archives of the Atlantic Synod, of which he was then clerk. Dr Cameron wisely initiated a project to microfilm Synod minutes, which was taken up and carried through to completion by Joan Cho, Synod convener of history. Dr J.J. Edmiston shared reminiscences of and papers relating to his years in Halifax as minister of Knox Church and clerk of Presbytery. Dr George McNeill shared information and insight on evangelist Tom Allan's 1961 mission to Halifax; Maggie Boulter, Tom Allan's daughter, did likewise. Dr L. George Macdonald, until January 2007 minister of Knox Church, Halifax, shared reminiscences and provided access to Knox's records. The Reverend E.M. Iona MacLean, the first woman ordained in the Atlantic Synod, shared reminiscences of her own early ministry, as well as of her father's long pastorate at Knox Church.

Professional research assistance was provided by Taunya Dawson, the Reverend Janet DeWolfe, Maggie DeWolfe, Heather Long, and Bill Naftel (Halifax); Marlene Chisholm (New Glasgow); Donna Beal (Sackville); Gillian Liebenberg and Graeme Somerville (Saint John); Jody Perrun and Jeff Noakes (Ottawa); Diana Fancher (Toronto); Carolyn Webber (Victoria); Jennifer Irwin (Belfast, Northern Ireland); and Jean Brodie (Edinburgh, Scotland). Kim Arnold and Bob Anger, respectively archivist and assistant archivist at The Presbyterian Church in Canada Archives and Records Office (Toronto), were unfailingly helpful, as were Judith Colwell (archivist, Maritime Conference Archives, United Church of Canada, Sackville, New Brunswick) and Cheryl Ennals (university archivist, Mount Allison University). The committee extends very special thanks to Twila Buttimer, of the Provincial Archives of New Brunswick, and to Garry Shutlak, senior archivist, Reference Services, Nova Scotia Archives and Records Management, who generously shared his vast personal knowledge of architectural history and his unpublished research on David Stirling. Line Francœur of Casavant Frères Ltée (St-Hyacinthe, Quebec) responded to many queries and supplied copies of documents from the file on Saint David's 1928 organ.

A substantial grant in aid of research was awarded by Halifax Regional Municipality in 2003 under its Community Grants Program. Generous financial support was also received from the Session and Board of Saint David's, as well as from the Presbytery of Halifax and Lunenburg. Judith Moreira provided a generous gift in aid of publication. She also shared many invaluable reminiscences. Individual members of Saint David's have been more than generous in their personal support and encouragement; alas, they must remain anonymous.

As in any work with a collective author, the committee members are indebted to each other in ways both great and small, tangible and intangible. In every sense, however, our greatest debt is to the members and adherents of Saint David's past, present, and future. This book was written for them and is theirs. *Amen – Glory to God.*

The Presbyterian Church of Saint David
   Records Management Committee
Barry Cahill, convener
   for and on behalf of
The Reverend D. Laurence DeWolfe, DMin
Murray W. Alary
†Dr Elizabeth A. Chard
Lois K. Yorke

Note: Shortly before her untimely death on 5 May 2007, Elizabeth Chard arranged for a substantial gift in aid of publication. She offered this in memory of her parents, Robert Reid and Mamie (Withrow) Hutton, and her paternal grandparents, William Wallace and Laura (Boutilier) Hutton, who were pillars of Saint David's and who would have taken great pride in Elizabeth's role in bringing this work to fruition.

Abbreviations

AST	Atlantic School of Theology
CGIT	Canadian Girls in Training
DUA	Dalhousie University Archives
MCA	Maritime Conference Archives (of the United Church of Canada)
NSARM	Nova Scotia Archives and Records Management
PCA	Presbyterian Church Association
PCC	The Presbyterian Church in Canada
PCOSD	Presbyterian Church of Saint David
PYPS	Presbyterian Young People's Society
RCCO	Royal Canadian College of Organists
RCO	Royal College of Organists
SDA	Saint David's Auxiliary
SMU	Saint Mary's University
UCC	United Church of Canada
VON	Victorian Order of Nurses
WMS	Woman's Missionary Society
WPA	World Presbyterian Alliance

Frederick B. Schell, "Halifax, from Citadel"; etching [after 1879]; from an unidentified periodical of the period. Grafton Street Methodist Church appears towards the upper right-hand corner.

"From St Mary's [Roman Catholic Cathedral] Spire, Looking Northwest"; reproduced from *Halifax, Nova Scotia and Its Attractions* ([Halifax?]: Howard & Kutsche, 1902). Grafton Street Methodist Church appears at the lower left.

The Reverend James Campbell of
Glencairn Parish Church, Scotland,
who was called to Saint David's in 1925
but declined (PCOSD archives)

West interior of the second Grafton Street Methodist Church
before the 1911 renovations (PCOSD archives)

Dr Kerr (left), caught in an informal pose,
probably during the annual meeting of
the Maritimes Synod held at Saint David's
in October 1935 (PCOSD archives)

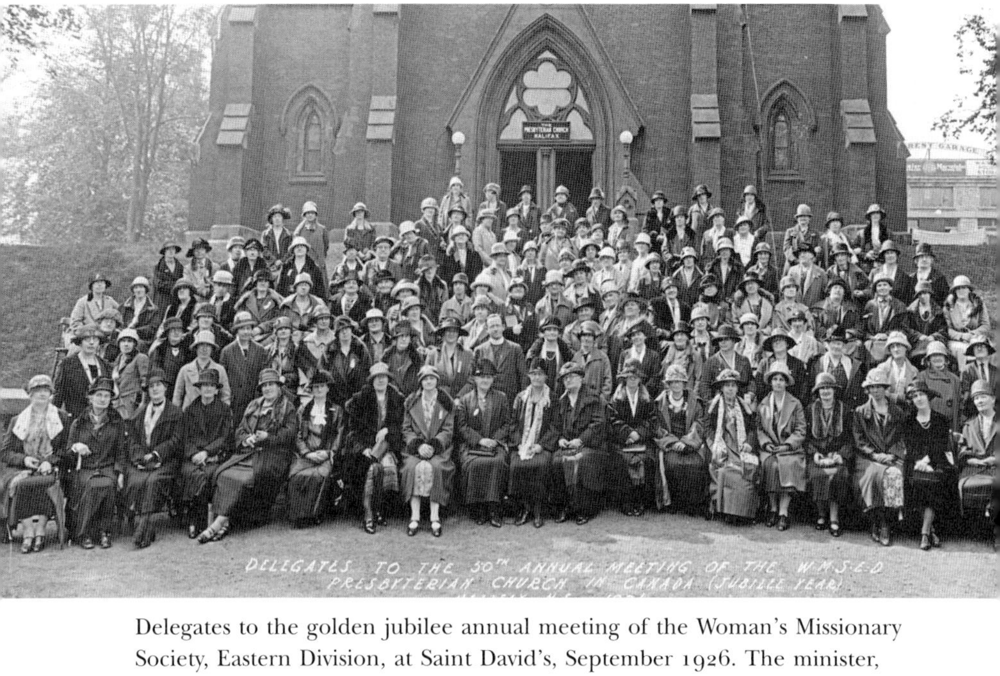

Delegates to the golden jubilee annual meeting of the Woman's Missionary
Society, Eastern Division, at Saint David's, September 1926. The minister,
Dr Colin Kerr, is in the middle of the second row. (PCOSD archives)

Manse housewarming, October 1946; the minister, Frank Lawson, a bachelor, had arrived a year earlier. J.W. Merrimen photo (PCOSD archives)

Saint David's twenty-fourth birthday celebration, 28 February 1949. Mrs James McGregor Stewart Sr (Julia Creelman) is flanked by Elizabeth Ann Hutton (Chard), afterwards elder, superintendent of the Church School, and chair of the Board, and the minister, Frank Lawson. (PCOSD archives); reproduced by permission of The Halifax Herald Limited

Saint David's Choral Christmas. E.A. Bollinger photographer, 1949 (NSARM, Edward A. Bollinger fonds, 1975-307, negative no. 49229); used by permission

Saint David's in winter (after 1950). Edu Ali Godfrey photo
(PCOSD archives)

Saint David's silver jubilee celebration, 28 February 1950. Cutting the anniversary cake is Mrs Henry Delby Creighton (Helen Robson), granddaughter of the minister of the first Presbyterian church in Halifax. Flanking the ladies are clerk of Session W.J. Kane (left) and the minister, Frank Lawson (right). (PCOSD archives)

Saint David's Sunday School picnic at the MacKeen estate ("Maplewood"), 7 September 1957. Photograph by Dr Forest W. Fyfe; reproduced by courtesy of his son, Mac Fyfe

Saint David's east wall facade, from Grafton Street (after 1965).
H.P. Snider photo (PCOSD archives)

Ross Nelson MacLean early in his tenure as director of music
at Saint David's, 1961–2006 (PCOSD archives)

Commissioners to the 96th General Assembly of the Presbyterian Church in Canada, held at Saint David's, June 1970. Photographic Associates photo (PCOSD archives)

The Presbyterian Church in Canada centenary year congregational portrait, May 1974. Wamboldt-Waterfield Photo (PCOSD archives)

MINISTER
REV. D.B. MACKAY C.D., D.D.
PUBLIC WORSHIP
SUNDAY   28 TH MAY
A.M.   WHERE IS JESUS ?
ORGANIST ROSS N.M.LEAN
EVERYBODY WELCOME

Saint David's diamond jubilee congregational portrait, Palm Sunday, 31 March 1985. Blair Davis Photo (PCOSD archives)

Ordination of Catherine Calkin, 18 October 1989. On the left is the Reverend John Pace, minister of Saint David's, and on the right the Reverend D. Lawrence Mawhinney, moderator of Presbytery, who conducted the ordination service and preached the sermon. Wamboldt-Waterfield Photo (PCOSD archives); reproduced by permission of The Halifax Herald Limited

On the tenth of June in 1925 The Presbyterian Church in Canada was rent in two. The proposed union with the Methodists and the Congregationalists in the formation of the United Church of Canada gave rise to more bad feeling than any other issue in the history of those churches. The feeling that this controversy aroused has not altogether subsided even yet.

Revisiting the subject obviously involves some risk. I certainly have no desire to reopen old wounds. I do hope to suggest why the positions of the two sides made sense to them at the time so that this may encourage good relations between the current successors of the parties involved. At the very least I hope that people will gain a better understanding of what happened.

John Webster Grant,
Divided Heritage: The Presbyterian Contribution to the United Church of Canada
(Yorkton, Sask., 2007), preface; reprinted by permission

"The Church on Pizza Corner"

The Presbyterian Church of Saint David in Halifax, Nova Scotia, has been, through its history, both a sign of the times and a sign of contradiction. The city's churchless anti-church-union Presbyterians of 1925 found sanctuary in a Methodist building that had become vacant and surplus because of church union. For eighty years since, Saint David's has stood as a beacon on the little hill overlooking Grafton Park, once the Poor House burying ground and afterwards home to the Spring Garden Road Memorial Public Library. Yet Saint David's arrival on the southwestern corner of Grafton and Blowers streets was as accidental and unforeseen as the first appearance of Grafton Street Methodist Church on the same site was not. For fifty years, 1793–1844, it was home to the Old Methodist Burying Ground of Halifax. Here William Black, the "Apostle of Methodism" in the Maritime provinces, lies buried. The ground on which Saint David's stands is thus among the holiest sites of Methodism in eastern Canada.

Today Saint David's remains as striking and imposing as ever, but its environment is much more problematic than in 1869, when the second of the two church buildings on the site was dedicated, or in 1925, when the congregation found a home there.[1] Given its situation, Saint David's has probably never been near the residences of most of its members, and its being Jonah in the belly of the whale is both a blessing and a curse – an opportunity and a challenge. "God in the city" is not fashionable. It may not have occurred to the graffitist who once scrawled "F*** God" on the pavement outside the church door that neither God nor the worshippers within repay in the same coin. The church shares the intersection of Grafton and Blowers with fast-food eateries and is within easy walking distance of hotels, restaurants, taverns, coffee bars, and shops both trendy and quirky. Its property hosts street people and diners and intermittently serves as a public convenience, garbage drop, and venue for dealers and their clients – the church is smack in the midst of the downtown drug corridor. Nevertheless, though it suffers the ravages of casual or even directed vandalism and burglary, the church, thanks in part to its very intrusiveness, remains the still point of the swirling world around it.

Saint David's' inner-city identity belies the makeup of its congregation: few, if any, members reside in the area of the church, and some travel a considerable distance to attend. The worshipping community consists of members (communicants) and adherents (supporters) new and old alike, Presbyterian travellers from out of province, and the unchurched. The congregation includes many men and women whose parents or grandparents founded the church; the last of the charter members survived until 2002. The church welcomes all people to worship and all Christians to the communion table.

Despite its traditionalism and apparent conservatism, Saint David's is and has always been strongly evangelical. It is keenly aware of what it is and, more importantly, *where* it is. Its home mission field is the wide, messy world just outside the door. The weekly chowder luncheons conducted by the Ladies Guild during Lent are a downtown Halifax institution. The Blue Christmas Service, inaugurated in 2000, reaches out to people bewildered if not traumatized by the holiday season. Saint David's tries to get to know those who cross the threshold. Though far more regulars – not to mention all the leaders – now enter through the church hall door rather than the front door of the church proper, climbing the steep staircase in order to shake hands with the "welcoming elder" is worth the effort. For unaffiliated Christians seeking the public worship of God, it is a rite of passage from the unbelieving world.

Declining and aging membership helps explain why Saint David's strongly emphasizes intergenerational transition, families as collective members, and children and youth as prospective members and leaders. The active part of the congregation may be shrinking, but it looks hopefully forward rather than smugly backwards to a heroic past. No future could have been or have appeared more uncertain than that facing the fathers and mothers of 1925. Had Presbyterianism been completely extinguished in Halifax, it would not have been especially missed or mourned.

Indeed, non-Presbyterians were bemused by the schism in The Presbyterian Church in Canada (PCC), in 1925 the largest Protestant denomination in the country. Only the Baptists understood what the non-uniting minority Presbyterians were *really* fighting for – evangelical preaching; not a purely social gospel, nor saccharine pietism, nor secular humanism, but

"Christ crucified, unto the Jews a stumbling-block, and unto the Greeks foolishness" (1 Corinthians 1:23). Regardless of whether the social gospel or any other variation on gospel themes was to blame for the church union disaster – as many Presbyterian resisters thought – the resistance to church union climaxed in a revival, a great reawakening. And what more appropriate venue to launch an evangelical renewal than a Wesleyan sanctuary. A viable Presbyerian congregation was planted, put down deep roots, and gradually became acclimatized to and identified with its new-found home.

Over its eighty-year history, the physical and social environment of Saint David's has changed beyond all recognition. It has had to "morph" from an accidental congregation in the inner city to an inner-city church, a transition fraught with difficulty. Saint David's is from another time and place – or, rather, places. Though an ad hoc response to a moment of extreme crisis in the history of a mainstream Protestant denomination, Saint David's has always striven not to be constrained or constricted by its past.

Among the paradoxes of the church is the discrepancy between the real and the official congregation. The real congregation is the body of people present at traditional worship on Sunday morning. Its numbers and makeup vary from Sunday to Sunday and season to season. Today's Presbyterians are not strict Sabbatarians. It is more important to maintain one's formal connection with the church through professing membership and financial support than by attending worship on a frequent or regular basis or even at all. Affiliating non-attenders are proud of their affiliation and reluctant to have their names struck off the communion roll.[2] But this official, "social" membership is generally inactive and non-participatory.

Attendance at worship is seasonally adjusted. In summer it plummets, but it is restored when public school and church school resume in the autumn. The high holy days of Christmas and Easter and personal or congregational milestones such as the induction of a new minister or the golden-jubilee rededication of the marriage of a senior elder draw the infrequent or first- or only-time worshipper. The memorial service, on a Saturday afternoon in August, for the much-loved widow of a former minister of the church could fill the sanctuary, but the church be largely empty the following Sunday morning.

"The family that worships together stays together" might be the church's motto. Families, nuclear or intergenerational, usually attend as a group or not at all. The church is a community of families and individuals and is both a worshipping and a social body. Members and adherents know and help each other, not only in the church but also in the world. As a group, they minister to other Presbyterians, other Christians, and other people.

More than one friendship leading to marriage has been forged in the church. The age and gender imbalance – older and female – though palpable, enriches rather than debilitates the congregation. No effort is spared to welcome visitors, encouraging them to share in worship and post-worship fellowship and, most importantly, to return again.

Who are the members of St David's? On the face of it, the congregation is rather unselfconsciously upper middle class. The independently wealthy jell and jostle with the corporate, legal, medical, and professional elite. At least two lieutenant-governors have worshipped here, one of them a charter member. Politicians are in evidence, especially around election time, as are backroomers and bagmen on a more regular basis. Elite lawyers have always been prominent. The congregation includes a former chief justice and a former attorney general, sitting and retired judges, and a former president of the Canadian Bar Association. In earlier days the chair of the board of governors and the president of Dalhousie University were both members, and Dalhousie's faculty was well represented. Like Fort Massey United in its Presbyterian heyday, Saint David's is a church of choice for the Halifax establishment. It is nothing if not dignified; it has cachet. Appearances, however, can be deceptive. Saint David's is not embarrassed by who it is, yet it remains consistently open and responsive to those who it is not.

As an inner-city church, Saint David's shares its territory with street people and pub-crawlers. When it sleeps, the city is wide awake. By nine o'clock on Sunday morning, when an informal communion service takes place in the chancel, the street is deserted, except for the flotsam and jetsam: gulls, garbage, and, on occasion, a homeless person, sound asleep, curled up on the sidewalk against the retaining wall below the front of the church. By eleven o'clock, when traditional worship takes place, the world is finally waking up. In a city of joggers and coffee-shop habitués, the Sabbath is honoured more in the breach than the observance. Despite its brownstone eminence above the street, Saint David's is criss-crossed and encircled by people who pound the pavement in search of drugs, fast food, money, and shelter.

This book follows Saint David's from its beginnings as a new congregation and the only site of Presbyterian witness in metropolitan Halifax. It focuses not only on the resumption of congregational life for churchless Presbyterian resisters but also on the survival and reconstruction of the church. In Halifax, continuing Presbyterians were not just a minority but a rump; on 10 June 1925 the PCC as it had existed for fifty years simply vanished from the scene. Saint David's, once established, represented a new birth of Presbyterianism.

The very existence of Saint David's highlights the ambiguities and contradictions of church union in Atlantic Canada. How could the Presbyterian Church rise from near-death in a city that was as solidly unionist as any in the country? Saint David's was not a congregation that voted out of the new United Church; it was a brand new congregation consisting of Presbyterians who voted with their feet when their home congregations all voted to confirm their membership in the United Church. So "The Presbyterian Church, Halifax" (as it was originally known) counted among its charter members persons from all nine existing Presbyterian churches.[3]

Another focus of the book is how the congregation coped with the negative memory of its conflicted origins and learned to offer a positive, non-sectarian message of Christian hope. The long struggle for survival and reconstruction of the church cast an even longer shadow over the congregation's equilibrium and sustained an ongoing identity crisis: twenty years later, church union was still seen as a destructive struggle for true-blue Presbyterian witness. The foundational myth of Saint David's, as with all congregations that came into existence during and as a result of the Disruption, was that church union was a recession from those Scottish Reformation principles underlying The Presbyterian Church in Canada.

Saint David's is heir to no less than four Scottish Presbyterian traditions which, in the half-century after 1800, each gave rise to congregations in Halifax – the Secession,[4] the Relief,[5] the Kirk, and the Free.[6] These four streams converged in the establishment in 1875 of The Presbyterian Church in Canada. That merger was followed fifty years later by a disunification crisis that split the church and many of its congregations. The Presbyterian Church, Halifax, was a patchwork made up of seceders from nine congregations, ranging from the very old (St Matthew's) to the nearly new (Stairs Memorial), each with distinctive house traditions at once generally the same but differing in detail. Saint David's was neither more nor less than the sum of its parts, and its parts did not coalesce overnight.

The new congregation, which could call itself "The Presbyterian Church, Halifax" because there were no longer any others, was a frozen-in-time snapshot of The Presbyterian Church in Canada on the eve of the Disruption. From Park Street and Fort Massey came the Chinese Sunday School. From St Matthew's came the style of administering communion, "debts" rather than "trespasses" in the Lord's Prayer, and the Christmas Coffee Party and Bazaar, founded in 1911. The first, provisional Kirk Session comprised all those who had been elders in their former congregations; the first clerk of Session had held the same office at Park Street.[7]

A final focus of the book is Saint David's place in the community. It has cooperated with other churches in social-service ventures such as the Interfaith Housing Corporation and the Interchurch Group Home for Boys (Genesis House). For a decade it offered a Wednesday afternoon playschool aimed at underprivileged children in its own neighbourhood. More recently, it has joined with the Halifax Victorian Order of Nurses (VON) to offer a weekly Friday morning clinic for the benefit of downtown Halifax's underclass.

Saint David's principal outreach, however, apart from presbytery pulpit exchange and anniversary services, has been to Presbyterian congregations that are smaller, less advantaged, or more recently established. Having begun by keeping Presbyterianism alive in Halifax, Saint David's has since 1925 been the mother church, giving moral and financial support to six other new PCC congregations in what is now Halifax Regional Municipality.[8]

Saint David's has also assimilated or co-opted social change and is more a mirror of shifting attitudes inside The Presbyterian Church in Canada than in society at large. It has provided two moderators of the Maritimes (Atlantic) Synod, and its members have served on standing committees of the PPC's governing body. It has also been a loyal and generous supporter of the schemes, ministries, and special initiatives of the PCC. Thus it gives to the world through the larger church of which it forms part, and in whose survival and reconstruction it played so significant a role.

Yet reaction against what its founders believed to be the secularizing tendencies of the social gospel has had a lingering effect on how Saint David's people view the world around them. Saint David's is known for its proclamation of a spiritual (though not pietistic) message, rather than a social or political one, and thus its principal contribution to religious life in Halifax has been liturgy and music.

The focus is therefore the congregation ministering to itself, but that ministry is by no means exclusively spiritual or worship-related. Saint David's carries on an extensive program aimed principally at supporting the life and mission of the congregation and building community among its members. The orientation is internal, yet the program is diverse and fosters socialization as well as personal and communal growth. The most popular activity is Sunday's post-worship coffee hour, the chief means by which the congregation keeps in touch and encourages new worshippers.

The history of Saint David's is rich in examples of collective and collaborative effort well beyond the strict confines of public worship and the official workings of Session and Board. Outreach is usually delivered through organizations internal and specific to the congregation, but may also spring from initiatives at the Presbytery, Synod, or General Assembly level. The largest, hardest-working, and most successful undertaking has always been the Ladies Guild, whose late autumn fundraiser, the Holly Tea and Sale, is the high-water mark of the congregation's year. Likewise, the Guild's Lenten chowder luncheons and Christmas Families program typify the congregation's subtle and understated approach to outreach.

In the process of replanting and growing Presbyterianism in Halifax, Saint David's has reprised its own early history. It is still resisting; it has not conformed. The 1925 downgrading, almost overnight, of The Presbyterian Church in Canada from a large, prestigious, and influential institution in the local, regional, and national community to the shadow of a name was traumatic for the non-uniting minority Presbyterians. The reduction of the number of Presbyterian churches in metropolitan Halifax from nine to nil posed an immense and immediate challenge. Yet the Presbyterian resisters were determined to stand firm "like the Covenanters of old" and to be the rock on which The Presbyterian Church would rebuild itself in Nova Scotia.

Saint David's appreciates its unique historic character and takes pride in its enduring Presbyterian witness, however contingent and historically conditioned it is. The purpose of this book is to explain why Saint David's exists and what it means. Part one of *The Blue Banner* ("Origins") is a chronological narrative that sketches the background and sets the stage. Parts two ("The Ministers") and three ("Congregational Life") are strictly thematic, treating broad subject areas over the first seventy-five years of the congregation's existence. *The Blue Banner* frames Saint David's as the conserver of Presbyterianism in Halifax. There the Presbyterian witness that once blazed was rekindled and still burns brightly, though the flame is smaller.

It is fitting that this history should be written from a Presbyterian, rather than a unionist, perspective, unlike most studies of church union – even some Presbyterian ones. Historically speaking, church union remains contested ground between The Presbyterian Church in Canada and the United Church of Canada. Both institutions stand as living proof of the schism that rent The Presbyterian Church in Canada in 1924–25. The two mainstream Protestant denominations that emerged represent the continuation of The Presbyterian Church in Canada in two quite different, if not contradictory senses, which are matters of perspective and interpretation. Three denominations – Presbyterian, Methodist, and Congregational –

were reduced to two: Presbyterian and United. Church union was not achieved cleanly or Christianly, and the price was high.

Opposition and resistance were part of the larger and much longer story of the church union movement. However, there is no modern study of either church union or the United Church that resulted. The standard general work on anti-unionism is N. Keith Clifford's *The Resistance to Church Union in Canada, 1904–1939*.[9] Clifford has next to nothing to say about Atlantic Canada, focusing instead on Ontario, where resistance was strongest, and the West, where it was weakest. His reason for factoring out Atlantic Canada seems to have been that only about one-seventh of PCC members resided there, all the while allowing that the East Coast "dissidents [non-uniting minority] had more support than on the Prairies."[10] Any national study of the Presbyterian resistance to church union that excludes Atlantic Canada is therefore fundamentally unbalanced and flawed.[11]

The best monograph on the subject remains unpublished. In March 1981 Douglas F. Campbell, then associate professor of sociology at the University of Toronto (Erindale Campus), announced in a letter to the editor of the *Presbyterian Record* that he was conducting research for a book about church union. Campbell devoted a dozen years to the project before abandoning it. Thirty-odd substantial "working papers" preliminary to an integrated work on the sociology of church union were eventually deposited in The Presbyterian Church in Canada Archives and Records Office and in the United Church's central archives at Victoria University. A few found their way into print as stand-alone articles.[12]

Excepting Clifford's study of western Canada,[13] no regional studies of church union exist and only three provincial ones – Stinson's for Nova Scotia,[14] Cameron's for Prince Edward Island,[15] and Gunn-Walberg's for Manitoba.[16] A notable exception to this general rule is John R. Cameron's study of Pictou Presbytery.[17] The only scholar to treat the resistance to church union as the disruption of The Presbyterian Church in Canada is Donald S. Moore in "Disruption in the Canadian Presbyterian Church."[18] More than thirty-five years later, Gunn-Walberg's observation still holds true: "The study of the movement for organic church union in Canada has suffered from the lack of regional studies."[19]

There is no history of Presbyterianism in Nova Scotia, much less Halifax, comparable to Frank E. Archibald's "Contribution of the Scottish Church to New Brunswick Presbyterianism."[20] For Reformed Presbyterianism, Eldon Hay's *The Chignecto Covenanters*[21] is definitive. Likewise, for early Cape Breton is Laurie Stanley's *The Well-Watered Garden*.[22] The Pictou County heartland is well covered in A. Douglas C. Earle's thesis, "The Story of Pictou Presbyterianism from Its Beginnings to the Union of 1875."[23] An especially useful older work is James Robertson's *History of the Mission of the Secession Church to Nova Scotia and Prince Edward Island from Its Commencement in 1765* (Edinburgh, 1847). Congregational histories proliferate, but most – one may say all – are unscholarly and useful only as sourcebooks.

The only modern general study is John S. Moir's *Enduring Witness*.[24] The articles in the volume edited by William Klempa, *The Burning Bush and a Few Acres of Snow;* that edited by Charles H.H. Scobie and G.A.Rawlyk, *The Contribution of Presbyterianism to the Maritime Provinces of Canada;* and John S. Moir's *Early Presbyterianism in Canada* should all be consulted,[25] as well as the essays by Duff Crerar and Barry Mack in G.A. Rawlyk's *Aspects of the Canadian Evangelical Experience*.[26] An important continuing series is the annual *Papers* of the Canadian Society of Presbyterian History, beginning in 1975.[27] Article, essay, and thesis literature aside, the scholarly history of Presbyterianism in Halifax, in Nova Scotia and in Atlantic Canada remains to be written. Micro-historical case studies of continuing or new congregations making up the post-Disruption church are at least a baby step towards the goal of achieving a satisfactory general history.

PART ONE

Origins

1

Church Union: Movement and Resistance

The prehistory of the church union movement in Canada may be considered to have begun with the Presbyterian and Methodist unions of 1875 and 1884 respectively. The intellectual and ideological origins of the movement have been thoroughly analyzed by historian Burkhard Kiesekamp and need not be gone into here.[1] Initial Anglican and Baptist interest in the project was defeated by ecclesiastical and doctrinal objections, and Congregationalist interest did not become significant until after the formation of the Congregational Union of Canada in 1910; but Presbyterians and Methodists persevered throughout. The Methodist Church and the Congregational Union were centralized, legislated corporations in which opposition to church union was negligible or quickly suppressed. The Presbyterian Church in Canada, on the other hand, was a decentralized, unincorporated body in which the only real power was held by hundreds of local presbyteries. They sent delegates ("commissioners") to the annual meeting of the General Assembly, which governed the church by consensus. Significant opposition to church union grew with the movement and led to a countervailing resistance. The church union movement resulted ultimately in disruption and schism in The Presbyterian Church in Canada and its reconstitution by the non-uniting minority.

Church union in Canada was a child of its time, beginning in the opening years of what has been called the ecumenical century of the Christian Church. The previous century had seen Presbyterians from different traditions, often bitterly and even violently divided, begin to converse, cooperate, and talk and to achieve union after a history of hostile separation, division, and competition.[2] Within The Presbyterian Church in Canada, the real spur to "organic" church union was not Methodist openness to or promotion of the idea but the union in Scotland in 1900 between the

United Presbyterian Church and the Free Church. The Scottish emigrant minister who, during a courtesy call on the Methodist general conference meeting in Winnipeg in 1902, brazenly suggested that The Presbyterian Church in Canada was a cherry ripe for the picking had arrived in Canada to become principal of Manitoba College (University of Manitoba) in 1900. A liberal unionist with a roving eye, William Patrick wished to see the Scottish ecclesiastical miracle replicated in Canada, where there were no more Presbyterians to unite, except a few Covenanters and dissenting Kirkmen, so that the next thing to be accomplished was the extramural union of Protestant Reformed evangelical churches.[3]

Scotland, which until 1900 had three Presbyterian bodies, was still twenty-five years away from achieving full denominational union when The Presbyterian Church in Canada embarked on a course leading to ecumenical union.[4] Yet if partial denominational union could result in schism in one of the uniting churches, as in Scotland, how much greater the dangers inherent in "organic," interdenominational union. In 1904, when the union movement within The Presbyterian Church in Canada was officially launched, the House of Lords, the supreme judicial court in the United Kingdom, awarded the non-uniting minority in the Free Church – the "Wee Frees" or "Legal Frees" – the entire property of the former Free Church of Scotland. There followed a commission of inquiry, remedial legislation, and an executive commission to divide the property of the Free Church (1843–1900) between the continuing Free Church and the new United Free Church.

Scotland's "Free Church Case" was a long, dark shadow hanging over the entire church union movement in Canada from its inception in 1904 to its consummation in 1925. The movement for Protestant evangelical church union in Canada was launched concurrently with schism within the uniting Free Church of Scotland and the secession of its non-uniting minority; the continuing Free Church of Scotland persists to this day. It was the shape of things to come in The Presbyterian Church in Canada. Unlike their Scottish counterparts, however, who looked to the courts to protect the rights of the non-uniting minority, Canadian Presbyterians who opposed and resisted union would look beyond courts and legislatures to continue the church.

THE CHURCH UNION MOVEMENT

The Canadian church union movement was at its weakest in Ontario and Quebec and its strongest in the west and the east. Halifax Presbytery, and the city of Halifax in particular, was the business headquarters of the Presbyterian Church in Atlantic Canada, and as such, it lay in the eye of the storm from start to finish. The church union movement in Halifax may be considered to have begun the evening of Thursday, 31 March 1904, when an informal conference of Presbyterian and Methodist ministers, together with elders and "leaders," took place at the home of Methodist businessman Andrew Mackinlay Bell.[5] The host presided, while Walter C. Murray, elder of St Matthew's, acted as secretary. The *crème de la crème* of the Halifax Presbyterian intelligentsia attended: Murray himself, professor of philosophy at Dalhousie University; Allan Pollok, former moderator of the General Assembly and retiring principal of Presbyterian College; R.A. (later Sir Robert) Falconer, professor and principal-designate of the college; John McMillan, minister of Chalmers and incoming chair of the college board; Robert Murray, editor of the *Presbyterian Witness* and Halifax Presbytery's unordained "minister of everything"; President John Forrest of Dalhousie University, for fifteen years a city pastor and the single most influential minister in the presbytery since Peter Gordon MacGregor; and Professor Robert Magill of Presbyterian College, a leading proponent of the social gospel and a future principal of the college. All spoke strongly in favour of union; there were no naysayers.

From the roll call alone it is clear that Presbyterian College was in the vanguard of the church union movement. According to Sir Robert Falconer's biographer, who refers to the March gathering as "something like an ecclesiastical pep rally,"[6] "the men of Pine Hill were quick off the mark. In a twinkling, professors, trustees and students alike rallied behind the unionist banner."[7] None was more active than Allan Pollok, the old émigré Kirkman who would remain in harness to the end of his long life in July 1918.[8] Pollok was the first of four successive principals of Presbyterian College who, over the twenty years of the union movement, would be in the forefront of its leadership, both intellectually and practically. In addition to Pollok himself (1894–1904), these were Falconer (1904–07), Magill (1907–09), and Clarence MacKinnon (1909–37), the last pre-Disruption moderator of The Presbyterian Church in Canada and the principal who oversaw the college's transition from Presbyterian to United.

The Halifax church union conference in March 1904 was one of a series taking place in cities across Canada where unionist sentiment was considered to be especially strong. Their purpose was to drum up enthusiasm in advance of the General Assembly in Saint John, New Brunswick, in June. In April members of the Assembly's committee on correspondence met with their Methodist and Congregationalist counterparts to consider church union. This provisional joint conference reported unanimously in favour of union as both possible and desirable. In order to help keep up the momentum generated by the March meeting, Principal Patrick visited Halifax in June, on the eve of the General Assembly, and preached at Fort Massey; its minister, James W. Falconer, was an avid unionist. Patrick then went on to second the motion in the General Assembly that a church union committee be established.

The deed was done. The General Assembly appointed a sixty-member committee, on which Halifax was well represented: Robert Murray, John McMillan, Principal Falconer, Thomas Stewart, deputy clerk of Synod, Walter Murray, and John F. Stairs, dean of the Maritimes' corporate elite and elder of Fort Massey. The first official joint conference of the individual Presbyterian, Methodist, and Congregational committees on church union was held in Knox Church, Toronto, in December 1904. Falconer, McMillan, Stewart, and both Murrays attended. Five joint study committees – doctrine, polity, the ministry, administration, and law – were constituted to prepare the way for developing a basis of union. Walter Murray was named convener of the subcommittee on polity.

No sooner had the 1904 General Assembly completed its work, however, than the shape of things to come became apparent. Frank Baird, the young minister of Chalmers in Sussex, New Brunswick, though not a commissioner, had attended the "sederunt" (session) at which church union was discussed, and the Sunday following the Assembly's closing, he preached to his people on the evils of the proposal. Baird is said to have been the first Presbyterian minister in Canada openly to criticize the union scheme, and years later he would play a significant role in the regional resistance to it.[9]

THE 1910 GENERAL ASSEMBLY

Up to 1909 the General Assembly was more or less quietly receiving the annual report of the church union committee, congratulating the committee on its labours, and encouraging its members to persevere. The fifth and last trilateral conference of union committees, in December 1908, reported that union was practicable. The following June the General Assembly discharged the committee from its five-year task and ordered the Basis of Union placed before congregations for information purposes. Thomas Sedgwick, a charter member of the union committee and one of only two major leaders in the church to oppose organic union from the very beginning, ridiculed the proposed Basis of Union as "Alice in Wonderland."[10]

In June 1910 the General Assembly convened at St Matthew's in Halifax for the fourth and final time before the Disruption. Dalhousie's president, John Forrest, a radical unionist, was elected moderator. In his capacity as convener of the union committee, Principal Patrick reported that no meeting had been held since the 1909 General Assembly and that it was necessary for the Assembly to consider what action should now be taken.[11] During debate on the committee's report, Patrick moved that the Assembly set union formally before the presbyteries as recommended policy for approval. Nova Scotia's lieutenant-governor, Duncan Cameron Fraser, elder of St Matthew's and member of the union committee, seconded the motion and spoke to it.[12]

The vote on Principal Patrick and Lieutenant-Governor Fraser's motion stood at 184 to 73 in favour. Peremptorily sending church union down to the presbyteries as the recommended policy of the General Assembly would prove, according to Keith Clifford, "one of the most serious tactical errors in the entire controversy."[13] The purpose of the so-called Barrier Act was to make haste slowly on matters such as constitutional reform, not to bring into question the church's very existence. John Mackay, principal of Westminster Hall, Vancouver, entered the main collective dissent from the Assembly's finding. Of the 41 protesting commissioners who signed it, only one was from Halifax – Robert Johnston. Former Moderator Sedgwick entered a personal dissent, citing Mackay's reasons and adding one of his own which went straight to the heart of the matter: "adequate discussion of the vital issue involved, namely the continued existence of The Presbyterian Church in Canada, was not permitted many members of Assembly who desired and had a right to express their views." Unlike Sedgwick, Mackay could be mistaken for neither "old nor reactionary,"[14] and when it came time to select a president for the newly formed and short-lived Church Defence Association, the opponents of union looked to Mackay rather than Sedgwick for leadership.[15]

The 1910 General Assembly was the swan song of Presbyterian Halifax. Once the Assembly had committed itself to church union, serious opposition began to develop. It soon became resistance, and the struggle a spiritual and political one for religious freedom – not within the state but within the church. The unionists never forgot that opposition to church union began in Halifax in 1910, nor the resisters that the first General Assembly vote favouring union occurred there. The General Assembly did not come east again for sixty years, long after the church union movement had climaxed in disruption and schism in The Presbyterian Church in Canada.

CHURCH UNION IN THE MARITIMES SYNOD

In October 1904 the Maritimes Synod met in the old shire town of Pictou and received fraternal greetings from the Methodists.[16] The regional Methodist Conference sent a delegation, including its president, no doubt hoping that Synod would follow the lead of the General Assembly meeting in Saint John the previous June and appoint its own union committee. But the time had not yet come. Not until 1907 was Synod prepared to appoint a committee on "cooperation" with the Methodists.[17] Among its seven members was John S. Sutherland, minister of St John's, Halifax – appointed convener no doubt because he was also convener of Synod's home mission committee – and James W. Falconer, the former minister and an elder of Fort Massey. It was clear that the city of Halifax would lead the union movement not only within Halifax Presbytery but also within Synod.

The "committee on cooperation with the Methodist Church" was not really a church union committee; its main achievement was to get itself reappointed at each succeeding annual meeting. Synod's energy and attention were instead diverted first by issues touching social service and evangelism[18] and secondly by the European war. The social gospel ruled; church union was still a top-down movement generating little interest or controversy among ministers and representative elders, the large majority of whom supported it more or less unquestioningly as the de facto policy of the General Assembly. Synod had more important and more pressing matters to which to attend. The connection between the social gospel – at its height in the last pre-war decade, 1904–14 – and the church union movement was entirely subterranean. Finally, in 1917 the General Assembly declared a truce; the church union movement went into remission until the first Assembly a year after the end of the war.

In 1909 the convener of the Methodist cooperation committee had reported that he had no report to present and suggested that the committee be enlarged – with two representatives from Prince Edward Island and two from New Brunswick.[19] In 1910 Sutherland moved to St John's, Newfoundland; he was succeeded as convener by Professor Falconer, a constant and effective agitator and propagandist for church union, just as Presbyterian College itself was the engine driving the movement in Atlantic Canada. Though the committee remained inactive for the next thirteen years, Falconer's watching brief and tireless work behind the scenes preparing for union when it should come bore fruit. A union committee ("committee on church union matters remitted by the General Assembly") was finally appointed in 1923 to select delegates to the first General Council of the proposed United Church of Canada and to nominate Synod representatives on a regional joint union committee with the Methodists and Congregationalists. The Maritimes joint committee on church union held its organizational meeting in Saint John in October 1923.[20] It was chaired by John Macintosh, clerk of the Presbytery of Sydney, member of the General Assembly's union committee, and convener of Synod's union committee.

The same Synod meeting that saw the formal reactivation of the church union committee also witnessed the climax of the Gillies affair. By 1922 the tiny unionist minority in St Paul's Church, Glace Bay, was so unhappy with its long-time minister, Donald MacMillan Gillies, a staunch "anti," that it prevailed on the seamlessly unionist Presbytery of Sydney to ask for his resignation.[21] Gillies, who had been minister since the congregation's founding in 1903, refused and took his protest and appeal from the decision of Sydney Presbytery to Synod, which in 1922 met in Halifax. Synod's judicial committee, to which Gillies's case was referred, recommended the appointment of an investigative commission. Alive to the delicacy of the situation, Synod agreed and proceeded to appoint a commission of five, including both unionists and antis, but with Robert Johnston as convener.

The commission departed for Glace Bay as soon as the Synod meeting had ended and reported in October. It concluded that Gillies, though indiscreet, was not culpable and urged members of the congregation to settle their differences amicably. That was too much for Sydney Presbytery, whose clerk, Macintosh, had spearheaded the attack on Gillies. Sydney lodged a strong dissent from the report and recommendations of the commission but forbore appealing to the General Assembly.[22] In 1924, partly on account of *Gillies v. The Presbytery of Sydney*, Macintosh was elected moderator of Synod, the last before the Disruption. Despite casting aspersions on unionist ministers in Sydney presbytery, Gillies – one of only three who stayed out of the United Church – retained his pulpit. In 1925 St Paul's voted massively not to enter the United Church.

CHURCH UNION IN THE PRESBYTERY OF HALIFAX

In December 1905 the Presbyterian, Methodist, and Congregational union committees, holding their second annual joint conference in Toronto, had produced nineteen articles of doctrine to serve as the working draft of a Basis of Union.[23] The following month, a public meeting was held at St Matthew's in Halifax to hear reports from local members of the three committees. This gathering was informal, unofficial, and unauthorized;

Thomas Sedgwick, former moderator, clerk of Synod, and a member of the union committee who had attended the Toronto meeting, delivered a strongly worded protest against its taking place. It went ahead regardless; Principal-Emeritus Pollok presided, while Principal Falconer, President Forrest, and Professor Murray spoke for the Presbyterians.[24]

By January 1907 the question was being discussed in presbyteries far and wide. In February Pictou met to consider the statement on church union sent down for information purposes by the General Assembly's union committee.[25] St John had already appointed a committee for the same purpose. In September 1907, the week following the fourth joint conference of union committees in Toronto, Halifax Presbytery appointed a committee of two ministers to report on the General Assembly's "remit" on church union.[26] In December the committee submitted its report, study subcommittees were struck, and in February 1908 Presbytery held a special meeting to discuss the question. Thereafter the pace slowed considerably until 1910, when the General Assembly's resolution favouring church union was carried in Halifax Presbytery by a vote of twenty to three. One of the three was Robert Johnston, then moderator, who asked that his dissenting vote be recorded.[27]

For the next thirteen years, partly on account of the war and the wartime moratorium on discussion of church union, which lasted from 1917 to 1921, Halifax Presbytery minutes are silent on the subject. Finally, in November 1923, complying with a request from the convener of the General Assembly's union committee, Presbytery appointed its own union committee – not to study church union but to prepare for it. Consisting of five ministers and two elders, its convener was John Alexander Clark, who had succeeded John W. Macmillan at St Matthew's in 1916. The ministers of St James and Stairs Memorial, Dartmouth, were also members, while the two elders were from Halifax city churches. Both of them – Charles Head Mitchell (St Matthew's) and Horace Flemming (Fort Massey) – were members of the General Assembly's church union committee. It is clear that, from start to finish, church union in Halifax Presbytery was a metropolitan movement, neatly dividing urban and suburban communities from rural ones. The only congregation in the entire presbytery (excluding Newfoundland and Bermuda) to vote decisively out of union was situated in rural Hants County.

THE CHURCH UNION PLEBISCITES

In United Church mythology there were three church union votes. In fact, there were only two. The "third" vote – to be taken in the six months before 10 June 1925, when the United Church of Canada became a *fait accompli* – was merely to allow any non-uniting majority congregation to opt out of the new body. The actual number of votes cast as such had no standing; so it is false and misleading to refer to a "third vote" as if it were the last of three plebiscites on church union. The congregational vote was at best a straw poll indicating those who would have rejected union had the vote been an actual plebiscite.[28] Church union was enacted five months before the congregational voting could begin and came into effect at the end of the six months during which it could take place. So the fictitious third vote affected only individual congregations choosing to hold a vote, not the church at large, which was going into union, vote or no vote.

The first plebiscite was in two parts: whether union and, if so, whether on the proposed basis. The former attracted more support than the latter. Many loyal Presbyterians favouring, or at least not opposed to, union conceived it as the Methodists and Congregationalists joining *them* in a greater Presbyterian church with perhaps a new name; they would have preferred to export the Basis of Union of 1875 rather than replace it with a new, composite one less than the sum of its parts. In metropolitan Halifax the 1912 vote showed 72 per cent of Presbyterians in favour of church union (see table 1.1). The only city church that voted strongly against was St Andrew's, where Robert Johnston was minister; the only other city church in which there was strong opposition was Park Street, where Johnston would become minister in 1914. In all but one of the others there were lopsided majorities in favour of union; the exception was new Chalmers (Coburg Road), whose minister, Robert J. Power, was, like Johnston, an Ulster emigrant who would remain Presbyterian at the Disruption. In Halifax Presbytery at large the vote was nearly 75 per cent in favour, though support for the proposed basis was less strong.[29]

After the General Assembly gave final approval to the revised Basis, a second vote was held, in 1915, on the question of union solely (see table 1.2). The 1915 plebiscite in metropolitan Halifax showed 58 per cent of Presbyterians in favour of church union. In relative terms, opposition had significantly increased. Three congregations, instead of one, voted decisively against union, including the newest, Stairs Memorial (1913), an offshoot of St James, Dartmouth. Two of them – Bedford and Park Street – had staunchly anti-union ministers,[30] a fact that may help to explain the strength of anti-union sentiment within their congregations. In Halifax Presbytery at large the vote was 67 per cent in favour of union, a slight decrease from 1912.[31]

Table 1.1
The 1912 plebiscite

Pastoral charge	For	Against
Bedford and Sackville	21	23
Bethany and Rockingham	89	15
Chalmers	53	34
Fort Massey	146	50
Grove	91	0
Park Street	170	111
St Andrew's	64	139
St James	157	15
St John's	174	16
St Matthew's	157	36
Total	1,122	439

SOURCE: *Presbyterian Witness;* Session minutes; official returns.

Table 1.2
The 1915 plebiscite

Pastoral charge	For	Against
Bedford and Sackville	19	68
Bethany and Rockingham	95	20
Chalmers	57	29
Fort Massey	209	59
Grove	119	47
Park Street	68	251
St Andrew's	54	58
St James	177	81
St John's	91	31
St Matthew's	149	58
Stairs Memorial	21	54
Total	1,059	756

SOURCE: *Presbyterian Witness;* official returns.

THE RESISTANCE ORGANIZES

The rising opposition made clear to the unionists that another plebiscite
was necessary, while to the Presbyterians it signified that church union
should not be merely deferred but abandoned. A new resistance movement, the "Organization for the Preservation and Continuance of The
Presbyterian Church in Canada," was established on the fringes of the
General Assembly meeting at Toronto in June 1913.[32] The aim of this bloc
was to prevent another vote, the assumption being that since the first vote

was insufficient, a second would be unnecessary. Though the resisters failed either to prevent or to win the second plebiscite, it was a pyrrhic victory for the unionists in that opposition rose to 40 per cent.[33] The resisters did not believe union could proceed in the face of such a verdict. The unionist-dominated General Assembly saw things differently.

Instead of hastening towards a third referendum in the hope of substantially decreased opposition, the Assembly hurried to proceed with consummating union. How different from the response to the 1912 plebiscite, when fully 45 per cent of the church's membership did not vote![34] When opposition was less and voter turnout lower, the General Assembly resolved on another vote. When opposition was more and voter turnout higher, the Assembly set its face against further consultation with the people. Not only was the General Assembly not democratic; it was not representative, except of presbyteries. Nor were presbyteries representative. They comprised all the ministers, among whom support for union was overwhelming, and an elder from each congregation forming part of the presbytery. The role of the "representative" elder was to advance the interests of the presbytery and the church, not to act as spokesman for his session, much less his congregation.

Such was the nature of Presbyterian polity. Presbyteries ruled, and ministers ruled the presbytery. It was not congregations, sessions, or even synods that sent commissioners to the General Assembly, but presbyteries. So the 1916 General Assembly could safely decide to proceed with union despite the fact that more than one-third of Presbyterians voting had voted against it. Ironically, the Assembly met in Winnipeg, the same city where, fourteen years earlier, William Patrick had first draped himself in the unionist banner. By a margin of 404 to 89, the commissioners voted to discontinue The Presbyterian Church in Canada. "Strategically," as Keith Clifford rightly observes of the "dissidents" (his term for the non-uniting minority), "their case would gain strength only if the unionists proved their unfaithfulness to the church by going ahead with union and by unjustly silencing all dissent."[35] That, indeed, is exactly what was to happen.

The decisive vote in the General Assembly was the signal to the opponents of union to reorganize themselves as a radical resistance along the lines of the Solemn League and Covenant of 1643, to maintain Presbyterianism in Canada. In the autumn of 1916 the Organization for the Preservation and Continuance of The Presbyterian Church in Canada reconstituted itself as the Presbyterian Church Association (PCA), the third, final, and by far the most effective of the resistance organizations.[36] In September 1916 a circular letter was issued by the Maritimes executive of the "committee organized for the continuance of The Presbyterian Church in

Canada." Signed by three ministers – Baird, Johnston, and Sedgwick – and seven elders, it went to every minister in the Synod with the request that it be read from the pulpit on a Sunday.[37] Hard on the heels of the letter was a flyer advertising a pre-Synod congress: "Convocation for the Preservation and Continuance of the Presbyterian Church in Canada. At Truro, Tuesday, Oct. 3rd, In the County Academy Hall, at 3.30 o'clock." The opening meeting of Synod took place later the same day. Thus was inaugurated the custom of the PCA's assembling in the same town as and on the eve of Synod's annual meeting.[38]

This first general meeting of Maritime Presbyterians opposed to union was held in anticipation of the PCA's founding national congress in Toronto later the same month. Robert Johnston chaired the regional organizing committee, which in turn nominated a provisional executive to represent the Maritimes at the national level. Its convener was John McKeen (1849–1924), the most prominent lay leader in the resistance to church union in Nova Scotia.[39] McKeen, a retired banker and future elder of Fort Massey, was also a member of Halifax's board of control[40] and chair of the Presbyterian Council, established in 1913 to plan the church's expansion in the north and west of the city. He coined the apt phrase "dominating ecclesiastical junta" to characterize the unionist leadership.[41] Secretary-treasurer of the new regional resistance body was Edgar Kaulbach, CA, elder of Fort Massey and the only prominent resister in Halifax to change sides and go into the United Church.

Though a central coordinating committee of resisters is known to have existed in Halifax as early as 1915, by and large early resistance there was too narrowly focused to be really effective. In Nova Scotia at large, where Presbyterians were most numerous and where seven of the eleven presbyteries in the Maritimes Synod were to be found, resistance was concentrated in two of the less populous ones – Pictou and Lunenburg-Yarmouth. The other five – Halifax, Truro, Wallace, Sydney, and Inverness – were strong for union. Yet in every presbytery other than distant, missionary Trinidad, resistance was active, and no presbytery except Trinidad was to be left without at least one continuing Presbyterian congregation.

The driving force behind the organization of the Presbyterian Church Association in the Maritimes Synod was Robert Johnston, until 1918 minister of the staunchly anti-union Park Street, Halifax. Nationally, few ministers played a more active or prominent role in the resistance to church union and the preservation and reconstruction of the church.[42] In Atlantic Canada he was the leader of the resistance. It was, for example, Johnston who served as president of the Maritimes branch of the PCA throughout its existence and who initiated the great newspaper war on church union in Halifax in November 1922.[43] It was also Johnston who masterminded the plebiscitary strategy that the Presbyterians followed in the final pre-legislation phase of the resistance;[44] who led the "anti" forces in the Maritimes Synod; and who, in October 1924, led the secession of the Presbyterians, becoming moderator of the provisional synod.

THE STRANGE CASE OF ST ANDREW'S

By the end of the First World War in November 1918, church union was definitely in the air; Grove Presbyterian and Kaye Street Methodist were on the verge of uniting, though for reasons that have nothing to do with the union principle. Halifax Presbytery considered union with the Methodists to be only a matter of time. The period of grace, which saw the union question deferred until the first General Assembly held a year after the end of the war, was soon to expire. Exploratory meetings among Presbyterian and Methodist churches in Halifax began to be held.

As early as January 1919, the annual meeting of St Andrew's appointed a committee to confer with representatives from Grafton Street and Robie Street Methodist churches, to investigate the possibility of merger sooner rather than later.[45] Two meetings were held, but nothing came of them; so the matter was quietly dropped. Then in April 1920 St Andrew's suddenly raised the stakes. A special congregational meeting appointed a new committee to resume merger discussions with the Methodists. The Presbyterian representatives candidly told their Methodist counterparts that, so pressing was the need of St Andrew's for a new, larger, and more expensive church building and annex, they could not wait for national church union. They needed union at ground level, and they needed it now. The joint committee on the proposed merger, which met several times during May 1920, unanimously recommended full union sooner rather than later.[46]

But "The Union Church" was not to be – at least, not yet. In October 1920 the St Andrew's representatives advised the Methodists that they could not agree among themselves to refer the proposed union to Presbytery, which would have had to approve it. Opposition to congregational union in advance of church union became so intense that some members of the committee concluded that to proceed further would induce a disastrous schism. As the crisis deepened after 1921, the pressure on ministers increased. Much – indeed, almost everything – depended on them. The General Assembly expected them to deliver their congregations undivided to the United Church, while congregations expected them to provide both spiritual guidance and moral leadership from the pulpit and within the session.

"PROTESTANT ECCLESIASTICAL CIVIL WAR"

Looming large in the intensification of resistance between 1921 and 1924 was the determination of the unionists not to hold a third plebiscite.[47] Understandably, it was deemed a risk not worth taking. The earlier votes had been democratic referendums on the idea and its terms and conditions. A simple majority against union in 1925 would have scuttled it forever, just as the simple majority in favour of it in 1915 was considered a mandate to proceed. The resistance, therefore, concentrated its efforts on securing a third vote. When the resisters failed to do so, they turned to opposing parliamentary legislation, the heavy-handed substitute for another plebiscite. When that too failed, the resisters turned to continuing the church. Like the union movement itself, the resistance evolved and changed over time. Only the goals were different. In the one case, it was to achieve church union by whatever means necessary; in the other, it was to prevent its arbitrary imposition, with the accompanying certainty of disruption and schism. Only when it became clear that the uniting majority in the General Assembly had arrogated to itself the power to extinguish the church did the non-uniting minority resolve to continue it.

Dormant after the "armed truce" effected in 1917, the Presbyterian Church Association came back to life in the spring of 1921.[48] Rightly anticipating that the forthcoming General Assembly would reopen the union question, the Presbyterians met in conference in Halifax in May 1921, on the eve of the Assembly's meeting in Toronto, to reiterate their opposition to the 1916 decision to proceed with union.[49] Instead, the 1921 Assembly, the first after the end of the wartime truce to reopen the question, resolved to consummate church union without delay. In direct response to the Assembly's decision, the Maritime Presbyterians met again in Halifax in September 1921 to establish a separate and autonomous regional branch of the PCA.[50] The ancient and venerable Thomas Sedgwick, just two months away from his death at age eighty-three, was named honorary president, and Robert Johnston, president.

By 1922 it was clear that a third vote would not take place. The General Assembly took the view that the second, 1915, vote had conferred a mandate to decide the question in favour of union and to proceed with consummating it when the time was right. This interpretation explains the Assembly's action in 1916 and again in 1921, 1922, and 1923. From 1910 onwards the unionists had always commanded a substantial majority among commissioners. The scale of opposition and resistance, however, guaranteed that the new arrangement could only be completed by act of Parliament, folding the unincorporated Presbyterian Church in Canada into a new, incorporated church. Meeting in December 1922, the Maritimes PCA resolved on maximum effort to turn the legislative struggle for church union against the unionists.[51]

Shortly after the General Assembly in June 1923 approved the draft of the bill incorporating the United Church of Canada, Johnston issued a pastoral letter. In his capacity as president of the Presbyterian Church Association in the Maritmes, he advised Presbyterians that, as a result of the General Assembly's action, the PCA had committed itself to continuing The Presbyterian Church in Canada.[52] The letter resonated even in strongly pro-union congregations in Halifax. In August and September 1923 the trustees of St Matthew's passed pointed resolutions against church union legislation of any kind whatsoever.[53]

The success of the unionists in imposing their agenda with the full authority of the official church provoked a backlash. There was an upsurge of activity among non-uniting minorities in uniting majority congregegations. Resisters in Halifax began to organize to preserve the church at the congregational level. A local chapter of the Presbyterian Church Association was formed in March-April 1923. Within days, a women's league was also organized.[54] Unionist ministers in the metropolitan area responded to this challenge by issuing a four-point pastoral letter ("cautionary statement") on the church union issue, reminding Presbyterians that the General Assembly was the church legislative. It was read from all the Presbyterian pulpits on Sunday, 29 April.[55]

Two weeks earlier Presbyterian resisters had held a grand meeting in – of all places – St Matthew's.[56] The principal speakers were the Reverends Alexander James MacGillivray of Guelph, general secretary of the Presbyterian Church Association, and Walter George Brown of Red Deer, "by far the most effective opponent to church union in the west." Brown was a western Robert Johnston, so brilliant an organizer that later in 1923 he was offered the post of national organizer for the association.[57]

NOVA SCOTIA'S UNITED CHURCH OF CANADA ACT

On 17 March 1924 John Brown Douglas, Liberal member for Halifax County and sometime trustee of St Matthew's, introduced in the House of Assembly Bill no. 52, "An Act respecting the union of certain churches therein named."[58] Its purpose was to vest in the United Church of Canada the entire property in Nova Scotia of the three uniting churches – Presbyterian, Methodist, and Congregationalist. Though technically a private member's bill, the United Church of Canada Act was a government bill in everything but name. It was based on a template developed by the Joint Committee on Church Union in Toronto for the purpose of vesting provincial church property in an ecclesiastical corporation. The principle of church union was not at stake. That was to be dealt with in the United Church's act of incorporation ("federal act"), then still three weeks away from being introduced in Parliament. Under the British North America Act (1867), however, property and civil rights lay within the exclusive powers of provincial legislatures. Nova Scotia's United Church of Canada Act ("provincial act") was in the nature of a gigantic expropriation of private property on behalf of a private organization. Among many other serious and severe losses, it would cost the church Presbyterian College, Halifax.

The bill provoked a firestorm. Petitions against it were received from forty-seven Presbyterian congregations, including Fort Massey, Park Street, and St Matthew's (two); the largest – from Park Street – carried 105 names. These petitions had been opened for signing at a meeting of the Presbyterian Church Association held a week after the introduction of the bill, at which the principal speaker was the Reverend William Fishbourne McConnell, the PCA's national organizer.[59] Opposition to the bill was led by two Presbyterian cabinet ministers, from Cape Breton and Pictou respectively: Daniel Alexander Cameron, provincial secretary, and Robert Malcolm MacGregor, minister without portfolio. MacGregor, a great-grandson of the patriarch, the Reverend James, was an elder in Robert Johnston's church – United, New Glasgow. A successful businessman and even more successful politician, he was to the lay resistance what Johnston was to the clerical.

Premier Ernest Howard Armstrong, a loyal Methodist, was determined that the bill should pass unamended, and the majority of Presbyterian members on both sides of the House agreed with him. Yet the bill was resisted every step of the way by the minority who did not agree with him. On 31 March the bill reached the committee on private and local bills, the chair of which was a Presbyterian resister from New Glasgow. The following day public hearings before the assembly committee began. It was a great debate, with numerous eloquent speakers for and against the motion.

The unionists spoke first, while Johnston led for the Presbyterians: "'You can never build up a church of God on broken promises, promises torn to shreds,' and 'What is morally wrong cannot be ecclesiastically right' rang through the chamber in a voice quivering with emotion."[60] Among others speaking against the bill were Dr John Stewart, elder of Fort Massey and Nova Scotia vice-president of the Presbyterian Church Association,[61] and W.F. McConnell. Among those speaking in favour were Principal MacKinnon of Presbyterian College, soon to become moderator of the General Assembly, and John Pringle, a former moderator.

On 15 April, while the bill was still before the committee on private and local bills, the General Assembly's union committee further poisoned the atmosphere by taking out a full-page advertisement in the pro-union *Halifax Herald* which began, "Presbyterians stand by Union / Church Union Will Go Forward – People, Presbyteries and General Assembly Determined."[62] The committee attempted to report the bill with amendments but was thwarted by the premier, who moved that the bill be reconsidered in committee of the whole house, where it was reported without amendments. On 29 April, in order to delay third and final reading, MacGregor and Cameron launched a filibuster against their own government. Nine amendments were proposed and voted down one after the other. It was all to no avail; the bill passed 18 to 9 and went up to the Legislative Council.[63]

Council refused to pass the bill without amendments, and the government had to compromise. The only amendment agreed to, however, was quite meaningless – except in the unlikely event that the bill to incorporate the United Church of Canada, which was then going through the House of Commons, failed to be enacted. The provincial act, as amended, provided that congregations might vote to withdraw from the United Church within six months after 10 June 1925. The act of incorporation, on the other hand, provided for a vote either *before* 10 June 1925 or *after* that date if a provincial act (as in Nova Scotia) so provided. The failure to recognize that there could only be one effective vote in any congregation caused endless problems, especially in congregations with uniting minorities. It was erroneously supposed by unionists losing the vote under the federal act that they could hold a second vote under the provincial act, in the hope of a more favourable result.[64]

Nova Scotia's United Church of Canada Act was passed on 9 May 1924,[65] to come into force on 10 June 1925. Politically, the bill was a disaster. It not only divided Presbyterians across party lines in the legislature; it also divided the Liberal cabinet and caucus. Worst of all, it landed R.M. MacGregor in an early grave. Aged only forty-eight, he dropped dead of exhaustion and worry on 9 September 1924, weeks before the meeting of Synod that initiated the disruption of the Presbyterian Church in the Maritimes. His church, however, did not die with him; it was about to take a new lease on life.

2

The "Union" Disruption

THE MARITIMES SYNOD DISRUPTED

When Synod met at Fort Massey in September 1921, Robert Johnston, newly appointed president of the Maritimes branch of the Presbyterian Church Association, attempted to obtain approval for an "overture" (petition) calling for a third referendum on church union. By a margin of nearly four to one, Synod refused to adopt the overture, instead deciding to transmit it *simpliciter* (without prejudice) to the General Assembly. The overture did not, however, reach the floor of the 1922 General Assembly; it was decided that, instead of a third referendum on church union, there would be an act of Parliament merging The Presbyterian Church in Canada in the new "United Church of Canada." The overture was referred to the new committee on church union, which, packed with unionists, read and ignored it.[1]

No further action on church union or resistance to it was taken at the next Synod meeting (again held in Halifax) in 1922. It was the lull before the storm. At the Synod meeting in Saint John in October 1923 the resisting commissioners – all twenty-two of them, out of some three hundred – failed to prevent the appointment of a union committee, the nomination of prospective commissioners for the first General Council of the new United Church, or the selection of representatives to serve on a joint union committee with the Methodists. The members of this committee, whose task it would be to oversee integration of the Presbyterian synod and the Methodist conference, included the ministers of St Matthew's and Fort Massey and a number of Halifax elders. Johnston accomplished little more than Synod's accepting his offer to host its 1924 meeting in his own church in New Glasgow.

By June 1924, when the Presbyterian Church Association met in New Glasgow, enactment by Parliament of the United Church of Canada bill was a foregone conclusion. In light of that inevitability, it was proposed to form a shadow synod with power to act as and from 10 June 1925, when the United Church of Canada Act would come into force.[2] On 7 October the Maritimes PCA held its annual meeting in First Presbyterian, New Glasgow; Robert Johnston was appointed convener of a committee to consider setting up a "provisional" prospective synod.[3] On 8 October, at a private dinner, the Presbyterian leadership decided to move forward with preparing to succeed and replace the Synod when the time came.[4] It was Caesar crossing the Rubicon.

The official Synod opened on the evening following the annual conference of the Presbyterian Church Association on the 7th. Some twenty-four commissioners signed a protest against any further union proceedings, while Johnston resigned as chair of the board of Presbyterian College, a unionist citadel.[5] Professor James W. Falconer introduced the report of the union committee by stating one of its purposes to be "to hasten on the crisis. We do not need to prolong the crisis unduly. We are increasingly impatient of the long delay."[6] The gauntlet had been thrown down. The Presbyterians were not slow in taking it up. When the moderator called for a vote on the fourth of the eleven resolutions put forward by the union committee, it was clear that the parting of the ways had come.[7]

Well aware that voting on a prejudicial resolution would give it the colour of right, Johnston asked the non-uniting minority to abstain, and all but one commissioner complied. There were more abstainers than active resisters. Later on, Johnston announced that the non-uniting minority commissioners intended to constitute a provisional synod, but he was ruled out of order by the moderator. Finally, towards the end of the meeting, Frank Baird resigned as clerk of Synod, "in order to preserve his moral integrity in the matter of church union and that he might be free to pursue the course dictated by conscience."[8]

After Synod adjourned near 11:30 PM, fifteen ministers and nine representative elders continued in session and unanimously elected Johnston moderator.[9] Synod meetings were not open to the general public, but townspeople converged on United Church hall when the faithful remnant reconvened on the morning of Friday, 10 October.[10] The new parallel, "shadow" synod ensured that the church in eastern Canada would be ready to continue from and after 10 June 1925.[11] On the very day the United Church was to be born, the provisional Presbyterian synod would become official and permanent.

In April 1925 Johnston, moderator of the provisional Maritimes Synod, presided at the last regional conference of the Presbyterian Church Association.[12] He had already commenced negotiations with John Gresham Machen, a conservative Presbyterian divine at Princeton Theological Seminary, for divinity students to come to Nova Scotia to supply pulpits that would be vacant after 10 June 1925. Indeed, they might be needed before, if unionist ministers in non-uniting majority congregations were to resign their pulpits as a result of the upcoming congregational vote on membership in the United Church.[13] Nationally, too, the continuing church was preparing for reconstruction. In May 1925 Johnston formed part of a blue-ribbon delegation sent to the United Kingdom to brief Presbyterian bodies there on the disruption of The Presbyterian Church in Canada.[14] In June he was appointed to an ad hoc national commission that was to govern the "Continuing Church in Canada" until the 1926 General Assembly.

HALIFAX PRESBYTERY DISRUPTED

In Halifax Presbytery itself, matters had come to a head in April 1924 while the provincial United Church of Canada bill was still before the Private and Local Bills Committee of the legislature.[15] On 23 April formal charges that he had slandered Presbytery during the committee's public hearings were laid against Robert Johnston.[16] A committee of Presbytery – in reality, a subcommittee of its union committee – was appointed to draft a resolution of censure. Johnston, who was not amused ("It is a communication very remarkable from every point of view"), declined to answer the charge and appealed. However, Synod, disinclined to add fuel to an already blazing fire, concurred with the recommendation of its judicial committee to let the matter lie. Johnston was not to be controlled by Halifax, and his own presbytery, Pictou, dared not act against him, given the overwhelming strength of anti-union sentiment among Presbyterians in that county.

Out of thirty-four congregations in Halifax Presbytery, six were already united in fact if not in form. The General Assembly's final decision in 1923 to compel union by act of Parliament acted as a spur to de facto congregational unions where Presbyterian resistance was negligible or non-existent. In Halifax Presbytery a mere three congregations voted not to become United Church, while eighteen did not vote at all.[17] Among ministers, only three out of thirty-seven remained Presbyterian.[18] Small wonder that the same correspondent further observed, "Probably no Presbytery in the Dominion has been less affected by the Church Union struggle than Halifax."[19] Yet, in the ten years since the second of the two referendums in 1915, resistance had steadily increased – partly in response to the growing awareness that the General Assembly was too apprehensive of the outcome to allow a third referendum. Even in areas such as metropolitan Halifax, where pro-union sentiment was exceedingly strong, the "anti-union party" was not quite so small or feeble as the unionists assumed.

For various reasons both logistical and ideological, the anti-union party in Halifax Presbytery was concentrated in metropolitan Halifax. The local chapter of the PCA was a sect within a church – a cadre of committed Presbyterians in "revolt," as George Pidgeon, convener of the General Assembly's union committee, would say – against The Presbyterian Church in Canada. In November 1924 the PCA took rooms in a downtown Halifax office building, advertised in the daily newspapers, and invited Presbyterians to subscribe; eventually some five hundred did so. The declaration read, "We, the undersigned, hereby record our opposition to the present form of church union and our desire to perpetuate The Presbyterian Church as at present constituted."

The month before the local PCA chapter was formally organized, Johnston, in his capacity as Maritimes regional president, came to Halifax "and opened an office from which he carried on a vigorous propaganda throughout the Province against Union. His cohorts in this city were well organized and disciplined."[20] Halifax may have been the centre of the resistance organization, but it was very far from being the centre of the resistance movement. Indeed, the PCA's efforts were largely concentrated outside Halifax Presbytery. Its limited resources could not be wasted fighting a losing battle where its strength was weakest. The local PCA, for its part, focused its efforts on the one or two metropolitan congregations it thought it could win.

On 31 October 1924 the Halifax chapter of the PCA addressed a letter to all sessions asking for permission to hold anti-union meetings in Halifax Presbyterian churches. Few if any replies were received, and only one such meeting is known to have been held – at St Andrew's.[21] Undaunted, on the 6th of that month the PCA launched what was intended to be a series of weekly meetings in Halifax. The inaugural one was addressed by Baird, Johnston, and Dr John Stewart, Nova Scotia vice-president of the PCA and senior elder in the presbytery.[22] In the aftermath of passage of the United Church of Canada Act, the Halifax PCA set to maximizing the No vote in all the congregations, hoping thereby to ensure that at least one city church was preserved for the Presbyterians. When all else failed, the PCA encouraged Presbyterians to renounce their congregational membership and organize for independent Presbyterian public worship.

In the city of Halifax, the overconfident unionists organized later and less effectively than the Presbyterians. Indeed, they did not think that they needed to organize at all; they had the entire resources of the official church at their disposal, and no body, including the ministerial association, was friendly to the "antis." So it was not until November 1924 that a unionist organizer was appointed.[23] In October, Halifax Presbytery had instructed ministers to declare their intention to enter the United Church. Unionists hastened to do so, but the Presbyterians delayed until congregational voting was over. On 25 March 1925 Baird of Bedford resigned, followed in March by Donald MacOdrum of St Andrew's, Halifax, and R.W. Anglin of St John's, Windsor; and in April by D.B. Marsh of St Andrew's, Hamilton, Bermuda. Of the four, only Marsh was the minister of a non-uniting majority congregation.

THE CONGREGATIONAL VOTE

The act of Parliament incorporating the United Church of Canada (federal act) permitted congregations to vote themselves out of the United Church, provided the requisite number[24] of communicant members requested that a vote be held and that a special meeting of the congregation was called for the purpose. Beginning in December 1924, the congregational vote was a "winner-take-all" electoral-college process resting on a simple majority of the votes cast. Had there been a third plebiscite, or had the congregational vote been reckoned as such, church union would probably have been lost in Atlantic Canada and certainly in Ontario and Quebec.[25] Many anti-union Presbyterians deplored the prospect of schism and chose to remain with the official Presbyterian Church in Canada "whither it goest." Nevertheless, after passage of the United Church of Canada Act, schism was not preventable. Many devout and sincere Presbyterians who were not active resisters resented not being consulted on the extinction of their own church. But as a matter of conscience, they were not prepared to oppose the General Assembly.

Since not all congregations with majorities favouring union voted, the congregational vote cannot be represented as a third referendum on church union. Since it was a dedicated and defined procedure for staying out of the United Church – in other words, defeating the very purpose of the United Church of Canada Act – the congregational vote did not need to take place at all. Individuals voted only as members of congregations deciding to hold a vote. Congregations that did not vote went into the United Church automatically. This meant that all congregations with majorities opposed to union had to hold a vote whether they wanted to or not; otherwise, come 10 June 1925, they would have found themselves in the United Church.

The congregational vote option in the federal act was not intended by either side as a substitute for a third plebiscite. Without it, however, the act would not have passed, and it did make possible the reconstitution of The Presbyterian Church in Canada. Without continuing congregations or significant non-uniting minorities in uniting congregations, there could not have been a continuing church to found new congregations to replace the lost ones. Unionist leaders understood only too well that a third plebiscite might have defeated union, while the one-off congregational vote on joining or not joining the United Church gave the Presbyterians carte blanche to continue a church that, according to the law of Canada, was ending. Ultimately, what defeated the unionists was the decentralized and centrifugal nature of Presbyterian polity. If non-uniting majority congregations had the right to leave the church, then they also had the responsibility to continue. And if they had ministers, they could form new presbyteries. Had it been up to the unionist leaders, there would not have been another vote of any kind.

In the final year, from passage of the United Church of Canada Act in July 1924 to its coming into force in June 1925, the resistance to church union became a struggle for survival through and beyond it. The prospect of the congregational vote claimed everyone's attention and the full resources of both the union committee and the Presbyterian Church Association. At its last pre-Disruption meeting, in October 1924, the Maritimes Synod adopted a resolution from the union committee that presbyteries hold a vote in all the congregations as soon as possible after 10 December 1924. The final decision as to whether to vote, of course, lay with congregations. In adopting the resolution, Synod simply tore a page from the book of the Presbyterian Church Association, which had unanimously resolved to press for an every-congregation vote. The union committee's *volte-face* looked like a significant political victory for the PCA because it ran counter to the wishes of most if not all presbyteries within the Synod. Being solidly unionist themselves, however, they looked to ministers to use the power of the pulpit to convince congregations that, since the vote was not a referendum on church union, it was a pointless exercise. Union was a *fait accompli,* and The Presbyterian Church in Canada would be entering the United Church regardless of what action individual congregations decided to take. On paper, at least, there would not be a "Presbyterian Church in Canada" after 10 June 1925.

THE CONGREGATIONAL VOTE IN METROPOLITAN HALIFAX

Though Halifax Presbytery did not favour Synod's policy of promoting a congregational vote and would subsequently show its displeasure by not recording the votes in its official minutes, it did not insist on the requisite number of communicants petitioning their session to hold a special congregational meeting. Sessions were encouraged to proceed with summoning the special meeting. But they were not compelled to do so; Presbytery would go that far. Presbytery saw Halifax as a unionist town in which congregational voting, whether voluntary or compulsory, represented a gratuitous moral and psychological victory for the Presbyterian Church Association. It feared that voting would be seen to be a failure on the part of the unionists to make their case. If failure it was, it could not be blamed on the pulpit propaganda of local resisting ministers. The only strong "anti" minister to be found anywhere in metropolitan Halifax was Frank Baird (Bedford-Sackville), and even he could not carry his people with him. Regardless of its annoyance, Presbytery complied, recommending to sessions in October 1924 that the congregational vote be taken as soon as possible after 10 December, the earliest day on which voting could legally occur.[26]

On 8 December 1924 the General Assembly's committee on church union issued a special statement on voting under the federal act. It was to begin on 22 December, and all congregations were encouraged to proceed without delay. For its part, the joint committee on church union of the three uniting churches tried to expedite matters by publishing an eight-page pamphlet entitled *Method of Taking the Vote on Church Union under the Federal Act in the Province of Nova Scotia*. The Presbyterian Church Association countered with a twenty-four-page pamphlet entitled *Suggestions to Congregations as to the Method of Taking the Vote as to Whether or Not the Congregation Shall Enter the United Church of Canada*. A second vote (under the provincial act) trumping or superseding the first was an outlaw fantasy in which both some unionists and some Presbyterians on the losing end of the poll participated. In general, unionists saw the congregational vote as an opportunity to confirm the wisdom of the General Assembly's decision on church union by demonstrating how strong support for it was "on the ground." For Presbyterians, it was their last chance to preserve congregations (and, scarcely less important, congregational property) for the continuing church.

The first vote in Halifax was a straw poll by members of the Pine Hill Theological Society, a secret ballot taken symbolically on 10 December 1924. By a margin of 50 to 2, the ministerial candidates declared for union; there were no abstainers.[27] Special congregational meetings were held on the evening of 22 December 1924 in every Presbyterian church for the purpose of commencing the vote.[28] The first votes cast in five of the six Halifax city churches were dropped into the ballot boxes at the close of the special congregational meeting, which stood adjourned for two weeks while voting continued. The rule was one member one vote, and a simple majority of votes cast sufficed to prevent the congregation's staying out of the United Church of Canada.

Alone among congregations in not holding a special congregational meeting was St Andrew's. The "auld kirk" had as yet made no decision as to whether, much less when, such a meeting would be held.[29] It was generally assumed that the Presbyterians had targeted St Andrew's as the one congregation they could win and so wished to defer the vote until June if necessary, or until certain of a win. The unionists, already confident of a majority, wished to bring the vote forward for the same reason.

The first congregations to report were St James (Dartmouth) and Bethany, both showing large majorities in favour of the United Church. By 14 January Bedford, St Matthew's, Fort Massey, Park Street, and St John's had also reported.[30] Voter turnout was as high as 80 per cent in some congregations. Overall, the turnout stood at 65 per cent, which meant that 35 per cent of professing members abstained. Unionists did not believe that any congregation in metropolitan Halifax was seriously at risk. Only in Park Street and St Andrew's did the No vote stand as high as 35 per cent. The case of St Andrew's was unique: 95 per cent voter turnout and – in violation of the federal act – adherents as well as members voting.[31]

DISRUPTION IN ST ANDREW'S

Donald MacOdrum, minister of St Andrew's from the time of the 1917 merger with Chalmers, feared that the proposed extramural union was exacerbating tensions between the Presbyterians from old St Andrew's and the unionists from new Chalmers. He was not a resister, much less a prominent resistance leader like Robert Johnston or Frank Baird, but a loyal churchman who was prepared to accept union – provided it did not lead to schism and disruption, either in the church or in congregations.[32]

Though he voted for union at the 1924 General Assembly and, later, at Synod, MacOdrum was thought by the unionists to be a unionist and by the Presbyterians to be a Presbyterian. He was in fact an "anti-disunionist," and he took very seriously George Pidgeon's animadversion that ministers who resisted the union policy of the General Assembly were traitors. MacOdrum's crisis was one of conscience and pastoral concern for the spiritual welfare of the Presbyterians in St Andrew's – by far the largest group of "antis" within Halifax Presbytery – after the uniting majority had voted the congregation into the United Church.

There the matter rested until the question of the congregational vote arose in December 1924. There was a sharp division of opinion between Presbyterians and unionists, not as to whether a vote should be taken but when: before or after 10 June 1925. On 13 January a special meeting of Session was held to decide whether to recommend a vote to the congregation. A unionist motion that the vote be held sooner rather than later carried eight to five. Session was unequally split between unionists and Presbyterians, the latter wanting to defer a vote for as long as possible – until they were ready – if necessary, until December 1925. A special congregational meeting was called for Monday, 26 January, to decide whether to accept Session's recommendation for a vote.

On Sunday, the 18th, MacOdrum concluded his sermon at the evening service by speaking to congregational membership in the United Church for the first and only time. Contending that to preserve the status quo was preferable to disrupting the congregation, and that natural justice demanded that provision be made for the significant non-uniting minority, he advised St Andrew's not to enter the United Church.[33] For MacOdrum the real issue was not church union but the disruption of The Presbyterian Church in Canada. The latter was the greater of the two evils. Since the PCC was going to continue, however, the only way St Andrew's, *as a congregation*, could avoid the schism that was overtaking the PCC was to remain out of the United Church. MacOdrum, for his part, would remain if St Andrew's voted No and leave if it did not.

At the special congregational meeting of St Andrew's held on 26 January, Session's recommendation of a vote was accepted, and voting commenced.[34] St Andrew's membership stood at 390; adherents at about 46. The Presbyterians saw to it that adherents were enfranchised, and for the sake of peace, the unionists complied. Had the vote gone against them, the unionists could have raised the hue and cry of electoral fraud. The vote concluded on 9 February. It was announced at the reconvened special congregational meeting on the 10th that the vote in St Andrew's was one of the largest in proportion to the size of the congregation in the entire Presbyterian Church in Canada, and perhaps even the largest. Out of 436 eligible voters, 413 voted, giving the United Church a majority of 123, a margin of almost 2 to 1.[35] Up until the decision to vote early was taken, it was the earnest hope of the Presbyterians, and the well-founded fear of the unionists, that the Presbyterians would carry one Halifax congregation with them, and that it would be St Andrew's.

MacOdrum immediately announced his resignation ("It seemed to me that one church in Halifax should be preserved as a home for those hundreds of people who said they must otherwise build for themselves"). He would not lead a congregation that would not follow him, nor would he remain to minister to the new Presbyterian congregation, then in process of formation.

THE DISAPPEARANCE OF PARK STREET

Despite the same relative strength of the non-uniting minority, the situation in Park Street could not have been more different from St Andrew's. The Disruption sealed the fate of Park Street as a separate congregation. So intense was its minority opposition to church union that, once the congregational vote in favour of the United Church had taken place and the Presbyterians withdrew, the unionists realized they could not sustain the church on their own. The withdrawal of the Presbyterians was both the cause and the occasion of Park Street's merger with St John's, which was strongly unionist. It had been common knowledge ever since Robert Johnston's departure in the spring of 1918 that Park Street was situated beyond convenient reach for many of its members. The city had been expanding rapidly in the area of the new site of St John's on the west side of Windsor Street, a principal north-south thoroughfare. Yet in unionist demonology, sustained efforts to merge these two "midnorth" congregations following the 1917 Halifax Harbour Explosion – in which both church buildings were badly damaged – were frustrated not so much by urban demography as by those followers of former minister Johnston, who afterwards withdrew when Park Street voted to enter the United Church.

The pulpit of St John's fell vacant in October 1924 and – purposely – was not filled. The then minister of Park Street, Alexander Louis Fraser, was slated by Presbytery to become minister of the soon-to-be-merged congregations. A staunch unionist tailor-made for St John's, Fraser had such an impact at Park Street that after six years in the pulpit (1918–24), he had completely undone Johnston's careful work, turning a 79 per cent

vote against church union in 1915 into a 64 per cent vote in favour of
the United Church in 1924. In March 1925 Park Street merged with
St John's, and Fraser took over as first minister of what would soon be
St John's United. The eighty-two-year history of Park Street had come to
a premature end.

DENOUEMENT

On 24 May 1925 the unionists celebrated the jubilee of The Presbyterian
Church in Canada at St Matthew's.[36] For obvious reasons, the date was
brought forward by three weeks; the church's official birthday was 15 June,
which would have been five days too late for unionist purposes. Some
unionist ministers close to the struggle were embittered by their encounter
with the Presbyterian resistance. Writing in the inaugural issue of the *New
Outlook,* the United Church's weekly magazine, R.W. Ross of Fort Massey,
who had organized the jubilee service, castigated the Presbyterians.[37] As
the chief unionist organizer in Halifax Presbytery, Ross was keenly aware
that the non-uniting minority Presbyterians exercised an influence out of
all proportion to their numbers.

The 51st and last pre-Disruption General Assembly of The Presbyterian
Church in Canada was to meet in Toronto in June 1925. In February the
national chair of the Presbyterian Church Association announced that the
first General Assembly of the "Continuing Presbyterian Church in Canada"
would begin in Toronto on 10 June. It was to be preceded by a pre-
Assembly congress that would plan for the reconstruction of the church.[38]
The Presbyterian congress not only admitted women as delegates but also
accredited commissioners from congregations with non-uniting majorities.
The Maritimes were well represented and submitted encouraging reports.
The three delegates from Halifax, where there were no continuing con-
gregations, were Donald MacOdrum and Frank Baird (both of whom had
long since resigned their pulpits) and Mary Moore, president of the
Women's Missionary Society.[39]

On 9 June, the General Assembly having declined to hear or receive an
official protest against its dissolution, the uniting majority commissioners
adjourned and paraded out of the Assembly hall, completing the disruption of The Presbyterian Church in Canada. The non-uniting minority
commissioners remained in place, attempting to transact business despite
former moderator Charles William Gordon's mean-spirited instruction to
the organist to strike up the "Hallelujah" chorus from Handel's *Messiah* in
a vain effort to drown them out. The faithful remnant, like the disciples

in the upper room,[40] moved to Knox Church and resumed sitting over midnight, when, according to act of Parliament, The Presbyterian Church in Canada passed out of existence. David George McQueen, the last opponent of union to be elected moderator (in 1912), was now acclaimed provisional moderator, and the 51st General Assembly carried on.[41]

WHY THE RESISTANCE TO CHURCH UNION SUCCEEDED

The biographer of George Monro Grant, Barry Mack, subtitled his study of twentieth-century Canadian Presbyterianism "from preaching to propaganda to marginalization."[42] Exemplifying the transition from preaching to propaganda was the movement towards church union, while the transition from propaganda to marginalization was reflected in its achievement. "Church union" was the most decisive, divisive, and destructive event in the 125-year history of The Presbyterian Church in Canada: both an end and a beginning – or neither – depending on one's perspective. For Mack, the question posed by church union is how The Presbyterian Church in Canada survived its own suicide. For David Brian Marshall, on the other hand, the union movement – clergy-instigated and clergy-led – epitomized a "crisis of belief," its end time "an era of drift" and union itself the final act of "secularizing the faith."[43]

It was lost on unionists that The Presbyterian Church in Canada, as the largest Protestant body in the country, already was "the united church of Canada." In the year of its disruption, the PCC had already been a united and uniting church for fifty years. Ecumenical union at the cost of disruption and schism was too high a price to pay for an idea whose time had come and gone. All that the unionists were really capable of doing was destroying the church, and in that they very nearly succeeded. It would have been more constructive for the Presbyterians to have invited the Methodists and Congregationalists – and indeed, all Protestant evangelicals – to join *them.* Instead, the tide of secularism and "mergermania" rose so high that it crested a disruption and schism which engulfed and nearly drowned the church.

The Presbyterian Church in Canada which existed on and after 10 June 1925 was a conserved presbyterian worshipping community. It laid claim to historical and ecclesial continuity with the Church of Scotland, as reformed in 1560, and The Presbyterian Church in Canada, as formed in 1875. The United Church, on the other hand, sought to replace the Presbyterian Church without succeeding or continuing it. Those Presbyterians who preserved the church in Canada were a grassroots movement of clergy and laity who defied a largely clerical intelligentsia – officialdom and the professoriate – who placed ecclesiasticism before evangelism, theology before doctrine, and, in Robert Johnston's memorable dictum, machinery before light. For the non-uniting minority, church union was pure "treason by the intellectuals."

The resistance to church union had nothing to do with sectarianism, denominationalism, ethnic determinism, or anti-ecumenism. It was neither progressive nor conservative, in theology or ecclesiology. Presbyterians were not fighting for *a* church – much less a Scottish-Canadian church – but for *the* Church, the spiritual body of Christ. The Presbyterian Church in Canada was a witnessing, confessing, and evangelizing church – and never more so than during the conflagration of 1923–25, when the burning bush was nearly consumed. The preservation of The Presbyterian Church in Canada was the triumph of ecclesiology over ecclesiasticism.[44]

Church union was achieved only through disturbing the delicate balance of church-state relations. Canada was not Scotland, and no Presbyterian church was, or ever had been, established. Indeed, the Canadian Presbyterian tradition, even within the Kirk, had been distinctly anti-establishmentarian. While the creation of the United Church of Canada depended no less on parliamentarians than on unionists, the preservation of The Presbyterian Church in Canada depended on Presbyterians, and on them alone. The Presbyterians were an unsilent minority who refused to be cowed or coerced. The unionists' ability to deploy state power could not prevail against the resolve of Presbyterians to preserve their church. Through its people, the church proved indestructible, but now it had to be rebuilt from the ground up – congregation, presbytery, synod, general assembly. Continuation was a matter of surviving long enough to commence and complete this reconstruction. The Presbyterians were Covenanters, fighting anew the battle for separation of church and state, which everyone thought had been won long ago. It was a typical Scottish reformation and post-reformation scenario.

Ironically, however, in seeking a new identity to distinguish it from its former discredited self, The Presbyterian Church in Canada became for all practical purposes the Church of Scotland in Canada. It was both returning and reverting to the tangled roots of Presbyterianism in British North America. It is no coincidence that, from and after 1925, the official collective title of congregational elders has been "*kirk* session."[45] What emerged from the ashes of John Moir's "smouldering bush" was a latter-day Kirk of Canada. After the Disruption, The Presbyterian Church in

Canada would not only be much smaller than it had been before but also very different. It had undergone a psychologically traumatic near-death experience from which it would at length recover, but with which it would afterwards be identified – and identify itself. If the promise of survival was reconstruction, then the price was retrenchment.

3

Death and Resurrection

Ironically, the significant anti-union vote in St Andrew's would pave the way for friendly relations between St Andrew's United and the new "Presbyterian Church, Halifax." As in the other congregations, not every Presbyterian who voted against the United Church left St Andrew's – at least, not immediately. Of the 145 who voted against the United Church – the largest "anti" vote of any congregation in the presbytery – only 101 actually left. The pull of congregational loyalty was exceedingly strong, as were inertia, convenience, and the seductive principle that the devil one knows is preferable to the devil one doesn't. Some Presbyterians left only after a decent interval, when they concluded that the United Methodist Church and St Andrew's Presbyterian were unequally yoked and that St Andrew's United was more Methodist than Presbyterian; or when they learned, to their relief, that the Presbyterian Church was continuing in Halifax against all the odds. They could not forsake their old church home unless and until they were sure of another, which would stand for, and in some sense be, the continuation of the auld kirk.

In mid-February 1925 the national office of the Presbyterian Church Association announced a plurality of 2,362 against, among Presbyterians in congregations voting on membership in the United Church.[1] The news would have proved cold comfort to Presbyterians in Halifax, "an island surrounded by unionists."[2] In no congregation other than Musquodoboit Harbour in rural Halifax County, which had gone United Church by a mere 7 votes, was there a non-uniting minority strong enough to form a new congregation, which was soon done. Of the 1,715 Presbyterians in the metropolitan region who cast ballots, only 421, or 24.5 per cent, voted

against the United Church, and not all of those left their congregations –
at least, not right away.

The question in Halifax was whether there would be a new Presbyterian
congregation or merely isolated anti-union Presbyterians dispersed among
nine different uniting majority congregations.[3] The matter was pressing.
While Parliament made ample provision for non-uniting majority congregations to vote themselves out of the United Church, no provision had been
made for the non-uniting minority in uniting congregations, except to
remain where they were. The rights of non-uniting minorities were not
protected, and they were left to fend for themselves, if they had the will
and the means to do so. Even before congregational voting was over, the
focus of the resistance in Halifax began to shift from the near-hopeless task
of salvaging even one congregation to reconstructing the church at the
congregational level.

No sooner had the results of the congregational vote in Halifax been
announced on 8 January 1925 than the local executive of the Presbyterian
Church Association met and unanimously resolved to take steps to prepare for organizing a congregation.[4] The necessary first step was organizing public worship. Though the PCA hoped to begin with a congregation
of more than two hundred,[5] it could not expect the non-uniting minority
in the various Presbyterian churches to abandon their congregational
homes unless and until it could offer a consistent alternative venue for
Sunday worship. A search committee was struck, while it was announced
that public worship would be held on Sunday, 18 January. For obvious
reasons, unionist sanctuaries were closed to remanent Presbyterians. First
Baptist, a large church then at the corner of Spring Garden and Queen
in the downtown, volunteered. That was the beginning of close relations
between First Baptist and what would become the Presbyterian Church of
Saint David.

On Saturday, 17 January 1925, the following advertisement appeared in
Halifax newspapers:

PRESBYTERIAN CHURCH

———

First Service of the New Presbyterian Congregation

FIRST BAPTIST CHURCH

SUNDAY AT 3 P.M.

Sermon by Rev. Robert Johnston, M.A., of New Glasgow.

Service of Praise led by Mr.
Fred M. Guildford.
All are Welcome.[6]

As many as seven hundred turned out. The moderator of the provisional synod, who had spent the larger part of his ministerial career in Halifax, began by reading a prepared statement on behalf of the Presbyterian Church Association.[7] Johnston preached from John 14:27 ("Let not your heart be troubled …"), a strongly Christocentric sermon in which the word "Presbyterian" was not so much as mentioned.[8] For Johnston, there was no dissonance between witnessing to Presbyterianism and proclaiming the gospel of salvation. Nothing less than first principles were at stake. The gospel was a message that found its purest articulation and most perfect distillation in Presbyterian worship, work, and witness. The resistance to church union was the symbolic renewal in twentieth-century Canada of the Solemn League and Covenant in seventeenth-century Scotland. Halifax's "new Presbyterian Congregation" was a broad church in which all were indeed welcome.

A provisional session was soon appointed from among those elders willing to serve who had been members of Session in their former congregations. Convened by Frank Baird, one of only two "anti" ministers in the city, this "committee of elders" functioned until 14 July 1925, when it was succeeded and replaced by an official Kirk Session. A.D. Falconer, formerly clerk of Session at Bethany, chaired the committee. Eleven strong, it was dominated by elders from St Andrew's, where the resistance to church union had been loudest and strongest.[9] All the existing Presbyterian congregations were represented except St Matthew's, whose minister was chair of the presbytery's union committee, and St John's, where there had been no resistance and little opposition to church union. It seems probable that the committee of elders included most of the executive of the Halifax PCA, of which Falconer was president and W.J. Kane (Park Street) treasurer.

The cooperative arrangement with First Baptist lasted for just over two months, from 18 January through 29 March. Pulpit supply proved to be more of a problem than supplying a pulpit. "Anti" ministers, whose ranks were decidedly thin and who were more than usually in demand all across the country, had to be supplemented by Baptists and even the occasional Anglican. Helping local Presbyterians continue The Presbyterian Church in Canada proved a fashionable cause among Anglicans and Baptists, both of whom had exited early on from the church union discussions.

Presbyterian services were well attended by sermon-tasters and church-shoppers, as well as by committed Presbyterians. The Church School was inaugurated on 22 February, when nearly a hundred children were in attendance; the Wednesday evening prayer meetings probably began soon after. On Sunday morning and evening, 8 March 1925, Donald MacOdrum preached his last sermons in St Andrew's; in the afternoon he presided at the continuing Presbyterian communion service in First Baptist Church. On that occasion Frank Baird preached as fighting and partisan a sermon as Johnston's inaugural one, which had been given over to spiritual uplift. The Presbyterians took leave of the Baptists at a reception on 17 April, at which Johnston was guest of honour. The Baptists were presented a handsome pulpit Bible bearing on its front cover, in golden letters, "PRESENTED TO THE FIRST BAPTIST / CHURCH BY THE PRESBYTERIAN / CHURCH, HALIFAX IN APPRECIATION / OF COURTESIES EXTENDED DURING / THE TIME OF NEED, JANUARY, / FEBRUARY AND MARCH 1925."[10]

"THE PRESBYTERIAN CHURCH, HALIFAX"

A decisive step was taken on 26 February 1925 when the Presbyterians met further to Nova Scotia's Religious Congregations and Societies Act for the purpose of organizing a congregation.[11] They were not alone, nor were they the first, in Canada or in Nova Scotia. No sooner had the six congregations in Regina voted United Church than the non-uniting minority met on 5 January and decided to proceed with organizing a Presbyterian church. Ten days later Stellarton did likewise,[12] followed at the end of January by Sydney. The die was cast.

The Halifax meeting, delayed until after the result of the vote in St Andrew's was known on 10 February, had to address a situation as unprecedented as it was delicate. As a matter of federal law, The Presbyterian Church in Canada would remain in existence until 10 June 1925. No precedent or provision existed for disaffected members in good standing to form a congregation outside the church. Collectively, the non-uniting minority from the uniting majority congregations were following the most divisive course imaginable – rebelling against the church and its discipline and order. The proceeding was wholly un-Presbyterian.[13] Such a meeting could only be authorized by Presbytery and only take place after Presbytery had approved the formation of a congregation and appointed an interim moderator from among ministers on the constituent roll of Presbytery to convene the meeting and organize a provisional session. A provisional synod may have existed, but there was no provisional presbytery to which the intending congregation might appeal for assistance.

Halifax Presbyterians tried to circumvent these church-legal difficulties by having Frank Baird, still a member in good standing of Halifax Presbytery, preside. By doing so, Baird was risking censure and even suspension, but if he thought that Presbytery would not dare take action against him, he was right.[14] The meeting was chaired by lawyer Robert David McCleave, a prominent non-uniting elder from St Andrew's. "Eight Resolutions," drafted by Baird, were passed constituting "The Presbyterian Church, Halifax."[15] The meeting concluded with the singing of "O God of Bethel," the Scottish psalm most frequently heard at moments of sorrow or crisis in the life of the church. The final resolution was a prayer of surpassing eloquence that still resonates.[16]

After the meeting was over, the elders assembled for the first time and appointed W.J. Kane provisional clerk. Kane also became treasurer of the congregation, thus inaugurating a tradition of office-holding by elders that has continued to the present day. The elders were inevitably less representative of the membership than the trustees, 73 per cent of them coming from St Andrew's (five) and Park Street (three), where resistance to church union had been strongest. Together, the elders and trustees were to act as a joint management committee until such time as a mainland Presbyterian presbytery could be re-established after 10 June 1925.

Elders and trustees were kept busy building the infrastructure of the new congregation and preparing for 10 June, after which they – and they alone – would be the Presbyterian Church in Halifax. On 18 March an official letter over the signatures of the chair and the secretary of the trustees went out to the "Members and Friends of the Continuing Presbyterian Church" inviting all those who had not yet done so to join the Presbyterian Church, Halifax, and providing an up-to-date status and situation report. As the question of securing a permanent church home had not yet been settled, financial concerns were paramount.[17]

FINDING A CHURCH HOME

Park Street, surplus as of 29 March 1925, had been home to prominent resisters such as R.A. Guildford and W.J. Kane, clerks of Session there for thirty years. The Presbyterians could have purchased it for half of what they eventually paid for Grafton Street Church had its current lessees, the Full Gospel Church, not held an option to buy. Park Street, a wooden structure just over forty years old, had been substantially refurbished after damage sustained in the great explosion of December 1917. On top of everything else, it had also been Robert Johnston's church. It had, to put it mildly, cachet.

Grafton Street Church lay scarcely a block away from First Baptist (at the northeast corner of Queen and Spring Garden), where the Presbyterians had been worshipping since January. No sooner had the non-uniting minority commenced public worship on 18 January 1925 than the Methodists offered the Halifax PCA the use of Grafton Street Church free of charge for Sunday afternoon and evening worship.[18] The Presbyterians, wary of Greeks bearing gifts, deferred responding until they had organized as a congregation. A mere four days afterwards, on 2 March, they inquired about the possibility of leasing Grafton Street Church from April through June.

Built on and over the Old Methodist Burying Ground (1793–1844), Grafton Street Church had been a centre of Methodist witness in Halifax for seventy-three years. In June 1924, however, after a decade of negotiations, Grafton Street Methodist, shorn of its former wealth and numbers, had reluctantly merged with its daughter congregation, Robie Street, to become the United Methodist Church.[19] Public worship services alternated between Grafton Street and Robie Street. In January 1925, in anticipation of a further union with its near neighbour, St Andrew's Presbyterian, the United Methodist Church decided to rebuild on the site of the Robie Street church; Grafton Street would be sold to help finance the project.[20]

United Methodist agreed to the Presbyterians' request, and arrangements for the three-month lease of the Grafton Street premises at $50 per month were soon formally completed. Grafton Street's last Methodist service was held on 29 March 1925. The following Sunday the building was occupied by the Presbyterians for the first time. The short-term lease, renewed and extended for a year to the end of June 1926, could be neither renewed nor extended indefinitely. Though the Presbyterian Church, Halifax, as lessee, had first refusal, it had to exercise its option to buy before another prospective purchaser offered. There was widespread concern that the building and property might be converted to commercial use.

There were four disused or former church buildings then on the market: Park Street, Temple Baptist (in the North End), The Auditorium (old St Andrew's), and Grafton Street. Though the oldest of the four, Grafton Street was built of brick and stone. The elders and trustees were satisfied with the general condition of the fifty-six-year-old building, with its central and attractive location near Grafton Park and especially with the brick "schoolhouse" (1866) close behind the church, which served as the hall. Under the terms of the $1,500 lease, however, the congregation had also assumed responsibility for all repairs, taxes, water rates, and assessment, which provided further incentive to stick with the devil they knew and stay where they were.

There was not a moment to lose. At the end of September 1925 the following advertisement appeared in Halifax newspapers: "Sealed tenders will be received until October 20th for the purchase of GRAFTON STREET CHURCH PROPERTY Corner Grafton and Blowers Streets, in the City of Halifax, either for the buildings alone or for the buildings with all fittings, including pipe-organ, seats and electric fixtures. Highest or any tender not necessarily accepted." In October St Andrew's United sought and received permission from the United Church presbytery to sell Grafton Street Church. In November it offered to sell the church building with all its fittings to the Presbyterians for $30,000. At a special congregational meeting held on 2 December to consider the offer, the Presbyterians voted to remit the matter to the joint management committee. As the offer was time-limited, the subcommittee on the church building wasted no time accepting it.[21]

The agreement of sale, executed on 11 January 1926, was to have become effective on 1 July, but transfer of the property was delayed until the spring of 1927. Not only did the Presbyterians have to raise the money; doubts arose as to whether St Andrew's United had the legal right to sell property formerly held in trust by and for the Methodists. This obstacle necessitated the passage of an act to confirm and declare the title warranty. *An Act to Vest the Grafton Street Methodist Church Property, so-called, in the Trustees of the United Church of Canada at St. Andrew's Church, Halifax* was passed on 11 March 1927.[22] In order to finance the purchase, the Presbyterians met on 23 March to authorize the trustees to execute a mortgage.

On top of everything else, however, the lawyers were concerned that the power to mortgage, which the act of incorporation gave the trustees, might not be "ample and sufficient." The act was therefore amended to provide for a majority vote by a majority of those entitled to vote and present in person or by proxy at a special meeting called for the purpose.[23] The $20,000 mortgage, amounting to two-thirds of the cost, was taken by the University of King's College, evidence of the high esteem in which the continuing Presbyterians were held by the Church of England establishment. The conveyance was executed on 14 April, and the mortgage nine days later. After two years the Presbyterian Church, Halifax, finally had a home to call its own.

CALLING A MINISTER

The great unsolved mystery of the early history of Saint David's is why Donald MacOdrum did not become its first minister. A free agent as of 8 March 1925, MacOdrum was without a pulpit and the new Presbyterian congregation in Halifax without a minister. But the inevitable did not happen. MacOdrum believed until the last moment that St Andrew's would continue and seems to have been deeply disappointed that the same resisters who now loomed so large in the newly minted congregation had failed to deliver enough votes to keep St Andrew's out of the United Church. It is telling that after a brief stint as interim moderator of the new First Presbyerian, Stellarton, MacOdrum opted for a continuing congregation in Ontario such as he had vainly hoped St Andrew's would become.

The double departure of MacOdrum from the Maritimes and of Frank Baird from Halifax to fill the vacant pulpit of First Church, Pictou, a continuing congregation where both the minister and the entire Session had resigned in consequence of the vote, meant that the Presbyterian Church, Halifax, was without a minister or even the prospect of one. Continuing ministers were scarce throughout the Synod, except in Prince Edward Island, where resistance among ministers and elders had been strongest. A nationwide official census of Presbyterian ministers taken on the eve of the congregational vote showed that fully 80 per cent were unionists.[24] Not to be outdone by this bit of timely propaganda from the General Assembly's church union committee, the Presbyterian Church Association announced that it would turn to the United States, especially to ministers who been born or educated in Canada. In the end, however, few came and fewer stayed, though some ministerial candidates from Princeton Theological Seminary supplied pulpits in Nova Scotia in the summer of 1925.

Psychologically, it was perhaps understandable that a new congregation made up of tried and true Presbyterians from diverse and not necessarily compatible congregational backgrounds should look back to a time before Presbyterianism in any form had arrived in Canada and, moreover, look to the Church of Scotland for a minister. What was needed was one who would not only meld the scattered remnants into a coherent whole but also be able and disinterested enough to meet the unionist intelligentsia – the MacKinnons and Falconers – on their own terms. Many of the continuing Presbyterians were exhausted front-line veterans of the resistance to church union; their minister needed to be someone with no first-hand knowledge of or personal involvement in it.

Finding such a person in Canada would have been a tall order. Predictably, the task of carrying out the search in the old country fell to Robert Johnston, then en route to Britain as part of a blue-ribbon deputation to the British General Assemblies and the Pan-Presbyterian Council to assure them that the PCC was still functioning. Fortunately, he had some assistance on the ground. Henry Gibson Bauld's brother-in-law was George Duncan, son of the Reverend Thomas Duncan, a former minister of old St Andrew's. George, having spent his early years in Halifax, had come back to Canada to serve as minister of St Andrew (and then St Andrew and St Paul, Montreal) in the years 1914–24. A strong "anti," he would act as go-between for the Presbyterian Church, Halifax, in its quest for a minister.

With Johnston as plenipotentiary and Duncan as talent scout, the search for a minister proceeded.[25] Duncan's "find" was James Campbell, the minister at Glencairn, Dumfriesshire, where Duncan himself had formerly served. On 4 June Johnston telegraphed that he was sailing for Quebec on the *Athenia* and bringing with him a Kirk minister for Halifax. The arrangement was that he would supply for the summer, preach for a call, and accept it if offered. James Campbell, his wife, and seven-year-old son travelled from Quebec via the Maritime Express, arriving in Halifax on 16 June. They were accompanied as far as Truro by Johnston and from there to Halifax by W.J. Kane, and were met at the station by a great throng of Presbyterians. The Campbells were received as guests of A.D. Falconer, president of the Halifax PCA, before taking up a rented apartment. Campbell preached his first sermons on Sunday, the 21st, and made a profound impression. His preaching even attracted favourable comment from John A. MacGlashen, minister at Stairs Memorial United and clerk of Presbytery. MacGlashen, whose weekend column in Halifax's *Morning Chronicle*, "Chimes from the Belfry," was much read, went out of his way to praise Campbell.[26] Indeed, this was the first occasion on which MacGlashen had deigned to notice the existence of the Presbyterian Church, which he otherwise airily dismissed as "Halifax Scotsmen of the Blue Banner brand." In MacGlashen's eyes, Campbell had the decisive advantage of being a Presbyterian minister far removed in every sense from the resistance to church union in Canada; he was *persona grata*.

On 30 June James Campbell, bearing fraternal greetings from the Church of Scotland, addressed the inaugural meeting of the newly reconstituted Presbytery of Pictou and was added to the ministerial roll as an associate. However, the statesmanlike advice he gave his fellow ministers – to put the resistance to church union behind them – was followed neither then nor later. Presbytery soon took steps to establish formally the

Presbyterian Church, Halifax, as a congregation. Robert Johnston was appointed "assessor" (interim moderator), and on the 13th he formally constituted the Kirk Session. W.J. Kane was confirmed as clerk.

The prospective minister was decidedly high kirk, really a Scoto-Catholic; his quasi-mystical sermons in the Presbyterian Church, Halifax, on unconventional topics such as the stigmata attracted attention. High kirk Presbyterianism had the virtue of novelty, and Campbell's brief, foreshortened ministry remains the great "what if" of Saint David's. So impressed were the trustees by his preaching that, after three Sundays, they were encouraging Session to recommend to the congregation that he be called. Anticipating that Campbell would be in place for two months or more, Johnston stepped down as interim moderator on 13 July. Campbell told a newspaperman that he had to report to his presbytery in Scotland no later than 15 October;[27] he would be gone long before that. Barely two weeks after taking over from Johnston, Campbell unexpectedly left; Mrs Campbell had found herself quite unable to tolerate Halifax any longer.[28] Her husband preached his last sermons on 26 July; he had given the congregation a mere six Sundays. The congregation, however, had reason to hope that his departure would be temporary, that he would honour his undertaking. It was not to be. On or about 19 August Campbell sent a telegram declining the call that had been offered him. In the eyes of W.J. Kane and many others, he was guilty of bad faith. Johnston, both hands already overfull, had no alternative but to resume his duties as interim moderator.

"A SUPERMAN FROM SCOTLAND"

The provisional Synod of the Maritime Provinces was already flourishing when, on 10 June 1925, it became permanent. By September there were a hundred congregations,[29] while the number of ministers stood at forty-five.[30] Synod met in Robert Johnston's church in New Glasgow – fittingly renamed "Westminster" – in October. Breaking with tradition, Synod re-elected him moderator, recognition that he was both head and heart of the continuing Presbyterian Church in the Maritimes.

Since the Presbyterian Church, Halifax, was still without a minister, A.D. Falconer attended Synod as acting interim moderator, together with R.D. McCleave as representative elder. On behalf of the congregation, Falconer extended an invitation to Synod to meet the following year in Grafton Street Church. Though contested by Pictou, with no less than two continuing congregations, Halifax's invitation was accepted. If W.J. Kane

was the business leader of the Presbyterian Church, Halifax, then Falconer –
Kane's senior by a generation – was its spiritual leader. A native of
Hopewell, Pictou County, Alexander Duncan Falconer was a wealthy
retired building contractor already seventy-three years old. But his energy
and determination belied his years. A true son of the Kirk, into which he
had been born, Falconer in April 1925 attended the final gathering of
the Maritimes PCA, called to coordinate preparations for Disruption day,
10 June 1925. He was the only resisting elder from Halifax to attend the
pre-Assembly congress of the national PCA in Toronto in June 1925, and
he would soon be instrumental in procuring a Kirkman from Scotland as
permanent minister.

Minister or no minister, the Presbyterian Church, Halifax, went from
strength to strength. By the middle of September 1925, when the first communion service according to the rules and regulations of The Presbyterian
Church in Canada was held, there were 259 professing members.[31] Yet the
Campbell debacle saw the unity that had hitherto prevailed in the collective
leadership of the congregation evaporate almost overnight. Elders and trustees, as well as members and adherents, were dividing into two factions: the
St Andrew's–Park Street group, who – once bitten, twice shy – wanted to
look harder at home for a minister, and the St Matthew's–Fort Massey
group, who wanted to look again in Scotland for another Kirkman. Almost
certainly behind the latter initiative were Falconer, with whom Johnston and
Kane did not see eye to eye, and Dr John Stewart of Fort Massey, the most
eminent lay resister in the Synod and dean of the Session.

The search for a minister resumed on two fronts, while further pulpit
supply was requisitioned. Among them was J. Keir Fraser of Knox Church
in Galt, Ontario, an important continuing congregation. Fraser, whom
Johnston, Baird, and Kane all wanted to see called, supplied three consecutive Sundays in October and was willing to accept a call, but would brook
no competition. A native Prince Edward Islander whose brother was principal of Presbyterian College, Montreal, he was a veteran of the resistance.
However, at sixty-one, Fraser was thought too old for the demanding job
of bringing up a congregation whose genesis was sufficiently exceptional
to be described as a "virgin birth." The Presbyterian Church, Halifax, was
not a continuing congregation but a new congregation made up of continuing Presbyterians who had been thrown together, willy-nilly, by the force
of circumstances. In terms of group dynamics, the congregation's history
had to begin on a positive note – as if church union was but a bad dream
and the Disruption had never happened; as if the congregation's birth was
a purely routine development responding to demographic considerations.

But it was not for these reasons alone that no call to Keir Fraser was forthcoming. Behind the backs of the official leadership, influential persons such as Falconer and Stewart were carrying on negotiations with George Duncan in the hope of procuring another "Scotsman," as W.J. Kane wryly referred to the prospect. Risky though it was to call a minister without having heard him preach, the congregation could not afford to be skewered twice. There was no question of inviting another to cross the ocean to preach for a call, only to have him decline it, as Campbell had done. Fortunately, among Duncan's broad circle of ministerial acquaintances was the former assistant of the parish where Duncan himself was currently minister – Govan, Glasgow. The Reverend Dr Colin MacKay Kerr was willing to take the plunge.

The upshot was that on 3 November 1925 the elders and trustees placed before a special congregational meeting one name and one name only. A unanimous call was extended, sight unseen, to the minister of St George's-in-the-Fields, Glasgow, a large and flourishing urban charge. A native of Aberdeen and three-time graduate of its famous university, Colin Kerr was more down to earth and perhaps more adventurous than Campbell – or perhaps it could be said that Mrs Kerr (Elizabeth Cargill) was more adventurous than Mrs Campbell. Kerr had served in the Great War for two years, not as a chaplain but in the ranks. In India from 1909 to 1911, he taught at the Scottish churches college in Calcutta, served as secretary of the Calcutta Philosophical Society, and was a chaplain to the Indian Army. He afterwards acted as examiner in church history and systematic theology at Aberdeen and as a member of the examining board for students entering and leaving the divinity halls of Scottish universities. A protege of Henry Cowan, Regius professor of divinity and church history at Aberdeen, Kerr was on the rebound from failing to be appointed Cowan's successor. He was ready to shake the dust of Scotland off his feet and came complete with a testimonial from John White, minister of the prestigious Barony Church, Glasgow, moderator of the General Assembly, and the "dominant figure" in the Church of Scotland.[32]

Eight days after the call was extended, Kerr cabled his acceptance; in December he resigned his Glasgow pulpit. The call was signed by 320 communicants and concurred in by 72 adherents. By the time it went before Pictou Presbytery on 12 November, the collective total had reached 400. That Campbell and Kerr could be offered the usual Church of Scotland stipend of $5,000 (£800 sterling),[33] six weeks' vacation, and a manse gives some idea of the financial resources which the trustees commanded. W.J. Kane was not exaggerating when he told one correspondent that the congregation was the cream of Halifax Presbyterians; he might have gone further and said that the continuing Presbyterians were the cream of Halifax society. Though the new congregation resisted George Duncan's suggestion that "kirk" be added to their name, they fully intended to be a Kirk church in everything *but* name. Indeed, no Presbyterian congregation in Halifax ever included the word "kirk" in its name, and of the three streams that converged to make Presbyterianism in Halifax, the Kirk was the weakest-flowing. How ironic it was that in the end it should triumph, that the survival and reconstruction of Presbyterianism in Halifax should depend on it.

George Duncan's father, Thomas, had been the last Kirk minister from Scotland to fill a Halifax pulpit. Fifty years on, history was repeating itself. Colin Kerr, his wife, Elizabeth, and nine-year-old daughter, Isobel Margaret, set sail for Halifax in the new Anchor-Cunard liner *California* on 9 January 1926. On Sunday, the 10th, Kerr conducted divine service shipboard. The passengers endured severe winter weather all the way across, but Kerr himself was cheered by a cablegram of welcome which reached him in mid-Atlantic. Arriving on Sunday, the 17th, the Kerrs were immediately swept off to Maplewood, the North West Arm estate of Mrs David MacKeen, widow of one lieutenant-governor and mother of another. There was no thought of a rented apartment this time round; the Kerrs were to remain guests of Mrs MacKeen until they had the leisure to select a manse. Three weeks later the Presbyterian Church, Halifax, took an interim three-month lease on the fine Queen Street house formerly occupied by William Lester Kane (a distant relative of the clerk of Session), which lay within easy walking distance of the church. By March a new, two-year lease had been secured at a better address, and in May the Kerrs moved to 127 (6345) Coburg Road.[34] A permanent manse would not be obtained until the spring of 1928.

MacGlashen ("Bellman"), writing privately and in his official capacity as clerk of the United Church presbytery, was sarcastically unwelcoming to Kerr, whom he saw as a cross between Superman and Judas Maccabaeus.[35] Kerr's imminent arrival was attracting a high degree of press interest. He was, after all, not coming to supply for a season and preach for a call, but to be the permanent minister. He even got a complimentary editorial in the *Herald* newspapers,[36] whose proprietor was a unionist from St Andrew's.

The first year in the life of the Presbyterian Church, Halifax, concluded with the induction of C.M. Kerr as minister on 18 January 1926, a year to the day after Robert Johnston had unfurled the blue banner of the Covenant in First Baptist Church. Johnston, as moderator of Synod, presided, conducted the induction ceremony, and addressed the new minister; Woodbridge O. Johnson, a young minister from Los Angeles (Northern Presbyterian Church of the USA) who had recently been inducted into the new congregation at Stellarton, preached. With amazing power of face, Clarence MacKinnon and other prominent ex-Presbyterian United Churchmen occupied front pews, provoking Frank Baird, clerk of Presbytery, who addressed the congregation, to wonder aloud whether this was not another instance of betrayal with a kiss.[37] Johnston's address to the new minister, pronounced "one of the finest ever delivered at a Presbyterian induction service in Halifax," made a profound impression.[38] The presence at the service of those very ministers deemed most to blame for the situation in which the Presbyterians found themselves can only have fired Johnston's eloquence.

THE END OF THE BEGINNING

Three days after Kerr's first appearance in the pulpit, on 27 January, the congregation met for its first annual general meeting. The act of incorporation stipulated that such a meeting be held within one year after the coming into force of the act – 7 May 1926. So rapid was the progress of the congregation, however, that it did not take nearly so long. Formal reports were tendered by the Kirk Session, the Church School, the Woman's Missionary Society, the Young People's Missionary Society and Guild, the Ladies Guild, and the Trustees. During its first year the congregation had raised more than $10,000.[39] *The First Annual Congregational Report 1925 / The Presbyterian Church, Grafton Park, Halifax N.S.* was a handsomely printed booklet, running to thirty-seven pages and illustrated with fine photographs of both the church exterior and the new minister.

The "Memoranda" that introduced the report shows how completely congregational life had sprung into being fully formed. The acquisition early in the year of a well-functioning church building and hall, which had not lain unused for even one Sunday, meant that the full range of congregational activities and events began immediately and were carried forward uninterruptedly. There was public worship on Sunday morning and evening; a Church School with two departments; a Wednesday evening prayer meeting; quarterly communion; the WMS auxiliary monthly meeting; the Young Peoples' Missionary Society and Guild, CGIT (Canadian Girls in Training), Tuxis (the CGIT equivalent for boys), and Ladies Guild weekly meetings; the Kirk Session quarterly meeting; and the Trustees' monthly meeting. On the face of it, there was nothing to suggest that the

conception, birth, and infancy of the Presbyterian Church, Halifax, had
been in any way exceptional, much less unique – except its name. It may
not have been a PCC congregation, but otherwise the Presbyterian Church,
Halifax, was a seamless web.

Synod convened in Grafton Street Church on 5 October 1926. Kerr was
invited onto the platform to join the moderators of the General Assembly
and Synod and the clerk of Synod, a unique honour. After two long and
difficult years as moderator, Robert Johnston was ready to step down. Having
surpassed all others, he, in his farewell sermon, surpassed himself. Taking
as his text Revelation 2:4 ("Thou hast left thy first love") and as his theme
Christ the crucified leader, he implicitly compared the United Church of
Canada with the new civic religion that the more radical ideologues among
the French revolutionaries had tried but failed to invent or sustain.[40]

Johnston's work was done and he knew it. Despite the washout of the
congregational vote and the teething troubles, no one realized more
clearly than he the strategic necessity of re-establishing the Presbyterian
Church in Halifax – and soon. By the end of 1926, membership had risen
to 397, an increase of 53 per cent over 1925. Johnston took leave of the
Presbyterians of Halifax on Sunday evening, 17 July 1927, a few weeks
before his departure for Ottawa – preaching on "Man's self-respect." Earlier
that day he had dedicated the new church at Musquodoboit Harbour. The
Presbyterian Church, Halifax, was so distressed about the prospect of his
departure from the scene that the Kirk Session sent a letter of concern to
the Presbytery of Pictou and placed a copy of it in the Session minute book.

On 10 June 1925 the continuing Presbyterian Church in Atlantic
Canada was a synod with one presbytery, Prince Edward Island. Three
weeks after the United Church came into being, Pictou Presbytery was re-
established, with jurisdiction over all of mainland Nova Scotia. Without a
congregation and settled minister in Halifax, however, re-forming Halifax
Presbytery would have been unthinkable. By January 1926 there was both
congregation and minister. At Pictou Presbytery's meeting in April, Kerr
moved that the General Assembly be overtured to divide the Presbytery of
Pictou in two.[41] The General Assembly remitted the matter to the next
meeting of Synod, which nominated Kerr as first moderator.[42] In October
1926 the Presbytery of Halifax – "and Lunenburg" (a tribute to the continuing congregation of St Andrew's) – was set off from Pictou, and Kerr
acclaimed moderator.

The new Presbytery of Halifax and Lunenburg met for the first time at
Grafton Street Church on 2 November 1926. The representative ruling
elders from the Presbyterian Church, Halifax, were H.D. Wallace and

Dr John Stewart. Wallace was elected treasurer. Presbytery showed its grateful appreciation of Robert Johnston by nominating him for moderator of the General Assembly.

THE FUTURE OF THE PAST

The fathers and mothers of the Presbyterian Church, Halifax, were a faithful remnant, and the congregation they founded a conscious and deliberate act of Reformed witness. In effect, therefore, the 1925 Disruption of The Presbyterian Church in Canada was not wholly negative. Seen as a purification by fire, it had a salutary impact. The PCC became less so that it might, by growing in grace, become more. Church union may have divided Presbyterian congregations, as it divided the church into two unequal parts, but it also renewed Presbyterians. It turned them away from the secular and materialistic "One Big Church" model of Christian unity to a personal and communal rededication to the worship of God in spirit and in truth.

Among continuing Presbyterians, in Halifax as elsewhere, it incited something of a spiritual renewal. The PCC from and after 1925 would be again the witnessing and confessing church that it had been at its birth in 1875. It would rediscover its roots – not in Scottishness but in preaching, prayer, and worship. It would not turn back the clock but instead restart it. For its part, the Presbyterian Church, Halifax, had no tradition, only a congeries of nine different congregational traditions – partly complementary, partly conflicting. The new congregation was to be a richly interwoven tapestry.

PART TWO

The Ministers

4

Colin MacKay Kerr

In its first eighty years Saint David's has had five ministers. Three have been new Canadians, one Canadian-born, and one a Nova Scotian. All have been men; women only became eligible for ordination to the ministry of word and sacrament in the first year of the third pastorate, 1966. All but one of the ministers were in their forties when beginning their pastorates; the oldest was fifty-seven, the youngest forty-one. The length of the four completed pastorates ranged from twenty-two years to nine; the average has been seventeen years. None of these four ministers died in office: the first and second resigned; the third and fourth retired. With one exception, a new pastorate has always signalled intergenerational change; the first minister was born in 1880, the second in 1899, the third in 1908, the fourth in 1928, and the fifth in 1958.

Saint David's Pastorates

Minister	*Begun*	*Ended*	*Duration*
Kerr	Jan. 1926	Mar. 1944	18 yr 2 mo.
Lawson	Sept. 1945	Sept. 1965	20 yr 0 mo.
Mackay	Feb. 1966	June 1975	9 yr 4 mo.
Pace	Apr. 1976	Sept. 1998	22 yr 5 mo.
DeWolfe	Sept. 1999		

In January 1927 the Presbyterian Church, Halifax, celebrated its second anniversary and its minister his first. In the course of the anniversary sermon, preached on Exodus 12:26 ("What mean ye by this service?"), Colin Kerr reflected on the congregation's brief history and his own as its minister.[1]

It had, indeed, been an eventful year. On Sunday, 24 January 1926, Kerr preached his first sermons.[2] In addition to announcing changes to the order of service, which Kerr was at pains to point out were not carved in stone, he also declared his intention to speak briefly to the children each Sunday, as he had been accustomed to doing in Scotland. The practice established itself quickly and persists to this day. Kerr began to devote five minutes before the regular sermon to this Children's Address: "The girls and boys gave him their full and interested attention from first to last, and it may be observed that he has a gift for arresting and holding their attention and that his talks are becoming a telling feature of the morning service each Sunday."[3]

No sooner had Kerr ascended his pulpit than the congregation held its first annual meeting, on 27 January 1926. Of course, he could take no credit for the "notable progress" that had been made during the first year when the congregation was without a regularly called and inducted minister. From the start, Kerr never attended annual congregational meetings, but his "Message to the People" was printed in the first annual report. The feature would not reappear for half a century.

Front-line soldier, preacher, pastor, teacher, and scholar,[4] Colin Kerr seemed to promise all things to all people. Indeed, his first secular engagement after his arrival in Halifax was to address the Halifax branch of the Overseas League on the impact of the Great War on Scotland; even the Church of England archbishop attended.[5] Kerr could hardly have made a more positive first impression.

As if to stress to his flock that in the Kirk there was neither Jew nor Greek, he preached a series of Lenten sermons on the Westminster Confession, the Presbyterian creed. Beginning on 28 February 1926 with chapter 1 ("Of the Holy Scriptures"), he offered sermons with titles such as "Vision of the unseen," "Divine interventions, or the religion of signs," "The need and the power of spiritual vision," "The reasonableness of prayer," and "The nature and being of God." If Kerr was not quite the divinity professor lecturing ministerial candidates, then he was determined to save the souls of his people by at least improving their minds. Oral tradition around the reconditeness of his sermons persisted for years: "It has been said of him that he would study such works as Einstein's Theory of Relativity for months to enable him to preach a 20-minute sermon on this difficult topic."[6] But Kerr was also at pains to emphasize that the sermon, however learned, was not an end in itself.[7]

The local press quickly took stock of the new Presbyterian minister: "Rev. Dr Kerr of St David's Church is one of our clergy who keeps himself in touch with world happenings."[8] As early as September 1928, he was preaching against the forthcoming Lateran Treaty ("Democracy, Christian liberty and Mussolini"),[9] which made Vatican City a sovereign state. His two-part series of evening sermons on "Bolshevism" (March 1930) attracted wide interest and favourable comment. In July 1932 the substance of "a striking sermon" that Kerr gave on Soviet Russia as the Antichrist (1 John 2:22) was published "by request of many."[10] As early as May 1933, a mere four months after Hitler became chancellor of Germany, Kerr was preaching against the persecution of the Jews as unchristian and indefensible. By November 1936 he was teaching his people that the Nazi regime in Germany was the enemy of Christians no less than of Jews: "What is Nazism and what is its relation to Christianity?" By November 1938, when the war scare was at its height, he was offering a series on "The religious situation in Germany." No less deeply committed a Scoto-Catholic ecumenist than an anti-fascist, Kerr repeated by request the following week the address he gave at evening service on the 27th dealing with the attack on the Roman Catholic Church in Germany.

Though he did not shy away from political and social issues, many of Kerr's sermons – especially Sunday evenings' – were highbrow. Half in fun, wholly in earnest, his hearers wondered loudly to themselves what he was talking about.[11] Saint David's was not the lecture hall of the divinity school of the University of Aberdeen, nor was the pulpit a lectern. Nevertheless, Kerr believed that the church must engage fully with the world and that the life of the intellect was a window on that world as surely as the gospel was the rule of life. Of particular timeliness early in the twenty-first century would have been the subject of Kerr's "Christianity and the Moslem world" (1929). Wearisomely new-age was the question "Do you believe in angels?" (1939). One cannot help wondering what might have been the subtext of his July 1929 sermon "Detractors," in which Kerr warned his audience that it was "impossible to undo the mischief done by idle gossip." Some sermon titles appear to have been tongue-in-cheek: "What college did to my religion," "The foolishness of preaching," and "The dangers of middle age" (the minister was fifty-three at the time).[12] One Sunday in December 1934 he preached morning and evening sermons, respectively, on "The foolish virgins" and "What men most desire."

Kerr also contributed at least four "short sermons" to the "Churches" page of the Halifax *Evening Mail*.[13] In the spring of 1934 he was one of six Halifax ministers – three of them professors at Pine Hill Divinity Hall – who took part in a Lenten series of lectures, "What the church believes," sponsored by the Pine Hill Theological Society. Kerr's contribution was to have been "What the Church believes about science."[14] In January 1935 he became the first Presbyterian minister to preach from a United Church pulpit, exchanging with the new Scottish minister of Fort Massey.

Kerr was an ecumenical Kirkman who took seriously his self-defined role as goodwill ambassador for The Presbyterian Church in Canada. Not only did he bring Saint David's into the annual week of prayer sponsored by the Halifax and Dartmouth Ministerial Association, a fixture among Reformed churches since 1847. Beginning in 1926 he represented the PCC at meetings of the Western (North and South American) section of the World Presbyterian Alliance.[15] In February 1930 this role took him to Atlantic City, New Jersey, where, at the invitation of the president, Alfred Gandier (a pre-Disruption moderator of the General Assembly), he conducted the opening services. In June he attended the thirteenth quadrennial general council meeting of the WPA in Boston. Kerr travelled less in the summer of 1930, however, for in August he had surgery for a sudden and serious illness, which kept him away from his pulpit for a month. As in 1926, he made a complete recovery. In 1931 he took his wife and fifteen-year-old daughter to Scotland for two months. In February that year he attended the WPA conference in Washington, DC, and a year later, in Richmond (Virginia). In the summer of 1933 Kerr, one of whose four languages was French,[16] spent a month in Quebec City as pulpit-exchange preacher. In March 1934 he celebrated the silver jubilee of his ordination. Kerr was not having a good year, however, and his nerves had deteriorated to the point where Session advised him to go south for three weeks.[17] While he recuperated in Bermuda, his pulpit was occupied by elder Herbert L. Stewart, professor of philosophy at Dalhousie and an unordained licentiate of the Presbyterian Church in Ireland. For reasons that cannot now even be surmised, Stewart was the bane of Kerr's existence; ten years later he would be instrumental in procuring his resignation. One wonders what prompted Kerr to preach on "Is life worth living?" one Sunday morning in November 1935.

Kerr was determined that he and his new-model congregation would take their rightful place among Halifax's mainstream Protestant churches. Even before he became inaugural moderator of the new Presbytery of Halifax and Lunenburg in November 1926 (a post he retained until February 1929), he was assuming a leadership role commensurate with the status and significance of the high kirk parish of Halifax. He served as moderator of Presbytery again in 1938–39 and in 1939 became clerk-treasurer, a dual post he filled until his departure in the spring of 1944. In June 1939 Kerr and his family were presented to Their Majesties during the royal visit, an unusual honour. The Kerrs had met HM Elizabeth, the Queen Consort, before. As Lady Elizabeth Bowes-Lyon, she had worshipped at Kerr's church and accepted his invitation to open the parish fair, the first public engagement of the young royal-to-be.[18]

The newborn "auld kirk" was to be to Presbyterian Halifax what St Giles' was to Edinburgh – the parish church. To this end, Kerr's influence also showed indirectly in the choice of the name "Saint David," which was adopted in April 1929. The preceding January, Kerr used Anniversary Sunday to suggest that the time had come to chose a proper name for the kirk. The selection committee, which Kerr chaired, recommended "Saint Columba."[19] Columba was probably Kerr's personal choice; one Sunday evening in November 1926 he had devoted his sermon to Columba and his mission at Iona.[20] But the special congregational meeting on 10 February rejected the suggestion. Saints such as Columba, Cuthbert, and Giles – Kerr's proposals – were rather more identified in the Presbyterian mind with the Roman Catholic heritage of Scotland than with the Scottish heritage of the Christian Church. Presbyterians who would not have settled for a Scottish saint were willing to accept a saintly Scot. A subsequent congregational meeting chose King David I (ca. 1085–1153), a "sair sanct for the croun."[21] King David's mother, St Margaret, was "Scotland's sole canonized saint."[22] Thus did the Presbyterian Church, Halifax, became "The Presbyterian Church of Saint David."

The choice of name was also a subtle way of making an unsubtle point about church-state relations in the post-Disruption era. The Presbyterian ideal was not a Protestant state church such as had been imposed in 1925 but a Christian nation inspired and affirmed by the Church. No modern Western country could be the medieval theocracy that Scotland was under King David. Nevertheless, the whole issue was hotly debated in the early post-Disruption era. At the General Assembly in 1927, for example, one minister objected to the commissioners' singing the national anthem in response to a message from the governor general, rather than "Stand Up, Stand Up for Jesus."[23] Presbyterians were citizens of no earthly kingdom and subject to no earthly king.

By January 1930, Kerr's fourth anniversary, Halifax newspapers were lauding his pastorate as "a period during which the many-sided work of the church has been organized by his masterhand and mind, cohesion effected, the church building transformed, a new organ installed, and the church grounds made beautiful."[24] The flavour of public worship during Kerr's heyday was perfectly caught by "Bellman"/ MacGlashen in "Sunday Morning at Saint David's."[25]

As the Great Depression set in, Kerr began to remit as much as one-fifth of his $5,000 stipend to the Trustees; the congregation was never able to afford the sum it had committed to pay him. Gratified as he was by the busyness of the various congregational organizations, he was also at pains to remind the people "that our church exists primarily for worship. Let *both* our Divine Services, our Diets of Worship, be well attended. There is both the morning and the evening sacrifice."[26] On more than one occasion Kerr had reason to caution his people against overemphasizing the social side of church life.

Informal congregational timelines treat the period 1930–44 as one in which no significant event occurred. The real problem is not that too little happened but that too few records have survived. In 1939 the Maritimes Synod met in Sydney, and Kerr was elected moderator, the first of two ministers of Saint David's to hold the post.[27] His synod sermon, "The genius of Presbyterianism," was preached on 1 Timothy 4:14.[28] Kerr was offering a short, sharp course in comparative religious history. One wonders, however, whether he was not also reflecting on his own experience of Saint David's.[29]

When it came to the United Church, Kerr was a liberal ecumenist, quite unlike most indigenous Canadian Presbyterian ministers of his time. He had always been active in the UCC-dominated Halifax and Dartmouth Ministerial Association and saw no reason why relations with the United Church should not be close and cordial. Indeed, during his last year in Halifax, Kerr addressed one of the association's regular monthly meetings on the "Episcopal-Presbyterian approach to unity."[30] Though his closest ministerial friendships were with professors at Pine Hill Divinity Hall, he did not favour church union; he believed in Christian unity and in the catholicity of Presbyterianism.

Visiting UCC ministers, especially former Presbyterians, were welcome in Kerr's pulpit. Perhaps the most remarkable appearance was that of James W. Falconer in July 1939. After Clarence MacKinnon, Falconer was the leading unionist in eastern Canada. The invitation to him probably had more than a little to do with the amendment to the United Church of Canada Act, which was passed in April 1939. The Presbyterian Church in Canada formally regained the legal right to use its name and could finally deal with the United Church on an equal basis. Coming hard on the heels of the first General Assembly at which it was possible for The Presbyterian Church in Canada to accept fraternal greetings from the UCC, Falconer's preaching at Saint David's was highly symbolic.

The outbreak of war in September 1939 found Kerr the convener of the ministerial association's committee on the work of the churches in relation to the armed forces. The outline of the committee's report sounds like Kerr and was probably written by him. It began, "The spiritual aspect of this work is more important than the social."[31] It was an agenda for Christian social action by local churches to which Saint David's adhered strictly throughout the Second World War. It impinged in ways both small and large. Members and adherents of the congregation lost their lives in combat and, in another sense, the minister himself was a casualty. In May 1942 the moderator of Presbytery was instructed to forward to Ottawa's controller of supplies (Wartime Industries Control Board) a unanimous resolution asking that he rescind his refusal to allow Kerr to purchase new tires for his car, which was "required for ministerial duties."[32]

It was also in May 1942 that a potentially disastrous fire of unknown origin destroyed the choir room at Saint David's and made necessary the reconditioning of the organ.[33] There followed five months of redecorating the chancel and paying down the debt. A special Thanksgiving service to commemorate "burning the mortgage" was held 4 October 1942. Kerr preached on Proverbs 29:18 ("Where there is no vision, the people perish").[34] Later that month Saint David's hosted the Interchurch Area Conference on World Missions, and Kerr entertained the guest speaker, Dr John Raleigh Mott, the American Methodist who was instrumental in founding the World Council of Churches.[35]

The double-edged tribute to Kerr at the 1942 annual congregational meeting gave some hint of the pressure he was under.[36] Minutes of the annual congregational meeting of January 1943 do not survive, but the usual resolution of appreciation of the minister is known to have passed. It would be Kerr's last. Earlier that month the Trustees unanimously passed an extraordinary resolution reflecting on both minister and Session and ordered it sent to the clerk of Session.[37]

Kerr returned from six weeks' holiday in August 1943 perhaps unsuspecting that the game was nearly up. In September he announced in a pastoral letter (his first) that he intended giving a series of sermons "on the more fundamental truths of our Faith. These will centre round 'The spiritual being of man,' 'God as revealed in Christ,' 'Sin and redemption,' and 'The Kingdom of God and its meaning.'"[38] These sermons seem never to have been delivered. Kerr, out of step and perhaps out of touch with the rising generation, clung to his firm belief that sound doctrinal sermons could only enhance the attractiveness of public worship. Increasingly, however, leading members were taking a quite different view of the spiritual health of Saint David's. It was not only the Church School that had fallen on hard times; attendance at divine service was in free fall. The minister was coming to be seen as part of a problem, the existence of which the minister himself did not acknowledge.

The sharpest statement of disaffection appeared in the Trustees' report for the year 1943.[39] At a time when cross-membership between Session and Trustees was still the exception rather than the rule, a joint committee of four was appointed to analyze the results of an informal "goodwill canvass." Conducted over the course of the year, it was for all practical purposes an opinion poll on the effectiveness of the minister. In 1943 there were four elders who were also trustees: Frank Ashworth (vice-chair; president of the choir), Fred Guildford, Herbert L. Stewart, and Herbert D. Wallace. It was undoubtedly they who comprised this committee and probably they whose combined efforts induced the minister to resign. Of this small group of *agents provocateurs*, only Ashworth – an elder since 1939 – was not a charter member of the congregation.

The joint committee found "that the results of the visitations to the Members and Adherents of the Church do not explain the lack of attendance and interest in the services of St. David's Church." Meeting on 14 September to consider the report of the committee, the elders and trustees came to an inflammatory resolution. The "urgent action" the joint meeting had in mind was clearly the retirement of the minister. Session met on 23 September to consider the resolution from the joint meeting. At a further meeting on 3 October it passed a resolution of appreciation in favour of the minister. The battle lines were drawing up.[40]

On 5 October 1943 John Scott Chisholm, long-time chair of the Trustees, died. An old Kirkman who had seceded from St Matthew's, Chisholm was among Kerr's staunchest supporters. Scandalized and entirely out of sympathy with the "dump Kerr" movement, which was gaining ground among the trustees, Chisholm had given up the chair in disgust in the autumn of 1942. In his morning sermon of 1 November that year, Kerr warned his people of the dangerous results "of talking without knowledge and acting on hearsay." The retirement and, within months, death of Chisholm was the last straw; Kerr began to look for another pulpit – in Scotland, not Canada. In November 1943 he sought and received a testimonial from his closest friend in Halifax, Carleton Stanley, president of Dalhousie University and an adherent of Saint David's.[41]

Few ministers would vacate their pulpit a month before Easter, but Kerr's situation was desperate. He was being hounded out by a small group who laid at his door the entire blame for the congregation's apathy and decline. Shocked and appalled by Session's acquiescence in the trustees' involving themselves in the spiritual oversight of the congregation,[42] Kerr decided to resign. The precise timing would be dictated by arrangements for his acceptance of a call in Scotland. An intrepid traveller, he was undisturbed by the perils of crossing the North Atlantic during wartime. He preached his last regular sermon in Saint David's on 5 March 1944. Two days later he submitted to the quarterly meeting his resignation as clerk and treasurer of Presbytery as well as minister of Saint David's. Kerr immediately went to Montreal to visit his daughter, leaving the pulpit to be occupied by Ian MacKinnon, professor of church history at Pine Hill Divinity Hall.

"The blow has fallen," W.J. Kane, a strong supporter of the minister, wrote sadly.[43] The "Irishman" whom the clerk of Session blamed for the current, unhappy situation of Saint David's was Herbert L. Stewart, elder and, by some accounts, a licentiate of the Presbyterian Church in Ireland. Stewart, formerly of St Andrew's and the only elder of Saint David's who ever preached in Kerr's absence, seems to have nursed a grudge over the defeat the anti-Kirk faction had suffered in 1925. The St Andrew's group – Edgar Holloway, Stewart, Clifford Torey, Wallace – had never fully accepted Kerr as minister. The difficulty for Kerr was that by 1944 his strongest supporters – A.D. Falconer, W.E. Maclellan, Frank K. Warren, Chisholm, Mrs Senator MacKeen, and Dr John Stewart – were all dead. He had few friends to keep close, while his enemies moved ever closer.

On Sunday, 12 March, the clerk of Session mounted the pulpit and announced that the minister would not be returning. He read Presbytery's statement of appreciation of Kerr's services and expressed the congregation's "sincere and unanimous regret" over the loss of its minister.[44] Kerr preached his farewell sermons on the 26th, Passion Sunday; his resignation took effect five days later. The ministerial association gave him a complimentary luncheon on the 31st;[45] no such courtesy was extended by congregation or Presbytery. Nevertheless, the Trustees voted him an *ex gratia* payment of $2,000, which Torey, the chair, hand-delivered. It must have been a chilly encounter, as there was no love lost between the two men. With almost indecent haste, a special congregational meeting was called for 12 April to authorize the sale of the manse. It was a course of action that the trustees had been considering as early as November 1943, when they, or at least some of them, hoped or suspected that the minister would shortly be eased out.

Having begun on the most positive note, Kerr's pastorate ended prematurely and badly. Only a vocal minority wanted to see him go, but Kerr had had enough, as had his wife. Like Caesar's wife, the wife of the minister had to be above suspicion, and Mrs Kerr had thought the better of continuing as treasurer of the Ladies Guild. Writing to his friend President Stanley of Dalhousie University a year after his resignation, Kerr stated that "the best thing I did was to leave H[alifa]x. My wife often wonders now why we stayed there so long, & it makes us appreciate all the more the kindliness & friendliness there is elsewhere."[46]

Kerr was still in Halifax on the 1st of May 1944, but it looked to W.J. Kane as though he would be sailing soon. Obtaining passage could not have been easy, as commercial service was suspended for the duration of the war. It is understandable why Kerr's first choice was Scotland, not Canada. He was going home, the circumstances that had driven him away years before having long since been forgotten. He spent the next nine months ministering to a church in the suburbs of Dundee, obtained for him by his good old friend Dr White. In 1925 John White had helped Kerr escape to Canada; now he was helping him escape back to Scotland.

Kerr's brief, almost inappropriately terse obituary in the *Acts and Proceedings* in 1966 suggests how little known or well remembered he was.[47] He was too cosmopolitan a minister for a Presbyterian church as parochial as Canada's. Despite – perhaps because of – his great intellectual gifts, he was not really a success as a pastor. He preferred the company of scholars and intellectuals, and his peremptoriness could easily be mistaken for hauteur. In his relations with his congregation, he tended to be dour and schoolmasterish. Nor was he an emigrant by choice. His very presence at Saint David's spoke to mid-career frustration. As the English used to say of one who had not quite made the grade at home, "He failed and went to America." Unlike Stuart Crawford Parker and William Gordon Maclean, emigrant Kirk ministers who rose to become moderators of the General Assembly, Kerr was not at home or especially active in church office. He limited his participation to service on the Board of Education.

Kerr would not have been at home anywhere but in academe, his true vocation and first love. He might have been less ill at ease in the pre-Disruption Presbyterian Church in Canada, when Presbyterian College, Halifax, routinely called Scottish ministers to the professoriate. If the post-war scheme to establish a new theological teaching faculty in Halifax had gone forward, Kerr might have had more meaningful work to do. (As it was, he had been invited in the spring of 1930 to lecture at Pine Hill Divinity Hall.) Generally speaking, however, he was out of his depth in a congregation as yet too young and unsophisticated to appreciate or benefit from his immense gifts. His intellectual passion and erudition were more a hindrance than a help in the pulpit. His congregation, aged eighteen in 1943, was growing up while he himself, at sixty-three, was aging. As a pastor, Kerr did not know and could not learn how to be the father of a adolescent congregation on the cusp of full adulthood. The war both accelerated and complicated the process. He could not recognize, much less manage, the intergenerational transition that was taking place under his nose; as the Depression gave way to the war, his work became more demanding and difficult. He was a restorer and a preserver, not an innovator; so inevitably, opportunities for growth and development were missed. Much more was needed than the reassertion of the Kirk tradition in Canadian Presbyterianism.

Kerr was the first Scottish Presbyterian minister to fill a Halifax pulpit since Thomas Fowler at St Matthew's (1891–1908). Saint David's, the living ghost of nine disappeared congregations, was old wine of mixed vintage in a brand new bottle. Saint David's could not rebecome the pre-1875 Kirk; Halifax was not Glasgow. Kerr's legacy would be mostly undone during the twenty-year pastorate of his successor, an Irish evangelical whose sympathies lay with the Covenanters, not the Kirk. Yet the character of Saint David's as a "wee kirk," formed and nurtured by its first minister, survives to this day. Twenty years after his death and forty after the end of his pastorate, the people of Saint David's remembered Colin Kerr. A brass plaque in his honour and memory was raised at the entrance to the chancel on Anniversary Sunday, 27 April 1986. Some still remembered him, though perhaps not fondly.

5

Frank Lawson

The sudden loss of Colin Kerr in March 1944 could hardly have come at a worse time. "We do not want a long vacancy," W.J. Kane wrote Frank Baird the day after he had had to announce from the pulpit the minister's resignation.[1] It would, however, prove the longest and most difficult vacancy in the congregation's history. That Kerr had been more or less forced to resign meant that achieving consensus on the choice of a successor would be next to impossible. Those who had not wanted him to leave wanted another Kerr; those who did, wanted anyone else but. The congregation was deeply divided, with considerable bad blood between the two factions.

Kerr had been gone for over a year when Frank Lawson, a "brilliant pulpit orator" of Kitchener, Ontario, preached for a call. Unlike the other candidates who had preached by invitation of the vacancy committee, Lawson invited himself. At a special meeting on Sunday, 6 May 1945, Session considered Lawson's letter and decided to hear him on consecutive Sundays in June. In addition to travelling expenses and board, he was to be paid an honorarium of $30 per Sunday.[2] Postcards announcing the event were sent to each household in the congregation.

Born at Tircreven, County Londonderry, in 1899, the youngest of four sons of a farmer, Francis Lawson Jr emigrated to Canada in 1928. Five years later he graduated BA from the University of Western Ontario, where he was a leader in the Student Christian Movement.[3] He was a native son of the Presbyterian Church in Ireland, having been connected with it first as Sunday school teacher and superintendent and then, after his arrival in Canada, as a student preacher in The Presbyterian Church in Canada. "I was fond of public speaking, an art which I practised prior to my entering the ministry," Lawson wrote in his application for admission to Union Theological Seminary.[4]

Frank Lawson was certified as a candidate for ministry about 1930. Graduating BD from Union Theological Seminary in New York City in 1936, he had had among his teachers Paul Tillich, professor of philosophical theology, in 1933–35. His first pastorate was St David's, Campbellville-Nassagaweya (just outside Milton, Ontario), where he was ordained and inducted in May 1936. Up the road was the United (formerly Methodist) Church, in local parlance "Sodom" to the Presbyterian "Gomorrah," a joke Lawson enjoyed telling.[5] After resigning from Campbellville in January 1941, he spent the rest of the Second World War as stated supply at St Andrew's, Kitchener, while the minister, Finlay G. Stewart, was on leave of absence to serve as a chaplain in the armed forces. A pacifist and conscientious objecter, Lawson himself would never have volunteered for such duty.

At the end of January 1945 Finlay Stewart returned to his pulpit, and Frank Lawson began to cast about for one of his own. Saint David's was still unsettled – in both senses of the word. It was an opportunity Lawson could not afford to ignore. So he came, saw, and conquered, bringing with him his motto: "Whatever your creed or denomination you are cordially invited to attend these services." That was the pure distilled essence of Lawson's evangelicalism, and it would stand as the theme of his entire pastorate. The essence of his evangelicalism was also nicely captured by one of his early bulletins (2 December 1945): "In the Church of Saint David we have no pride nor conceit; we seek to worship God in the manner of our Fathers – with reverence and simplicity. If you are a member of another Church, or belong to no church, we extend to you a hearty welcome. Something in our service may minister to your needs; then come as often as you please." Lawson was endeavouring, from the very start, to appeal to Everyman and Everywoman.

The titles of his two sermons preached at Saint David's on 3 June are not known, but those of the 10th are: "Is life a lucky chance or a divine plan?" (morning) and "Is there a key to happiness and success?" (evening). While Lawson waited in expectation of a call, Presbytery became so concerned with the overlong vacancy at Saint David's that on 22 June it conducted a visitation. The consensus seemed to be that everything would be fine once the congregation had a settled minister. The congregation met again on the 27th to discuss the vacancy and decided to ask Session to summon yet another meeting, this time in order to moderate in a call. This meeting took place on 11 July, and the recommendation of a call to Frank Lawson was approved; it was signed by 199 members and 56 adherents, less than half the respective totals. The call came before Presbytery on 30 July; as Lawson was without a charge, the mills of Presbytery ground less slowly than usual. Frank Lawson was inducted as minister of the

Presbyterian Church of Saint David on Friday, 7 September, and occupied his pulpit for the first time the following Sunday. Presiding at the induction service on behalf of the moderator of Synod, the interim moderator of Saint David's alluded to the fact that, despite the overlong vacancy, the congregation had never faltered in its duty to the church.[6]

Under normal circumstances, Lawson would never have become minister of Saint David's. The course of events, however, had been anything but normal. By the summer of 1945 it was imperative that Saint David's have a minister, any minister. Frank Lawson – without a charge and on the appendix to the roll – was available. He needed Saint David's as badly as it needed him. He was ready, willing, and able, and it would not be taking him sight unseen, like Kerr. In Lawson, Saint David's had someone completely different. He was not a scholar like Kerr, but a charismatic preacher pure and simple. It is difficult for any minister to excel at being both preacher and pastor, and Lawson was emphatically the former, not the latter, believing that the essence of pastoral ministry was preaching.

Like Robert Johnston, Frank Lawson was an Ulsterman who feared God but no man, and who spoke to power the truth that was in him. Beginning under unpropitious circumstances, his twenty-year pastorate turned out to be the golden age. Saint David's went from being on the verge of schism to being the premier Reformed church of Halifax. Lawson quickly reversed the downward trend that had set in towards the end of Kerr's pastorate. Thanks to his "progressive leadership," halfway through Lawson's pastorate, in 1955, members and adherents of Saint David's purportedly exceeded a thousand.[7] The 1950s were a believing, churchgoing time when ministers were opinion-makers, if not quite public intellectuals, and worshippers looked to the pulpit for guidance on the great issues of the day. Lawson avoided no subject, regardless how controversial it was or how controversial his views on it. His question always was, not what would Jesus have done, but what must Christians do as followers of Jesus.

Lawson had a dry wit, as two sermon titles from early in his Saint David's years suggest: "Your money and your life" (morning) and "O Protestantism, what deeds have been done in thy name?" (evening). Some thought him a trifle eccentric, and his humour could be quirky. Soon after coming to Halifax, he was invited to address a public meeting in a small town with a strong continuing Presbyterian congregation. Lawson arrived late, was dressed more casually than his hosts thought appropriate, and began his address by saying how pleased he was to be there, because it was "known far and wide for its millionaires and fat women."[8]

Politically, if not quite a socialist, Lawson was a decidedly left-wing liberal years ahead of his ministerial colleagues. In May 1945, in his capacity as convener of the standing committee on evangelism, church life, and work of the Synod of Toronto and Kingston, Lawson had ghostwritten a report urging toleration of the Soviet Union, a report that became a bugbear in the conservative press and caused deep embarrassment to the church.[9] Lawson, for his part, was unrepentant. Laughingly telling the reporter from Toronto's *Telegram* "that he was literally deluged with letters of protest," he stated in a more serious vein, "I would gather that the Presbyterian Church has been awakened by the report so that something was accomplished."[10] The church took rather a different view, the moderator of the General Assembly having been in Synod when the report was tabled and approved and Lawson given a vote of thanks. Synod soon repented, but Lawson had burned his bridges. Small wonder he wanted to get away from the Synod of Toronto and Kingston as soon as possible. Saint David's offered a means of escape and sanctuary in more ways than one.

Lawson did not modify his political views one whit after coming east. Addressing the Halifax Kiwanis Club in 1946, he quoted his synod report, telling his audience that "the minds of millions of people have been poisoned against Russia by one great church [Roman Catholic]."[11] Speaking at the monthly meeting of the Halifax and District Ministerial Association in February 1951, Lawson "told them that the Church was poorly equipped to meet the future, mostly because it had lost the common touch and drawn away from the working man."[12] In March 1953 he preached a panegyric on the death of Stalin ("The man who shook the pillars of the world"), and in September 1959 another, "If Khrushchev had come to Canada" – rather than to the United States and the United Nations headquarters in New York. Exactly a year later, he preached on the question "If Mr Khrushchev were at evening worship." in June 1961 he devoted an evening sermon to "Christianity and Communism: is it a fight to the death or is there a common ground?" As late as May 1965, shortly before his departure, he was preaching on "Taking a leaf out of the Communists' book."

At the height of the Cold War, Lawson was a peace warrior, and one Sunday evening in September 1951 he preached on the question "Is our trust in arms taking away our trust in God?" (By then Canada was already involved in the Korean War.) On Remembrance Sunday over the years he preached, not about good wars and those who died in them, but about peace and how to achieve it: "The victory that overcometh the world" (1 John 5:4–5), "Peace is the Christian's business," "The stupidity of war," "A sword or a cross," and "Right is stronger than might." Nor was Lawson opposed merely to war. At a time when convicted murderers were still being hanged in Canada, he opposed capital punishment as no less a breach of the Commandment than murder itself. His concept of Christian socialist politics was well summed up in an evening sermon delivered in June 1954: "Two things a Christian can never be: a Communist or a panic-stricken anti-Communist."

Frank Lawson was no stranger to Nova Scotia when he arrived in Halifax in September 1945; in the summer of 1931 he had served as student-in-charge at St Paul's, Merigomish. Saint David's, the first kirk of Atlantic Canada, was opportunity writ large, and he knew it. But he had his work cut out for him. Several members, including at least one trustee, had left, and Saint David's was in worse shape than it had ever been. So serious was this crisis of confidence in itself that Saint David's was in no condition to host the seventy-second meeting of Synod early in October. Saint David's was without a minister when the decision to meet next year in Halifax was made, and at the last moment the venue for 1945 had to be switched back to New Glasgow.

Lawson's first sermons, on 9 September 1945, set forth the agenda of his pastorate: "The business of a Christian church in Halifax" (morning) and "The Church of Saint David: her creed and commission" (evening). His vision of a Christian community is well summed up in John M. Moore's "The Church of My Dreams," which Lawson afterwards reprinted in the church bulletin. He met the Trustees (board of managers) for the first time on 4 October and stated his pastoral needs. Though his relations with them were to be good until near the end of his pastorate, minister and Board were sometimes at cross-purposes, as in September 1948: "Minister had ordered painter to remove floodlight from top of arch in front of church. Chairman [H.D. Wallace] instructed Property Committee to replace light as same had been placed there for benefit of elderly people who were finding lower steps too dark for safety."[13]

Lawson reintroduced the adult Bible class and the Chinese Sunday School and also succeeded in re-establishing the Sunday bulletin, though not yet permanently. In December, in a notable departure from custom, he hosted a "social" for organist, choir, music committee, and their spouses. Later that month Lawson (a Freemason himself) preached at the Masonic service in Fort Massey United. Reflecting sadly in the Kirk Session's annual report for 1945 – "we have much to recall regarding a year of exceptional difficulty" – W.J. Kane nevertheless had to admit that in less than four months Lawson had turned things around.[14] January 1946 saw another break with tradition in that the minister attended the annual congregational meeting.

Lawson was concerned about how best to "mainstream" The Presbyterian Church in Canada. He was making progress. On 20 January 1946 divine service from Saint David's was broadcast over the national network of CBC Radio for the first time since before the war ("Mr Lawson has received a great many letters and telegrams from all over Canada regarding our National Broadcast of last Sunday. They all speak in glowing terms of our Service"). Once the power and potential of broadcasting was realized, Lawson was quick to deploy it further. He became a regular speaker on *Morning Devotions,* the daily program on CBH radio sponsored by the ministerial association, and was a tireless advocate of evangelism over the airwaves. Broadcasting of the Sunday morning service over CJCH Halifax began in October 1946 ("The policy of the Kirk Session and managing Board is to extend the influence of our Church as widely as possible. Thus they have initiated 'Acadian Vespers'"). Small wonder that within a year of Lawson's arrival Halifax newspapers could comment that "much credit for the progressive spirit abroad in Saint David's Presbyterian Church is being given to the minister ... for his initiative and dynamic personality."[15]

Lawson's engagement and marriage in 1950 to a doctor, Jean Macdonald, may have prompted him to reflect on spiritual healing. One Sunday evening in May that year, Saint David's held a service of intercession for the sick and suffering at which he preached on "Divine healing." He explained a type of service for the sick that had originated in the Iona Community in Scotland under the leadership of its founder, the Reverend George Fielden Macleod (Lord Macleod) in 1938. Lawson was trying to introduce a sophisticated prayer-and-worship concept that viewed faith healing as neither a substitute for medical treatment nor magic or miracle. In the winter of 1952 he devoted a six-week series of evening sermons to "Modern methods of healing." In June 1958, when the Canadian Medical Association, then meeting in Halifax, held its annual Protestant church service at Saint David's, Lawson preached on "Religion and healing." In April 1963 he preached an evening sermon on "The Good News is a declaration of health for those sick of body, mind and spirit." Lawson's view was that all physical illness is psychosomatic and the product of sick minds or sick souls. Divine healing ("a faith that heals the sick") affected the body indirectly, through mind, soul, or spirit.

Lawson had visited Iona in the summer of 1949, when together with other visitors to Macleod's mission, he worked on the reconstruction of the sixth-century abbey.[16] On Remembrance Sunday later that year he preached the evening sermon on "The marvellous story of Iona." Many at Saint David's would have said of Lawson, as was said of the Iona Community itself, that he was "halfway towards Rome and halfway towards Moscow." His critical curiosity about the more *outré* Roman Catholic notions (prayers

for the dead, purgatory, the stigmata, and the bodily assumption of Mary –
all subjects on which he preached) certainly raised eyebrows.

The zenith of Lawson's obsession with Roman Catholicism came in
February 1959, when he preached one Sunday morning on "The call to
Christian unity and the pope's invitation." (John XXIII had only just
announced his intention of summoning an ecumenical council at which
Reformed churches would be invited to observe.) In this as in most other
things, Frank Lawson was in the vanguard of The Presbyterian Church in
Canada. He was also a voice crying in the wilderness. Advanced thinkers
such as Arthur Cochrane, who was to be an official observer at the Second
Vatican Council, had long since moved to the United States.

In December 1946 Lawson was elected moderator of the Presbytery of
Halifax and Lunenburg. Unusual though it was for a minister newly arrived
in the synod, much less the presbytery, to be placed in the moderator's
chair, the circumstances were unique. Presbytery was faced with the
unpleasant duty of disciplining one of its younger and most popular ministers, Perry F. Rockwood. "A favourite young people's speaker," Rockwood
was especially active in Youth for Christ, a conservative Protestant young
people's mission. The subsequent career of Canada's "radio pastor" is too
well-known to require elaboration; what is less well-known is that before
Rockwood founded the People's Gospel Hour in 1947, he was for four
years and one month a minister of The Presbyterian Church in Canada.[17]
A biblical fundamentalist, he resigned from the ministry of the PCC after
being found guilty of breaching his ordination vows by "following a divisive
course." Lawson, who was moderator of Presbytery at the time, initiated
the proceedings against Rockwood. Sixty years after he left the ministry of
the PCC, Perry F. Rockwood still casts a long and solitary shadow. The
Missionary Bible Church, long since relocated to downtown Halifax,
thrives, as does the People's Gospel Hour. In 2004 a former associate of
Rockwood's who seceded to the Presbyterians in 1990 was elected an elder
of Saint David's. The wheel had turned full circle.

His victory over Rockwood made Lawson a bit of celebrity and greatly
enhanced his prestige. No one could deny Saint David's had a star for a
minister. He had shown that to be against the church was to be against the
gospel, that a minister could be an evangelical without being a fundamentalist, and that The Presbyterian Church in Canada could be an evangelical
church without being Luddite in matters of theology or biblical criticism.
Unlike unreconstructed fundamentalists such as Rockwood, Lawson
believed that interchurch cooperation and developments in biblical scholarship helped, rather than hindered, proclamation of the gospel of salvation.

Anniversary Sunday 1947 signalled the changing of the guard. The generation of Kerr, Kane, and Johnston was giving way to a new generation scarcely old enough to have fought in the Resistance. Lawson himself was the Anniversary preacher, speaking on "The Protestant witness." In February 1950 Saint David's celebrated its silver jubilee, spread over three Sundays.[18] Lawson preached at the second of them, in the evening, on "The principles to which I would rededicate the pulpit of Saint David's." The golden age was marked by two significant anniversaries. On Sunday, 11 June 1950, Presbyterians celebrated the seventy-fifth birthday of The Presbyterian Church in Canada, while Uniteds the twenty-fifth birthday of the United Church of Canada. In the morning Lawson preached on "Canada's experiment in Christian unity" and in the evening on "Facts and fallacies of church union."[19] Like Kerr before him, he was at pains to distinguish between Christian unity and church union and to point out that Canada's experiment in the former had failed precisely because of confusion with the latter. Christian unity had nothing to do with church union, and even "church union" had produced schism in the largest of the three uniting churches.

Typical of Lawson's half-in-fun-wholly-in-earnest style was the "Help Wanted" advertisement that appeared in the Thanksgiving Sunday bulletin, 10 October 1948. He was the consummate developer, in every sense of the word. The designation of a deaconess at St James, Truro, in the spring of 1949 – the first in the presbytery since the Disruption – prompted Lawson to wonder aloud why Saint David's had given no one to the ministry. There would be none until December 1955, when George Arthur Tattrie, a child of the congregation and son of an elder, was certified and recognized as a candidate for ministry. The Presbytery of Halifax and Lunenburg was clearly thinking along similar lines, for in May 1957 the nineteenth presbyterial conference of laymen heard an address by Lorne Clarke[20] of Saint David's on "Recruitment for Christian service."

Suggestive of Lawson's role as a Christian public intellectual was his evening sermon, broadcast locally, on Hugh MacLennan's "Are We a Godless People?" (*Maclean's*, 15 March 1949).[21] MacLennan had grown up in The Presbyterian Church in Canada and remained a Presbyterian after the Disruption. Like Kerr before him, Lawson saw preaching as the very heart and soul of all pastoral work. Kerr had occasionally written for the newspapers or had his sermons published in them. Lawson did so frequently. Among the earliest of his sermons on paper was "A Lenten message," in March 1950.[22] He inaugurated "The Clergy Comments," a weekly feature of the "Religion" page in Saturday's *Mail-Star* in November 1959, and his contributions to it over the remaining half-dozen years of his pastorate were remarkable for their breadth of interest and sympathy and their psychological depth. The first of them, questioning why university students did not attend Sunday morning worship, laid the blame entirely at the feet of the churches.[23] Among the most entertaining of Lawson's journalistic sermonettes was "Christmas – season of true joy," delivered in November 1960: "O, not again! Only thirty shopping days to Christmas and a parson about to tell us that we should make the festival tame, deadly dull and sanctimonious."[24]

A feature article by Lawson in the weekend magazine of the Montreal *Star* in September 1960, deploring the church's loss of moral authority, attracted much attention: "I have seen the Negro treated with condescension and toleration while he rots on the fringes of our cities, never tasting the good things of the civilization around him. If I were dropped into a black man's skin in a white community, I would rather be hated as in Little Rock than ignored as in Halifax."[25] The references are transparent: Halifax's Africville, whose residents paid municipal taxes without receiving municipal services, and Little Rock, Arkansas, where a pogrom against Black people, incited by court-ordered integration of the high schools, had led to President Eisenhower's sending in the army to uphold the constitution. One Sunday evening in October 1956, while the crisis in Little Rock was developing, Lawson preached on "Skin colour and Christianity – the greatest of modern heresies" and had as Scripture reader a Ghanaian law student at Dalhousie, Bredu Pabi. As early as February 1947, Lawson had invited the Reverend William Pearly Oliver, pastor of Cornwallis Street (African) Baptist Church, to speak after the evening service on "Race relations."

In general Lawson saw the evening sermons as ideal for addressing "practical matters under daily discussion." His "Vital questions" series in the winter of 1954 was designed to provoke and surely did: "The laws of Sinai or the laws of Dr Kinsey?" There cannot have been many Protestant ministers anywhere in Canada who preached on Alfred Kinsey's *Sexual Behaviour in the Human Female*. The same could be said of his series "Questions of religion and conduct" in the winter of 1957. Becoming both husband and father in his fifties made Lawson more conscious of and more interested in the problems of young people. In January and February 1962, for example, he preached a seven-week series of evening sermons on "Personal problems," leading the *Mail-Star* to comment, "Starting from the conviction that marriage should not be a gamble, one city minister [Lawson] is amazed that so little is done by the Church to help young people in their pre-marital and marital problems."[26]

Frank Lawson was making his mark. Entire pages of the church bulletin were taken up with lists of new members – either by profession of faith or by certificate of transfer. He was also a busy ecclesiastic. In the spring of 1951 Lawson served as chair of a special committee of the Halifax and District Ministerial Association preparing a feasibility study for an evangelistic campaign by all the Protestant denominations in the metropolitan area. The three-day crusade materialized in June 1952, during Lawson's presidency of the association. In the autumn of 1954 the association could not agree on a proposal to invite American evangelist Billy Graham to Halifax to conduct a more ambitious crusade. It would have been a Canadian first; Graham did not preach in Canada until 1955, when he led a crusade in Toronto. By 1960, however, enouraged by his success in Great Britain, the ministerial association was ready to invite him to Halifax; Graham was not available. The projected crusade could not go forward without a missioner. The Canadian Council of Churches helpfully suggested to the ministerial association that it instead invite Graham's Scottish associate, the Reverend Tom Allan, minister of St George's Tron, Glasgow.

Allan was his own best advance, coming to Halifax in January 1961 to meet with the ministerial association.[27] In order to allay fears among more conservative Presbyterians, the Presbytery of Halifax and Lunenburg asked Lawson – he had almost certainly met Allan on one of his frequent trips to Glasgow – to set down the church's official position on it.[28] The crusade was financed through the sale of $5.00 shares, which were available from association ministers and from elders of Saint David's. For three consecutive Sundays in October, evening service was reduced from one hour to thirty minutes so that worshippers could get to the Halifax Forum on time ("Crusade at the Forum at eight").

By April 1964, when the local office of the Billy Graham Evangelistic Association was sponsoring "cottage prayer plan" (house prayer meeting) groups to prepare for the "great evangelistic crusade,"[29] Frank Lawson was trying to stimulate the people of Saint David's by preaching on "The question: Are you saved?" He shared with both Allan and Graham a holistic view of evangelism according to which all people, good or bad, religious or irreligious, "need the transforming power of Christ" (George McNeill). That was what he aimed for in his own evangelical preaching.

Not to be outdone by crusading evangelists such as Tom Allan, Leighton Ford, or Billy Graham, Lawson became more stridently evangelical in his preaching. He was also becoming increasingly suspicious of ecclesiasticism, the Vaticanizing "one big church" concept. In June 1964 – the same month the PCC announced its decision not to enter union negotiations with the

United Church – Lawson wrote to the *Presbyterian Record* denouncing a pro-union article by Professor Allan Farris of Knox College, the church's principal seminary.[30] Lawson's preaching church was no place for defeatist denizens of the ivory tower. It was but another recrudescence of the "treason of the intellectuals" that had compromised the church in 1925.

Despite Lawson's disaffection with latter-day unionists, excellent relations continued to be maintained "on the ground" in Halifax with the United Church. In the autumn of 1964, for example, the Uniteds shared with the Presbyterians no less eminent a person than the moderator of the General Assembly of the Church of Scotland, then on an official visit to the United Church of Canada. It was an event unique in the history of Presbyterian Halifax. On Sunday morning, 6 September 1964, the Right Reverend Duncan Fraser, who had once lived in Canada, where his father was a Presbyterian minister, preached at Fort Massey United; on Sunday evening he preached at Saint David's.

By 1964, Frank Lawson was sixty-five and the father of three young children. The best years of his pastorate were behind him. Relations with Session were deteriorating. When Ralph Kane replaced his father as clerk of Session in May 1960, Lawson's departure was probably only a matter of time. An elder since 1948, Kane did not like and did not get on with the minister, the circumstances of whose call still rankled after twenty years. Ideologically, they were poles apart, Lawson strongly favouring the 1964 recommendation of the church's committee on the place of women that they be eligible for ordination, Kane viewing women elders as an unnecessary evil and women ministers as beyond the pale.

Towards the end of his pastorate Lawson criticized Saint David's for not measuring up to the high standards and ambitious program he had set for it. In the last Kirk Session report that he tendered (1963), he observed that while some gave generously to support mission and outreach, "in general there has not been a real sacrifice by our people."[31] Lawson needed a secretary, but the congregation could not afford both a deaconess/director of Christian education and a secretary on a permanent full-time basis. He was probably suffering, if not from burnout, then at least from frustration and overwork. At his last annual congregational meeting, in January 1965, Lawson "addressed the meeting on a number of church matters of concern to him."[32] One of his more fervent admirers, elder Robert W. Wright, openly implied that the minister was doing everything but his services were both underappreciated and, more importantly, under-remunerated.[33]

In 1964, in a last-ditch effort to conciliate the minister, the annual congregational meeting had instructed the Board to strike a special committee to meet with Lawson to discuss his grievances. Lawson, however, was unresponsive. Though he was already the highest-paid minister in the synod, he was seeking a $1,000 per annum increase in his stipend. The Board doubled his expense allowance from $600 to $1,200 but drew the line at also increasing his salary beyond an additional $600.[34] It was not enough. Before the annual congregational meeting in January 1965, the chair and another member of the Board interviewed Lawson on the subject of his stipend. Lawson told them that while he was not interested in an adjustment to his pension, he *was* interested in a pay raise. Givings were down, however, and the Trustees could not oblige.

In June 1965 both Lawson and an influential elder of Saint David's went to Toronto as commissioners to the General Assembly. On Sunday morning, 4 July 1965, Lawson preached on "Honest religion: is it having your vote or is it not?" Then in a theatrical gesture he told Saint David's he was resigning as its minister. There was pandemonium in the church afterwards: all were in shock; some were in tears. His wife, who arrived late and went up to the balcony rather than taking her usual pew downstairs, was visibly affected.[35] While Jean Lawson must have known of her husband's decision, she may not have been forewarned of the manner and timing of the public announcement of it.

Lawson was spared having to face his distraught congregation for a second time that Sunday. He and the minister of St Matthew's United had already drawn up the summer schedule for alternating Sunday evening services, the first of which was to be held at St Matthew's later that day. Nor had Lawson previously advised Session of his intentions; so an emergency meeting had to be held Monday evening. Following the adjournment of the Session meeting, there was an "informal gathering" of sixteen elders with Randolph D. MacLean, minister of Knox Presbyterian, who agreed to act as interim moderator should Presbytery accept Lawson's resignation. The meeting also appointed a four-person pulpit supply committee.

Lawson penned his letter of resignation to Presbytery on or about 7 July and then went off on vacation to the Macdonald family cottage at Pointe-du-Chêne in southeastern New Brunswick. Ever ready to fill the breach was the minister who had supplied Saint David's most frequently during Lawson's pastorate – Dr John Bruce Hardie, professor of Hebrew and Old Testament at Pine Hill Divinity Hall. No minister, perhaps not even Lawson himself, stood in higher or more general esteem at Saint David's than Hardie. In a symbolic act, the church bulletin of 11 July omitted from its standard timeline, "1945 The Reverend Frank Lawson called to Saint

David's." Though he remained a lame duck for two more months, Lawson's pastorate effectively ended the Sunday morning he announced his resignation.

The resignation came before Presbytery on 9 September. Lawson "spoke at some length about his happy heritage of coming from a Christian home, his career and ministry in Halifax. He ended his remarks by saying, 'I wish to be set free from Saint David's and to have my name placed on the Presbytery Appendix Roll.'"[36] Four elders from Saint David's were present but spoke not a word. The silence was deafening. One of them, Murdoch McLeod, clerk of Presbytery, seems to have nursed a guilty conscience over the callous treatment accorded Lawson. At the annual congregational meeting in January 1971, he proposed an annuity to the former minister of $100 a month for life or a lump-sum payment of $15,000. The proposal received no support, and McLeod withdrew it from consideration.[37]

Ralph Kane was not sorry to see Lawson go and privately said good riddance in no uncertain terms.[38] Session had had enough of Lawson and he of them. His resignation took effect the following Sunday, 12 September, when he preached his farewell sermons: "The worship of God in spirit and in truth" (morning) and "The worship of God in forms ancient and modern" (evening). Two days later Session met and passed a resolution of appreciation for his pastorate.[39] A special committee, chaired by trustee (afterwards elder) Robert Kennedy, was given the task of raising money for a farewell gift and organizing a social on 12 October. Session asked the trustees to continue paying Lawson's stipend until the end of November. They concurred and sought Session's permission to carry it through to the end of the year. Session and Board, however, drew the line at recommending to the congregation an *ex gratia* payment to the retiring minister.[40]

On Anniversary Sunday, 17 January 1971, Frank Lawson returned to Saint David's as preacher. Ambivalent though he may have been, he had no excuse not to accept the invitation. He was already in Nova Scotia, having spent 4–10 January as guest preacher for the annual week of prayer hosted by Westminster Presbyterian, New Glasgow.[41] For Lawson, Saint David's represented both success and failure, and his return was bittersweet. He could not draw all men to himself. The minister sent out a special letter, and the church bulletin gave Lawson a laudatory full-page biography, pointing out that during his pastorate yearly givings had increased eightfold. Kirk Session even restored the defunct evening service to accommodate him, and so he preached two sermons rather than one: "The sign of the cross at the centre of [the] city's life" (morning) and "Is the new generation moving to the front of the stage?" (evening). Lawson would have agreed with those young adult observers at the 1970 General Assembly (held at Saint David's) who pointed out that Christian education was a joke and that the church was failing to address their needs.

It was his swan song. But Halifax was not done with Frank Lawson. Ten years after his departure, the afternoon newspaper quoted these memorable and altogether typical words of his: "One day the curse of war, the clash of race and clan shall cease. His Kingdom is bright with promise. To it we must give ourselves, with heart and soul and mind and strength."[42] Lawson was a radical evangelical at a time when few Presbyterian ministers were evangelicals, radical or otherwise. In his estimation, Jesus, the "strange man" who "disturbed his own time and haunts ours," was a life-long radical – one whose faith was not blind but seeing. Christians were called to be no less radical than Jesus of Nazareth. For Lawson, "Christianity was an invitation to adventure rather than a goal to be achieved."[43]

Frank Lawson began inauspiciously and, like Kerr, went out on a sour note. But the years in between were outstandingly successful. Saint David's benefited from the profound differences of style and substance between its first and second ministers. The same number of years that separated the beginning of their pastorates – nineteen – also separated Kerr's and Lawson's ages. Intergenerational transition in the pulpit was needed, and it had unintendedly taken place. Just as Kerr had been the man for 1926, so Lawson was the man for 1945 – in a world that the Second World War had changed beyond all recognition.

Unlike Kerr, the haughty academician, Lawson suffered fools gladly – provided he could make them repent and believe. Though by no means a scholar, he was nevertheless highly intelligent, articulate, deeply read, and deep-thinking and as charming and personable as Kerr was dour; the very difference, one might say, between Irishmen and Scotsmen. Lawson was a latter-day social gospeller, with the important qualification – common to all evangelicals – that the social gospel was not the gospel and must not be confused with or substituted for it. Sin is the root of all evil, social as well as personal, and Christianity the only solution to all of life's problems ("Life's big questions: the gospel's final answers," "Christianity still the hope of those who have lost the way").

6

Donald Bruce Mackay

The membership of Saint David's reached its greatest extent, 632, during 1967, Canada's centenary year. Frank Lawson had departed in 1965, but his impact continued to be felt into the next two pastorates. The people of Saint David's reacted to his departure with confusion and uncertainty. The devil they knew was gone, and they missed his vigorous presence and the success Saint David's had experienced during his heyday in the 1950s. The second vacancy, however, would be as short and painless as the first had been long and difficult. Despite the unexpectedness of Lawson's departure, Session and congregation alike were much better prepared than they had been in 1944. A valuable lesson learned the hard way had not been forgotten. Session saw to it that Saint David's got the interim moderator they wanted, in the hope that they would also get, and get quickly, the minister they wanted.

Donald B. Mackay, of First Presbyterian Church, Chatham, Ontario, was the fourth of the five prospective ministers to preach and did so on 7 November 1965. The congregation's attention may have been a little distracted, as the following day a federal election was to take place in which a prominent member of Saint David's, Robert J. McCleave, was seeking to win back the Commons seat he had held from 1957 to 1963.[1] Though not an extrovert like Lawson, Mackay had "people skills" that were intuitive and well honed; the convener of the vacancy committee noted with satisfaction that Mackay, during his visit, had taken care to speak individually to all members of the committee, not just the convener. A special congregational meeting held on 8 December 1965 saw three of the remaining four candidates nominated and a secret ballot held in which Mackay led by a wide margin.[2]

A few years younger than Lawson, Mackay seemed the least unacceptable of the would-be successors. He represented neither nostalgia for the old nor the shock of the new, but instead a happy medium between preacher and pastor. His was the comfortable pulpit to match the "comfortable pew" of the early 1960s. In essence, the Mackay pastorate was destined to be a prolonged cooling-off period.

Donald Bruce Mackay was born in August 1908 at Windsor Mills in Quebec's Eastern Townships, where his father, Malcolm Mackay, practised medicine.[3] His mother, Verena May Caswell, descended from New England stock and was a native of the area. Dr Mackay had been born in Brighton, where his father, Alexander Bisset Mackay, a minister of the Presbyterian Church of England (now the United Reformed Church), served until called to Crescent Street Church, Montreal, in 1879. A.B. Mackay was a Free Church evangelical of the old school. He died suddenly in July 1901, seven years before the birth of his grandson.

When Donald Mackay was still a small child, the family moved to nearby Sherbrooke, where his father became an elder in the Presbyterian Church. After the premature death of Dr Mackay in 1922, young Donald was greatly influenced by his father's sister Katherine and her husband, John Duncan Anderson, a continuing Presbyterian minister who served Beauharnois for nearly thirty years until the Disruption. Their son, Llewellyn K. Anderson, a student for the ministry, set an example for Donald to follow. Graduating from high school in 1927, Donald worked for three years in Montreal in the actuarial department of Sun Life Assurance, in order to save enough money to attend Bishop's College (University). These were the early days of the Great Depression; so it was not until 1935 that Mackay graduated BA from Bishop's and was able to realize his ambition to attend Princeton Theological Seminary. Once accepted as a candidate for ministry, he took student placements in mission fields such as Cochrane and Bar River, Ontario.

While at Princeton, Mackay met and became engaged to Mary Jane Beattie of Shaker Heights (suburban Cleveland), Ohio, a student at Westminster Choir School; they married in November 1938. The preceding June he had been licensed, ordained, and inducted to Georgetown Presbyterian, Howick (Presbytery of Montreal). In December 1939 Mackay was commissioned a chaplain in the Canadian Army Active Force and assigned to the 1st Battalion, Royal Highland Regiment of Canada (Black Watch). He went overseas in the summer of 1940 and the following year resigned his pastorate, from which Presbytery had given him a leave of absence. In 1943 he was appointed assistant senior chaplain, 2nd Canadian Infantry Division, and promoted major. In May 1944 he became staff chaplain, First Canadian Army headquarters, Northwest Europe. Rotated home in May the next year, Mackay arrived in Montreal, where his wife had been engaged in war work, and was called to St Andrew's, Quebec City. Two children – Malcolm Beattie (Mac) and Mary Mossman (Molly) – were born there.

While at St Andrew's, Mackay served as moderator of the Synod of Montreal and Ottawa (now Quebec and Eastern Ontario). He never lost his interest in army life and remained an active chaplain until 1965. In 1950 he was called to Knox Church, Stratford, where he remained for eleven years. During that time he served on one of the committees that helped organize the Stratford Shakespearean Festival, acted as chaplain of the Perth Regiment, and was awarded the Canadian Forces decoration for his services. He was also the guiding force behind a huge restoration project for Knox Church, which had been rebuilt in 1916 after a disastrous fire.

In 1961 Mackay accepted a call to First Presbyterian, Chatham. First Chatham was a very conservative continuing congregation; it was not a good fit, and Mackay's pastorate there was neither happy nor successful. He could not emancipate it from its victory in a long-ago war. By contrast, Saint David's had no prelapsarian idyll to inspire it. Indeed, it had no history at all before 1925 and so could only look forward – and always did. Existence was its victory, and even that had been grasped from the jaws of defeat. This was a pyschological advantage that "new" congregations seemed to possess over continuing ones, which believed they had fought harder and scored the greater victory. Donald Mackay saw Saint David's as the cutting edge, which – thanks to twenty years of Frank Lawson – it undoubtedly was. Mackay also had incidental connections with Saint David's. His brother-in-law, Frank Donaldson, was an elder of Saint David's from 1953 to his death in 1958. In the summer of 1954, while on a visit to his sister May, Mackay had guest-preached at Saint David's one Sunday during Lawson's vacation.

Frank Lawson left Saint David's in much better shape than he had found it. By the 1960s it was in many respects the most prestigious and progressive, though by no means the largest, Protestant church in Halifax, able to balance the contradictions and be both evangelical and mainstream at the same time. This was Lawson's achievement and his legacy, and it seemed both non-repeatable and non-renewable. Frank Lawson was an impossible act to follow, and his successor was cut from a different cloth. As reserved and understated as Lawson had been flamboyant, Mackay was far from being a pulpit orator and stormy petrel like his predecessor.

Indeed, they were as fire and ice. Apart from their liberalism and ecumenism, they had little in common.

Donald Mackay was inducted to Saint David's on Thursday, 17 February 1966. He preached his first sermon the following Sunday morning, on "The fateful power of words"; his farewell sermon at First Chatham two weeks earlier. In the evening he preached on "The high cost of allegiance." On Sunday, 6 March, following evening service, a welcoming organ recital was given as a greeting to Mackay, who was very fond of keyboard music and an enthusiastic amateur pianist himself.

His first annual congregational meeting was in January 1967. After conducting devotions, he "expressed his pleasure in attending the first Congregational meeting since becoming pastor of Saint David's." Symbolic of the new beginning that Mackay, like all ministers, wanted to make in the life of his new congregation was that, for the first time since 1933, the annual report was printed. The entire Mackay family threw themselves with gusto into the work of the church. Mary Jane Mackay ("Mrs D.B.") swiftly re-established and took charge of the junior choir and within the year could pronounce it "the happiest organization in Saint David's." In June 1971 she was instrumental in introducing the post-worship social hour.

The Presbyterian Young People's Society (PYPS) also took a new lease on life, holding a picnic to welcome the new minister's teenaged son and daughter. Molly, for her part, when a senior at Acadia University, undertook the first scholarly research that had ever been done on Saint David's. In December 1970 she received permission from Session to distribute a questionnaire. A copy of the resulting sociology paper was given to the clerk of Session.[4] Mac and Molly would be the only "PKS" (preacher's kids) in the history of Saint David's to be married – in 1970 and 1974 respectively – by their father in his church.

In June 1968 Donald Mackay celebrated the thirtieth anniversary of his ordination. It was the Age of Aquarius. In the rebellious 1960s Lawson was in his natural element – hot water – while Mackay was out of his depth. Like Lawson, however, Mackay was an ecumenist, and ecumenism was in the air. But the idea remained controversial among Presbyterians old enough to remember 1925, for whom ecumenism equalled anti-denominationalism. In October 1965 Synod voted, by a majority of two, not to accept an invitation to join the Maritime (now Atlantic) Ecumenical Council.[5] Synod was deeply divided along metropolitan/hinterland and progressive/conservative lines. For conservatives, ecumenism was the thin edge of the church-union wedge. For liberals such as Halifax's A.O. MacLean and Dartmouth's James Goldsmith, it was in the best traditions of the pre-

Disruption church. For ministers such as they, the continuing church meant continuity with The Presbyterian Church in Canada as it had developed in the fifty years after 1875.

Shortly before Mackay's arrival, at the end of the annual week of prayer in January 1966, an ecumenical conference called "Who Are the People of God?" took place at Saint David's. There was little further activity until 1972, when, on 3 December, Saint David's played host to an "Ecumenical Service of Repentance" for the churches of south-end Halifax, in which Anglicans, Catholics, Uniteds, and Salvation Army all participated. It was among the preparatory events for "KEY 73," an interchurch campaign to evangelize all of North America.[6] Sponsored locally by the Halifax-Dartmouth Council of Churches, of which the minister of St Andrew's Presbyterian, P.A. McDonald, was then first vice-president, KEY 73 was the last and least successful of the "crusades for Christ" that had begun with the Tom Allan mission twelve years earlier. Less ambitious ecumenical initiatives, such as joint services with St Matthew's and Fort Massey United during Holy Week, continued throughout Mackay's pastorate but did not survive it.

Another sign that "the times they are a-changin'" came one Sunday in March 1969 when Mackay exchanged pulpits with the Reverend Wrenford Bryant, pastor of Cornwallis Street (African United) Baptist Church. Two days later, Presbytery met at Saint David's and heard a stirring address by Marvin Schiff, director of Nova Scotia's Human Rights Commission: "Black power is no different than Jewish power, Presbyterian power, white power or any other type."[7] Yet another sign was the trend away from evangelicalism, whether conservative or radical. When the Reverend William Fitch of Knox Church, Toronto, an evangelical whom many Presbyterians considered a fundamentalist, came to Halifax in May 1969 in his capacity as president of the Evangelical Fellowship of Canada, he spoke not in a Presbyterian church but in Trinity, a Low Church Anglican parish.[8]

The common-sense philosophy of Mackay's Scottish forebears taught him that charity began at home; that Christianity was about individual repentance and belief. Seeing the minister's chief responsibility as the stewardship of the Christian community, Mackay was shrewd and experienced enough to realize that the greatest problem facing Saint David's was not lack of openness to the wider world but poor internal communication. In January 1969 Session recommended publishing the newsletter ("as and when necessary, or when the spirit moves"), a vehicle of communication that had not been seen for nearly forty years. Volume 1, number 1, was duly mailed to each member and adherent; it was the only issue to appear.

Doubtless at Mackay's behest, Saint David's decided to invite the 96th General Assembly to meet in Halifax in 1970. It would be the first time since 1910 that the General Assembly had met east of Montreal. The Maritimes in general and Halifax in particular were no longer the citadel of Presbyterianism they had been in the fifty years preceding the Disruption, when the General Assembly had convened in Halifax on no less than four occasions and in Saint John, New Brunswick, on three.

In April 1969 Mackay received a DD from Presbyterian College, Montreal. In June he attended the General Assembly meeting in Toronto, where he was named to the moderator's committee to determine the date and place of meeting for the next Assembly. Supported by Session and Presbytery, Mackay extended a formal invitation for 1970. The invitation was accepted, and in March of that year Session played host to a native Maritimer who was the most influential bureaucrat in the church. The Reverend Dr L.H. Fowler, chair of the Administrative (now Assembly) Council, came to town to make initial arrangements for the General Assembly meeting three months later; it was expected to attract some 250 commissioners.[9]

The June 1970 issue of the *Presbyterian Record* had as its cover illustration a photograph of Halifax's old town clock and featured a short article on Saint David's and its antecedents, probably written by Mackay: "The congregation has entered on several co-operative programs with other churches in the neighbourhood. A slum area was torn down to make way for Scotia Square. With the advent of several high-rise apartments a new form of ministry is envisaged."[10] Mackay was also keen to reverse what Session (or at least some elders) saw as "the decline in interest in Church affairs by members of the congregation."[11]

Mackay's peaceable disposition showed in his invitation to Herbert M. McInnes to serve as general chair of the local arrangements committee. A former elder, McInnes had resigned from Session in June 1966 after what was apparently a rather bitter dispute with the powers that were. Though mediation by Mackay failed to induce him to withdraw his resignation, McInnes graciously agreed to the minister's request to organize the event and was chiefly responsible for its success. The entire congregation was mobilized to assist. Even the former organist, Harold Hamer, was brought out of retirement to direct the combined choirs of the five Presbyterian churches in the metropolitan area.

Mackay himself, as minister of the host church, was the guardian spirit and guiding hand throughout. Two weeks before the General Assembly, he delivered a sermon on "What is a General Assembly?" and then made himself available in the church hall after worship to answer questions arising. He wanted all of Saint David's to understand and appreciate why it was important for the church to be hosting the General Assembly, which he saw as pastoral ministry in the broadest sense. Saint David's would minister to the commissioners just as the church at large ministered to Presbyterians in Halifax simply by being there.

The 96th General Assembly of The Presbyterian Church in Canada opened at Saint David's on Sunday evening, 7 June 1970. Mackay assisted the outgoing moderator in conducting public worship and administering the sacrament of the Lord's Supper. The new moderator was then acclaimed; predictably, the Presbytery of Cape Breton protested electing a moderator on Sunday. Official greetings were received from civic representatives, the Anglicans, the Catholics, the Baptists, the Uniteds, Principal Nicholson of Pine Hill Divinity Hall (a former moderator of the United Church of Canada), the Halifax-Dartmouth Council of Churches, the Canadian Bible Society, the Korean Church in Japan, and – of all people – George Pidgeon, then in his ninety-ninth year, "quite frail and almost wholly blind." Needless to say, Pidgeon was styled "moderator, 51st General Assembly [1925]" – a polite fiction – rather than first moderator of the United Church. Most of the commissioners, 240 strong, were housed in the new residence and classroom complex at Saint Mary's University, whose chair of history and dean of women, Elizabeth A. Chard, was an elder of Saint David's. Business meetings were shared between the university and the church proper.

Historically, the 96th General Assembly is important for two reasons. First, the Ross Report (*Ministry of The Presbyterian Church in Canada*) was tabled. In John Moir's words, the Ross Report "provided a statistical and ideological self-portrait of the Presbyterian Church in Canada."[12] Tendered in October 1969, this 130-page consultants' report was based on a scientific sample of responses to a wide-ranging and widely distributed questionnaire. A blueprint for radical reconstruction of the church, it was the logical follow-up to the Declaration of Concern and other pronouncements of the 1968 pre-Assembly Congress of Concern. In some respects it was a little too radical. The proposal for open Session meetings and deleting the word "kirk" from the term "kirk session" did not commend itself. Though its recommendations were implemented only gradually – and never completely – the concept and practice of ministry that prevail in The Presbyterian Church in Canada today were inspired by the Ross Report. Among the detractors of the report was the new moderator, Dr Dillwyn T. Evans, who believed the church was part of the solution, not part of the problem. Evans felt "the report missed the basic point of the Church – that is in society to heal and to be the conscience of society."[13]

Secondly, the new system for electing the moderator of the General Assembly was introduced. Previously, candidates for moderator had to be nominated from the floor, and unless all but one nominee withdrew, balloting took place then and there. Beginning in 1970, however, candidates were nominated by the presbyteries, and the candidate receiving the most votes became the official nominee and was routinely acclaimed moderator once the Assembly got underway.

By spring 1974 celebrations for the centenary of The Presbyterian Church in Canada were about to begin. Sounding a cautionary note, Mackay gave an interview to a Halifax newspaper in which he observed that while Saint David's people were affluent, most church people in the neighbourhood were poor and Roman Catholic.[14] This was what would now be called a "reality check": the church's business was not to celebrate its own history but to change lives. Earlier that month, on Palm Sunday, Mackay had delivered the same message to his own flock, writing in the bulletin under the heading "Jesus Christ – Lord of Our Future."[15] As ever, he was looking to the pastoral aspect; the Presbyterian centenary was an opportunity for the Presbyterian Church as a whole to witness to Canada.

The new mood of self-congratulatory optimism suffusing The Presbyterian Church in Canada was nicely caught by R.J. Anderson in an article for the Canadian Press at the outset of the centenary year: "That there is a Canadian church to celebrate a centennial is viewed with thankfulness by Presbyterians looking back a half-century to the 'civil war' of 1925 when the issue of church union rent the Church. It is now the third largest Protestant denomination in Canada with about 180,000 communicant members in 1,071 congregations."[16] The church's survival testified to its size, strength, and vitality when it had been the largest Protestant denomination in Canada in 1925. Had there not been dozens of new congregations formed out of the ashes of the great schism, there would have been no centenary to celebrate. Continuing congregations alone were not enough to make the church's reconstruction feasible.

As the founding of Saint David's had led directly to the re-establishment of the Presbytery, it seemed appropriate that the Presbytery's centenary communion service should take place at Saint David's. Moderator of the 100th General Assembly, Dr Hugh F. Davidson, preached there on 8 October 1974. Presbytery's "service of thanksgiving and witness to celebrate the 100th anniversary of the formation of The Presbyterian Church in Canada" also took place at Saint David's, on 4 May 1975.

By the time the church's centenary year officially began on 1 June 1974, the jubilee of Saint David's was already in full swing. On 26 May, a damp Sunday morning, a "family photograph" was posed and shot professionally outside the front of the church immediately after divine worship. Indoors, a luncheon followed, graced by the presence of a former moderator of the General Assembly, Dr A.D. MacKinnon.[17] While a student at Presbyterian College, he had attended the first Presbyterian service at Grafton Street Methodist Church on 5 April 1925. Fifty years later, to the very day, he would preach the jubilee sermon in Saint David's.

The culmination locally of the national celebration came on Sunday, 20 April 1975, when Saint David's joined with St Matthew's United in a joint service of worship commemorating Presbyterian origins in Halifax. It was a backhanded compliment to the two "Presbyterianisms" – one old, the other new – which skilfully circumvented both the church union and the Disruption events. It also came at a time when progressive clergy on both sides of the denominational divide were exhorting people to hear what the Spirit was saying to the churches: Reconcile![18] The year 1975, the jubilee of the United Church of Canada and the centenary of The Presbyterian Church in Canada, should have been the one in which the two churches took their first steps towards reunification. As in 1925, however, advanced clerical and professorial opinion was so far ahead of everyone else's that no one on either side paid them much attention. Instead, both Uniteds and Presbyterians just got on with the more immediate and agreeable task of celebrating *la différence.*

Donald Mackay, undemonstrative to the end, was not given to what is now called "networking," but his wide and long experience, combined with his profound pastoral intuition, enabled him to recognize a crisis of confidence when he saw one. By the autumn of 1972 it was clear that not even its minister's deep faith and deeper prayerfulness and spirituality could retrieve the situation at Saint David's. Though he could not have known it, Mackay was history repeating itself at almost the same age Kerr had been when the writing on the wall appeared in 1943. The end result would be more or less the same, though amicable in spirit.

In August 1973 Mackay turned sixty-five and decided it would be best for Saint David's and for himself if he were to retire – though gradually, not immediately. Making haste slowly was typical of the man. His health had begun to fail; in June 1973 his physician ordered him to leave at once and not return to his pulpit until after the end of summer.[19] Mackay's request for permission to retire was approved by Presbytery in November 1974. The centenary celebration banquet in May 1975 was to serve double duty as a farewell banquet given the minister. News of Mackay's impending retirement was received with regret and sympathy, but also with understanding and appreciation for the devoted service he had rendered. Donald Mackay preached his farewell sermon ("All our ways") on 22 June 1975, one week to the day after the church's one-hundredth birthday; his retirement took effect on 31 August. His nine-year pastorate, the shortest of the four yet completed, would seem in retrospect the lull between the storms.

Though disappointed at not being made minister emeritus, Mackay had the satisfaction of seeing his son elected an elder of Saint David's in 1977. Malcolm B. (Mac) Mackay had previously served a three-year term as trustee and was convener of the all-important property committee. In January 1976 Mackay senior left for Christ Church, Wabush, Labrador, contributing to the Board of Congregational Life a Sunday bulletin cover ("Ministry in a Mining Town") which was used at Saint David's in November 1976. His wife wrote that "we responded to a challenge and went, for the winter, to Wabush … to fill in for a young couple who had 'cabin fever.' One of the happiest experiences of our ministry, which we are glad to have had."[20]

Since the early 1970s Mackay's pastorate had been in decline. The five years before 1971 were more energetic and productive. Yet the hegemony exercised by Kane, McLeod, and Macleod – the "Big Three" – gradually wore Mackay down and sapped his strength. The departure of D.A. Macleod in 1970 was hurtful, and there were three other withdrawals from Session, all in favour of Calvin Church, where, under Lawson's old comrade, A.O. MacLean, the great tradition carried on. Despite skill, experience, and too hard work, which took a toll on him, Mackay never really "caught on" at Saint David's; never captured the imagination of the congregation, especially the younger generation. He was perhaps a little too old, older than any of the congregation's four other ministers, before and after, when he began his pastorate.

Mackay deliberately kept a low public profile, and under him Saint David's accordingly had much less visibility than under Lawson. For example, he did not write for the newspapers, and apart from the 1970 General Assembly, there was little press coverage of congregational events. A case in point is the 1975 celebrations. The golden jubilee of the United Church of Canada attracted a full-page feature in the local newspaper, but the centenary of The Presbyterian Church in Canada did not.[21] Protestant Halifax was still a United Church town, and the *Herald* newspapers, whose proprietor was a member of St Andrew's United, quite sincerely believed that the Presbyterian Church had died the day the United Church was born. The mere continued existence of the PCC was an awkward sign of contradiction that had been neither forgiven nor forgotten and, worse, was not understood.

Many members and adherents who had been present and active during Frank Lawson's watch took a furlough during Mackay's. Simply put, the difference between Mackay and Lawson was that Lawson wanted to draw people – all people – to Saint David's, while Mackay sought to reach the people who had already found their own way there. A telling gesture was Mackay's replacement in February 1969 of Lawson's trademark motto ("Whatever your creed or denomination you are invited to these services") with the Celtic cross. Branding made the church more attractive to church-shoppers with a concept, a sense of what they wanted. Mackay was interested in conserving market share, attracting lapsed or intending Presbyterians; Lawson – the continuous evangelical – in cornering, monopolizing, and expanding the market to the whole of humanity. For him, preachers made Christians, not Presbyterians.[22] The essence of Christianity was public worship, and the essence of worship was preaching.

The Presbyterian Young People's Society, the Men's Club, and the senior Church School all disappeared on Mackay's watch, as did evening worship and the preparatory service for the Lord's Supper. Of course, the minister was not to blame, nor was he blamed, for the decline – the world, after all, had ceased to be Christian – but he was identified with it. Against the fruits of retrenchment, however, must be set a record of significant achievement: ordination of the first woman elders in the Synod and among the first in the entire church, complete restoration and rebuilding of the organ, establishment of the Interchurch Group Home for Boys ("Genesis House"), the 96th General Assembly, and the highly successful dual celebration of the centenary of the church and the jubilee of the congregation. Mackay's pastorate was a time of radical, almost revolutionary change in church, community, and world. Yet it was a time of stasis at Saint David's.

Undemonstrative by nature, Mackay maintained a dignified reserve that was sometimes mistaken for hauteur. He took very seriously the gospel admonition to do good in secret lest one attract praise. He hid his light under a bushel and did not court and cultivate publicity as Lawson had done. Aiming to conciliate rather than provoke, he thought "inside the box," measuring everything in pastoral terms. Blessed or cursed with the demeanour and discipline of a retired army officer, he was a quiet, highly principled, and very determined man. A gifted pastoral visitor, he practised his craft silently and invisibly but with supreme assurance and to excellent effect. He was at his best when dealing one-to-one. Though he had strong supporters among the deeper and more discerning spiritual souls at Saint

David's, they formed a distinct minority. Among them was the clerk of Session, for whom Mackay's ministry – entirely without flash or flair – was an oasis of calm and a blessed relief by comparison with Lawson's.

The day for preacherly pyrotechnics was also over and done. Unlike Lawson, for whom the more controversial a subject, the better material it was for a sermon, Mackay was careful to confine his sermons to spiritual themes. If he had political views, the congregation never heard them. A possible exception was an anti-abortion sermon ("How to murder a baby") preached in January 1972 around the theme of the Holy Innocents.[23] Access to abortion was a continuing, hot button issue on which The Presbyterian Church in Canada had taken a firm oppositional stance. The United Church, on the other hand, struck a committee and published a study. The liberal policy recently adopted by the UCC's General Council was controversial within and outside the United Church, and especially so in the Presbytery of Halifax. Abortion was the gay-marriage issue of its time, but Mackay viewed it in straightforwardly pastoral, rather than ethical or legal, terms: it prevented little children from coming to Jesus.

No word appears more frequently in Mackay's sermon titles than "Jesus." He viewed preaching less as evangelism and exhortation than as spiritual direction, advice to Christians on how to live the Christian life. Such was Mackay's reputation as a spiritual counsellor that, towards the end of his pastorate, he was appointed convener of Presbytery's special committee on "The Work of the Holy Spirit." This was the measured Presbyterian response to the "Charismatic Renewal," the Pentecostal new wave then engulfing the Roman Catholic Archdiocese of Halifax with the full support of its very liberal archbishop, James Hayes.

Mackay was more collegial than Lawson and was therefore more popular with his fellow ministers. He had the good fortune not to be Irish and rarely if ever found himself a minority of one. He was a consensus builder, inside Presbytery and out. His pastoral care and concern extended to candidates for the ministry, and among the new clergy he mentored was P.A. (Sandy) McDonald, whom he had known as a youth during his eleven years at Knox, Stratford. Mackay was largely responsible for McDonald's coming to the Presbytery of Halifax and Lunenburg, where in 1968 he was appointed ordained missionary at St Andrew's (Dartmouth) and Musquodoboit Harbour. In November 1969, when Mackay declined the nomination in his favour, McDonald, age twenty-five, became the youngest minister ever to serve as moderator of Presbytery.[24]

Donald Mackay made history simply by being at Saint David's: he was the first native-born Canadian to be called as minister. His tenure, brief by comparison with the other three completed pastorates, was an interregnum.

He did not impress his stamp on the congregation – perhaps he did not especially try to – nor did he ever gain its wholehearted support. He was neither the charismatic preacher nor the benevolent despot that Frank Lawson had been. Yet he was selfless to a fault and inculcated with a discipline that induced him to give too much too often. He did his duty as God gave him the light to see that duty.

Much as Mackay had to offer, Saint David's needed more than he had to give. He was no Frank Lawson, nor would he have wanted to be; to that extent his pastorate, half as long as his predecessor's, was pure anticlimax. A year and a month after Mackay's death, on 17 March 1985, a plaque in memory of his nine-year pastorate was unveiled by his family and dedicated. It was a telling riposte to the unintended implied slight delivered at the annual congregational meeting two months earlier, when a prominent elder thanked Mackay's successor for his "support and leadership over the last 9 years which had done so much to re-establish Saint David's congregation as a vital and alive entity."[25]

7

John Pace

Donald Mackay preached his farewell sermon on 22 June 1975 and never occupied the pulpit of Saint David's again.[1] Unlike Lawson's departure, which had been marked by shock at the suddenness and sadness over the untimeliness of it, Mackay's allowed Saint David's plenty of time to prepare for it. Yet the shortest pastorate in the congregation's history would be followed by a longer vacancy than the one that had preceded it. The circumstances were unusual in that seven months elapsed between the minister's resignation in November and his departure in June. Presbytery immediately set up a "pastoral relations committee" to liaise with Session until an interim moderator could be appointed. Mackay offered his full cooperation, inviting the special committee to meet with Session whenever it wished and authorizing Session to hold these meetings in his absence.

On 7 December 1975 the congregation had heard preach for the seventh time since 14 September the Reverend John Pace, newly appointed project coordinator for the Metropolitan Regional Board on Drug Dependency. So impressed were they by the man himself and his sermons that enthusiasm for a call to anyone other than Pace all but evaporated. "It was," according to elder Robert J. McCleave, "a case of love at first sight between many of the congregation and the young man in the pulpit."[2] Pace, of course, was not young, but he was twenty years younger than Donald Mackay.

He had taken care to present his presbyterial certificate from Waterloo-Wellington so that his name could be added to the appendix to the roll of Halifax and Lunenburg. In light of the failure to call either of the invited preachers, an informal but irresistible consensus was emerging and coalescing around a supply preacher who was not even a candidate. Pace supplied for the last time on 4 January 1976. The vacancy committee then set about persuading him to reconsider his refusal. This time the answer was yes. The recommendation in favour of Pace went before Session on 1 February, the following day he attended his last meeting as metropolitan region coordinator, and the day after that he tendered his resignation. On the 6th the clerk of Presbytery issued the notice of moderation in the call to Pace. On Sunday the 15th he preached for a call; as it was by then a mere formality, the usual order of the steps could be inverted – preaching coming after the call, rather than before. The text of "A symphony for 10 fingers" is not extant, but according to one who was present, Pace "called for people to be more than observers or spectators – they must become involved."[3]

The special congregational meeting held on 22 February was unanimous in accepting the vacancy committee's recommendation. The call to Pace went before Presbytery on 11 March and was supported by a bevy of enthusiastic commissioners from Saint David's. On Thursday, 1 April, a few weeks shy of his forty-eighth birthday, John Pace was inducted to the Presbyterian Church of Saint David as its fourth minister. Donald Mackay, ever the old-fashioned gentleman, sent a letter to be read publicly. The prophetic aspect of the event was emphasized by the induction preacher, R.K. Anderson, of First Sackville Presbyterian Church, a newish congregation in outer surburbia which Saint David's had done much to help establish: "Today in your very hearing" (Luke 4:14–30).

On Passion Sunday, 4 April, John Pace preached his inaugural sermon. His texts were Numbers 11:1–17 and Mark 1:14–22 and his theme was leadership. For Pace, the minister was leader-preacher. "I will hold high the banner of our Lord," he concluded. "I will dream dreams for you, and I trust that we will walk in shared responsibility into a new day for the Church of Saint David and for her Lord, Jesus, the only King and Head of the Church."[4] That Easter Sunday, 18 April 1976, Pace preached on "Christus Victor" (from the old Latin antiphon "Christ wins, Christ reigns, Christ rules"). It was an auspicious beginning to a new pastorate.

John Pace was born in Belfast in 1928, the only child and namesake of a newsagent. The family was Methodist, not Presbyterian, and John junior ("Jack") was educated at the Euston Street public elementary school and Methodist College secondary school. A "bank boy" who emigrated in 1947, he "burned with Presbyterian zeal for advancement."[5] Working as a teller at the Royal Bank in Hamilton, however, was too tame, too predictable, and too monotonous; soon he was on the move. From 1948 to 1953 he was employed by International Harvester Company, from 1953 to 1955 by the Commercial Credit Corporation, and from 1955 to 1959 by the Hamilton *Spectator,* where he was credit manager.

No sooner had he arrived in Hamilton than Pace began to worship and socialize at New Westminster, a continuing congregation. He became a professing member of New Westminster in 1948 and met his future wife, Margaret Evelyn Logan, daughter of an elder, whom he married in June 1951. Pace also served on the board of managers and was convener of the property committee. He personally attributed the call to ministry to his acceptance of a challenge thrown down by a business colleague twice his age.[6] In order to qualify as a student for ministry, Pace began to work part-time towards his BA at McMaster University. In 1959 he was certified by Presbytery as a candidate for ministry and became a full-time student. Graduating from McMaster in 1961, he went off to Knox College. Graduating BD (MDiv) in 1964, he took the Goldie scholarship, the W.W. Bryden prize in history of religion, and the Agnes and Lindsay Torrance endowment, a post-graduate scholarship.

In February 1960 Pace moved from New Westminster to St Paul's as student assistant. St Paul's was the oldest and most prestigious Presbyterian pulpit in Hamilton; its minister since 1949 was perhaps the best-known Canadian Presbyterian preacher of his time, Dr Stanley Vance (1918–76). Vance, ten years Pace's senior, was colleague, mentor, and friend. It was Vance, Pace wrote in 1986, "whose preaching shaped and created who I am today."[7] Pace had his hands full at St Paul's, preaching at least once a Sunday and serving as superintendent of the Church School, which was in disarray.[8]

It was at St Paul's that he began the youth ministry that would afterwards make him something of a local hero. On the very eve of his arrival, he had been appointed director of senior youth activities for the Presbytery of Hamilton. In his early thirties and ten years older than most of his Knox College contemporaries, Pace was considered just the right age to "connect" with teenagers. He was ordained at St Paul's in May 1964 but did not remain in Hamilton; instead he was appointed missionary at St James, in Préville, Quebec, a suburb of Montreal. St James was a mission field that did not get off the ground, and within two years Pace was back in Hamilton, serving as assistant at St Paul's.

In July 1967 he was inducted to St Paul's, in Ingersoll, a small town east of London. There he would continue and diversify his youth ministry – only to have it implode. A promoter of the Teen and Twenty Chapel move ment,[9] John Pace has good claim to be considered the first dedicated, and certainly the most advanced, youth minister in The Presbyterian Church in Canada. He saw before almost anyone other than young people them-selves that the church was losing them because it was making no credible effort to engage them. Sadly, his worship-and-music-focused youth ministry ("Rev. John beats a mean tambourine") was to be a victim of its own success. In his efforts to be all things to all young people, Pace got himself into waters as deep as they were hot. The end came in February 1970; he resigned from St Paul's and spent the next six months ministering to a United Church congregation in Woodstock that had an active youth program.

The spring and summer of 1970 were a cooling-off period. Pace was a minister in good standing in the church whom no presbytery had on its constituent roll. His future as a minister of The Presbyterian Church in Canada hung in the balance. In October 1970 he went to London to work for the Lake Erie Region of the Addiction Research Foundation (ARF), an Ontario government agency now merged in the Centre for Addiction and Mental Health. Though he had neither academic nor professional qualifications in the field, addiction research was in some respects the continuation in the secular sphere of Pace's youth work in the pastoral ministry. In 1973 he moved to Kitchener as program director for the Midwestern Region of the ARF. But by the end of 1974 he was looking for a more substantial change of scene.

After considering and rejecting potential employment opportunities in Manitoba and New Brunswick, Pace decided to pursue one in Nova Scotia. Established in 1972 and given a broad mandate to deal with problems of substance abuse, the Nova Scotia Commission on Drug Dependency (NSCODD) was equivalent to Ontario's Addiction Research Foundation. The new Metropolitan Regional Board (MRB) on Drug Dependency (a subsidiary of the commission) was seeking a regional project coordinator of drug dependency services in Halifax-Dartmouth. In March 1975 Pace was offered and accepted the post, and in June he began work. The commission removed the "Reverend" and in its place conferred on him an MA, which he did not – and did not claim to – possess.

In due course, Pace was discovered by the interim moderator of Saint David's and invited to supply-preach. P.A. McDonald, busy at the best of times, was getting ready to entertain the moderator of the General Assembly as well as host the Synod meeting at his home church and was glad to have a new face "within the bounds" who was willing and able to help. Pace did so for the first time on 14 September 1975, just two weeks after Mackay's retirement officially took effect. Thus the congregation got to see and hear a natural-born preacher who was *not* a candidate a full two months before either of the two ministers who were.[10]

Pace preached again on two Sundays in October and the first three in November. He also presented to the young people of Saint David's two sessions on alcoholism and other forms of substance abuse. On 6 November his name was added to the appendix to the roll of Presbytery. He would no doubt have preached the remaining two Sundays in November as well, had he not had to stand aside for the invited candidates. Unfortunately for them, the congregation no longer had ears or time for anyone but Pace, who was back in the pulpit on 7 December and again on 4 January. Saint David's began the year 1976 with John Pace in the pulpit. He preached in the morning and again at the evening communion. During the course of that month, Pace made up his mind to become a pastoral minister again. Assured by the vacancy committee that the call was a foregone conclusion if he were but willing to accept it, he summarily resigned from the MRB.

Pace moved quickly and worked hard not to disappoint the great expectations that Saint David's held of him. It helped that he was a known quantity and that first impressions had been so positive that he did not even have to apply – he was recruited. It also helped that the competition was perceived as weak by comparison. "When I was first approached by the Vacancy Committee of Saint David's," Pace wrote, "and was asked as to my aspirations for the congregation, I replied, 'To create a caring community.'"[11] He set about doing so by visiting each household in Saint David's, restoring to the worship service the conversation with children (which had lapsed years before), reintroducing the Wednesday evening prayer meeting (which had not been seen since A.D. Falconer's time), and promoting schemes such as a congregational orchestra and an art show. He had caught the vision and thereby captured the imagination and support of his people.

The charisma that had made Pace especially effective as a youth minister was put to excellent use. No sooner had he settled in than elder Elizabeth A. Chard, in her capacity as registrar of Saint Mary's University, recruited him to act as de facto chaplain to Protestant students at what had been until recently a Roman Catholic institution. Pace was thus the latest accrual to what was jocularly known among undergraduate wags as the "God Squad," the "Holy Trinity," or the "Rebel Revs."[12] The bulletin for 31 October 1976 announced, "We will be happy to know that our congregation will have a closer relationship with Saint Mary's University now that our Minister has been named interim Chaplain to assist with the Protestant students."[13]

In the first of his pastoral letters (Christmas 1976), Pace expressed his gratitude and satisfaction that the baby had been brought to term. In January 1977 he chaired his first annual congregational meeting. None of his predecessors had done so, because the congregation's tradition was completely against the practice. Congregational meetings were one thing; the Board of Managers ("Trustees") was another. The minister's attendance at trustees' meetings was purely discretionary and barely respectable. Pace was the first minister to attend as a matter of course and threw himself with gusto into the work of administration. No regular trustee was busier or more attentive than the new minister, and no matter, small or large, escaped his attention. On at least six occasions over the years, Pace found himself chairing meetings in the absence of both the chair and the vice-chair; on other occasions he acted as secretary. For years, trustees' meetings took place in the minister's study. Pace's close and continuous interest in the work of the trustees began with his induction and persisted throughout the twenty-two years of his pastorate.

The congregation showed its approval of his job performance by voting Pace a $1,000 increase in his stipend after less than a year in the pulpit. So consistently high was his approval rating that his compensation was increased by $3,000 in 1983 and a further $3,000 in 1984. Saint David's also financed an annual overseas study leave – a personally directed continuing education program, most often in an academic setting. Though it was unheard of in the church, the congregation thought this perquisite well worth the expense, if only because Pace himself believed it to be a necessary aspect of continuing education. In 1977 he attended an international ecumenical seminar in Vienna. The summers of 1978, 1979, and 1981 through 1984 found him at Christ Church, Canterbury, England, attending the Canterbury Ecumenical Summer School (CANTESS).[14] In 1985 Pace went instead to the American Institute of Theological Studies near Geneva; he returned there in 1987 to hear Marcus Barth, son of the famous theologian. In 1986 he was at St Andrew's (the oldest university in Scotland) to hear Murdo McDonald on the Gospel of John. In 1991 he went for the second time to Oxford to hear lectures on medical ethics. Pace also attended a colloquium on the life and death of Dietrich Bonhoeffer given by Bonhoeffer's cousin.

Characteristic of Pace's innovations was the pastoral letter, addressed to the congregation at set times during the liturgical year. His annual pastoral, printed in the annual report, became the minister's opportunity to speak his mind. It was what would now be called a scorecard – the minister's measuring the congregation's progress and appraising its performance over the course of the year. Pace's public letters were candid and sometimes highly personal, and collectively they amount to a serial autobiography written in instalments over twenty-two years. They also compensated for the want of a congregational newsletter in all but six of the twenty-two years of Pace's pastorate.[15]

Like Frank Lawson, though less frequently, John Pace sermonized from the headlines, a case in point being the hostage-taking crisis at the American embassy in Iran in the autumn of 1979. Three weeks into the crisis, Pace preached on "Insight into Islam," and the sermon was published in the local newspaper under the title "God help the hostages, God help us all if the call for a Holy War is heeded."[16] Despite strongly held opinions, Pace was no ideologue and his principled conservatism was distinctly enlightened. He was a strong believer in the cult of the leader, going so far as to preach in March 1981 a sermon with the daring title, "Jesus Mein Führer."

This outlook explains both his intense monarchism and his admiration for strong leaders as far apart politically as Margaret Thatcher and Chairman Mao. For him the quality of leadership, whether in a Presbyterian church or in a nation-state, had little to do with ideology, much less political correctness, but with the desire, the determination, and the capacity to lead effectively. Politically, he was, in the Canadian jargon of the time, a "red Tory." He did not make a virtue of consistency. He was anti-papist without being anti-Catholic; opposed to the Orange Order and the Reverend Ian Paisley but a proud Ulsterman for whom the British connection was paramount.

Pace was keenly interested in relations between church and state, which he considered inseparable and intermingled,[17] though not in the same way as the covenanting theocracy with which he had grown up. In May 1977 he designed a Service of Thanksgiving in honour of the Queen's Silver Jubilee, but despite the intercession of elder Robert J. McCleave, MP, he was unable to carry out his plan to invite HRH Prince Andrew, then studying in Canada, whom HM the Queen had forbidden to undertake any official engagements.[18] Nevertheless, the lieutenant-governor, the premier, and the leader of the Opposition all attended.[19]

In August 1978 the Canadian Bar Association held its annual meeting in Halifax. The report of its Committee on the Constitution (*Towards a New Canada*) caused a stir by recommending that the Queen should be replaced as head of state by a Canadian. Pace, stung to the quick by what he perceived as bad citizenship, preached a no-holds-barred sermon on the retention of the monarchy ("The fertile centre"). Four days later he published the sermon in Halifax's afternoon newspaper and sent a copy to Buckingham Palace.[20] He also sent it to Prime Minister Pierre Trudeau and received a thoughtful personal reply.[21] Of all his "political" sermons, this was the one of which Pace was most proud.

In January 1978 the joint annual meeting of Session and Board proposed to establish a special fund for the employment of an assistant minister "in future years."[22] A detailed proposal, drafted by Pace and accepted at the annual congregational meeting later that month, called for "a three-year pilot project for ministerial assistance." Among the seven parts into which the proposal was divided was an appendix giving the rationale for *calling* an assistant (a minister) rather than *appointing* an assistant (a deaconess). There were no women ministers in the Atlantic Synod at the time and only one "assistant minister," an ordained assistant to the minister in Moncton, New Brunswick.

The proposal envisaged an assistant who was a minister, and was written with Iona MacLean in mind. MacLean was the daughter of the minister of Knox Church, Halifax, and the first woman to be ordained in the Atlantic Synod. At the time serving in Ontario, she was receptive to the idea and had preliminary discussions with Pace.[23] The proposal was approved in principle at the annual congregational meeting in January 1979, and MacLean supplied on two consecutive Sundays that summer. In the end, however, she declined, and nothing more could be done. Few young clergy were willing to play assistant to another minister when they had a pastoral charge of their own. Pace had to settle for an assistant who was a woman but not a minister and to defer for fourteen years his dream of recreating the happy relationship between himself and Stanley Vance at St Paul's in 1966–67, when Vance was minister and he assistant.

The post was advertised in the *Presbyterian Record* for the first time in June 1979: "ASSISTANT MINISTER WANTED / The Presbyterian Church of Saint David, Halifax, N.S. is desirous of receiving applications for the position of Assistant Minister. Applicant should have proven ability in the field of music and be able to work with young people. Job description available upon request." Personal approaches were also made, but no applicants for the full-time employment opportunity came forward.[24] Pace appointed himself a search committee of one and went to Toronto in the winter of 1980 to interview graduates of Ewart College, a diaconal training institute. There he found what he was looking for. Amy Campbell had just graduated with a diploma in Christian education and was about to graduate from the University of Toronto with a BA in religious studies. Though only twenty-two years old, she had already served two internships and came highly rec-ommended by her minister, Bruce Miles. Of particular interest was that she was musical. Campbell, in short, was nothing if not well qualified.

The employment of Amy Campbell as pastoral assistant went before a special joint meeting of Session and Board on 2 March 1980. Pace's "Progress Report and Search for Ministerial Assistance" was received, and he was authorized to act. "I would further recommend," he reported, "that she be responsible directly to myself and through me to the Session. That the job description be furnished closely resembling the job description already prepared for the Assistant Minister."[25] The pastoral assistant was a two-year renewable appointment, with salary and benefits at the going rate for deaconesses. The thirteen-point description of the position seemed to cover everything falling outside the ministry of word and sacrament. Campbell was to assist with worship, if necessary conducting it during the minister's absence, and to undertake visitation, especially of hospitals and senior citizens' residences.[26]

Her appointment having been announced in March 1980, Deaconess Campbell set to work in September. On Sunday, the 28th, she contributed "A Litany for the Educational Ministry of Our Church" to the Church School and Rally Day celebration of the bicentenary of the Sunday School movement. It was the first of several special litanies she would prepare for use in public worship. Two days later she was welcomed at a congregational dinner, and a Presbytery service installing her as pastoral assistant was held.[27]

Campbell conducted worship services monthly at Grace Maternity Hospital, occasionally at the Victoria General Hospital, and about every six weeks – when it was the "turn" of Saint David's – at one of the senior citizens' residences. Nevertheless, being unordained, she saw herself as second banana; she once upset the minister by telling someone, in his hearing, that her job description consisted of everything Pace did not want to do. A case in point was her limited opportunity for preaching, a privileged task that Pace did not want to share with her. Campbell conducted services during the minister's annual vacation only during the second of the two summers she was at Saint David's. There were also a couple of winter opportunities when Pace was away on holiday. Typically, however, he left the opening part of the service to Campbell (hence her authoring a number of litanies), taking the rest of it for himself.

By the spring of 1982 Amy Campbell had had enough. Deaconesses had never before been styled "pastoral assistants," nor had they served as assistants to ministers. That was a new concept and a new role; deaconesses were catechists and pastoral visitors who rarely participated in public worship and even more rarely preached. Even Presbytery seemed in two minds. Though Campbell attended both Session and Presbytery meetings, Presbytery had to agree formally that she be included when the right hand of fellowship was given during ordinations.[28] All of these factors prompted her not to seek a renewal of the posting; instead, she returned to university to obtain a degree in education. Campbell saw clearly enough that, as deaconess-assistant, she could accomplish little in a conservative congregation like Saint David's. The two roles seemed incompatible; a deaconess was one thing, a pastoral assistant another. At the bare minimum, the assistant to the minister would have had to be someone en route to ordination.

Campbell's last Sunday was 1 August 1982. (By November 1983 she would be back, serving as deaconess at Halifax's Knox Presbyterian.) The lessons learned from her experience at Saint David's were not lost on Pace. The next assistant to the minister would not be a deaconess and therefore not styled a "pastoral," but rather a "lay," assistant. Instead of a service of installation, there would be a service recognizing her certification as a student for the ministry. Campbell found it difficult living in the shadow of what might have been, had Iona MacLean become the assistant as Pace desired. He certainly wanted to work only with a woman, ordained or otherwise; hence his visit to Ewart College when he could not find a minister who was interested in the position. Saint David's was a learning experience for Campbell, and she continued to receive a warm reception from people there when she supplied. But she was definitely more at home in churches with a less formal and traditional style of worship and music than Saint David's.[29]

Despite Pace's most sanguine hopes, it proved no easier to find an ordained assistant in 1982 than it had in 1979. The new lay assistant was a native of Belleville, Ontario, and nine years older than her predecessor. Judithe Adam had taken her RN at Kingston in 1971, and two years later she came to Dalhousie University to take her diploma in public health nursing. From 1976 to 1980 she studied and worked in Calgary, before returning to Halifax and Dalhousie to continue working on the bachelor of nursing degree she had begun at the University of Calgary. By the time she graduated in the spring of 1983, her professional career had taken a decisively different turn.

Unlike Amy Campbell, Judithe Adam was not a cradle Presbyterian. Introduced to Saint David's by a nursing colleague, she was worshipping there when Campbell arrived, and she was received into membership by profession of faith in December 1980. Over the next two years Adam got involved in the Saint David's Auxiliary, a lively new organization of younger, mainly single professional women. She also caught the eye of the minister, who, faced with Campbell's impending departure, in the spring of 1982 drafted for Adam a detailed "Proposal for Pilot Project for Lay Assistant / September 1982–September 1984." Adam having offered herself as a candidate for the ministry, Session approved the proposal and recommended it to the Board, which accepted it unanimously. Adam herself appended a six-part series of objectives stating the means by which she would carry them out. It was an auspicious beginning to a sixteen-year tenure, eleven as lay/pastoral assistant and five as ordained assistant.

In June 1982 Judithe Adam was certified as a student for the ministry, and in September the Presbytery of Halifax and Lunenburg held a service of recognition at Saint David's. Counterbalancing her newness to the church was the fact that she was a health professional, and more particularly a public health nurse, for whom hospital visitation was routine. In May 1983 she wrote, organized, and composed the entire service for Christian Family Sunday. Half-time during the first year, Adam became full-time as of September 1983. Unlike her predecessor, who preached only occasionally in the minister's absence, Adam routinely did so long before she became a minister herself. Pace was impressed and said so in his 1983 annual pastoral.[30]

The rapport between Pace and the new lay assistant was good. Adam was reaping the harvest where Campbell had sown the seeds; the scope of the position was now broader and its content more diversified. It was also better understood, appreciated, and accepted by the congregation. Adam's not being a deaconess was a positive advantage, as was her having been a member of the congregation rather than a complete stranger; she was well-known and well-liked. Campbell had had the unenviable task of introducing a brand new concept, and she failed to dispel the congregation's preconceived notion that a deaconess was a deaconess was a deaconess. The assistant could be a minister, a licentiate, or a student – in short, what Pace himself had been at various times during his six years with Vance at St Paul's.

In June 1984 Judithe Adam was one of seven new elders elected, and that summer she supplied throughout the minister's study leave and vacation. In the autumn she commenced occasional part-time study towards the MDiv degree at Atlantic School of Theology. No one, herself least of all, seemed in a hurry for Adam to proceed to ordination. It was more important that she establish the position of *lay* assistant and herself in it. When her initial two-year term expired at the end of August 1984, she asked Session to extend it and Session agreed to do so.

Two months into Adam's second term, the clerk of Session reflected that when Saint David's first thought of a lay assistant, it had in mind an ordained minister, but none was available. Session then secured a graduate from Ewart who was with Saint David's for two years. She left to go back to university for an education degree. The new lay assistant was a graduate from Dalhousie in nursing who had worked in this field. She now intended going to Knox College to study for the ministry and had been certified by Presbytery as a candidate. These young women helped the minister in visiting, both sick and well, and assisted in leading some study groups and with other church groups. They took some part in each Sunday morning service and full charge of services during the minister's vacation. Neither took a major part in Church School work, but both assisted when needed.[31] Thirteen years after the termination of the second of the two deaconess-directors of Christian education, Saint David's was again ready for female ministry. Campbell laid a sure foundation, and Adam was building upon it.

In 1985, while Saint David's was busy celebrating its diamond jubilee, Pace decided to observe the upcoming tenth anniversary of his pastorate by publishing a representative selection of the over four hundred sermons he had preached "from a Nova Scotia pulpit."[32] In the task of selection and editing, he was assisted by the Calkins – Melvin (an elder since 1984), Patricia, and the eldest of their four children, Catherine, then president of the senior choir.

Catherine Calkin was Pace's true spiritual heir, having grown up under his pastorate. Received into membership at age fifteen, she designed the bulletin cover for the 1985 diamond jubilee of Saint David's. In November of that year she advised Session that she wished to become a candidate for ministry. In April 1986 Presbytery certified Catherine, then completing her MA at Dalhousie, as a student for ministry. Pace and the organist composed special music for the recognition service, and Pace preached the sermon, "Who's calling?" In May 1989 the Paces attended Catherine's graduation from Knox College as official representatives of Saint David's, a singular honour. Especially poignant was that she was awarded the Stanley W. Vance memorial scholarship for preaching. In June Catherine was licensed at First Sackville Presbyterian (then vacant), and on 30 July she preached at Saint David's. In October she was ordained – in the same church to which she had come as a child eighteen years earlier.[33]

Though Catherine Calkin did not linger in the Presbytery of Halifax and Lunenburg,[34] her prospective ordination had had one very important, if incidental effect. The lay assistant at Saint David's finally made up her mind to complete her theological studies so that she too could proceed to ordination sooner rather than later. In June 1988 Judithe Adam's certification as a candidate for ministry was revived, and she reverted to part-time status at Saint David's in order to accelerate her theological studies. Pace found the absence of his assistant burdensome and said so in his annual letter.

The annual congregational meeting in January 1990 heard the minister laud the fact that Saint David's, unlike so many other churches, was "devoid of divisiveness." Sadly, the harmony was not to endure. In the spring of 1991 Judithe Adam, now Adam-Murphy, sought and received an eight-month leave of absence (September 1991–April 1992) to enable her to complete at Knox College, Toronto, all the courses necessary for ordination. She returned to full-time service at Saint David's at Easter 1992. Pace advised the Trustees that she would graduate from AST on 24 April and be licensed in June, and that there would be a service at Saint David's in September.[35] There was to be no licensing, however, as it was not customary for the candidate to be certified for ordination unless she was actively seeking a pulpit. Nor was it customary for the licentiate to be ordained unless a call had been extended and accepted and approved. In Adam-Murphy's case, neither of these conditions applied.

Pace started the ball rolling in May 1992 by convening a "very important" special meeting of Session for 7 June; it was "for one purpose and one purpose alone … 'to discuss the future of the Ministry of Word and Sacrament at Saint David's.'"[36] The seriousness of the agenda was underscored by Pace's inviting the clerk of Presbytery to attend. Session responded to the minister's initiative by striking a select committee of six elders whose task it was to investigate "future ministerial options." Early in October the committee reported. Adam-Murphy's term as lay assistant was to expire at the end of December, and Session offered to appoint her *pastoral* assistant as of January 1993. This title was in keeping with the higher status that Adam-Murphy had acquired over the course of 1992 and was of course the one which Deaconess Campbell had held a dozen years earlier.

In November, despite opposition from its own special committee, Session complied with the personnel committee's recommendation to take the call to Adam-Murphy before the congregation. By December the cat was out of the bag. Pace wrote in his Christmas letter, "I believe you will welcome the news that the Session is recommending to the Annual Meeting that our Pastoral Assistant, Judithe Adam-Murphy, should be called and ordained as Assistant Minister."

The annual congregational meeting, supposed to take place in January, had to be deferred for a month while the financial and political aspects of the arrangement were worked out. It did not help matters that on 10 February the controversy reached the pages of Halifax's biweekly satirical magazine *Frank* ("Showdown at St David's").[37] It was widely believed that Pace intended to retire sooner rather than later and wanted Adam-Murphy to succeed him. Her ordination and call/induction as assistant minister were but the prerequisites.

A special congregational meeting was held on 21 February 1993, immediately following the deferred annual meeting, to decide whether to accept Session's recomendation to call Adam-Murphy as assistant minister. Four documents were distributed and spoken to by the minister, who, as usual, was chairing the meeting. The fourth – "National Presbyterian Church Protocol to be Used in the Retirement of a Minister" – contained words to the effect that it was the practice of The Presbyterian Church in Canada for an assistant minister to resign when the minister retired or resigned. (It was not.) The statement was meant to reassure the apprehensive that the promotion of the lay assistant was *not* an exercise in succession planning.[38]

The chair of Session's personnel committee moved, and a trustee seconded, that the steps be initiated that would result in a call to Judithe Adam-Murphy as assistant minister. A secret ballot was asked for; the vote was 77 in favour – about 39 per cent of the active membership – to 33 opposed. Some objected to an assistant minister as unnecessary, while others (including the treasurer of the congregation) to a second ministerial salary as unaffordable. Many simply boycotted the meeting. The "promotion" of the pastoral assistant to assistant minister was a nominal call that the congregation was being invited to rubber-stamp. There was no advertisement, no vetting of applicants, no leet (short list), and no invitation to preach for a call. The letter of church law was being followed but not the spirit. Pace was moderator of Presbytery at the time, and faced with a strong congregational vote in favour, Presbytery sustained the call when it came before Presbytery on 20 April 1993.

Judithe Adam-Murphy was ordained and inducted at Saint David's on the afternoon of Sunday, 30 May 1993 – appropriately, Pentecost, the descent of the Holy Spirit on the Apostles. Throughout the five years of her second assistantship, she capitalized on the extensive goodwill she had accumulated. She worked diligently and was accepted in both church and community. Metropolitan Halifax was not overstocked with women ministers, and at the time of her induction, she was one of only two in the Presbytery of Halifax and Lunenburg.[39] Pace, for his part, considered the assistant minister his greatest achievement. He was, so he hoped, creating a bright and certain future for ministry at Saint David's. Adam-Murphy had given exemplary service as lay assistant and now, as assistant minister, would have an authority commensurate with her responsibilities.

Though an elder of nine years' standing when ordained to the ministry, Adam-Murphy did not get on with the octogenarian clerk of Session, who strongly disapproved of the position that had been created for her. Their clashes both in and out of Session were legendary. The Kirk Session review for 1993 said it all with deafening silence: "The congregation would extend its congratulations ... to Judithe Adam-Murphy on her being ordained and inducted during this year."[40] As far as Ralph Kane was concerned, Adam-Murphy might just as well have been ministering on Mars. Kane resented what he perceived as her interference in the Church School, while she was unsympathetic with his old-fashioned ways. She abandoned teaching in the Church School after becoming assistant minister and did not resume it until Kane finally retired in the autumn of 1996. Church School aside, Adam-Murphy was the youth minister by default; such youth work as was done was done by her, and she left a deep impression on the many young people who grew up with her ministry.

On 12 May 1993, the 149th convocation of Knox College conferred the degree of doctor of divinity *honoris causa* on the minister of the Presbyterian Church of Saint David. A few days earlier Pace had turned sixty-five, but in his 1992 Christmas letter he had announced that retirement was not in his future plans. He spoke truer than he knew. Growing opposition to the planned promotion of the assistant minister meant that Pace might have to defer retiring indefinitely. Though it was against church law and custom that a minister should have any say at all in pulpit succession, Pace lingered for five more years, trying to arrange a seamless transition from himself to the assistant. After seventeen years, his legacy was secure; he had nothing further to prove or achieve. Shaping the future, however, was the mark that Pace most wanted to make on Saint David's.

On Palm Sunday, 31 March 1996, Saint David's marked the twentieth anniversary of Pace's induction with a special luncheon. The affair was muted by comparison with that of April 1989, when the silver jubilee of his ordination had been lavishly celebrated. In seven years nearly everything had changed. By April 1996 Pace had been minister of Saint David's longer than any of his predecessors, but the remaining two years of his pastorate would be neither easy nor pleasant. Though members and adherents remained constant at just over 600, active worshippers had fallen to 175. By 1998 they would drop to 125. Pace's friends continued to support him, but new accretions could not make up for the number of worshippers falling away.

The twenty years seemed longer. Pace was feeling the passage of time and growing a little weary. In June 1997 Ralph Kane died in his eighty-fifth year. He had been an adherent and member of the congregation since its establishment, superintendent of the Church School for fifty-two years, an elder for forty-nine, and clerk of Session for thirty-seven. No one found it harder to imagine Saint David's without Ralph Kane than John

Pace. During an awkward moment at the last annual congregational meeting that Pace chaired (January 1998), he was overheard to mutter, "Where is Ralph Kane when you need him?"

Pace sustained a more affecting personal loss in March 1997 when Ian Palmeter died. Judge Palmeter,[41] son of an elder and an elder himself since his father's death in 1980, was Pace's staunch supporter and close confidant. Though it did not officially conclude for another fifteen months, Pace's pastorate symbolically ended in the spring of 1997. Revealing of his deep sense of personal loss is that his December pastoral letter alluded to Palmeter's death before Kane's. An unflattering squib in *Frank* magazine in November ("St David's: Bummed Out") was the last straw;[42] later that month Pace and Adam-Murphy told Session they were resigning. The year 1997 was indeed one of "painful memories."

Judithe Adam-Murphy, for her part, had agreed to retire with the minister as a condition of her call. Her swan song was the 124th General Assembly (June 1998), which she attended as sole minister-commissioner from Halifax and Lunenburg. Adam-Murphy went quietly and gracefully but not willingly; some felt she was being hurried, if not harried, out of the congregation. At the wake following her last Sunday (28 June 1998), she spoke with deep feeling of how utterly impossible and self-defeating it was to try to decline a call from God.

In February 1998 Presbytery gave Pace permission to retire. He departed at the end of September, chagrined enough over the miscarriage of his plans to allude to it in his remarks at the complimentary dinner given him by the congregation and in his farewell sermon two days later. He believed, and a substantial minority of the congregation agreed with him, that Saint David's had made an error in judgment by not calling Adam-Murphy to be minister; that the congregation's rejection of her was a reflection on him. Pace's philosophy was that leaders lead and the led accept their leadership. Some of Adam-Murphy's more fervent, but less knowledgeable admirers thought that there was no need to declare the pulpit vacant; that the assistant could simply be promoted minister. There was no question of her serving as stated supply, which she might well have done. Session, in consultation with the interim moderator, moved quickly to make other arrangements for filling the pulpit during the vacancy.

John Pace was not another Frank Lawson, but his impact on Saint David's was similar and certainly no less positive. They each found a struggling, moribund congregation and brought it to spectacular rebirth. Lawson left before his time, while Pace remained after his. One regrets that they never met; they would have had a lot to talk about. It is an irony of history that an "artificial" Presbyterian congregation like Saint David's, thrown together by the force of circumstances and designed by its first minister to be a Scottish kirk, should have fared better under two Ulstermen. Unlike Kerr, who fled to Scotland after the failure of his Canadian experiment and stubbornly remained an aloof expatriate after nearly forty years in Canada, Lawson and Pace both became true Canadians. It is, one suspects, the difference between Scotsmen and Irishmen – the latter at once rooted and rootless; travellers and citizens of the world.

8

Donald Laurence DeWolfe

In February 1998 the clerk of Presbytery, Dr P.A. McDonald, was designated prospective interim moderator of Saint David's, reprising the role he had played during the third vacancy in 1975–76. A Presbytery advisory committee convened by the interim moderator and comprising two ministers and two elders was struck, and Pace gave McDonald permission to start the ball rolling. The pulpit was declared vacant the first Sunday in October, and an interim minister took over two weeks later. The longest pastorate in the congregation's history would be followed by a vacancy of just under a year's duration. Collective soul-searching and critical self-examination seemed required in order for Saint David's to determine precisely what it needed and wanted in a minister.

Session's first task was to arrange for pulpit supply. Rather than depend on the interim moderator or do what had been done in the past, and never quite successfully – recruit supply on a Sunday-by-Sunday basis – interim moderator and Presbytery had recourse to a third way: appointment of an interim minister. The accent that this exercise placed on recruiting and equipping ministerial leadership in the church found symbolic expression in the appointment of the Reverend Dr W. James S. Farris, professor emeritus of Knox College, to serve as interim minister of Saint David's from October 1998 through July 1999. Farris had completed a quarter-century's teaching at Knox,[1] followed by brief interim ministries, including two elsewhere in the Maritimes.

Thanks to a disinterested and efficient interim minister, Saint David's had room to manœuvre. The eminently satisfactory arrangement for pulpit supply meant that there was no need to fill the pulpit as soon as possible. To expedite the search for a new minister, Session in January 1999 established a large and representative search committee with two senior elders –

Kenneth Mader and Elizabeth A. Chard – as convener and co-convener respectively.[2] The committee prepared a substantial congregational profile, which included a detailed description of the position for the minister based in part on the responses to a survey-questionnaire distributed among members and adherents.

The Presbyterian Church in Canada had a surfeit of ministers of all ages, and Saint David's was still the plum posting it had always been. Some twenty expressions of interest were received. One candidate rose decisively to the top of the list and was unanimously recommended to and accepted by Session. Laurence DeWolfe – since 1990 minister of Saint Andrew's, Petrolia (a continuing congregation in southwestern Ontario), and Knox, Dawn Township (a small church in the midst of oilfields and soybean farms) – would be the only one invited to preach for a call. The committee felt that DeWolfe, at age forty the youngest prospective minister in the congregation's history, would bring to Saint David's "the tactful mix of respect for tradition and innovation necessary for [its] growth as a church; … that he [would] address the needs of the youth and the seniors in ways that meet their respective and our collective needs." DeWolfe interviewed well and was invited to spend a weekend at Saint David's. Session took the highly unusual step of posting to every household in Saint David's the candidate's complete resumé.

Laurence DeWolfe preached for a call on 16 May 1999, the Sunday after Ascension Day.[3] In his sermon he described a broad expanse of sky above the Mount of Olives, which he had seen from the spot where legend says the disciples of Jesus stood and watched as Jesus was taken up and away from their sight. He compared both that sight and the disciples' experience with the atmosphere of expectation present in a congregation looking forward to a new ministry. He challenged the congregation to look up and look forward, to grasp the boundless possibilities of the future. Three days later a special congregational meeting voted unanimously and enthusiastically to extend a call to DeWolfe. On 8 August he resigned his pastoral charge, a month to the day later he was inducted to his new one, and on Sunday morning, 12 September 1999, he preached his first sermon ("Some opening words") as minister of Saint David's. His text was Matthew 18:15–20, and he spoke of new beginnings. Taken together, these May and September sermons revealed the new minister's principal aspirations for Saint David's: building and being a true community and catching a vision of mission to the world outside the church.

Saint David's could not have chosen a minister more deeply rooted in Nova Scotian soil. The first native son to serve the congregation, DeWolfe shares paternal ancestry with the Irish Catholics of Halifax through the large and prominent Keating family. By the twentieth century, most of the DeWolfes of Halifax County were Roman Catholic. Malcolm Henry DeWolfe and Maria Gertrude Keating moved from Ship Harbour to Merigomish around 1910. Their second son, Donald Leslie, crossed over into the world of Pictou Presbyterianism and married Dorothy Harris, of Piedmont, in the manse of St Paul's Presbyterian Church, Merigomish, in 1940. Laurence DeWolfe's mother was a granddaughter of the stalwart Presbyterian, Deacon James McDonald, postmaster at Barneys River.

Laurence DeWolfe was born in New Glasgow in 1958 and grew up and went to school in Stellarton. His church home was First Presbyterian, Stellarton, a strong post-Disruption congregation prominently housed on the main street of the town. The Reverend D. Neil McCombie, a Scot who served First Presbyterian from 1968 to 1980, was a formative influence. McCombie was an emphatic low kirkman who preached frequently about the purity of worship. By "purity" McCombie meant simplicity and sincerity.

In the autumn of 1976 DeWolfe began his BA course at Saint Mary's University (SMU), a former Catholic institution where the then-new minister of Saint David's, John Pace, was "on call" as chaplain to the Protestant students. It seemed the natural thing for DeWolfe to attend the closest Presbyterian church. His first experiences of the liturgy, decoration, and design of Saint David's were a distinct culture shock. His innocence was further shaken during coffee hour when he saw the minister with cigarette in hand. John Pace was the first preacher DeWolfe had heard whose sermons were not strictly expository. Pace's preaching – not strictly textual, but topical, with great rhetorical flourish – was in stark contrast to McCombie's plain, expository preaching. Pace had a text, of course, but it seemed to provide only a framework for his oratory. He relied a great deal on illustrations from literature and philosophy and on theologians who were strangers to DeWolfe. His most memorable sermons included references to current events. If nothing else, DeWolfe learned from Pace the effect of alliteration, particularly of the more explosive consonants. No one spoke to him, but DeWolfe found some fellowship when he joined the choir, members of which made sure he had a drive from campus to choir practice and often collected him on Sunday mornings.

In 1976–77 a few meetings were held at Saint David's in an attempt to start a university-age youth group. DeWolfe and a fellow student met Pace in his study to propose a group aimed at university students. The minister recruited a former officer of the defunct Presbyterian Young People's Society (PYPS) to help with leadership and met a couple of times with five or six young people, but the project did not get off the ground. In the summer of 1977 DeWolfe served an appointment with the Board of World Mission in Kootenay Presbytery, in the interior of British Columbia. On his return to Halifax in the autumn, he began instead to attend services at All Nations Christian Reformed Church, then on Inglis Street.[4]

During that time DeWolfe had a love-hate relationship with Saint David's and The Presbyterian Church in Canada. He was under some strong evangelical and anti-denominational influences that had taken root in the synod's PYPS. Conservative evangelicals believed that the PCC was on the wrong course. Churches such as Saint David's were not truly Reformed, and liberals such as John Pace were to be avoided. Heavily influenced by these ultra-conservative and divisive voices in the church, DeWolfe did not attend Saint David's during his second year at SMU. He resumed, however, in the autumn of 1978, drawn by the liturgy if not the preaching, but meanwhile continued attending evening services and youth fellowship at All Nations Christian Reformed. He wrote to Pace hoping to initiate a student assistant position for himself at Saint David's, but received no reply.[5] DeWolfe passed judgment on Pace's apparent liberalism and turned a deaf ear to the sermons. He came to sing and to see Pace in action when he told stories from John Calvin Reid's *Bird Life in Wington* from memory at children's time during worship.

When DeWolfe arrived at Saint David's as a freshman undergraduate at what had been until very recently a Catholic university run by the Jesuits, he discovered that there was another way to worship, rooted in ancient tradition and just as Presbyterian as the worship he had known as a youngster. Even before the first prayer of the service, the sense of place that DeWolfe found at Saint David's carried him towards the holy. He learned the "why" of the high kirk tradition when he studied under James Thomson at Knox College, and it made sense because he had participated in the "how" of it at Saint David's. DeWolfe's approach to worship throughout his over twenty years of ministry were largely shaped by his early experiences at Saint David's. In every church where he afterwards served, he introduced two services he first experienced at Saint David's: the informal communion on Holy Thursday evening and Tenebrae on Good Friday morning.

In 1979 Laurence DeWolfe went off to Knox College, convinced he had been called to save the church from itself (and from liberals like Pace and many of the good people at Saint David's). Chief among the church's "sins," in his view, was the ordination of women, a highly divisive issue at the time.[6] DeWolfe took a stand for liberty of conscience and the freedom of those who resisted to resist. Going out on a limb – a literal "Here I stand!" – he found no one was behind him. Liberals, especially liberal women, were the only people who stayed around to catch him when the bough broke.

Among these women was Janet Allan, from Acton, Ontario, who was one year senior at Knox and would later become his wife. DeWolfe graduated MDiv in 1983, together with the Reverend Janet Allan DeWolfe. Then-compulsory ordained missionary appointments took them to adjoining pastoral charges in southern Ontario. Janet served the congregations of Palmerston and Drayton, while Laurence was appointed assistant minister at Knox Church, Listowel. He served in Listowel for one year and completed the two-year appointment, working half-time alongside his wife in what had been her own pastoral charge. The DeWolfes' daughter Mary Margaret (Maggie) was born during their year of shared ministry.

In 1985 Laurence DeWolfe was called to Erskine Presbyterian Church, Ottawa. While in Ottawa he was instrumental in the formation of the Dalhousie Food Action Group, which operated a food bank in Erskine's large church hall. Erskine's neighbourhood had once been a thriving working-class community, but by the mid-1980s Dalhousie Ward was one of the poorest neighbourhoods in Ottawa; urban gentrification had not yet begun to creep into the area.

Within Ottawa Presbytery, DeWolfe served on the busy Pastoral Relations Committee and was founding convener of the presbytery's Committee on Civil and Social Concerns. He also served as vice-chair of the Christian Council of the Capital Area, one of the oldest ecumenical councils in Canada. In 1987 he wrote the CCCA's *Beyond Charity to Change*, a resource guide used throughout the region to raise congregational awareness of poverty and the need for welfare reform. On behalf of the council he addressed Ontario's Thompson Commission on Social Assistance Reform.

DeWolfe left Erskine just months before major repairs to the church began. In 1990 the family moved to Petrolia, in the far southwest of the province. Janet DeWolfe served as a hospital chaplain and later as a congregational minister in Sarnia, while Laurence had the pastoral charge of Saint Andrew's, Petrolia, and Knox Dawn, in Dawn Township.

DeWolfe sought some relief from his extra-congregational commitments when he moved from Ottawa. The Presbytery of Sarnia gave him a year to catch his breath before appointing him to its ministry committee. Then a flurry of appointments followed. For three of his nine years in the presbytery, he was moderator. Between the second and third years in the chair he was also moderator of the Synod of Southwestern Ontario. He also served on Synod's staff support committee for four years, first as a member and then as convener. In 1997–98 he was a member of a synod judicial commission. For three years he was Protestant padre of the First Hussars, resigning in 1996 when he was elected moderator of Synod.

"One starry night in February 1999," DeWolfe recalls, "Janet and I were walking the dog. From somewhere came the inspiration to say, 'I think I'll give Sandy [McDonald] a call and see how things are going at Saint David's.' Janet said, 'Do it.'" The call to the interim moderator led to correspondence and, the following month, an interview. In that initial conversation, McDonald was blunt. The congregation was on shaky financial footing. There had been a serious division over John Pace's retirement and the compensation offered him at his departure. Communication within the congregation was poor.

Yet, according to McDonald, there were encouraging signs of unity at the recent annual congregational meeting (31 January 1999). He spoke in glowing terms of a plea that elder Frank Stalley had made at that meeting, and which received resounding support from all. Stalley, assigned to move a vote of thanks to the choirs and organist, prefaced his remarks by expressing the sincere hope that after airing opposing views on the annuity to the retired minister through a democratic process, the congregation might now close ranks to make Saint David's bigger, better, and more united. This sentiment evoked a standing ovation.[7] McDonald candidly admitted that had DeWolfe called him two weeks earlier, he would have advised him to stay away. After the annual congregational meeting, however, he felt there were signs of hope. He believed that Saint David's could move forward with "the right person" and the right kind of leadership, a factor on which McDonald placed great emphasis. Within four months of that meeting, the wheels of the church were turning towards a call.

Before coming to Halifax, DeWolfe entered the doctor of ministry in preaching program of the Association of Chicago Theological Schools. His thesis project, "Servant Leader/Servant Preacher," reflected work done in his former pastoral charge, but it would be principally drawn from his experience beginning a new ministry at Saint David's. A small group from the congregation (the "preaching project group") worked with him, preparing the sermons required by the program and reflecting with him on both the sermons and the task of preaching. In June 2001 DeWolfe was awarded the degree of doctor of ministry by McCormick Theological Seminary in a ceremony at Rockefeller Memorial Chapel, at the University of Chicago.[8]

Meanwhile, in September 2000 DeWolfe began to teach courses in preaching at the Atlantic School of Theology, which occupies the site of the former Presbyterian College, Halifax, and is supported by the Anglican,

Roman Catholic, and United churches. His participation both reverses history and continues a tradition. The last Presbyterians to teach there entered the United Church in 1925. But Saint David's has always had connections with AST and its United Church predecessor, Pine Hill Divinity Hall. Members of Saint David's have studied in lay programs at the school. Judithe Adam-Murphy was a 1992 graduate, while Pine Hill and AST faculty have filled the pulpit of Saint David's on many occasions.

Long pastorates shape congregations in the mould of their ministers. DeWolfe followed a pastorate of twenty-two years, which began on a high note and ended on a low one. Any minister who comes after one who served as long as John Pace did meets a congregation's entrenched expectations head-on. When a new minister is of a younger generation than his predecessor – and indeed, most of the congregation – the new minister's very presence means change. From the beginning, DeWolfe's ministry gave rise to complaints of too much change too fast. Others complained of too little change too slowly. In short, the minister was doing everything right. The introduction in 2000 of the 1997 *Book of Praise* became a focus of dissatisfaction for some members, who quickly identified the action with the new minister – this despite the fact that Session's decision to bring the new hymnal to Saint David's antedated DeWolfe's arrival but had been delayed, pending the new minister's advent and the availability of funds to stock the pews with copies.

In the autumn of 2001, DeWolfe's physician advised him to take several weeks' medical leave. Ten years earlier he had had to take comparable leave from his churches to recover from exhaustion. This time the general stress of ministry, the recent completion of his degree, and the death of his mother in March brought him once again to exhaustion. Predictably, the crisis led to controversy. In particular, some members of the congregation were dissatisfied with the insistence of the human resources committee of Session and Trustees that the minister's privacy be respected and that details of his situation not become public knowledge. It was, as well, a difficult time to be without a minister, in the first weeks of a busy autumn season inaugurated by the terrorist attacks on New York City and Washington. Yet worship and pastoral care continued. The autumn program of the congregation and Church School were delivered without clerical guidance. DeWolfe returned to the church half-time in October and was back to a full schedule by the end of that month.

Attitudes to the minister's leave of absence split along generational lines. Those steeped in older ways found it difficult to accept their pastor's vulnerability. Younger members were more familiar with the concept of "burnout" and in general held a less exalted view of clerical invulnerability. DeWolfe saw his return to work in the autumn of 2001 as a second new beginning. Previously, much of the work of the minister, Session, and Trustees had been devoted to addressing transitional issues. DeWolfe often described his work in the first two years as being more like interim ministry than the work of a settled pastor. Official interim ministers address issues of communication, organization, planning, and conflict resolution. They prepare the way for a fresh start after a long ministry. James Farris's ministry had been called "interim," but it was really more the work of a caretaker than stated supply.

In the relatively brief vacancy following Pace's retirement many issues were identified, and these were intentionally addressed after DeWolfe was called and inducted. One of these issues was stewardship. DeWolfe recalled that when he had met with the search committee and then with individual trustees, great emphasis was placed on the need for leadership with a view to increasing the church's income and educating the congregation in stewardship. He sensed a discomfort over talking about money in the church, but also felt that the time had come to talk about stewardship of financial resources, no matter how uncomfortable it made people feel.

Everyone seemed to expect the minister to lead the way. In the autumn of 2000 a stewardship task force was formed by Session and Board, but it met only twice. Chaired by the minister, this small group considered the various stewardship programs recommended by The Presbyterian Church in Canada and seized on the idea of sending a team to an event called "Stewards by Design" in Guelph in April 2001. A team of four was gathered – two elders, a trustee, and the minister.[9] Team Saint David's was impressed by the Stewards by Design seminar and in turn presented much of its content to both Session and Board. Because Presbytery had subsidized the team's attendance, the minister and one of the two elders also addressed a special presbytery meeting at Knox Church. Rather than promoting a fundraising program, the Stewards by Design team initiated a process through which the congregation's sense of mission and purpose would be stimulated. This was based on the principle that people will contribute generously to a cause with which they can identify and which they find worthy of their support. The cause must have a clear purpose and a plan to fulfill it. People will no longer support the church simply because it is the church. The Stewards by Design team promoted mission education before stewardship education and held think tank–style gatherings for the congregation. A booklet entitled *Christian Stewardship* was also produced and circulated.[10]

In a congregation like Saint David's, accustomed to long pastorates – the average has been seventeen years – it is premature to speak of a "DeWolfe era." It will be up to a later generation to judge whether the fifth pastorate was a good beginning to a new century.

PART THREE

Congregational Life

9

The Congregation

Among the paradoxes of the Second Disruption in Nova Scotia was that anti-union Presbyterians could not form congregations under the law of The Presbyterian Church in Canada. As of July 1924 the official PCC was going into the United Church of Canada as one body. Congregations, new and old alike, had to vote not *in* but *out*. So the radical resisters to church union turned instead to the only avenue open to them: the law of the state. The organizational meeting of the Presbyterian Church, Halifax, on 26 February 1925 took place further to section 11 of Nova Scotia's Religious Congregations and Societies Act.[1] This act provided for congregations to be constituted "by declaration" – in other words, by resolution passed at a public meeting called for the purpose after due notice given. The act also provided that any congregation thus formed could adopt a constitution and bylaws, appoint trustees, and vest property in them. At the organizational meeting a constitution (the "Eight Resolutions") was accordingly adopted, elders recognized and designated, and trustees elected. No further action seemed necessary. Nevertheless, sometime between the end of February and the middle of April 1925, the ad hoc joint committee of elders and trustees who were managing the congregation's affairs decided to apply to the legislature for an act to incorporate the trustees.[2]

The problem confronting the management committee was that since 1890 religious congregations and societies could only *acquire* real property if they were incorporated. The new congregation did not own any property but was looking to buy. It was not a corporation; so in order for it to be able to acquire property, it had to become one. The elders and trustees decided that they would seek a private act of the legislature to incorporate the trustees. Fortunately, among their number was a Liberal government MLA who was willing to do the needful. Henry Gibson Bauld, formerly of St Matthew's, had cast his lot with the non-uniting minority. On 15 April he introduced in the House of Assembly a private bill entitled "An Act to Incorporate the Trustees of the Presbyterian Church, Halifax." It passed easily and came into force on 7 May 1925, barely a month before the "legal" Presbyterian Church in Canada was extinguished.[3] No MLA on the United Church side of the church-union question, which had so divided government and legislature a year earlier, was prepared to reopen the controversy by denying Presbyterians the right to organize.

The act co-opted the eighteen-member board appointed in February and incorporated it, vested the congregation's property in it, gave it the power to hold property up to the value of $500,000, set the quorum for Trustees' meetings at eight, authorized the congregation to enact rules and regulations, and provided for the first annual meeting of the congregation to take place before 7 May 1926. In the eighty years since, the act of incorporation has been lightly amended on five occasions, mostly for housekeeping purposes. In the heat of the moment, however, it had gone unnoticed that the act was significantly at variance with the letter and spirit of the basic law of The Presbyterian Church in Canada – the Book of Forms.

DEMOGRAPHIC PROFILE

No mainstream Protestant denomination has ever declined as steeply as The Presbyterian Church in Canada between 1921 and 1931, when the Disruption combined to reduce it to a shadow of its former self and a fraction of its former size (see table 9.1). In that decade the number of Presbyterians in the city of Halifax fell 61 per cent, and the church from its customary third place behind the Church of England to fifth behind the United Church and the Baptists. The "legal" Presbyterian Church in Halifax, of course, disappeared on 10 June 1925, but Presbyterians did not. A persistent demographic almost immediately gave rise to a structural recrudescence.

The first post-Disruption census (1931) was a statistical nightmare, religionwise, as many formerly Presbyterian members of the United Church continued to describe themselves as Presbyterian. Thanks to the legal fact that The Presbyterian Church in Canada was now the United Church of Canada, the number of Presbyterians in Canada was certainly over-reported. There was also a category for "Presbyterians" (those outside the United Church), but the Dominion Bureau of Statistics had to admit the near impossibility

Table 9.1
Presbyterian population, city of Halifax, pre- and post-Disruption

Census	Number	% decrease
1921	6,628	
1931	2,607	60.6

SOURCE: Census of Canada, 1921, 1931.

of distinguishing accurately between Presbyterians who had gone into the United Church and those who had not.[4] It was not until the unionist generation had passed on that this anomaly finally corrected itself.

In 1925, when denominational survival was at stake, growth and increase were not at issue. The four hundred names on the membership roll of the Halifax chapter of the Presbyterian Church Association (established in November 1924) included many whose children and grandchildren continued active in Saint David's. Husbands and wives subscribed, though not necessarily as a couple. In all but a handful of instances, married woman members signed in their own right, not as "Mr and Mrs." At a time when the sexes were unequal and women had no standing in the church except as deaconesses, the gender balance of the roll lay 60 per cent in favour of women. Presbyterian Church women, though barred from eldership and from any official say, had been the backbone of the resistance, and they would be the backbone of new congregations arising from the Disruption.

Where did the people of Saint David's come from? Those Presbyterians who joined the Halifax PCA were asked to state their congregational affiliation, and most did so. The roll book therefore reveals something of the respective levels of anti-union sentiment within those congregations from which the members and adherents of Saint David's originated.[5] The larger and older the congregation, the higher the number of resisters. Unsurprisingly, St Andrew's ranked first; it accounted for fully one-quarter of those resisting church union. The new congregation of non-uniting minority Presbyterians would be comparable in size to St James, St Andrew's, or St Matthew's at the end of their Presbyterian existence. Stairs Memorial (Dartmouth), the only congregation that did not vote, was unrepresented in the membership.

When the inaugural communion roll of the Presbyterian Church, Halifax, was established in September 1925, there were 259 members, only 11 less than had participated in the new congregation's first communion service the previous March. When it was closed off in December 1932, there were 622, an increase of 140 per cent in seven years. At the beginning, however, the communion roll represented only 65 per cent of the membership of the PCA. The reason for the discrepancy is that not all conscientious objectors to church union were prepared immediately to abandon the official Presbyterian Church in Canada. Those 259 on the first communion roll were the vanguard – the forward resisters – who no sooner saw that there would not be a single continuing congregation than they set about building a new one.

THE KIRK SESSION

Regardless how homogeneous The Presbyterian Church in Canada was or became during the fifty years between its formation and the Disruption, the new-model PCC that emerged from the wreckage of 1925 has been, so to speak, the Church of Scotland in Canada. Whereas Presbyterian union in 1875 had forged a delicate balance between Kirk and non-Kirk elements, the chief factor in the preservation of the PCC was the paramountcy of the Kirk tradition in Canadian Presbyterianism. The triumph played out symbolically. While pre-union kirks had "*kirk* sessions" and the pre-Disruption Presbyterian Church in Canada, "sessions," the post-Disruption PCC has only had "kirk sessions." The very persistence of the term is a constant reminder not so much of the Scottishness of the Kirk as of the "Kirkness" of the post-Disruption Presbyterian Church in Canada. Survival in the present and persistence into the future is a function of rediscovering and returning to the roots – and putting them down deeper.

The role of the Kirk Session is not to speak for or answer to the congregation but to attend to its welfare and render to Presbytery an account of its stewardship. Session is stable and self-perpetuating in that the elders themselves decide when an election for new elders should be held. The quorum of a Session meeting is three, and the number of elders is determined by Session's evaluation of the congregation's needs; there is no maximum or minimum number of elders. No elder who dies, resigns, or retires is replaced immediately. Though leaves of absence and inactive status are sought and granted, one cannot resign from eldership, which is ministerial ("call of God"). Once an elder, always an elder. Mass resignations are unheard of and seem to have occurred only during the supreme crisis of church union.

Government by session is representative but not democratic. The role of the congregation's professing members does not extend beyond standing for election, nominating others, and balloting on the nominees. Session acts as the governing body of the congregation and is supreme in both spiritual and temporal matters. It decides whether and when new elders are needed; if so, how many and how to hold the election. It also approves those nominated or elected so that they may proceed to induction. Increasing the number of elders serves not only to recoup losses from mortality, intergenerational transition, resignation, demission, or inactivity but also to promote the congregation's growth and expansion and broaden Session's representativeness, both geographic and demographic, in relation to members and adherents.

Session formerly met quarterly, before Communion Sunday – as per traditional Scottish practice – but since Frank Lawson's pastorate, it has met more or less monthly except in summer. Session meetings are always held in camera, and access to the minutes of its proceedings is restricted for fifty years. Within Session, like any other executive council, the principles of collective responsibility, secrecy, and collegiality apply. Short of resigning, as some have done, on matters of personality, policy, or principle, elders may only signal their disaffection by taking a leave of absence or becoming inactive. Session votes are deemed to be unanimous, even when they are not, and no elder may publicly dissent from a decision once made or divulge the substance of deliberations of Session meetings. The quorum of a Session meeting is three – the minister and two others – regardless of how large or small the number of active elders.

The third of the Eight Resolutions that form the constitution of Saint David's dealt with the eldership. Those ordained and inducted elders who had seceded in 1925 from uniting majority congregations were set apart as a "committee of elders" and in due course comprised the first official Kirk Session. They came mostly from congregations where the resistance had been strongest: St Andrew's (five) and Park Street (three) – 73 per cent of the total. Neither then nor now is there a set number of elders. The first eleven who took office in February 1925 grew with the years, to a high of thirty-five in 1990. In 2003 the number was twenty-one, a decline of 40 per cent largely as a result of attrition. Just as any communicant member of the congregation is eligible for election as elder, so too at the beginning any ordained and inducted elder could have added himself to the provisional session.

The first election of elders at Saint David's took place by ballot in the autumn of 1926. Session had determined to add four to its number, and it ranked the nominees in descending order of votes received. Two of the four who topped the poll declined, as did the next two. Two of the three who were trustees preferred to remain so, though one of them – W.L. Harper, then secretary of the Trustees – became an elder in 1946. Session had to settle for the bare minimum of two new elders, two – R.D. McCleave and F.W. Christie – having died within weeks of each other the previous June and July. The ordination and induction service on 5 December 1926 saw F.M. Guildford and H.D. Creighton welcomed to the Kirk Session. Creighton was to represent members and adherents from Dartmouth, while Guildford those from Bedford, where Christie had been clerk of Session and the only elder to follow his minister, Frank Baird, out of Bedford Presbyterian. Fred Guildford had also been the first choirmaster at Saint David's.

Between 1926 and 2004 there were nineteen elections for elder. Given the nominees' poor response to the ballot in 1926, the second election, in 1928, was by co-option. A nominating committee consisting of the minister, the clerk of Session, and a senior elder recommended whom to approach, while those who agreed were announced to the congregation during public worship.[6] The group included one elder already ordained and inducted elsewhere.[7] The highest percentage of elders ever elected at any one time coincided with the longest period between elections: the decade 1929 through 1939. Several times through the 1930s, Session sought to add to its number, but it proved impossible to find suitable members willing to serve. Finally, in January 1939, in advance of the annual congregational meeting, Session nominated four men. The members wanted a secret ballot, however, and Session acquiesced. Eight new elders were approved as elected, but two declined to serve. The six included the four who comprised Session's original slate.

Session decided the number of elders needed and provided an up-to-date copy of the communion roll for each member. Only professing members could vote and be voted for. Members perused the roll and voted for whomever they wished. Those with the highest number of votes were approached; those who accepted were ordained and inducted. Despite the misstep in 1939, this procedure was followed in 1946, 1948, 1952, and 1953. Experience showed, however, that it was best to nominate only those willing to serve if elected. Beginning in 1955, nominations for elder were received at the annual congregational meeting and afterwards voted on by secret ballot.

The nadir was reached in 1963, a question having arisen as to whether a disgraced former member of Session who was a convicted thief might return. At the annual congregational meeting of 30 January, at which no more than 40 out of a communicant membership of 587 were present, the clerk of Session brought up the matter of the election of six new elders. Session had recommended that elders were to be nominated at this meeting, that the meeting should then be thrown open to further nominations, and that all names offered should be voted on there and then. Considerable discussion ensued as to whether this was an acceptable procedure, considering the small number in attendance, but it was finally decided to proceed on the basis outlined.[8] The "election" resulted in the return of the former elder, whose ten-year exile from Session was deemed punishment enough. Irregular practices were also followed in 1967, 1971, 1977, and 1980. The secret ballot was restored in 1984.

Among the original elders was W.J. Kane, penultimate clerk of Session at Park Street, who became secretary of the provisional "committee of elders" and in due course clerk of Session. William John Kane had been baptized and raised a Roman Catholic and converted in order to marry Miss Waterman. Thereafter he acted with all the zeal of a convert. A warm-hearted but tough-minded and practical man of business, he quickly put the Disruption behind him; to the end of his life he never lost his sense of perspective or his ability to think "outside the box." He was forward-looking and always receptive to new ideas and to new and better ways of doing old things. He was an expansionist, a builder of the church; during his tenure one congregation in metropolitan Halifax became four, thanks in no small part to his own efforts. Despite Kane's differences with Frank Lawson, his junior by a generation and worlds apart philosophically, the two got on and worked well together.

W.J. Kane died with his boots on in May 1960. At the time of his death, he was convener of the stewardship and budget committee of Presbytery, clerk of the assessor (interim) session at Calvin Presbyterian Church, and representative elder from Saint David's. Kane was succeeded by his son, Ralph Waterman, superintendent of the Church School since 1944 and an elder since 1948. The younger Kane was a leader in youth work and had been instrumental in the establishment of the Presbyterian Young People's Society in both Synod and Presbytery.

Ralph Kane was born in 1912, the year his father became an elder and Park Street voted narrowly in favour of union. Spending his early childhood under the ministry of Robert Johnston, Ralph was bred in the bone to be a continuing Presbyterian. His mother's family, the Watermans, had been pillars of Park Street for generations. Ralph never quite got over how, as a young teenager, he had lost his church home. Old enough to remember well but too young to have fought in the resistance to church union, he lived for seventy years with the memory and the consequences of it. He saw change as, at best, a necessary evil and identified it with the forces of chaos that had produced the Disruption. For him, the ideal congregation was Park Street as it had existed in December 1924, when the non-uniting minority led by his father, then clerk of Session, departed. By comparison, the minority's first worship service in January 1925, which twelve-year-old Ralph attended, was the inauguration of a dystopian brave new world.

Unmarried during the war and married but childless after it, Ralph Kane had as his patrimony his ecclesiastical heritage. He had neither hobbies nor, despite his high intelligence and excellent education, an intellectual life in any way separate from the spiritual and devotional. Throughout his nearly fifty years as elder, he affected an impossibly high sense of the dignity of his position. A senior civil servant in the workaday world, Kane found the bureaucracy of the clerkship attractive. The ministerial side of eldership did not appeal to him, however, and he tended to leave it in the capable hands of older "pros" such as Murdoch McLeod, who served for years as his assistant.

In other respects, however, Ralph Kane was even busier than his father had been. He served as president of the Halifax Association for Improving the Condition of the Poor, the Nova Scotia District of the Canadian Bible Society, and the Halifax-Dartmouth Council of Churches. Within The Presbyterian Church in Canada, he was a member of the Administrative (now Assembly) Council and of the Board of Congregational Life (now Life and Mission Agency). He was utterly devoted to the memory of his father, even to the extent of serving on the pastoral planning committee for the papal visit to Halifax in September 1984.

In 1966, after thirteen years of dithering, the General Assembly finally passed a declaratory act admitting women to eldership and ministry. In December 1967 Saint David's became the first church in the Atlantic Synod to elect woman elders. Session directed its selection committee "to include, if possible, the names of two women in their list of nominations."[9] A special congregational meeting was held, chaired – unusually – by the minister, and it fell to the clerk to introduce Session's nominees: five men and two women. Ralph Kane was implacably opposed to women elders, but to no avail. It was an idea whose time had come. It is not known how many women were approached, though at least one declined. The two whose names appeared at the bottom of the list – the men's names were presented in alphabetical order above – were a generation apart: Nora Ashworth and Elizabeth Ann Chard (née Hutton).

Ashworth was both the sister of a prominent minister, the late Dr T.H.B. Somers (a former moderator of Synod), and the widow of a prominent elder, Frank Ashworth. She herself would be the first woman elder-commissioner to the General Assembly from within the Atlantic Synod. Mrs Chard, junior superintendent of the Church School, had no elders in her family closer than her paternal great-great-grandfather. Her family were staunch "antis" from St Andrew's, where her grandmother had nearly become the first woman trustee. After 1925 four generations of Huttons worshipped at Saint David's. Chard's late father, Robert Reid Hutton ("one of the most faithful and devoted members that this Church has ever known"), had been trustee and chair of the property committee and was the driving force behind the construction of the 1951 church hall; her grandfather, William Wallace, was an original trustee; and her grandmother, Laura, was president of the Ladies Guild at the time of her premature death in 1929. Chard's mother, Mamie Hutton, was a Saint David's institution in her own right. Superintendent of the Cradle Roll in the Church School for nearly fifty years, she taught in the junior school until her eighties.

Ralph Kane was unimpressed by his youthful assistant's pedigree. He told Chard that while he totally disapproved of women in the eldership, if it were going to happen, she was the best he could pick.[10] The service of ordination and induction, on 14 January 1968, was memorable – especially for the women. Elizabeth Chard recalls, "Since hairspray was relatively new on the market at that time and big, fluffy hairstyles were all the rage, I was sporting a very elaborate hairdo for my big day and had lacquered it with lots of heavy, gooey hairspray. When Ralph Kane proceeded with the laying-on of hands, he really pressed down hard on my head with the result that when he lifted off his hands, he took my hair with him."[11] As a young woman elder, Chard did not have an easy time. Doors were slammed in her face when she tried to deliver communion cards, and some worshippers refused to allow her to serve them on Communion Sunday.

No subsequent election failed to return woman elders. It was not until 1997, however, that the same number of women and men were elected and not until 2004 that more women than men were chosen. Three of the six women elected elders between 1968 and 1980 were the widows of elders, but the custom of electing elders' widows did not persist beyond the 1970s. It was largely a matter of decorum; elders' widows were deemed to possess special status, almost a form of dower. The totemic number two persisted (with one exception) for twenty years, through six elections. One wonders whether the 1993 promotion of a woman elder to assistant minister did not break the mould, effecting substantive attitudinal change between the elections of 1990 and 1997.

The decline of widows' entitlement incidentally gave rise to the development of new and broader kinship networks. These were not without precedent. The Guildfords of Park Street and Bedford were a veritable dynasty – three generations of elders. Father Robert A. and son Robert D. were members of the original Session. Son Frederick Moir, ordained and inducted in 1926, was an elder for fifty-four years. Another son, David, was elected in 1939 but declined to serve. Fred's son Thomas was elected in 1963. The Kanes, father and son, were Session colleagues from 1948 to 1960. There would be nothing comparable until 1980, when a daughter joined her father. In 1990 an engaged couple were elected. In 1997 a wife joined her husband and a son his father.

Among the seven elders elected in 1967 was Murray W. Alary, then secretary-treasurer of the Church School. Like Ralph Kane before him, Alary was very active in the Presbyterian Young People's Society at presbytery and synod level. After becoming a member of Saint David's in December 1961, he was soon serving as president of the congregational PYPS. Like other young people, he found Frank Lawson more congenial than his successor. Restive during the Mackay pastorate, Alary in 1971 transferred his membership to Calvin. Saint David's in general and Frank Lawson in particular had been heavily involved in establishing Calvin Church, where Lawson's close friend, A.O. MacLean, was minister for twenty-five years. Alary soon became clerk of Session. After MacLean retired in 1982, Alary rejoined Saint David's. Re-elected elder in 1984, he immediately became Kane's right-hand man, assuming the post of assistant clerk in 1985. In June 1997 Ralph Kane died, and Alary succeeded him after a contested election and a decision that the clerkship would be a five-year term appointment, a highly unusual step in a congregation where term appointment of elders was never seriously considered. The clerkship, formerly for life, is no longer so, "unless explicitly stated."

The 1967 election elevated the chair of the Board, Robert Kennedy, to Session; he immediately resigned as a trustee. Though the congregation's rules and regulations were silent on the subject, trustees elected elders customarily stood down. The trustees were a "prep" or vocational school for elders, and over the years a majority of elders served first as trustees. The taboo against trustee-elders gradually disappeared as the congregation decreased in size and the number of active and willing church workers declined commensurately. In the early days, however, concurrent or cross-membership between Session and Board was the exception rather than the rule. Elders might be elected trustees, but trustees "promoted" to Session were expected to resign – and did.

By 1944 the number of elders among the trustees had risen to four; by 1999 it stood at five. The number varied little over the half-century. Elders have served as chair, vice-chair, secretary, or treasurer, and have filled different offices at different times. In 1943, for example, elder Frank Ashworth was vice-chair of the Trustees but failed in his bid to be elected chair. In February 1946 Clifford Torey, an elder (though not of Saint David's) and former chair who had resigned from the Board, resumed the chair and the following month was inducted elder. Torey was the first elder to serve as chair of the Board. In 1948 he was succeeded as chair by another elder, Herbert D. Wallace. Of the twenty-three chairs since 1925, however, only seven have been elders, though several became elders during their term as chair or afterwards. The longest serving chairs – John Scott Chisholm (1931–42) and Michael de la Ronde (1992–2000) – both non-elders, were succeeded by a non-elder and an elder respectively.

The relationship between Session and Board at Saint David's was sometimes strained by poor communication and blurred lines of responsibility. By the late 1950s, attempts were being made to bring the two solitudes into some sort of constructive relationship. The chair of the Board wrote in his annual report for 1958 that the Board agreed that two members of Session should be invited to attend its monthly meetings. "In this way the two administrative bodies within the Church would be kept informed of the thinking of each other."[12] Nothing seems to have come of this proposal.

By 1962 Session and Board were having annual joint meetings. As late as 1970, however, the Board could hold a long discussion "concerning the matter of responsibilities of both the Board of Trustees and the Session. It was felt that it was the duty of the Board of Trustees to consider all financial matters in relation to the operation of the Church and that the Session should be particularly concerned with spiritual matters."[13] According to church law, Session and Board were not a partnership inhabiting separate but equal spheres. Everything the Board did or could do was by explicit or implied delegation of Session. From this notional regime of Presbyterian neo-congregationalism, due subordination was conspicuously absent.

Anxiety over the Board's independent spirit and "attitude problem" came to a head at the annual congregational meeting in January 1986 when elder Frank Stalley, the previous chair, proposed adding three elders, all former officers of the Board, to the slate of nominees for Board membership. This proposal forced a secret ballot, unheard of since the 1920s, in which two of the Board's nominees were defeated and all three elders elected. The then chair of the Board, one year into his three-year term, immediately resigned, and elders afterwards loomed large among Board members. Despite the difficulties, however, there is little evidence that Saint David's ever suffered the degree of tension between Session and Board that led congregations such as St Paul's, Hamilton, to merge its board of managers into the Session.

THE BOARD OF MANAGERS ("TRUSTEES")

In The Presbyterian Church in Canada, the Kirk Session is responsible for *all* matters relating to stewardship and works closely with the board of managers – if there is one.[14] Session's oversight extends to finance and property maintenance, and it is no more necessary that there be a board of managers than that the trustees exercise the functions of one. Under church law the board of managers (deacons) and the trustees (property-holders) are supposed to be separate and distinct. At Saint David's they have always been one and the same.

The notion that the Session and Board are separate but equal – supreme in their different spheres – was introduced at the very beginning of the congregation's existence. There are sound historical reasons why so un-Presbyterian a practice became deeply entrenched so quickly. The affairs of the congregation between organization in February and formalization in July 1925 were managed, not by the provisional session exclusively, but by a joint committee consisting of the "committee of elders" and the trustees. Many of the leading men who did not care to become elders willingly served as trustees, a sort of shadow cabinet or board of control. The Board provided an alternative forum for movers and shakers to influence the course of events without incurring the responsibilities of eldership. The trustees were also replete with lawyers, whereas the only lawyer on Session, R.D. McCleave, died in June 1926, too soon to make a real difference. On top of everything else, the Trustees became a legal corporation a full two months before the committee of elders became a legal Kirk Session.

One of the original three lawyer-trustees, Robert F. Yeoman, chaired the committee of trustees that prepared the congregation's rules and regulations, authorized by the act of incorporation and approved by the congregation at its first annual meeting in January 1926. Of critical importance was section VIII, which made the Trustees a board of managers. The trustees were to take direction from the congregation, not the Session. No evidence exists that the rules and regulations went to Session, much less to Presbytery, for approval before being presented to the first annual congregational meeting.

Colin Kerr made a point of not attending Board meetings, which he would have deemed an impropriety. Having grown up in the Church of Scotland, he found the idea of a "board of managers" not strictly subordinate to the Kirk Session bizarre. In the Kirk, Session and Session alone was in charge, and the minister, as moderator, was first among equals. Over the years 1933–41, Kerr's relationship with the Board was deteriorating. As much is suggested by his "Genius of Presbyterianism," reprised in 1940 as the Synod sermon.[15] By 1943, when Kerr's difficulties with the Board were reaching their height, the clerks of Assembly were drafting as per instructions a "Memorandum Defining the Relationships of Kirk Sessions and Boards of Management of Congregations," which was approved by the General Assembly. The problem was clearly not confined to Saint David's.

The original eighteen trustees appointed at the organizational meeting of the congregation in February 1925 were more representative than the elders, comprising as they did two each from all nine of the Presbyterian churches in the metropolitan area. The Board met monthly and served a three-year term, one-third of its number being replaced at each annual congregational meeting. Thus it gave the members and adherents a direct voice in managing the congregation's affairs. Anyone – member or adherent – could be a trustee if nominated and elected, and the trustees in turn elected their own officers. This was Presbyterian democracy at work. The Board introduced a formal committee structure almost immediately, the principal ones – then as now – being property and finance.

Through the 1980s, unease between Session and Board over the congregation's finances gradually increased. For the first time since the "dirty thirties," Saint David's found itself in a deficit position, the result of three decades of too generously helping to finance church extension in the metropolitan area. Endeavouring to work together to remedy the situation, Session and Board in 1987 established a long-range financial planning committee comprising three elders and three trustees. Then in 1989 an influential elder who enjoyed the minister's complete confidence took over as chair of the Board.

Financial management and accountability standards, however, continued to deteriorate – to the point where Price WaterhouseCoopers was engaged to conduct an audit of the 1998 financial statements. The report was accompanied by an eight-point memorandum "on internal control procedures and other matters," the recommendations of which were implemented. Following a $600,000 gift in 1997, the Board began to pay much closer attention to the stewardship of financial resources. Though it had been decided in 1986 to capitalize all unrestricted bequests, it was not until 1998 that the Board established an investments committee and the portfolio was placed under the supervision of a professional investment counsellor.

Generally speaking, over the first half-century, Saint David's trustees were a board composed of elders and persons of substance or influence who did not care to become elders, but wished nevertheless to exercise power vicariously and by and large did so. The trustees have always thought themselves – and acted as if they were – much more than a board of managers. Kerr could never understand why such deference was paid to the Board, took offence, and turned it against him, to his cost; Lawson and Mackay kept their distance, knowing that the Board did not appreciate their presence at meetings even on the few ocasions when they chose to attend; Pace, more astute and with far greater experience of boards of managers, jumped into the deep end, assuming – rightly – that he could bring the Board round to his way of thinking if need be.

It was during Pace's long pastorate that elders became more numerous among the trustees than they had ever been before. By 1998 the secretary and treasurer, as well as the conveners of finance and property, were all elders. While human resources management became a joint responsibility of Session and Board in 1998, property and finance remained the exclusive responsibility of the Board. In April 1998, faced with a still-rising deficit and reduced givings, the all-important finance committee was reorganized with the treasurer of the congregation as ex officio convener.

THE CHURCH SCHOOL

"Very soon after our congregation began holding church service in the First Baptist Church," wrote superintendent George Douglas Wallace in his first and only annual report, "the need of a Sunday School was clearly recognized and on Sunday Feby. 22/25 the first session was held in the School room of the First Baptist Church and I can say that success was assured from the very beginning."[16] It was only the sixth Sunday on which the non-uniting minority Presbyterians had met for public worship and days before they met to organize a congregation. Nearly a hundred children were present. Elder Robert D. McCleave was made acting superintendent and served until October, when Wallace, formerly superintendent at St Andrew's, was appointed to the office on a permanent basis. McCleave thereupon took over the Young Ladies Bible Class.

The tragic death in June 1926 of both Wallace and McCleave was deeply felt. Wallace was replaced by elder Robert D. Guildford, formerly superintendent at Park Street.[17] In February 1927 Saint David's celebrated the second anniversary of the Sunday school, the minister preaching on "Christ's view of children and their witness of the Truth." During Guildford's six years as superintendent, the structure of the school assumed more or less the shape it has held ever since: the Cradle Roll[18] ("little new Presbyterians"), Primary Department (junior school), main school, and officers (superintendent, assistant/junior school superintendent, secretary-treasurer, and librarian). Another import from Park Street–St John's was the Chinese Sunday School, which survived until 1932 and was briefly resurrected by Frank Lawson in February 1946. It continued until October 1947.

In November 1932 Guildford took over the senior Bible class and was to have been succeeded as superintendent by Frank Ashworth, trustee and president of the Young People's Society. Ashworth, however, declined, and Guildford was instead succeeded by his former deputy, Edgar Holloway. No reports of the Sunday school exist for the years 1934 through 1942, though membership is known to have declined sharply – from 142 in 1933 to 40 in 1942. Having the Sunday school meet in the church for the first part of morning service failed to quicken general interest among young people. (This innovation, introduced in the autumn of 1941, became permanent.) Session's dissatisfaction with poor levels of attendance in the Sunday school became so pronounced that in February 1943 Holloway was replaced as superintendent by the minister, a highly unusual move. Over the ensuing year, membership in the Sunday school almost tripled. "Revival" (Kerr) was not too strong a word to describe the increase; the chair of the Board used an even stronger one – "resuscitation."

Kerr vacated the superintendency in March 1944 and was succeeded by Ralph W. Kane, who had been serving as librarian. He accepted the appointment on condition that Session cooperate with him in building up the school. The post of assistant superintendent, which Holloway briefly held after his demotion, went into abeyance. "The year that has closed," Kane wrote in his first annual report, "finds the Sunday School in a slightly better condition than in the past few years, though there remains much yet to be done … if our School is to be worthy of the Congregation." Ralph Kane took his new responsibilities very seriously, viewing Sunday school teaching as a form of professional pedagogy. As early as January 1939, he was chair of the Local Boys' Work Board, a subsidiary of the Maritimes Religious Education Council. Throughout his half-century as superintendent, he strove continuously to augment the numbers of teachers and pupils and to improve delivery of the curriculum.

From the very beginning of his pastorate in September 1945, Frank Lawson took a close interest in the Sunday school. He immediately inaugurated not only an adult Bible class, which he taught, but also monthly meetings of the teachers at which he reviewed the lessons for the month and led discussion on program planning. Lawson's attentiveness and Kane's supervision saw the school expand, at least in number of members if not in levels of attendance. In 1946 the post of assistant superintendent was refilled. Arthur Tattrie, formerly elder and superintendent at First Presbyterian, New Glasgow, held the post until 1961, resigning only after Kane himself failed to do so on succeeding his father as clerk of Session. The offices of clerk of Session and superintendent of the Church School were incompatible and by custom were never held by the same person. Kane's determination to carry on explains why Tattrie relinquished the post of assistant and abandoned the Church School completely.

"It is unfortunate," Kane wrote in his 1948 report, "that when boys and girls reach the age of sixteen or seventeen they consider they are getting too old for Sunday School." In 1948 enrolment in the senior school declined from 38 to 30. Fluctuating over the years, it was a perennial source of concern to Ralph Kane, who had remained a Sunday school student throughout his later teenage years. Membership in the senior school continued to increase during most of Lawson's pastorate, and the class itself survived until 1969.

In 1949 Edgar Holloway rejoined the officers as secretary. In July 1951, on the death of Herbert D. Wallace, he became treasurer as well. Scandal led to his abrupt departure from Session and Church School in the spring of 1953, the very year in which enrolment reached its highest point. (Though reinducted to Session in 1963, Holloway never again worked in the Church School.) In 1954 Lawson was obliged by pressure of work to give up the Bible class, and the monthly teachers' meetings fell by the wayside.

The years 1960 through 1963 were the zenith of the Church School. When it reopened in September 1960, the bulletin announced, "We are in the process of reorganizing the School, and intend to make it one of the best in Halifax." The process began in March 1960, when a deaconess was hired as "director of Christian education." Roberta Shaw was W.J. Kane's parting gift to Saint David's. The idea, if not his, was promoted by him, and among his last official letters was one responding to her acceptance of the offer and setting forth terms and conditions of employment. The clerk of Session died the month before Shaw's arrival. It was his son and successor, Ralph, who had gone to Toronto earlier in the year to seek out and interview prospective candidates.

Newly graduated from the Presbyterian Missionary and Deaconess Training School (Ewart College), Roberta Shaw had spent the summer of

1959 working at Armagh, the PCC's home for single mothers (now abused women) in Mississauga.[19] On arriving at Saint David's in June 1960, she declared her aim to be "to assist teachers and leaders of youth organizations in presenting the Christian faith to young people as a dynamic encounter with the Living God through Jesus Christ."[20] Deaconess Shaw was to be for all practical purposes the congregation's youth minister. This intent meant finding an ex officio role for her in the Church School, as well as effectively putting her in charge of all other youth work. As program manager and chief operating officer in the Church School, she ranked fourth, behind the officers of administration.

At the first Presbytery meeting that Shaw attended, a motion was made to accept her as a full member, which gave her the privilege of participating in all the business of the court. She soon became secretary of Presbytery's Christian Education Committee. On 19 March 1961, the minister being absent, Shaw became the first woman to lead morning worship and preach the sermon ("The church and Christian education").[21] The event was historic and seen to be so.[22]

"The most important event in the work of the Church School," Ralph Kane wrote in his annual report for 1962, "was … the opening of the new addition to our Hall. We have now an adequate Christian Education Centre. Its value has been amply demonstrated in the short time it has been opened."[23] Construction began in May, and by autumn the extension was ready for use. There were nine new classrooms, more than half equipped for the very young.[24]

Officially opened on Anniversary Sunday, 18 November 1962, the Christian Education Centre was, according to the bulletin, "A BIG EVENT – For the first time ever, in the history of this Congregation, we have adequate facilities for the work of Christian Education." A month earlier Lawson had inserted in the bulletin an impassioned three-page plea on "The Right Way to Christian Education."

Sadly, the next important event in the Church School was the departure in October 1963 of Roberta Shaw, in order to accept what looked at the time like a better position elsewhere. "A great loss," Kane wrote, "was experienced in the work of the Church School through the resignation in October of Miss Roberta Shaw, Director of Christian Education. Her work in this field during the past three years was most efficient and she will be greatly missed."[25] Everyone at Saint David's was sorry to see her go. Shaw proved difficult to replace; in the end the position she inaugurated with such distinction fell victim to the great expectations engendered by her success.

The search for a successor to Roberta Shaw took two years. The post was first offered to but declined by a deaconess who in 1981 was ordained minister. It was then offered to Emily Drysdale, who at first had declined to apply when invited to do so. A native Nova Scotian, Drysdale was serving as Presbyery deaconess for Red Deer, Alberta, and had broad experience of church schools, vacation schools, teacher training, and summer camps. She had even led a junior choir. She looked right for the job; she had the misfortune, however, to arrive during a pulpit vacancy. Appointed in September 1965, just as Frank Lawson was walking out the door, Drysdale saw her recognition service deferred until May 1966. The new minister, Donald Mackay, had had no say in her hiring, and he and the new deaconess got off on the wrong foot. Mackay was not the women's libber Lawson was, while Drysdale was a lefty liberal with whom Lawson would have got on famously.

Drysdale assisted with worship during the five-month vacancy (though not afterwards) and, unlike her predecessor, taught in both the senior and junior schools. Her initiative soon led to the establishment of a Christian education committee of Session; she was also the driving force behind the Morris Project, an interchurch summertime playschool supported by the Summer of Service and Christian Youth Assembly, of which she served as chair. Session was happy with her work and in September 1966 renewed her contract. Tension between Drysdale and Mackay, however, seems to have begun early and mounted quickly, as did tension between Mackay and some elders on account of her. Influential Lawsonites such as T.K. Guildford, still smarting over the gratuitous loss of the former minister, were especially unhappy. The upshot was that after less than two years in the job, Drysdale was asked to resign.[26] The post of director of Christian education disappeared with her.

Emily Drysdale was not the diplomat and master of discretion that Roberta Shaw had been, and it seems probable that the Church School was suffering from too many chiefs. The teachers – all volunteers and mostly women – may have resented the director of Christian education as headmistress and teacher of teachers. Nor did it help matters that the interregnum between Shaw and Drysdale saw a significant reorganization of the staff of the Church School. In 1964 Elizabeth Ann Hutton (later Chard) had become superintendent of the junior school and de facto assistant superintendent. The year 1966 witnessed a wholesale exodus of teachers; Elizabeth Chard took a leave of absence to pursue doctoral studies at McMaster University and did not resume her post until after Drysdale's departure. The sacking of the director of Christian education brought about another mass exodus of teachers. Two of the teachers who had previously resigned returned, however. Drysdale's aggressive contemporariness had almost provoked a schism in the Church School. Youth work among the girls stopped altogether.

As if that were not enough, attendance at the Church School was in freefall – down 50 per cent in 1968. Enrolment in the senior school fell from 48 in 1966 to 39 in 1967, to 20 in 1968, and to 10 in 1969. The lone teacher of the senior school Bible class was an elder and elderly retired former minister who could be forgiven for not connecting with teenagers who listened to the Grateful Dead and dreamed of revolution. Discussing "current topics of vital interest to youth" at 9:45 on Sunday morning was not the way ahead. The senior school expired in June 1969, and its teacher, Cecil Howard Kennedy, died suddenly in December.

By 1970 the junior school had become *the* school. Elizabeth Chard, as junior superintendent, acquired an assistant in the person of Graeme Hicks, who had been active in the recently defunct PYPS. Further retrenchment occurred in 1971 when elder Murray Alary, who had been secretary-treasurer since 1963, removed to Calvin Church and was not replaced. Ralph Kane had to take over, the first time in the history of the Church School that it was without a treasurer. By the jubilee year, 1975, Kane had to concede, "The number of children attending our Church School is small – a result of the fact that Saint David's is not a youthful congregation."[27] The decline reflected the demographic, and celebrations over the centenary year, June 1974–May 1975, were more about what the congregation had been and might be again than what it actually was. Donald Mackay was a product of the pre-Disruption PCC, and his roots were showing. In 1925, the year of organization, there had been 123 pupils, sixteen teachers, and seven officers in the Church School; in 1975 there were 47 pupils, four officers, and four teachers – an absolute decline of 62 per cent.

Over the next few years, however, enrolment increased, and pedagogy was given a boost by the arrival in September 1980 of Deaconess Amy Campbell. Though she played no official role in the Church School – a direct legacy of the Drysdale affair – Campbell effectively marshalled and presented new educational resources from a church heritage perspective. A failed attempt was made to "capture" older youth by reintroducing the senior class, defunct for eleven years. A more successful attempt was also made to remedy falling attendance by introducing annual prizes for attendance, subvented by the Ladies Guild.

By 1980 Elizabeth Chard was in effective operational control of the Church School. Her influence had grown steadily after the forced exit of

Emily Drysdale in 1967 and her own elevation to Session later the same year. Though never holding the title, Chard was de facto the director of Christian education. In 1990 her mother, Mamie Hutton, retired after forty-six years as superintendent of the Cradle Roll. Chard herself, however, had to wait a few more years before entering upon her inheritance. Ralph Kane remained superintendent for fifty-two years, finally resigning in October 1996 in his eighty-fifth year. An educator by profession, he was perfectly at home in the Church School. He rarely actually taught, however, except to substitute on a few occasions, and even then the children were often rather scared of him.[28]

In 1997, thanks to the efforts of assistant superintendent Nancy Tindall, an inactive deaconess, a Resources Room was established on the second floor of the "new" hall. This was a timely reminder that the original intention and purpose of the 1962 hall extension were that it should serve as the Christian Education Centre. Senior youth were also encouraged to train as prospective Church School teachers, regular or substitute, and a number of them availed themselves of this opportunity. It had taken the better part of forty years for the Church School to aspire again to the heights it had reached during the all-too-brief ministry of Roberta Shaw.

10

Worship

"THE WORSHIP OF GOD
IN FORMS ANCIENT AND MODERN"

What continuing Presbyterians emphasized first and foremost was the continuity of public worship. But for that defiant assertion of minority rights, the public performance of the collective duty to glorify God, nothing more could have happened. Bringing non-uniting minority Presbyterians together for worship was the first step towards bringing them together to form a congregation. On Sunday afternoon, 18 January 1925, Presbyterians in Halifax declared their independence from the official church, which was perishing. Their very presence spoke to Presbyterian worship as Christian witness – praise and preaching.

No order of service survives from that occasion, nor for any of the succeeding Sunday afternoon services over the next three months. It was not until April 1925, when Presbyterians first worshipped in the former Grafton Street Methodist Church and both evening service and Wednesday evening prayer meeting commenced, that a generic order of service was printed. The Presbyterian Church, Halifax, was now a congregation with a permanent home and acted accordingly. The commercially printed order of service distilled the essence of the PCC's 1922 *Book of Common Order*, tinctured with the distinctive worship traditions of the seven old congregations whence the elders and trustees of the new one had originated: "Organ Prelude – Invocation – Hymn – Scripture Reading – Solo, if any – Prayer – Offering and Music closing with Doxology – Announcements – Hymn, followed by Lord's Prayer – SERMON – Prayer – Hymn – Benediction – Silent Prayer – Organ Postlude."[1]

Grafton Street Church, as delivered to the Presbyterians on the first Sunday in April 1925, would have suited most Presbyterian congregations, provided the communion rail was removed (it was, in the summer of 1927). Choir seating and communion table could both have been accommodated on the existing platform, with its central pulpit and organ behind. This arrangement was appropriately Protestant, as "Protestant" was understood in mid-Victorian times when the church was built. It placed front and centre the preacher as sole worship leader – barring a precentor, "the taker-up of the Psalms." The choir was ideally placed for its new-found role as singer of anthems; likewise the organist, who was visible at the console. Movement during the service was limited to the arrival and departure of the minister and choir and the brief appearance of the ushers (if the offering was carried forward for presentation after being collected). The usual order of service in this arrangement placed the sermon at the end as the most important element, to be heard and remembered without the distraction of any liturgical after-movement. The amphitheatrical configuration of First Baptist Church (Spring Garden Road at Queen), where the Presbyterians worshipped January through March 1925, lent itself to this order of priority. So did Grafton Street, despite its having a nave with central aisle. The entire church converged on the pulpit, where the Word was proclaimed and the Scriptures opened by the preacher.

The first minister, Colin Kerr, would have been aware of the Church of Scotland's new *Book of Common Order,* which went to press shortly after he left Glasgow in January 1926. In Canada the PCC's Committee on Public Worship and Aids to Devotion was one of the first to be re-established after the Disruption. Scoto-Catholic agitation, however, did not begin with the survival and reconstruction of The Presbyterian Church in Canada. The 1918 *Book of Praise,* intended by unionists to be the hymnal of the coming United Church, reflected the late nineteenth-century Catholic revival in worship in the Church of Scotland. The range of hymns was exceedingly broad but tended to reflect Scoto-Catholic attitudes towards liturgy. The full music edition allowed for chanted psalms, creed, and communion antiphons. Trends in PCC "aids to worship" mirrored developments in Scotland, where a further intradenominational church union movement was underway after 1900.

Once Presbyterians became fixed in their pews on Communion Sunday, there was even less movement in the course of worship. Elders served; the open space at the front of the sanctuary often became squeezed to accommodate choir from one direction and more pews from the other. Given the infrequent – usually quarterly – celebration of the Lord's Supper and that the table stood literally in the shadow of the pulpit, priorities were clear. Preaching was everything, the hearing of the Word in various forms the primary and exclusive concern in worship. From 1911, with the organ moved to the front and the choir (the strongest singers) facing the people, congregational singing became more difficult and less important. In the days of the precentor or at least of a cappella unison psalm-singing, the sheer effort of congregational praise reinforced its importance in worship. The construction of a chancel at the "business end" of the church forced the emerging choir back into its place as the leader of congregational singing – visible but not facing the congregation. Instead, they faced their other half across the same sacred space that the congregation also faced.

After 1928, the movement of minister between lectern and pulpit – gospel and epistle, church past and church present – and of the offering and elements of the sacrament – to and from the table, to and from the people – articulated the motion inherent in worship. Moreover, a centre aisle, with or without procession, emphasized the movement of "coming in and going out." Centring the communion table high against the west wall was a reflection of the high altar as the focal point of the church. The site of sacramental memorialization, the table became the visible focus of the church's worship and offering. More importantly, it positioned the Lord's Supper in a shared continuum with the Word – proclamation, praise, preaching, and witness. Whether communion is celebrated more frequently than seasonally or not, the table deep in the chancel at once demands and facilitates greater freedom of movement and more con-certed attention to the epicentre of action than would a small table com-plementing the woodwork of the high pulpit. What happens at the Lord's table dramatizes the Christian life, whether in the presentation of offerings symbolic of total self-giving or the anamnesis itself (take, break, share, serve, return).[2]

THE KERR PASTORATE

Colin Kerr met Session for the first time three days after his induction. Reminding the elders "that he had brought the traditions of the Church of Scotland," he proposed certain changes in the order of service, which were agreed to.[3] We do not know precisely what these changes were, other than that Kerr's first Sunday morning service, 24 January, opened with the sing-ing of the old Scottish psalm "All people that on earth do dwell," followed by the invocation. It must be assumed that a Church of Scotland minister who was a complete stranger to the country, church, and congregation simply applied the liturgy he had been been following at home. Under the circumstances, he could scarcely have done otherwise.

As his congregation was not yet fully cohered, Kerr had a golden opportunity to create a kirk in his own image. If the first minister of Saint David's had been a native brought up and ordained in The Presbyterian Church in Canada, the forms of worship would have been quite different. Halifax's new "auld kirk" was destined to be older in tradition and symbol than any kirk in the city had ever been. The symbols existed; the tradition would have to be invented. Even the church's name, "Saint David," adopted soon after the chancel was dedicated, evoked Kerr's Scoto-Catholicism, symbolizing as it did the transition of Scottish Christianity from the Celtic to the Anglo-Norman under St Margaret and her son, King David.

One of the most venerable Kirk traditions was the quarterly administration of the Lord's Supper. Communion was to be served the first Sunday in January, April, July, and October. On Easter Sunday, 4 April 1926, Kerr conducted his first communion service – strictly according to the Scottish rite; the number of communicants was 320, and 64 joined that day. In 1929 New Year's communion was moved from morning to evening, a practice that has continued ever since; April communion was also moved to the Sunday before Easter, in order to avoid inevitable collisions with Easter, a movable feast; and the first Sunday in December was added. The sacrament of the Lord's Supper was initially a threefold "communion season": preparatory, on Thursday or Friday evening; dispensing the sacrament proper, on Sunday morning; and thanksgiving, on Sunday evening. Communicants were expected to attend all three. The preparatory service was a relic of the Long Communion beloved of Gaelic-speaking Highlanders, Seceders, and Covenanters, all represented at various times in Presbyterian Nova Scotia. Preparatory service afterwards moved to the Sunday before Communion Sunday and survived until December 1981.

After a year in the pulpit, Kerr was unhappy with the level of congregational participation in divine service. Preaching was not performance art, nor worship mere spectacle.[4] In April 1927 Kerr (or an elder) suggested that the Lord's Prayer be chanted during communion. This innovation, forty-five years ahead of its time, was not agreed to. Another innovation was "Rogation Sunday," inaugurated in May 1928. While the rest of Protestant Halifax was observing Mothering Sunday, Kerr was preaching on "The efficacy of prayer." He made the same point differently in 1931, preaching on "The Ascension" (10 May) and again in 1937: "This Sunday is the last before the Ascension and will be known as Rogation Sunday and dedicated to the consideration of prayer."

Minister and liturgy aside, Saint David's could not be a kirk without a chancel: that part of the sanctuary where altars used to stand and which is separated from the nave by steps. High on Kerr's agenda for the reformation of worship and music was the construction of a chancel at the west (back) end of the church to accommodate a new organ, which was badly needed, a communion table, and the choir. The only Kirk artifact was the high pulpit of old St Andrew's, Tobin Street, designed by a Scottish Kirkman for a pre-union kirk and salvaged when the church was abandoned in 1917. Though, scalewise, the pulpit was a complete anomaly, it suited Kerr's plans admirably. Dating from 1871, the high pulpit was the ultimate symbol of the reborn "auld kirk."

In anticipation of the chancel's completion, Session in November 1928 held "a free conversation ... on the change in our order of service and suggestions made by the moderator [Kerr] were concurred in and left with him to work out and report."[5] The addition of a chancel in 1928 reflected the new direction of worship at Saint David's. The design, however, probably had as much to do with showing off the new organ and choir as with reflecting any Kirk bias on the part of minister or organist. The prevailing design in Canadian Presbyterian churches was that of St Matthew's kirk (1859): central pulpit, small communion table (if any at all), and the modern accretions of organ and choir somehow arranged below or behind the pulpit. Oral tradition explains the lack of a centre aisle as insurance against ritualistic processions, but it had more to do with sightlines and acoustics. If the real essence of worship was to look while listening, it made no sense to eliminate a prime seating area.

On the very Sunday the chancel was dedicated (20 January 1929), Session decided to adopt at once the Church of Scotland's new *Book of Common Order, 1928*. The sermon would henceforth be preached from the high pulpit and the offering collected after the sermon. Few bulletins from that time exist, but the one for spring Communion Sunday, 13 April 1930, reveals the extent to which Church of Scotland liturgy now dominated the order of service: "Organ Prelude – Introit (congregation standing) – Prayer (scriptural sentences and Invocation) – Hymn – Prayer (confession and supplication) – Praise – Scripture – Prayer (intercession and Lord's Prayer – congregation joining) – Intimations [announcements] – Hymn – Sermon and Ascription – Offering and Anthem – Offertory Prayer – [Fencing of the Table][6] – Hymn – THE COMMUNION – Hymn – Benediction – Silent Prayer – Organ Postlude."

In December 1932 the Wednesday evening prayer meeting, which had been in terminal decline, finally ended – over the strenuous objections of the clerk of Session. The service could not honourably have been dispensed with until after the death of its strongest proponent, A.D. Falconer, which occurred in September 1932. Though no part of Kirk tradition, the mid-week prayer meeting had been a staple of the Protestant Reformed experience in Halifax for a century. Kerr revived it during Lent 1935 and again in 1938, when it looked as if the grand old custom so dear to Falconer's heart was taking a new lease on life: the last Wednesday in March 1938 saw over a hundred people attend.

Christmas Day morning service, held intermittently from 1926 to 1940, disturbed the Presbyterian bias against immovable feasts involving public worship on any day other than the Lord's Day. Restored in 1943, it was the rule until 1967. By comparison, the Sunday before Christmas ("Christmas Sunday") was uncontroversial, though even it was unheard of before the nineteenth century. December 1932 saw the first Christmas Sunday evening choral service.

Good Friday morning service began in 1934 as reception and first communion for new members. This was a Kirk tradition that did not catch on, though for years afterwards new members were received on Communion Sunday. The year 1936 saw Good Friday service move to the afternoon.[7] In 1949 Kerr's successor, Frank Lawson, began holding a united Presbyterian evening or afternoon service on Good Friday. By 1955 Good Friday worship was again a morning service and has remained so ever since.

In 1938 the PCC had published a new *Book of Common Order*, and in April that year Saint David's began reciting the Apostles' Creed during communion; twenty years later it would be routine at all services. By 1999 it had been superseded during communion by the Nicene Creed. Kerr's Scoto-Catholicism was too much for one elder, Harry Oswald Pryor, who resigned from Session in October 1937 after eight years' service. Pryor was from Bedford, a distinctly low-church congregation, for which old-world Scoto-Catholicism would have been alien to the spirit of new-world Presbyterianism.

THE LAWSON PASTORATE

Just as Colin Kerr brought to Saint David's the traditions of the Church of Scotland, so Frank Lawson brought the traditions of the Presbyterian Church in Ireland. More significantly, he brought indigenous pastoral experience. All of Kerr's pastorates had been in Scotland; both of Lawson's were in Canada. Though he had grown up in the PCI, Lawson had worshipped in The Presbyterian Church in Canada for seventeen years and ministered in it for nearly ten. He also had some personal acquaintance with the heartland of Nova Scotian Presbyterianism in Pictou County. A newcomer but hardly a stranger, he put his accumulated knowledge, born of experience, to good use. He was an imaginative innovator and a daring experimenter, and he was nineteen years younger than Kerr. For him, the Kirk was but a variation on a theme, one among many and all of equal value and potential.

Though he could not sing and knew no music, Lawson was emphatic about the necessity of congregational singing in worship. It was not up to the choir to sing the hymns; choir members merely led the congregation in collective praise. An early bulletin (25 November 1945) asks the hard question: "MUSIC AND WORSHIP / The Congregational Hymn / Are you taking an active part in the singing of our Congregation's Hymns?" An honest answer would have been no; opening the book and lip-synching did not suffice. What mattered to Lawson was not whether one could sing but whether one did regardless of whether one could or not. The significant difference between choir and congregation was as between professional and amateur. The choir did not do all the work; it simply set an example for the congregation to try to follow. By 1957 the bulletin (5 May 1957) was announcing, "We are going to place more and more emphasis upon congregational singing: each soul must become conscious of the goodness of God, and sing their song of thankfulness." Congregational singing had barely existed before Lawson's time; not until March 1943 was mention even made of hymns being "specially selected for congregational singing." Choir or soloists sang, while the people listened and only joined in the singing of psalms or hymns if they were so inclined. Singing was for trained and rehearsed vocalists.

The better to make his point, Lawson also renamed the organist-choirmaster function the "ministry of music," an innovation that would not find acceptance for another forty years. It perfectly summed up his view of music in and as worship – not entertainment, edification, or enlightenment, but prayer and praise. Under all four of Lawson's ministers of music – Vivienne Fowler (1945–47), Arnold Bellis (1947–49), Harold Hamer (1949–61), and Ross Nelson MacLean (1961–65) – the central place of choral music in worship was emphasized. No seasonal music offering was more special or better loved than the Candlelight Carol Service. Successor to the Christmas Sunday evening carol service, which lapsed after Kerr's departure, it began in 1948 and endured until 1989. The Candlelight Carol Service was part and parcel of the invention of Advent, the four Sundays preceding Christmas. According to the bulletin of 17 December

1950, "For a long time the Advent Season was neglected by Protestant people. Once more we have recovered its values and hold it to be one of the great festivals of the Church year."

For the first ten years of Lawson's pastorate, the bulletin, which he restarted almost immediately upon taking over, did not as a rule print the order of service. That was in keeping with Lawson's principled evangelicalism, which had far more in common with Covenant than Kirk. Nothing, not even the sacraments, was comparable in importance to praise and preaching, worship's two foundations. As if in preference to a stated order of service, worship was generically described, on the outside back cover of the bulletin. It was typical of Lawson to render minister metonymically as "pulpit." For him, worship without preaching was as dead as music without congregational singing or works without faith. Sacraments aside, the minister led worship by preaching. In 1953 Lawson briefly renamed the sermon the "Message." As far as he was concerned, all that the worshippers needed to know was the titles of the sermons and the numbers of the hymns. The latter were given on the boards, and Lawson in any case was wont to change them without notice during the course of the service.

The bulletin for Christmas Sunday 1945 reveals some simplification of the standing order of service. The scriptural sentences and invocation were merged in the Introit, while the "Children's Address" (children's story) temporarily disappeared. On Sunday, 24 February 1946, Lawson read the Scriptures from the Revised Standard Version, then one week old. In March the Children's Address was restored, and the order of service was given more prominence in the bulletin. In June 1947 the Kirk order of service reclaimed first place, and – the better to highlight it – the order of service for both morning and evening was printed on the front cover of the bulletin. This practice lapsed in 1948, however, and did not resume for three pastorates. In 1947 Lawson introduced Christmas Eve midnight worship. It did not catch on, and the service was not repeated until Christmas Eve 1960, the first occasion on which Presbyterian worship in Atlantic Canada was televised. When Christmas Eve fell on a Sunday, Christmas Day morning worship was cancelled, as was evening service when Christmas itself fell on a Sunday. Otherwise, rarely if ever was morning service not held on Christmas Day.

By Christmas 1947 the processional hymn had been introduced. Though a permanent feature thirty years later, processions were initially confined to Christmas Sunday, Easter, and Anniversary Sunday. In 1950 Lawson anglicized the "Introit" to "Call to Worship." In 1953 a sung Introit separate from and preceding the Call to Worship was introduced. In 1954 the sung Introit was replaced by the "Little Entry" (entry of the Word). In 1956 the Apostles' Creed was added to the prayer of confession and supplication; later it was given pride of place after the Call to Worship. In 1957 the processional hymn was introduced at morning service, and the Lord's Prayer was being sung on an experimental basis during communion. By 1958 the order of service had achieved the form it would hold until 1966. Internal rearrangement or reidentification of the elements occurred from time to time, but the elements themselves were stable and permanent. Uncertainty persisted as to whether the Little Entry ("The Bible is brought in") should be separate from and simultaneous with or part of the processional. This question nicely symbolized the struggle for predominance between Reformed and Roman influences; between Word for proclamation and ritual for performance, with minister and choir as re-enactors. Eventually, the tension was resolved in favour of separate but equal actions: Bible-carrying beadle entering the chancel from the vestry while choir and minister processed down the nave towards it.

In 1958 Lawson gave Holy Week over to a Presbyterian mission "for the deepening of the spiritual life."[8] January 1961 saw the introduction of the Lesser Doxology (Gloria Patri) sung after the processional hymn. Good Friday morning worship was still occasionally used for the reception of new members by profession and first communion. In March 1962 (and again in May 1964) Lawson led worship by word and sacrament according to Celtic and Covenanter traditions.[9] In the autumn of 1962 he tried to ease the formality of traditional worship by holding evening service in the new Christian Education Centre (hall extension). Easter 1964 saw him introduce a sunrise service and breakfast for children and youth. Neither service nor breakfast caught on and were abandoned after Lawson's departure.

More frequent communion was tried, though the preparatory service disappeared over the course of 1965, Lawson's last year. It was restored early in the next pastorate, doubling as the evening service the Sunday before communion. The processional was immediately suspended on Lawson's departure and not restored for two pastorates. The same was true of the Children's Address, which Lawson himself seems to have dispensed with latterly.

In September 1948 Lawson devoted an evening sermon to "new horizons through great worship." Both of his farewell sermons in September 1965 dealt with worship, which he considered the highest exercise of the spirit of man, praise and thanksgiving being the only practical means to obey

the first and greatest commandment to love God. It did not matter
whether the forms were ancient or modern, only that the worship was in
spirit and in truth.

THE MACKAY PASTORATE

The PCC's third *Book of Common Order*, approved in 1964, arrived at Saint
David's early in Donald B. Mackay's pastorate. Three weeks after taking
over in February 1966, Mackay announced in the bulletin that next
Sunday morning (13 March) some minor changes would be introduced
into the order of service. He was at pains to emphasize that the new Order
of Public Worship was similar to that which had been in use in Saint
David's, subject to the following exceptions: the prayer of confession and
for pardon was placed immediately after the call to worship. As the offering was brought forward, it was suitable for the congregation to sing the
Doxology (Gloria Patri). If there was no celebration of Holy Communion,
the Apostles' Creed should be said in the same place in the service as it
would be if the sacrament were to be observed: that is, while the offering
was being brought forward. A brief offertory prayer would then follow.
The prayer of thanksgiving and intercession and the Lord's Prayer would
come after the Word of God had been proclaimed in Scripture reading
and sermon and after the ushers had returned to their places and the
congregation was seated.

The cumulative effect of this reorientation of elements – a limited eman-
cipation from the Kirk liturgy that had prevailed up to that point – was
that the sermon was unintendedly downgraded. Repositioned by default
as a result of other changes, it ceased to be the climactic be-all and end-
all of divine service; it was no longer first absolutely but first among equals.
Nevertheless, it followed immediately upon the reading of the Scriptures
and remained, in theory at least, another means of proclaiming the Word
of God.

In 1967 Christmas Eve fell on a Sunday, and Christmas Day morning
service – an "old tradition" – was replaced by an evening service on Christmas Eve. This innovation proved popular but did not permanently replace
the Christmas Day morning service until after Mackay's departure. By 1968
the future of evening service itself was in doubt. Though under Lawson it
had enjoyed a slight revival ("The evening service is geared to meet the
practical problems of young people and those who are not regular Church
attendants"), by 1968 attendance had been declining for ten years. The
prospect of a social hour afterwards kept the evening service alive, but when

that too disappeared about 1958, it was doomed. Not even the summertime evening services alternating between Saint David's and St Matthew's could withstand the tide of uninterest. On 29 September 1968 the bulletin announced that a change would be made in the form of evening service. The following Sunday evening a record would be used to start a discussion concerning "The Family." It was the beginning of the evolution from timeless worship to timely relevance.

Thus Sunday evening service ended as a teach-in on family values led by a professional educator. The idea that worship itself was sufficient to enrich Christian family life gave way before uncertainty as to what Christian family life actually was. This experimental substitution for divine service must have fallen rather flat, however, for the next next week Vespers was restored, only to be dispensed with again a week later – Laity Sunday. In November a sixth communion service, in non-traditional form, was added – to seduce the youth. Tellingly, it was relegated to the evening, when few adults and even fewer young people attended worship.

After an autumn and winter spent in inconclusive experimentation, Session took the bull by the horns in the bulletin of 23 March 1969:

Should the Session of the Church of Saint David continue to hold services on Sunday evenings? This question has been under consideration for some time. Discussions have been made this winter to use the hour from seven to eight for films, extra Communion services, special services, guest speakers, discussions and so on. Now that Spring is upon us and the Summer months approaching, the Session thought that members of the Congregation might like to express their views. As one elder says, "They have already voted to do away with evening services by not attending them." However, would you let us know your opinion? Do you plan to attend evening services in the summer – June through September? Are you unable to attend services in the morning and do you attend at night as a result? Have you any suggestions regarding the Sunday evening period from seven to eight o'clock that you feel would make that time more worthwhile for you to attend?

Do you feel that we ought to have an evening service all year round? Only in the Winter months? Not at all?

If you have any feelings regarding this matter, or any suggestions to offer – speak to an elder, or express it on the back of this sheet and hand it to an usher. The Session really want to know how the Congregation feel before they make their decision. But be sure you speak for *yourself*. If services are continued will *you* attend? If you usually come in the morning only, please say so.

The response from members and adherents was either minimal or decidedly negative. The congregation had already voted with its feet. Formally suspended on 22 June 1969, evening service was thenceforth restricted to the Sunday before communion (preparatory service) and the Service of Nine Lessons and Carols for Christmas. Sunday evening preparatory service endured until 1977. Anniversary Sunday 1971 saw evening service specially revived to accommodate the anniversary preacher, Frank Lawson. Though over seventy, Lawson still burned with holy fire and was not content to preach one sermon when he could preach two. So compelling was he on that occasion that in later years Anniversary Sunday included an evening service complete with sermon – more in tribute to Lawson himself than in recognition of the event. One Sunday evening in December 1972 saw "An Ecumenical Service of Repentance" for the churches of south-end Halifax, noteworthy for including Roman Catholics for the first time. Special events such as these aside, evening service survived only as the New Year's Sunday communion.

The "evening sacrifice" had gone the way of the Wednesday evening prayer meeting – and for much the same reason. Minimal attendance meant that the law of diminishing returns applied. The Wednesday evening prayer meeting could no more hold its own against radio in the late 1920s than Sunday evening worship could against television in the late 1960s.[10] There were also safety concerns, reinforced when the director of music was assaulted outside the hall door on Brunswick Steet after evening service.

The "depresbyterianizing" of worship was briefly arrested in 1970 when Christmas Sunday rather than Christmas Eve became again the focus of Christmas observance. By 1973, however, Christmas Eve had mounted a triumphant return. The outstanding event of the year 1972 was the introduction of the new *Book of Praise*, the first revision since 1918. It was dedicated on Sunday, 17 December, the Ladies Guild having generously undertaken to purchase three hundred copies for the use of the congregation. One Sunday evening in April 1973 Saint David's hosted a "hymn sing" to introduce some of the new hymns in the *Book of Praise*. The choirs of the five Presbyterian churches in the metropolitan area took part, and several of the new hymns were offered for congregational singing. The modernist folk-hymnal companion, *Praiseways*, published in 1974, was not seen at Saint David's, however, despite a personal visit from its editor, Alan H. Cowle, in August 1975.

Introduction of the 1972 *Book of Praise* occasioned two changes to the order of service. A responsive reading concluding with a sung Gloria Patri was inserted between the Prayer for Pardon and for Grace and the sung psalm or paraphrase, and the Lord's Prayer was sung rather than spoken during communion. The year 1973 also witnessed a far more daring innovation – a communion service on the Thursday evening before Easter. It is difficult to explain so radical a departure from Presbyterian ways, other than as an ecumenical gesture towards the downtown United Church congregations with which Saint David's had for most of twenty-five years shared special Holy Week services. The minister of Fort Massey United took part in the communion service, and in 1974 the service itself was held at Fort Massey. By Easter 1975 Holy Week services, including both Thursday evening communion and the Good Friday morning "service of meditation and prayer," were well-established. But there would be no more Christmas Day morning services. They and the Mackay pastorate closed together.

THE PACE PASTORATE

John Pace was inducted on the cusp of Easter 1976, and with his characteristic energy and imaginativeness, he moved quickly to impress his stamp on worship. As the most frequently employed supply preacher, he had already restored the processional, out of favour throughout the Mackay pastorate. He took up Holy Week Thursday evening communion, renaming it "Maundy Thursday" in fine traditional English style. Becoming less formal as it adjourned from sanctuary to Hall, Maundy Thursday communion took on a new and improved life of its own and continued after Pace. To the Good Friday morning service Pace added in 1977 the "ancient rite of Tenebrae" (The Extinguishing of the Candles), symbolic of the theophanic solar eclipse said to have occurred as Jesus hung on the cross. The ecumenical Holy Week services, in place for nearly thirty years, soon fell by the wayside, however, and did not resume until the end of the Pace pastorate.

Pace also restored the children's hymn and children's story, neither of which had been seen since Lawson's time. Moreover, in order to try to stimulate formation of a youth group, he introduced a Sunday evening communion service in contemporary style. It was held only intermittently, but an informal Wednesday evening worship service in May and June – shades of the midweek prayer meeting? – lasted until 1980.

In some respects, Pace was a conservative churchman sympathetic with the late nineteenth-century "Catholic revival" in worship that Kerr had introduced to Saint David's. The year of Pace's induction saw the adoption of the 1969 Roman calendar. In the words of the *Oxford Dictionary of the Christian Church*, this "did much to bring out again the importance of the great feasts of Christmas, Easter and Pentecost."[11] Christmas was followed by Epiphany, Lent by Easter, Ascension by Pentecost and then by the "first Sunday in Trinity." Pace had ritualistic inclinations, as evidenced by props such as the Advent wreath, the Jesse tree, and Advent candles, but these were intended to involve entire families in collective acts of public prayer. He designed worship around the seasons of the church year, a concept not indigenous to The Presbyterian Church in Canada. Not since Kerr's time had even limited recognition been given to Catholic feast days such as Ascension and Whit Sunday (Pentecost).

In December 1976 a second, earlier Christmas Eve service was added to accommodate families with young children. In January 1977 Pace restored the sung Introit – a bone of contention in Kerr's and Lawson's time – between the Call to Worship and the Prayer for Pardon and for Grace. It disappeared in June 1980 but was restored the following year. Advent 1980 saw the introduction of an informal communion service in the minister's study during the hour before public worship. In 1981 this expanded to Sundays in Lent. Advent communion services ceased in 1993, and the Lenten service in 1994. From 1980 to 1982 Holy Communion was also celebrated at the later of the two Christmas Eve worship services ("Christmas Eve Candlelight Communion Service"). It disappeared in 1983, when Christmas fell on a Sunday.

In 1980 the Prayer for Pardon and for Grace, following the Call to Worship, was renamed the "Prayer of Adoration and Confession." In February 1985 Pace went so far as to inaugurate a noontime Ash Wednesday service. "Marking the beginning of the pentitential season of Lent" was beyond the pale of Presbyterianism and seen to be so; the experiment was not repeated. New Year's Eve 1985 saw another one-off – the old Methodist Watchnight, a solemn service said to have been inaugurated by Wesley himself and kept many times in the former Grafton Street Methodist Church.[12]

An attempt to revive evening service on a monthly basis was made in the autumn of 1993 ("Prayers tonight are taken from the Scottish Book of Common Order"). This traditional "Service of Yesteryear" proved unsuccessful, though persisting into 1995. Other than evening service – "We also tried to put in place some informal evening services; however, these were so sparsely attended that they obviously were not filling a perceived need in our community" – there was little further action. Lawson's vision of mission and outreach as worship and worship as preaching and proclamation seemed outmoded and limited. Yet strenuous efforts were made to advertise worship services in the wider community, to bring the "C&Eers" (nominal members who worshipped at Christmas and Easter) into more frequent contact with the church, and to capitalize on burgeoning secular interest in what had once been Christian high holy days. Some wondered whether the emphasis placed on "family" services was in fact misplaced, questioning whether the purpose driving worship was to promote family values or to glorify God.

The mainstreaming of public worship, which had begun under Lawson and Mackay, continued under Pace. It reached its apex in the early 1990s, when The Presbyterian Church in Canada issued a new *Book of Common Worship* that betrayed a catholicizing tendency. The wheel of Scoto-Catholicism, which Kerr set in motion, had turned full circle under his third successor – not a Scot but a high kirkman nevertheless who, like Lawson, believed that whatever worked was good.

THE DEWOLFE PASTORATE

When Laurence DeWolfe was inducted on 8 September 1999, the moderator of Presbytery, who presided, used the order of service from the new *Book of Common Worship*.[13] In place of the customary preached charge to the inductee and congregation, the members of congregation and presbytery presented the new minister with symbols of ministry. A well-thumbed Bible represented the ministry of the Word. A basin and towel stood for pastoral ministry. Saint David's silver communion chalice, a gift from Bedford churchwomen in 1926, signified the ministry of the communion table. A copy of the Book of Forms represented the minister's role as presbyter and moderator of Session.

The choice of liturgy was appropriate. DeWolfe had participated in the development of the *Book of Common Worship* from the beginning of the project. In 1984 and 1985 he served, together with his minister-wife, on the task force drafting the marriage service. The years 1987 through 1990 saw him and his congregation in Ottawa study the preparatory documents for the BCW and evaluate the first drafts of services. At Saint David's, however, DeWolfe inherited liturgy based entirely on the *Book of Common Order, 1964*, introduced by Mackay after his induction. Saint David's customary communion liturgy was drawn nearly verbatim from BCO '64, shaped under the influence of David W. Hay, professor of systematic theology at Knox College for thirty-one years and another emigrant Kirkman who rose to become moderator of the General Assembly. A tattered copy of BCO '64 still resided at the organ. Minister and organist followed the same script at every communion service.

Congregational responses had long been a part of the communion service at Saint David's, though it mostly devolved on the choir to sing Merbecke's famous setting of texts from the Church of England's *Book of Common Prayer.* Though the minister did not sing the lines assigned, the choir and a few voices from the congregation responded to the spoken invitation, "Lift up your hearts," and sang the Sanctus and Agnus Dei (in English).

A trained baritone soloist, DeWolfe sang his assigned lines for the first time on 3 October 1999, Worldwide Communion Sunday. As if this were not enough to surprise the congregation, he also altered the prayers of the communion service. It was his custom to prepare communion prayers for each occasion, often choosing from among the seven eucharistic prayers found in the *Book of Common Worship.* The form and manner in which the Lord's Supper was celebrated went unchanged, but the content of the service was quite different. The congregation's seeing and hearing a new minister behind the communion table was perhaps change enough in itself. For a few, these minor variations in the common order of service were too much, while for others they portended radical change.

Worse was to come. Without announcement, DeWolfe also introduced the ancient Greek text "Kyrie eleison" (Lord, have mercy ...) to the Prayer of Confession as a way of expanding congregational participation beyond the responsive reading of the psalm. He also began to use "bidding prayers," inviting responses during the Prayers of Intercession, which he began to call "Prayers of the People." While some worshippers spoke positively to the minister about these changes, few brought their questions or criticisms directly to him. Elders Melvin and Patricia Calkin, co-conveners of Session's worship and music committee, kept track of all questions and complaints and faithfully shared them with the minister.

Concerns about "minor variations" to the liturgy were soon drowned out by contention over hymns. A product of Pictou County who had ministered in Ontario for sixteen years, DeWolfe knew two overlapping sets of "familiar" Presbyterian hymns. Neither set coincided exactly with the standard repertoire at Saint David's. When he sought advice from members of the congregation and the choir and from the organist, DeWolfe found little agreement as to which hymns the congregation knew best. The only consistent observation was that whatever the congregation were willing to sing, they did not sing well.

In the winter of 1996 Session had met to decide whether to acquire the church's new *Book of Praise* – the focus of considerable controversy even before its publication in 1997 – and the *Book of Psalms.* Session was reluctant, the congregation more so. In the autumn of 1997 the elders Calkin conducted an exhaustive study of the congregation's use of the 1972 *Book of Praise* since its introduction in 1973. The survey showed that while many of the hymns had been sung once or twice, a smaller number made up the congregation's hymnary within the hymn book. In May 1998 the Calkins drafted a report on behalf of the worship and music committee recommending that Session "reserve its decision for the moment" on the new hymn book and its companion psalter. The report did not specify how long the matter should be postponed, but it was clear that the advice or preference of the new minister might bring Session to a decision soon after call and induction. The recommendation also ensured that anyone who opposed the decision would lay responsibility for it at the minister's feet.

When DeWolfe was interviewed by the search committee in the spring of 1999, he was asked his opinion of the new *Book of Praise.* He replied that his congregations in Ontario were among the first to purchase it and enjoyed singing from it. He also commented that he would find it difficult to return to the old book, but that he could live with congregational custom and practice. He reiterated his belief that the church's public worship is, in part, witness to the community and a form of outreach, especially in a church such as Saint David's. Some change, including contemporization of both language and music, was necessary in order to reach people who knew little or nothing of the church's traditional language and hymnody.

As the year 2000 began, the hymnal landed back on Session's agenda. DeWolfe as moderator was asked to express his preference, and he spoke in favour of the new book. He urged Session to purchase it, but only if sufficient funds could be found without increasing regular expenditures. One senior elder immediately offered a memorial donation. The clerk of Session reported that there were also ample resources in the Memorial Fund, the purpose of which was to enhance congregational worship. On Palm Sunday, 16 April, the new *Book of Praise* was dedicated and introduced in worship. The congregation sang from the 1972 *Book of Praise* the first verses of "All people that on earth do dwell," the very same selection from the old Scottish Psalter with which Colin Kerr had opened worship on his first Sunday seventy-four years earlier, and then approached the chancel steps to exchange the old light-blue book for the new dark-blue one. The last verses of the psalm were sung from the new.

The advent of the *Book of Praise, 1997* raised the question of "amens." While most congregations had cut off the added cadences from the ends of hymns, Saint David's continued the Victorian custom. The 1972 book provided an "amen" with every hymn, but the new book supplied only a page of "Musical Amens in Various Keys." The organist, Ross Nelson

MacLean, asked whether the concluding "amen" would continue to be sung, but DeWolfe was reluctant to raise the issue with a worship and music committee already divided on the merits of the new book. It also seemed to him that retaining the practice might mollify some of the book's critics, who were legion. While DeWolfe did not join in the congregational sung "amens" at the end of hymns, he praised MacLean's skill at accompanying them, commenting that Saint David's organist was "the only Presbyterian organist [he had] heard who didn't make 'amen' sound like an apology."

The *Book of Praise, 1997* provided new music for the communion service, in hymn-like settings of the Sanctus and other texts. DeWolfe introduced these immediately, and they were met with a generally positive response. Those who had never tried to sing along with the choir during communion prayers did not change their practice, while others who wanted to sing quickly adapted to the new music. Hearing a strong voice lead from the communion table obviously helped. DeWolfe's policy since the introduction of BOP '97 had been to choose at least one hymn each Sunday that he was reasonably sure was new to the congregation. He did not announce this practice, and some members of the congregation took no notice of it. By December 2000, however, the worship and music committee had met (without the minister) and recommended to Session that every effort be made to ensure that there be *only* one hymn each Sunday that was in any degree new to the congregation. DeWolfe responded that he was already trying – without clear guidance or any consensus among those whose advice he sought – to comply. He also pointed out that congregational singing had improved overall, new hymns notwithstanding. The gradual, sometimes grudging, acceptance of new hymns and choruses in worship at Saint David's can be largely attributed to DeWolfe's skill in introducing and leading the singing of them. His first experience singing in a choir as a university student was at Saint David's, and when he returned there as minister twenty years later, it was as an accomplished soloist, with experience in several chamber choirs and symphony choruses.

One major change to worship early in the DeWolfe pastorate met with widespread support. The massive marble baptismal font, gift of the George MacGregor Mitchells in 1929, stood on the north side of the sanctuary, under the gallery and partly obscured by the piano. People complained that they often could not see a baptism in progress from where they sat. DeWolfe therefore advocated relocation of the font. Movers were called in to reverse the position of piano and font. With the font now in front of the lectern, closer to the centre aisle of the church, baptisms were more visible and audible to the congregation. In the summer of 2004 the font moved again, to the south side of the chancel steps, to accommodate a larger new piano on the north side. Removal of the front row of pews also increased the area where minister, parents and relations, elders, Church School children, and sometimes also godparents or family friends could gather to witness the sacrament. DeWolfe also began to employ the full baptismal service from the 1991 *Book of Common Worship*, distributing the text with the bulletin. The service of baptism thus became a more actively participatory feature of the congregation's worship.

Nor was the other Reformed sacrament neglected. On Easter Sunday 2000 Holy Communion was celebrated for the first time at a special morning service. Soon after his arrival at Saint David's, DeWolfe began to advocate more frequent weekly celebrations of the Lord's Supper. He also favoured an alternative liturgy for those who sought a less-structured service than Sunday morning's traditional public worship. Session agreed to initiate an earlier morning service at Easter, to continue at least until the summer. This weekly alternative communion service has persisted ever since, giving way only when the minister is on vacation or otherwise committed, and even then supply preachers often volunteer to lead it, as well as to conduct the Bible study that as a rule follows it. Attendance is rarely greater than a dozen, though in summer the service attracts visitors from downtown hotels who often have tours arranged to begin later in the morning.

After a twenty-year hiatus, the Lord's Supper again became part of the evening service on Christmas Eve 2001. On the recommendation of the worship and music committee, Session set Easter Sunday 2004 as spring Communion Sunday, the minister's preference. Spring communion had not moved since 1929, when it was fixed at the Sunday before Easter. Easter Sunday seventy-five years later saw a greater attendance than Saint David's had experienced for many years, constraining elders to a "loaves and fishes" exercise at the back of the sanctuary as the elements for serving ran low.

A survey of the congregation conducted after the "Stewards by Design" team returned from a national Presbyterian conference in 2001 revealed a strong commitment to the congregation's worship traditions. It was clear that Saint David's sense of identity was inseparable from its worship and the sanctuary in which it worshipped. Its sense of mission was also tied to social services and the church property where they were offered or prepared. Team Saint David's was encouraged to think of public worship as a form of outreach and of some services as potential sources of income for the congregation. Kennon Callahan, conference speaker, proposed a model for "Special Community Services" dedicated to a theme or interest that the congregation shared with the wider community.

The worship and music committee of Session took on the task of organizing several special community worship services in 2002 and beyond. Callahan challenged congregations to identify natural affinities with organizations whose aims were similar or whose needs the church might be able to meet. At Saint David's, services have been held to honour the work of the Victorian Order of Nurses, the wider health care community, and Missions to Seafarers. While these services have not been effective as fundraisers, the relationships formed and the publicity generated have greatly benefited Saint David's. The idea for "David's Place," a Friday morning drop-in clinic for street people, germinated at one of these special community services.

One such community outreach program through worship was already in place when special services became a congregational mission project in 2003. On winter solstice 1999 the first Longest Night, or "Blue Christmas," service was held. DeWolfe brought the practice with him, and Saint David's was among the first churches in Halifax to hold such a service. "Blue Christmas" is outreach to people who have difficulty joining others in the celebration of Christmas, because of grief, anxiety, or exhaustion. The service has continued to be an annual event, attracting worshippers from across Halifax Regional Municipality.

The preached word has always been central to Reformed worship, and a strong pulpit ministry has always been part of Saint David's tradition. While many of the congregation were uncertain what to make of DeWolfe as liturgist, they had few doubts about his ability as preacher. In his application to Saint David's, DeWolfe insisted that he could not separate preaching from leading worship. Generally speaking, Presbyterian congregations are more inclined to separate the two. When they consider candidates for calls, sermons often matter more than anything else. A congregation can accept a measure of innovation at the lectern, communion table, or prayer desk if pulpit ministry informs and inspires.

Saint David's fifth minister may be remembered more for his preaching than for any other aspect of his leadership of the congregation. In that respect, his pastorate would be fully in keeping with the tradition, for, as John Pace reminded the congregation in his sermon inaugurating the diamond jubilee (6 January 1985), "Saint David's has always been known for the high standard of its preaching."

11

Music

The first public worship service by Halifax's anti-union Presbyterians, on 18 January 1925, came complete with guest organist and soloist. The person responsible for arranging the choral music on that occasion was Frederick Moir Guildford. Lacking a choir, Guildford put together a quartette that included himself as tenor/baritone and his brother Robert as bass. The quartette served as the nucleus around which, over the next three months, Guildford built a choir.

The son and brother of elders, Fred Guildford (1885–1980) was a semi-professional vocalist. He sang as a child soprano at Fort Massey and in the choir of old St Andrew's kirk on Tobin Street before moving to Bedford in 1915. In 1934 he helped Harry Dean, organist and choirmaster at Fort Massey, to found the Maritime Academy of Music, where both organ and voice were taught. In later years he was a director of the Conservatory of Music (Maritime Conservatory of Performing Arts), where he had taken his formal musical training, and of the Nova Scotia Opera Association. An elder from 1926, Fred Guildford was long-time convener of the music committee and an influential presence on the music scene at Saint David's for twenty-five years. His solo rendition of "The Palms" became an Easter tradition in itself.

Over the years, Saint David's has had six organists, three organs, as many as four choirs, professional or semi-professional soloists, several pianos (including one electric), and a thriving music program comprehending and extending well beyond worship. Music has been no less integral to the mission and outreach of the church than to its worship. It has been in fullest sense a ministry of music, complementary to the ministry of word and sacrament.

THE ORGANISTS

During the course of Saint David's first ten months, money was spent on paying soloists, purchasing choir music and choir gowns, and hiring a piano. After the move to Grafton Street Church in April 1925, an organist was engaged and money spent on repairing and tuning the organ. Hugh Marshall MacKenzie Huggins, a law student at Dalhousie and gifted amateur keyboardist, presided at the organ until it became necessary to employ an organist full-time. The choice fell on Edward Waldemar (Ned) Schaefer, an Anglican who had trained at St Paul's (Church of England) under Frederick N. Clarke and C.M. Wright. Among the churches Schaefer served were St Andrew's (Coburg Road), St Matthew's, and St James (Dartmouth).[1] He remained at Saint David's until May 1927, when he accepted the post of organist and choirmaster at St John's United.

Schaefer's replacement came from Westminster Presbyterian, New Glasgow, home to the grandest Casavant Frères organ in Atlantic Canada (opus 339), installed in 1909. Born in Scotland in 1874, George Scott Hunter – he acquired the double-barrelled surname Scott-Hunter on emigrating – was educated at the Royal High School and Stanley House, Bridge of Allan. After entering the choir of Stirling's Holy Trinity (Episcopal Church in Scotland) as a probationer, by eight he was a full chorister and by eleven a soloist. When his voice changed, Scott-Hunter was apprenticed to the cathedral organist and master of choristers, Dr Charles Edward Allum. After serving the full five years as an articled student-in-music, he was appointed Allum's chief assistant and put in charge of training new choristers. Scott-Hunter probably left Holy Trinity in 1901 when he failed to be appointed successor to Dr Allum. His last two years before emigrating to the United States were spent as organist and master of choristers at St Mary, Star of the Sea, at Wemyss Castle in Fife, the private chapel of the Earls of Wemyss.

In April 1924 Scott-Hunter arrived in New Glasgow as organist and choirmaster at Westminster Presbyterian. The specifications of the Casavant Frères organ installed at Saint David's in 1928, written by Scott-Hunter, were based on Westminster's (1909), whose reconstruction he oversaw in 1926. Scott-Hunter left Westminster in June 1927, giving his farewell recital on the 27th. He guest-played at Saint David's the first Sunday in June and before the month was out, was hired at an annual salary of $1,200. He did not have an appointment at the Conservatory and so augmented his income through private teaching.[2] Scott-Hunter's first Sunday, 3 July 1927, was a banner occasion: the diamond jubilee of

Confederation. He gave his inaugural recital two weeks later at the School for the Blind, which had a thriving music education program and a much better organ than Saint David's.

Scott-Hunter immediately threw himself into the musical life of Halifax. In April 1928 he acted as adjudicator and rapporteur for the Philharmonic Society's Spring Music Festival. He also gave a remarkable recital with his successor in New Glasgow, the young Glaswegian Erik Chisholm (afterwards the famous modernist composer), in which they performed Charles-Marie Widor's duet *Marche nuptiale* for organ and piano.[3] Such music had not been heard in Halifax because there was no one capable of playing it. Of course, it helped that the venue – the Fraser Memorial Hall at Halifax School for the Blind – had a three-manual Casavant organ.

In December Scott-Hunter gave the inaugural recital on the new Casavant organ at Saint David's[4] and afterwards organized a series of recital performances by Halifax church organists alternating with himself. In 1936 a dispute over salary led him very unwisely to go on a wildcat strike, absenting himself for a Sunday without arranging supply. Session struck a special committee to investigate, and Scott-Hunter was cautioned. He sought refuge in liquor. One evening service in May 1936 found him presiding while under the influence; Session suspended him on half pay for a month and warned that a repetition would bring immediate dismissal. Scott-Hunter promised to become a "strict teetotaller"; it was a promise he had made before but one which he could not or would not keep.

Within days of Kerr's forced resignation in March 1944, Scott-Hunter's heart condition put him in hospital. He probably feared that, his strongest supporter out of the way, his own dismissal was only a matter of time. Knowing that he was indigent, the Board paid the hospital bill as well as his salary. Finally, in March 1945 he resigned, having obtained the post of organist and choirmaster at Centenary–Queen Square United Church in Saint John, New Brunswick, which also boasted a Casavant organ. The Board voted him a long-service award of $200 and the Ladies Guild, which he had cultivated by giving sponsored recitals for fundraising purposes, gave him a reception. His farewell recital was nearly derailed by the VE day riots, which caused its postponement from 8 to 22 May.[5] Scott-Hunter remained in Saint John until he suffered a fatal heart attack in August 1949.

George Scott-Hunter was essentially a choral conductor for whom the organ was a means to an end rather than an end in itself. Just as it accompanied singing, it also accompanied composing. Though he saw the organ "as an epitome of the orchestra" and relished playing the transposed orchestral parts of piano concerti together with a piano soloist, he was not a symphonist. He did not write for the organ, nor indeed did he perform on it except in a rather desultory and constrained manner. He saw the organ the way other Anglicans did, as operational support to choir and soloists – accompaniment writ large and if necessary very large indeed. The whole idea of congregational singing was too primitive to contemplate. He was devoted to sophisticated oratorio, not only Mendelssohn's *Elijah* and *Saint Paul* but even more ambitious and demanding works such as Haydn's *Creation.*

Scott-Hunter needed a good instrument on which to instruct his students, educate his audience, accompany hymns, and lead his choir. He needed an organ with which he was familiar and which was commensurate with his training, ability, experience, and purpose. His instrumental repertoire was limited and characterized by tuneful popular classics and orchestral transpositions, such as the overture to Rossini's *Guillaume Tell.* He knew Bach, Handel, and Mendelssohn but not the modern European musical literature, which did not interest him. Though an exceedingly polished performer, he was a technician rather than a virtuoso. Like all true dominies, Scott-Hunter was perhaps better at teaching than doing. His greatest achievement was neither his own compositions nor recitals but the choirs he led and the students he instructed. Among them was Delbert Jones, LRSM (1920–93), who in the 1970s occasionally supplied the organ at Saint David's.

George Scott-Hunter inaugurated the Saint David's musical tradition – an openness to and appreciation of the performance of serious but not necessarily sacred music far beyond anything that had been seen in Halifax Presbyterian churches before the Disruption. After Scott-Hunter, it was taken as read that the director of music at Saint David's would be a top professional – teacher, virtuoso, or composer or all three – and, in any event, far more than a mere church organist. Scott-Hunter set the bar high, a standard for others to follow no less severe than his pupillage under Dr Allum. When, for example, he inaugurated the prelude before divine service, it was improvised, not played from a score or from memory.

Scott-Hunter's would-be successor was his predecessor, E.W. Schaefer, who in 1943 had been sacked as organist and choirmaster at St John's United to make way for the interim minister's girlfriend. Hard done by, Schaefer and his entire family decamped to Saint David's, and he supplied in the hope, perhaps the expectation, of succeeding Scott-Hunter, twelve years his senior, when the time came. It was not to be. Schaefer, though competent and available, was not in Scott-Hunter's league, and Saint David's had grown accustomed to the flawed genius who had presided at their organ for eighteen years.

Saint David's third organist was Vivienne Marjorie Reid Fowler (1905–2001), of Sackville, New Brunswick. Musically gifted, Fowler at age fourteen was the youngest person ever to graduate in piano from the Conservatory of Music at Mount Allison Ladies College. Three years later she sat and passed the licentiate examination of the Associated Board of the Royal Schools of Music (London).[6] Vivienne Fowler was the first, and so far the only, woman to serve as minister of music at Saint David's and was well-known there for a dozen years before becoming organist and choirmaster. Though a pianist first and foremost, before leaving Sackville she studied organ with Harold Hamer, FRCO, head of music at Mount Allison.

Arriving in Halifax in 1931 to teach piano in the city schools, Fowler soon began to participate in the serious music life of the community. The fact that a relative of her father's, Charles A. Fowler, a prominent architect, was president of the local branch of the Mount Allison Alumni Society gave her an immediate entrée. In October 1932 she performed at Saint David's Weber's Piano Concerto no. 1 in C Major, an early Romantic masterwork probably not heard in Halifax before or since, with Scott-Hunter playing the orchestral part on the organ. She gave another recital in March 1933 and later that month played the piano part in the concert performance of Mendelssohn's *Elijah,* the first grand choral event at Saint David's.[7] On Saturday, 17 February 1934, the society page of the Halifax *Mail* carried a striking photograph of "Miss Vivienne Fowler" accompanied by the caption "who in association with Mr Scott-Hunter provided for the members of the [Halifax] Ladies' Musical Club on Thursday night one of the finest programs of the season." It was a duo recital – organ and piano – and Fowler's rendition of Anton Rubinstein's *Kamennïy-ostrov* no. 21 for piano ("Rêve angélique") made a deep impression.[8] It was a reprise; a year earlier she had introduced the work at a concert under the auspices of the Rotary Club – "quite unforgettable was her playing."

The four weeks in May–June 1936 when Scott-Hunter lay under suspension saw Fowler supply the organ at Saint David's. By 1937 she had a large stable of private pupils and was directing the choir of the Halifax Ladies' Musical Club. In the autumn of that year she was appointed organist and choir director at First Baptist, Halifax; by 1939 she was also teaching music at the Convent of the Sacred Heart. In March 1942 both organ and console were lost in the conflagration that destroyed First Baptist, and she soon gave up her post. After the deaths in quick succession of both of her parents, Fowler left Halifax in 1944, only to return the following year when summoned by Saint David's to supply the organ and then to replace Scott-Hunter permanently.

Vivienne Fowler may have enjoyed the confidence and support of Frank Lawson, a convinced gynophile, but she made life difficult for Session and Board by her continual importuning for money. She asked for $1,500 per annum and was offered $1,300 in addition to a $25 honorarium per Sunday; she grudgingly accepted. Fowler was at loggerheads with Session over complying with the "Broader Music Policy as outlined by the [Music] Committee of Session." Matters went from bad to worse; Fowler often procured substitutes, and in May 1947 she resigned. Asked to withdraw her resignation, in June she offered to do so provided three conditions were met: a studio where she could study and practise, paid tenor and bass soloists, and a substantial salary increase. Session was prepared to grant the first and second but not the third. When in August she told Session that she could not work for less than $2,000, her resignation was accepted. Minister and organist both went on vacation at the end of July, but only Lawson returned in September. Fowler's chief contribution to Saint David's was the Music Hour, inaugurated in February 1946 to enliven evening service.

The vacancy was advertised, at least five organists applied, and Schaefer supplied when the applicants were not "playing for a call." The successful candidate was Arnold Bellis, an eccentric Englishman about whom little is known beyond that he emigrated in August 1947. Bellis had connections to Saint David's through Robin C. Buchanan, a chartered accountant in whose firm Bellis worked. It was not he, however, but his wife, Hilda, who was the professional musician in the family. Lead contralto with the Liverpool Philharmonic Chorus, she had also been a founding member of the Liverpool Bach Choir. Mrs Bellis immediately became soloist at Saint David's and took charge of the choirs, while her husband presided at the organ. She was the de facto choirmaster. Bellis was prepared to accept a salary smaller than Fowler's, and the Bellises went out of their way to cultivate choir members socially, even holding choir practice in their home. They were gracious hosts, and their considerateness was appreciated by the choir.[9]

Sadly, Arnold Bellis's tenure was destined to be the shortest of all. Yet those eighteen months saw a significant increase in the number of choir members and the introduction of the exceedingly popular Candlelight Carol Service on Sunday evenings before Christmas, which lasted for forty years. Bellis's playing was sometimes criticized – though not by the choir – and he was no more a presence on the Halifax music scene than E.W. Schaefer. In May 1949 Bellis was summarily dismissed. He had either been or was about to be charged with a Criminal Code offence – perhaps indecency; Session made its decision after viewing the police evidence against him. Adding insult to injury, Session advised Hilda Bellis that she was welcome to stay on as soloist. She declined. Hers was a far more serious loss to the ministry of music at Saint David's than that of her husband. The Bellises soon left Halifax for parts unknown.

The suddenness of Bellis's departure could hardly have been more inconvenient. For one Sunday in May 1949 Saint David's was without an organist; Schaefer, passed over once too often, took himself off to J. Wesley Smith Memorial United. Moreover, Frank Lawson was about to go on extended leave to visit family in Ireland to announce his impending marriage and wanted the situation resolved before he left. Supplying the pulpit for three months was easy by comparison with hiring a full-time permanent organist and choirmaster on short notice. Then a *deus ex machina* appeared. Harold Hamer, FRCO, of Mount Allison University, who had just been appointed lecturer in music at Dalhousie, was asked to come down to supply; he did so, and his offer to fill the position permanently was gratefully accepted. He stayed for twelve years.

Harold Hamer (1900–80) was the first and so far the only fellow of the Royal College of Organists to serve as director of music at Saint David's. Scott-Hunter was gone, yet a new age of organ musicianship – in which Hamer and his successor at Saint David's, Ross Nelson MacLean, would figure prominently – was about to begin. The advent of Hamer and Maitland Farmer, whose appointment to the Anglican Cathedral Church of All Saints in the spring of 1946 marked the coming of age of church music in Halifax, led to the resuscitation of the moribund Halifax Centre of the Royal Canadian College of Organists.

A native of Leeds, Harold Hamer took his early musical training at the Durham Cathedral Choristers' School and became an organist and choirmaster at age sixteen. He was a student – afterwards deputy – of Dr Albert Charles Tysoe, organist and choirmaster at Leeds Parish Church, and achieved both the ARCO (1921) and the FRCO (1926). After emigrating in 1927 to take up an appointment as assistant director of the Conservatory of Music and professor of harmony and organ at Mount Allison Ladies College,[10] he also became organist and choirmaster at Sackville United Church. Sunday, 24 November 1929, found Hamer supplying the organ at Saint David's. It was the shape of things to come. After evening service he gave a brief recital comprising pieces Saint David's had not heard before and would not hear again for many years: Bach (Fugue in E), Guilmant (Pastorale and Finale, Symphony no. 1 in D Minor), Bridge (Adagio in E), Bernard Johnson (Pavane), and Widor (Finale from Symphony no. 3).

The war and postwar years were an era of "reappraisal" for both Mount Allison and Hamer himself, who at one point was seriously ill. Possibly suffering from what would now be called burnout, he concluded that a change was as good as a rest and that it was time to move on. The only question was where. He had had good offers, all from the West, where Hamer did not care to go.[11] Halifax was another matter. It boasted the region's largest university and two flourishing music training institutions – the Maritime Academy and the Halifax Conservatory. There were fine churches with fine organs and fine organists. Like his native Leeds, moreover, Halifax was a regional metropolis. So when President Kerr of Dalhousie University telephoned in April 1949 to offer him the post of lecturer in music and director of student musical activities, Hamer did not dither over accepting. The post carried with it a joint appointment as head of the theory and organ departments at the Halifax Conservatory.

Dalhousie's board of governors, professioriate, and administration were so well represented at Saint David's that Hamer's imminent move to Halifax quickly became common knowledge. One thing led to another, and Hamer soon found himself with three jobs and three salaries in Halifax. After a pair of false starts in quick succession, Saint David's needed a director of music on whom it could rely. Under the circumstances, Harold Hamer seemed almost too good to be true.

As early as November 1949, Hamer restored Saint David's Music Hour, defunct since Fowler's time. On that occasion he performed on a Remembrance Day theme: Basil Harwood (*Requiem Aeternam*), Harvey Grace (*Lament*), and Walford Davies (*Solemn Melody*).[12] Music Hour persisted for a few years as an occasional substitute for evening service and was often a forum for Hamer to "workshop" anthems of his own composing. By 1951 him was registrar as well as professor of organ and theory at the Conservatory, while also teaching classes in church music at Pine Hill Divinity Hall and directing the Dartmouth Choral Society. Easter evening service 1951 saw the choir perform a new anthem ("Look, ye saints! the sight is glorious") taken from a recent composition by Hamer. Palm Sunday 1955 saw him lead what was probably the first Canadian performance of I. Burnell's *For Us Men: A Passiontide Cantata* (1939). It was reprised on Palm Sunday 1961, Hamer's last at Saint David's.

Hamer could not have been pleased when Session reversed itself on the question of remuneration during his sick leave (November 1956 through February 1957) and he was asked to repay half of it. In the spring of 1957, moreover, he gave up teaching at Dalhousie altogether in order to devote himself to teaching music to schoolchildren. In September 1958, having received a better offer "from another church," he also resigned from Saint David's; he was dissuaded by a $600 increase in his salary, which brought it to $2,400. In April 1961 he carried through on his threatened resignation – his last Sunday at Saint David's was 18 June. Hamer was concerned lest his departure be misconstrued and asked Session's permission to issue a press release.[13] Session, for its part, was surprised and disappointed, and its disappointment turned to consternation when Hamer came out of premature retirement to assist at St Paul's Anglican. A planned official farewell and gift presentation did not materialize. Hamer went on to become full-time permanent organist and choirmaster at St Paul's Anglican, serving for nearly seven years.

It took the arrival of a new minister to make Saint David's forget Hamer's disingenuousness. In June 1970 Donald B. mackay invited hamer to direct the music during General Assembly worship. Hamer accepted and replied graciously to Mackay's letter, which thanked him for his services and enclosed a generous honorarium.[14] In December 1971 he returned again to direct a performance of Handel's *Messiah*. It was his swan song. Harold Hamer died in September 1980, leaving his personal papers, music library, and precious RCO yearbooks to his former pupil and successor, Ross Nelson MacLean.

The vacancy generated much interest among other church organists in Halifax. Replacing an organist and choirmaster of Hamer's consummate musicianship would not be easy, and invited by the music committee to act as consultant, Hamer communicated his views on who should succeed him. There was considerable discussion as to the relative importance of and the proper balance to be struck between organ musicianship and choir directorship; in other words, whether the new minister of music had to be another Harold Hamer, the epitome of both. The issue turned on which was more important – to have a good organist who was less effective as a choirmaster (e.g., Schaefer and Bellis) or a good choirmaster who was less effective as an organist (e.g., Scott-Hunter and Fowler). Though the consensus of opinion within Session was that the organist was chiefly a choral accompanist, in the end it was the organist rather than the choirmaster component that prevailed.

The choice fell on Ross Nelson MacLean, who was travelling in Europe when his appointment was announced in the bulletin of 3 September 1961. He began his ministry of music at Saint David's on 1 October, Communion Sunday. At twenty-seven, many years younger than any of his five predecessors when they began, MacLean had already served as organist at two city churches – St James Anglican (1953–56) and St John's

United (1956–61), where his family worshipped and his father was elder. As choirmaster at St John's in 1957, he made for London Records of Canada a recording of hymns that was well received and widely marketed and attracted a lot of attention locally.

Originally setting out to be a violinist, MacLean had attended the Maritime Conservatory of Music and had had the benefit of lessons from Maitland Farmer at All Saints Cathedral.[15] It was Farmer who introduced to Halifax and to MacLean the works of Marcel Dupré, organist at Paris's Saint-Sulpice and the greatest organ composer of the age. MacLean would devote much of his career to performing and promoting the works of Dupré, whose private pupil he became. He also took lessons from Hamer, and in October 1957 he became an associate of the Royal Conservatory of Music (University of Toronto), as well as licentiate and then fellow of Trinity College of Music, London. In 1959 MacLean went to England for advanced study under Harry Gabb, organist at HM Chapels Royal. Gabb and Sir John Dykes-Bower, organist at St Paul's Cathedral, were important formative influences.

MacLean's closest musical mentor, however, was Sir William McKie, organist of Westminster Abbey, who at Farmer's invitation had come to Halifax in 1952 to give a recital at All Saints. That was MacLean's introduction to McKie, who afterwards took special interest in Farmer's precocious pupil. MacLean's principal American teachers were Joan Lippincott (Westminster Choir College, Princeton) and George Markey. His musical education was cosmopolitan, comprehending two continents, four countries, and at least two distinct and incompatible performance traditions.

His five years at St John's United saw MacLean develop into a virtuoso with a sophisticated modern repertoire. His preference, reflecting summers spent in Europe, was for the French organ literature and the French performance style. As early as 1955, he was headlining recital programs at All Saints. In April of that year he also played the organ for the University of King's College Choral and Dramatic Society's performance of Handel's *Passion of Christ.* By the time he arrived at Saint David's, MacLean was teaching organ, theory, and piano at the Maritime Conservatory. He also took private pupils. In June 1964 he became associate of the Royal Canadian College of Organists.

It was during his years at St John's United that Ross MacLean became acquainted with Marcel Dupré, with whom he corresponded and whom he visited on several occasions. On 3 May 1971 MacLean gave an all-Dupré recital at Saint David's in honour of the master's eighty-fifth birthday, writing in the program notes, "It has been my good fortune to know Marcel Dupré personally, and to have studied privately under him at Saint-Sulpice and at his home in Meudon on a number of trips overseas. Sitting on the organ bench with him at Saint-Sulpice on Sundays as he improvises is an unforgettable experience." In May 1980 Graham Steed, FRCO, organist and choirmaster of St Mary's Basilica and the world's leading Dupré scholar, gave his inaugural recital at Saint David's. Studies with Steed led to MacLean's being awarded the ARCO in January 1982.

In 1968 MacLean, drawing on experience gained at St John's United towards the end of his time there, oversaw the complete reconstruction of the organ at Saint David's. In 1975 he took the unusual step of becoming church officer (custodian), a post he held for three years. In October 1979 he surpassed the previous record-holder, George Scott-Hunter – Saint David's first organist – in terms of longevity. On Worldwide Communion Sunday, 5 October 1986, MacLean's silver jubilee was celebrated. Ten years later he gave his thirty-fifth anniversary recital. By October 1997 he had served longer than his five predecessors put together.

In October 2001 Saint David's celebrated MacLean's "40 years on the bench." Elder Malcolm B. Mackay, long-time choir member and occasional tenor soloist, recalled the day in November 1965 when his father "returned from preaching for the call and spoke in glowing terms of the excellent young organist at Saint David's." In the autumn of 2004, MacLean's confreres in the Halifax Centre of the Royal Canadian College of Organists presented him with the RCCO's Distinguished Service Award. Early in 2006 he became ill with cancer and was obliged to take a leave of absence until 30 June. He died on 15 April 2006, less than three weeks short of his seventy-second birthday and in his forty-fifth year as director of music at Saint David's.

Given the length of his incumbency, it was almost inevitable that Ross Nelson MacLean should have presided over a decline in choral resources. The senior choir shrank to a fraction of its former size, the junior and intermediate choirs disappeared, and the quartet of paid professional or semi-professional soloists became a thing of the past. So straitened were vocal forces that it proved difficult to perform new or artistically demanding anthems, not to mention solos. Choir members left, died, or moved away and could not be replaced. Under circumstances such as these, which were beyond his control, it was only natural that MacLean should have concentrated on exploiting to the full his own superior talents as a virtuoso recitalist.

THE ORGANS

When the Presbyterians arrived at Grafton Street Church in the spring of 1925, they found a swell organ at the head of the sanctuary behind choir and minister's preaching desk. A two-manual electro-pneumatic Karn-Morris instrument, probably built by Charles Sumner Warren, it had been installed in the summer of 1911, when the interior of the forty-year-old church was substantially renovated and organ and choir relocated from the east gallery to the platform at the front. Seventeen years later the Karn-Morris instrument would return to where the organ had originally been – the east gallery facing the chancel – as an echo organ. The original console was also in the gallery. Since it antedated electrical-pneumatic connections, it had to be near the pipes and the air chest. It was also possibly a tracker-type console, with direct mechanical connection to some of the stops and other settings.

Replacing the 1911 organ would be part and parcel of the wholesale Presbyterianization of the old Wesleyan sanctuary. The older generation at Saint David's included former Kirkmen from St Andrew's, the first Presbyterian church in Nova Scotia to install an organ, in May 1867. Auld Kirkmen were almost certainly behind the move to ornament the new kirk with a cathedral organ too large for the space and the acoustic. Perhaps some had gazed enviously at the nearly new, if ill-fated Casavant (installed September 1920) in First Baptist, where they worshipped for the first months of 1925. Perhaps, too, they had been part of the capacity crowd on 17 December 1920 when the organ was inaugurated by Joseph Bonnet, successor to Alexandre Guilmant and at the time the most famous organist in the world.

Even before the matter of a new organ was brought before the annual congregational meeting in January 1927, officers of the Board had been in touch with Casavant Frères Ltée of Saint-Hyacinthe, Quebec, with a view to replacing the "obsolete" organ. For some reason, the venerable Warren Organ Company Limited ("builders of pipe organs since 1836"), still going strong in Barrie, was not thought of. The matter was remitted to the Board, which thereupon entered into discussions with Casavant's man in the Maritimes, G.R. Ledoux.

Nothing could have been done until the spring of 1927, when the Presbyterians acquired ownership of the church. Moreover, the arrival in July of Scott-Hunter, fresh from the reconstruction of the Casavant in Westminister, New Glasgow, acted as a spur. Technical specifications aside, he saw to it that the instrument had the "detached English console" that he had introduced at Westminster. Agreement between Casavant and Saint David's was reached by December 1927, and the contract signed in January 1928. "Opus 1284" was to be a three-manual organ – great, swell, choir – with pedal pipes and "electro-pneumatic action." The swell was to be installed above the console, and the choir organ opposite. An echo organ was not originally part of the specification. St Andrew's Presbyterian, Westville, expressed interest in acquiring the existing swell organ. At Scott-Hunter's urging, however, Saint David's decided to convert the swell to an "echo and chimes organ" and relocate it to the east gallery above the narthex, where the organ had stood before 1911. That would, in Scott-Hunter's words, "fill up the present ugly gap in the back gallery."[16]

It was Scott-Hunter, together with Aubrey DeWolfe Smith, convener of the music committee, who selected the parts and supervised their installation. By September 1928, much interest was being expressed in the imminent installation of the new organ, the specifications of which were unique in many ways. A large three-manual and echo organ containing forty-seven stops, thirty-five couplers, and electric pistons for both hands and feet, it included all the latest improvements known to contemporary organ-building. One of its many features was a chime of twenty-five bells known as "Class A" improved type.[17]

The new organ was installed over two weeks in November 1928; tuning then proceeded, and the organ was ready for use on 16 December.[18] Evening service that Sunday was broadcast over radio station CHNS, only the third time Presbyterian worship went live to air in the Maritimes. The organ had previously been inspected by the professional organist community of the city.[19] Scott-Hunter gave his inaugural recital on the new instrument on 27 December.[20]

From early days the Board had let a yearly service contract covering inspection, maintenance, and tuning of the organ. In May 1942 the organ was damaged by the fire that destroyed the choir room. The precise nature of the damage is unknown, but the necessary repairs and replacements were immediately carried out by Casavant and financed by the insurance payout. In later years the organ was maintained and tuned by Casavant's representative in Halifax, G.R. Ledoux. By 1964 the music committee was reporting that the organ required major restorative maintenance. Casavant wanted to repair or replace the echo division, then over fifty years old, which had not been used for some time. The Board however, preferred to wait on a report from Hill, Norman and Beard (HN&B), the premier English firm of organ-builders. Hamer was called in to offer an independent opinion.[21]

In September 1966 MacLean asked the Board to move the maintenance contract from Casavant to HN&B when the current contract expired. It agreed to do so. No further action was taken until December 1967, when the congregation voted to proceed with a "complete reconstruction" of the organ. One of the new elders, a professional engineer, wanted to know whether any thought had been given to a system of electronic controls, but that was an idea whose time had not yet come. The $30,000 contract went to HN&B; it would be the firm's fifth church organ in metropolitan Halifax.

The new organ was less a "rebuilding and revoicing" of the existing one than a replacement of it using the Casavant as building materials. Though the organ retained its basic structural integrity, it became in other respects a hybrid. The musical design was prepared by R. Mark Fairhead, HN&B's senior tonal designer and voicer, working in close consultation with MacLean and Hamer. It was Hamer who suggested the addition to the echo division of the *trompeta réal*, "seen and heard in many famous Spanish organs and for which there is an organ literature. The Trompeta is a fairly mild solo reed. We believe it to be the first of its kind in Nova Scotia and in Eastern Canada."[22] The detached English console beloved of Scott-Hunter was also redesigned in accordance with current RCO examination standard. The new organ was dedicated on Sunday, 15 December 1968, forty years to the Sunday after its Casavant predecessor. It was officially inaugurated on 29 April 1969 by Pierre Cochereau, organist at Notre-Dame de Paris and former star pupil of Marcel Dupré.

The HN&B edifice did not sit altogether comfortably on the Casavant foundation. Major repairs and pipe-cleaning were undertaken in 1978, deficiencies having been all too apparent when Cochereau returned for a second concert in April 1978, less successful than his first ten years earlier. A "Paean for Choirs and Organ" performed by organist and choir on Reformation Sunday afternoon (29 October 1978) marked the successful completion of this work. By 1983, however, the echo organ division was in danger of imploding. The second and far more radical rebuilding of 1968 had proved too much for the original instrument. In June 1984 Saint David's held a public auction to raise the $10,000 needed to restore the echo organ (wrongly described as being "well over 100 years old"). The poor condition of the echo organ, however, had little to do with its seventy-three years. It had been saddled with more equipment than it could bear – the *trompeta réal*. One wonders whether HN&B was properly briefed on the origins and history of the former swell organ of 1911–28. Saint David's did not retain the records of the 1928 installation, while Casavant Frères, having failed to receive the contract, were not about to share with a former client, much less the successful competitor, information from their extensive case file.

By 1998 the entire organ was in as bad shape as the echo organ had been in 1983. Session's worship and music committee had under consideration two proposals for how to deal with the situation, one from

Kingsway Organ Company Limited (Denis Anthony King), which had maintained the organ since 1968, and one from Casavant. The former was for renewal, the latter for rebuilding. Neither was destined to proceed; King died unexpectedly, and the Casavant proposal proved impracticable. In 1999–2000 a five-year organ restoration and modernization project, financed almost entirely by a member of Saint David's, commenced. The contractor was D. Leslie Smith, organ-builder of Fergus, Ontario, whose work was known to the new minister.

THE CHOIRS

A volunteer choir had been authorized by Session ten days before the move to Grafton Street in April 1925. In three years the choir doubled its numbers to forty-one, with voices in all four registers. Anthems and solos were sung on a regular basis. In the autumn of 1926 a junior (girls') choir was formed. Two years later the convener of the music committee proudly noted "the fact that we have one of the finest of VOLUNTEER choirs."[23] By 1929 the choir had reached its greatest extent – forty-three – and boasted not only officers but also an executive committee and even a "gown mistress."

The choir was busily adding to its repertoire sacred music from the cantata and oratorio literature. By January 1930 it had reached so "high a standard of excellence" that the minister saw fit to warn that the choir's role was not to perform for the listening pleasure of the congregation but to lead congregational singing, "in which all should join." Before long, Saint David's choir was singing out of doors. In December 1930 it performed at a concert in the Capitol Theatre, then the city's premier concert venue, and was a "hit." Little further is known until 1943, when an unsuccessful attempt was made to re-establish the junior choir. A second attempt in the winter of 1945–46 was successful; the junior choir sang for the first time on Palm Sunday 1946. But the early postwar period was unsettled: four choirmasters in as many years.

The Hamer years, by contrast, were a period of stability and growth. In 1953, for example, membership increased by two tenors, two basses, one contralto, and one soprano. Many new anthems were rehearsed and presented, including one written by Hamer and dedicated to Saint David's.[24] The anthem, "O brother man, fold to the heart thy brother," was a setting for five-part chorus of mixed voices and organ with incidental baritone solo of John Greenleaf Whittier's 1850 poem. It premiered on 17 May 1953.

In the autumn of 1954 an intermediate choir was organized. The later 1950s, however, were a testing time. Choir numbers fell below thirty, and in

November 1956 Hamer broke his leg badly in a car accident and was more or less completely indisposed for a few months. In November 1957 the lead soprano, Audrey Farnell, left for a year's advanced study in England. But the choir bounced back. Farnell returned, numbers rose to thirty, and in January 1959 Saint David's took the rose bowl for best choir at the Halifax Music Festival. Then in August of that year Farnell left for good.

The Hamer-MacLean transition was not an easy one for either organist or choir. Hamer's premature departure for no apparent reason had upset everyone. MacLean, though an able and experienced choirmaster, was less than half Hamer's age, was not a fellow of the RCO, and was also younger than many members of the choir, some of whom had belonged since before he was born. A measure of generational change had to occur before he was fully accepted; even Session was concerned at the outset that MacLean was insufficiently "aggressive" with his choristers. Numbers fell below twenty, though they were afterwards restored.

By 1964 tensions had eased and the choir was learning to appreciate MacLean's sheer musicianship and take pride in his considerable achievements as a virtuoso recitalist. "Our Director," observed the choir's annual report, "gave a very successful Organ recital with the Navy Band at St Mary's Basilica. The concert was well attended and of a very high order." At that recital, on 27 May 1964, among other more prosaic crowd-pleasers, MacLean performed four modern French masterpieces: Messiaen's *Celestial Banquet*, Boellemann's *Prière à Notre-Dame*, Dupré's eighth *Station of the Cross* ("Jesus Comforts the Women of Jerusalem"), and Langlais's *Te Deum*.

The arrival of Donald B. Mackay as minister in 1966 gave a boost to choral music-making at Saint David's. Mrs Mackay, a professional music teacher, immediately took charge of the junior choir, which had been reorganized in 1964, and in 1970 she re-established the intermediate choir, which had lapsed in 1959. The entire bulletin of 27 September 1970 ("Your Child Needs Music") was given over to the choirs.

The year 1968 was not a good one for the choir – the soprano soloist resigned. It was also caught up in a silly controversy over whether woman members should wear caps (since time immemorial they had worn mortarboards). The contention within Session was so fierce that the convener of the music committee, a new elder who, as chair of the Board, had overseen the successful rebuilding of the organ, left Saint David's altogether. The minister wryly observed, "All this in the name of Christianity."[25] Women's choir caps were not finally dispensed with until the autumn of 1989. Caps or no caps, the situation did not improve. The chief problem was revolving-door soloists, who could not or would not join or remain with the choir, where they were badly needed in order to provide not only vocal support but also artistic leadership.

By comparison with the senior choir, the junior choir was flourishing. Sadly, however, the autumn of 1971 saw the extinction of both the junior and intermediate choirs; Mary Jane Mackay's distress is evident in her report for that year. She promised to try again in 1972, but it was not to be. Three years later MacLean successfully reinstated the junior choir, consisting of both children and teenagers and on that account renamed the Youth Choir.

In 1976 senior choir numbers increased – they would continue doing so through the early 1980s – and the new minister's wife, Margaret Pace, who had lengthy experience of church choirs, joined the choir as occasional contralto soloist. In the autumn of 1979 Marian Beare, a registered music teacher whose father, Ronald, was long-time tenor soloist, formed a special choir, Saint David's Contemporary Music Group. Renamed Saint David's Singers, it gave its inaugural performance on Anniversary Sunday evening, 18 January 1980, as part of an ambitious program of choral and instrumental music arranged and directed by the minister. This small choir of young women mainly drawn from the senior choir was soon in demand in churches and elsewhere in and beyond metropolitan Halifax. Saint David's Singers survived until 1984, when its founder and director moved to Toronto.

The junior choir did not report in 1988 and the following year was again reorganized under a new director, Susan Chisholm, a clarinetist who sang alto in the senior choir. Chisholm built up the junior choir to the amazing number of fifteen, but was gone within the year and did not return as MacLean hoped she would. He resumed direction of the junior choir, while moral and logistical support was provided by Judithe Adam-Murphy, pastoral assistant and, from 1993, assistant. In 1997 another alto from the senior choir, Jocelyne Cross Lloyd, took over and the juniors carried on. Lloyd left in 1999 and was briefly succeeded by the lead soprano, Marilyn Drew.

By 2000, its seventy-fifth year, the choir was reduced to twelve – fewer than it had begun with. Yet all voice departments were represented, and the "small band of singers" coped bravely with the introduction of the 1997 *Book of Praise*.[26] Despite greatly reduced numbers, the choir continued to exhibit a high degree of professionalism and to attract not only fine ensemble singers but also exemplary soloists. Rarely, except during summer, has a service taken place at which there was not a least one soloist. At first, soloists were ordinary members of the choir with special training or vocal gifts. Of these none served longer or more faithfully than Fred Guildford, who organized the choir and served as first director of music. By the mid-1940s, professional or semi-professional soloists were being hired on retainer. The most distinguished of these were Audrey Farnell (lyric soprano) and Leonard Mayoh (baritone), both of whom are included in the *Encyclopaedia of Music in Canada.*

Audrey Farnell (1921–95) was born in Amherst, Nova Scotia, and began serious musical studies at the Mount Allison Conservatory when Hamer was director. She went on to the Toronto Conservatory of Music and was runner-up in the 1945–46 Singing Stars of Tomorrow, a nationwide voice competition sponsored by the CBC.[27] Before moving to New York to study with Lotte Leonard, Farnell appeared as soloist with Sir Ernest MacMillan and the Toronto Symphony, the Hamilton Bach Choir, the Toronto Mendelssohn Choir, the Montreal Elgar Choir, and the Ottawa Choral Union, as well as broadcasting over the national network of the CBC. She first appeared at Saint David's in September 1946,[28] while on a Maritimes tour. She again sang there to great acclaim on Anniversary Sunday 1949. That summer she was guest soloist at the bicentenary concerts of the Halifax Conservatory Choral Union. Settling in Halifax in September of that year to teach voice at the Conservatory, she joined Saint David's choir as lead soprano. In November 1951 Farnell was invited to sing at the civic reception for HRH Princess Elizabeth, afterwards HM the Queen.

In the autumn of 1956 Farnell took charge of the junior and intermediate choirs. A year later she was granted leave of absence to go to London for advanced study under Roy Henderson, "one of the most sought-after of teachers at the Royal Academy of Music," whose students included Kathleen Ferrier. Returning from England in 1958 as Mrs Chapple, Farnell resumed charge of the junior and intermediate choirs but remained at Saint David's for only one more year. Her last Sunday was 2 August 1959, whereupon she moved to Vancouver. During her decade in Halifax, Farnell also sang with the Nova Scotia Opera Association and starred on CBC Halifax's *Songs by Audrey Farnell* and, with Leonard Mayoh, on *Sketches of Songs.*

Leonard Mayoh (1918–78) arrived at Saint David's two years after Audrey Farnell. An associate of the Royal Manchester College of Music, he emigrated from England in February 1951 to become head of the voice department at the Halifax Conservatory of Music.[29] Hamer soon invited Mayoh to be baritone soloist at Saint David's, and his appointment was announced in the bulletin of 1 April. He had given his inaugural recital on 14 March[30] and sang for the first time at Saint David's four days later, Palm Sunday. On 14 April Mayoh performed the surpassing aria "Arm, Arm, Ye Brave" from

Handel's *Judas Maccabaeus*. On the 25th he joined Farnell and Diane Parker (contralto) in a concert of sacred music that also featured anthems by the choir and instrumental pieces by Ifan Williams and Arthur Fordham, violinists, and Carolyn Schurman, pianist, all directed by Hamer at the organ console. The bulletin (29 April 1951) modestly declared, "The Concert held last Wednesday evening was a great success. Seldom has there been such an evening of fine sacred music in Halifax."

Mayoh also took charge of the Halifax Conservatory Choral Union, renaming it in British fashion the Halifax Choral Society and conducting it until 1959. He remained with Saint David's through the summer of 1954, leaving to become choirmaster at Halifax's St James Anglican. He returned to Saint David's in April 1955 to sing the role of Christ in the Passiontide cantata *For Us Men* and again in November 1956 to direct the music during Hamer's four-month indisposition. In 1958 Mayoh received the Nova Scotia Bicentenary of Representative Government Medal for "distinguished service to music." That two vocal artists of the quality of Audrey Farnell and Leonard Mayoh should be recruited as soloists was testimony not only to the unrivalled stature of Harold Hamer but also to the vitality of the Saint David's music tradition. The choir was a warm and welcoming home away from home for both enthusiastic and gifted amateurs and accomplished professionals.

MUSIC AT SAINT DAVID'S

The first formal music event at Saint David's seems to have been a recital given by Mrs Thomas Guy, soprano soloist, and Mrs Gordon Page, pianist, in March 1927. (It was a fundraiser for the projected organ.) Before Scott-Hunter's arrival that summer, it was scarcely possible for the choir to undertake major choral works. The first was John Henry Maunder's sacred cantata *Bethlehem*, given at evening service Christmas Day 1927, which that year fell on a Sunday. It was so successful that it was repeated on Anniversary Sunday, 15 January 1928. *Bethlehem* was followed on Palm Sunday 1928 by French organist F.C.T. Dubois's sacred cantata *The Last Seven Words of Christ*. *Bethlehem* set the standard: "It is not difficult to see that this choir is undergoing very intensive training at the hands of the choirmaster." Christmas Sunday evening 1928 saw it repeated again, complete with a four-page printed libretto.

For as long as the requisite vocal talent remained available, the choir continued to offer cantatas or oratorios on special occasions, in addition to the regular Sunday anthems and solos, which themselves were often excerpts from an oratorio or cantata. Not until the late 1960s, when choral resources declined precipitately, would the emphasis change from choral to instrumental music and the focus from in-house to outside artists. The music program evolved, becoming less grounded in worship than in musicianship and virtuosity. The choir was reduced to its primary and original purpose – worship accompaniment – and even that under straitened conditions.

Easter evening service 1930 heard the Easter section of Handel's *Messiah*, while evening service on Christmas Sunday heard Parts I and II. Easter 1932 saw Sir John Stainer's sacred cantata *Crucifixion*. The choir's greatest success, however, was among its earliest and most ambitious: "Presentation of Mendelssohn's famous oratorio *Elijah* [at] Saint David's Church, March 30th [1933], at 8.15 p.m. under the direction of Mr George Scott-Hunter, Director, at the organ, and Miss Vivienne Fowler, at the piano." It was a tour de force, probably the first essay of this sublime and sophisticated work, rarely performed in Halifax afterwards. The augmented choir on that memorable occasion consisted of twenty-four sopranos, fourteen altos, five tenors, and nine bass-baritones.

Fresh from its triumph with *Elijah*, Saint David's Choir by September was planning something even more ambitious – a joint co-performance with St Paul's of Haydn's massive oratorio *Creation*. No English-language libretto was available, however, and the substitute, Mendelssohn's *Saint Paul*, proved a bridge too far for the Handelian music-tasters of Halifax. Despite the massed choirs of Saint David's and St Paul's and the same soloists save one, the performance at Saint David's in April 1934 attracted "a very small audience."[31]

The Second World War nearly put an end to special musical offerings, other than informal singsongs for the benefit of military personnel at Open Door hour after evening service. An exception was Anniversary Sunday 1941, an occasion made all the more special because it was the fifteenth anniversary of Kerr's first appearance in the pulpit. After evening service the combined choirs of Saint David's and the Cathedral Church of All Saints, supported by the string orchestra of the Halifax Conservatory of Music, sang the Nativity section of Handel's *Messiah*. However, it was not until Scott-Hunter's successor was appointed in August 1945 and Frank Lawson inducted in September that the music program resumed in earnest. Choral aspirations were less ambitious than they had been before the war, partly because neither Fowler (chiefly a pianist) nor Bellis (chiefly an organist) was a choirmaster of the order of Scott-Hunter before or Hamer after.

Holy Thursday evening, 6 April 1950, saw Saint David's host the Halifax Conservatory Choral Union's performance of Bach's *Saint John Passion*.

The director of the conservatory conducted, while Hamer played the organ. In December 1952 Leonard Mayoh conducted the Halifax Choral Society in the first full performance of *Messiah* at Saint David's. Harold Hamer played the organ, and the event was so successful it had to be repeated two days later.[32] Christmastime nineteen years later saw choir and people perform the work again. Though the Halifax *Mail-Star* commented, "The success of this venture indicates that it might become a permanent feature of the Christmas season in Saint David's," it survived only until 1974, when it was abandoned because of a lack of interest. On Palm Sunday afternoon, 12 April 1981, the combined choirs of Saint David's and West End Baptist repeated Stainer's *Crucifixion*. The work was performed again in 1995, this time in combination with St Matthew's United.

Organ recitals were rare after Scott-Hunter's time, partly because Hamer was uninterested and partly because the organ was not up to code. MacLean, already a polished recitalist, saw things differently. Despite the poor condition of the organ, he was able in April 1965 to present a remarkable series of recitals on Sunday evenings after worship. Everything changed with the Hill, Norman and Beard installation of 1968. The inaugural recital by Pierre Cochereau was followed on 27 May 1969 by MacLean's own, the second part of which he devoted to the modern French literature. In December of that year the Halifax Centre of the Royal Canadian College of Organists held a series of organ recitals at Saint David's inaugurated by MacLean. He also inaugurated the Halifax Centre's series of Lenten organ recitals in March 1970. Francis Jackson, organist of York Minster, came to Saint David's in May of that year, while in June MacLean gave an organ recital to the General Assembly. Though Hamer was summoned to direct the music for the General Assembly, MacLean's contribution was critical. The rapport, even chemistry, between the maestros was evident to the minister.[33]

The Dutch virtuoso Feike Asma came in November 1977; Pierre Cochereau paid a return visit in April 1978; Graham Steed gave a recital in May 1980, and Maurice Clerc in April 1981. Throughout the 1970s especially, MacLean himself offered recitals on a regular basis. Of particular significance was the Reformation Sunday organ recital, which continued until 1986. In May of that year Saint David's hosted the "College Service" of the RCCO Halifax Centre, in which three choirs participated; MacLean, Stillman Matheson, and David MacDonald all played; and John Pace preached on "The sound of music." Recitals thereafter seemed to become less frequent but were revived in the the autumn of 1993. A monthly series of four was offered, MacLean inaugurating it on 26 September.

June 1991 witnessed the beginning of "Noon at Saint David's," a month-long weekly recital series by young or student musicians – instrumentalists, vocalists, and composers alike. This yearly offering was the brainchild of James Calkin, the youngest of a musical family; all four children had sung in the choir, and the eldest, Catherine, had been president. James, an organ performance major at Dalhousie, began organ studies with MacLean in 1987. In the summer of 1990 he became a student of David MacDonald, then director of music at First Baptist, Halifax. By the time Noon at Saint David's got underway, he had completed the first year of his bachelor of music program. In the spring of 1991 he was awarded the Halifax Ladies' Musical Club prize for most outstanding performance by a first-year student. He was organ soloist in the 1991 Stars of the Festival concert of the Nova Scotia Kiwanis Music Festival and also found time to play the organ at Brunswick Street United Church.

Calkin realized the importance of being able to run such a series and decided to try it on his own. He sought permission from Session, which was granted, and set about rallying his fellow music students to the challenge. His parents agreed to underwrite the cost of posters, advertising, and paid professional accompanists, but the idea and of most of the work was Calkin's. He launched the very first concert on 5 June 1991 and served as artistic director of Noon at Saint David's until his departure for Montreal and graduate study at McGill in 1994. After ten successful years, Noon at Saint David's expired in 2000. Nothing short of MacLean's own recitals had demonstrated so vividly the power and potential of, and the community's need and desire for, music at Saint David's. The music program put Saint David's on the map and has helped keep it there ever since.

12

Mission and Outreach

As early as November 1927, Saint David's held a reception for Presbyterian students in Halifax. The spiritual and social welfare of university students has always been a concern and a special feature of life and work at the church. In March 1931 spring Communion Sunday evening saw a special students' service, sponsored by the local Student Christian Movement, at which elder H.L. Stewart preached on "The university and the church."

Colin Kerr was also interested in the Oxford Group Movement – alias "Buchmanism" or "Moral Rearmament" – and preached an evening sermon on the subject in January 1933. The Oxford Group Movement, begun at Oxford University in 1921, pioneered group therapy – the collective discussion of personal problems as a means of religious and spiritual development. Kerr himself was on stress leave in Bermuda in April 1934 when Frank N.D. Buchman and forty of his retainers descended on Protestant Halifax, a blitz sponsored by the Halifax and Dartmouth Ministerial Association that saw OGM representatives mount every Halifax pulpit except the conservative West End Baptist. That autumn Kerr preached a series of sermons aimed at students and young people in which he seems to have argued that Christianity was a challenge to the OGM, rather than vice versa. He preached on "Guidance and the Group Movement" again in March 1935. Nearly fifty years later John Pace reprised the theme in his sermon series "Jesus and logotherapy."

In February 1935 Kerr preached a series of two sermons on "The church and social problems," in them setting forth his concept of Christian social action: "Those then that pin their faith on the social gospel as the solution for this world's ills are really putting Christ's second commandment before the first … The chief need of the world today is that it be delivered from mere humanism and that it return into the Lord."[1] Shortly after war was declared in September 1939, Kerr held special meetings with the various organizations to address the role Saint David's was to play in promoting the social and spiritual welfare of troops stationed in and around Halifax. As the war progressed, there would be more and more of them, and the demands on the congregation's resources would increase commensurately.

The first organization to respond to this "call to arms" was Saint David's PYPS. In October 1939 the PYPS began to sponsor a post–evening service social hour ("singsong") aimed at military personnel in uniform and merchant mariners but open to everyone. This initiative was extremely popular. It was noted with pride one Sunday evening in April 1942 that "practically all the Provinces of Canada were represented." Among them was Sapper Allister Godfrey of Belleville, Ontario, who penned these verses, afterwards the subject of a drawing by Halifax *Herald* cartoonist Robert W. Chambers:

St David's Hall
Spr. E.A. Godfrey

In Halifax there stands a hall,
Saint David's Church folk own it,
A favorite young folks meeting place
For all the ones who've known it.

You'll find a welcome there, that's sure,
No matter what you're wearing,
They have a lot of good clean fun,
And that is what they're sharing.

A stranger in this city finds
At first, it's dull and dreary,
But come out to these meetings, and
You'll find a welcome cheery.

It matters not from whence you came,
Or where you go tomorrow,
The young folk of Saint David's Hall
Will help to banish sorrow.

Do you like fun, to romp and run?
You like to see some beauty,
Come right along, that isn't wrong,
In fact, should be a duty.

When you're alone, and far from home,
And slow the days are turning,
Don't stew and fret, come out and get
A little bit of learning.

So many thanks to you, my friends,
The best of luck for ever,
May words of cheer come to your ear,
And trouble find you never.

So successful was the singsong/social hour that the PYPS had to set up a special committee reporting separately from the parent organization. At its height in 1943, the social hour was attended by a total of 4,164 persons. Seeing the need and sensing the potential, other organizations and the congregation at large threw their weight behind the PYPS and both assisted materially and gave moral support. As the chair of the committee observed in his report for that year, "These figures show more than anything else the work our own Church is doing for these people who have no homes in Halifax and want to spend their Sunday evenings in a friendly and Christian atmosphere."[2] Kerr may well have fretted about the propriety of entertaining servicemen on the Lord's Day and striking the proper balance in ministering to their spiritual and social welfare. But war is a young man's game, and many were between life and death. In 2003 Saint David's received a letter from a woman in Toronto whose twenty-two-year-old brother, William Alexander Rose, a gunner in the Royal Canadian Naval Volunteer Reserve, was lost in March 1941 on his first tour across the Atlantic. In it she spoke of how her only brother, Bill, had been befriended by a prominent Saint David's family, the Palmeters.[3]

THE LAWSON PASTORATE

What began during the war continued after it, though on a reduced scale and aimed specifically at young people. Frank Lawson came to Saint David's four months after war's end determined that it should have an effective program of local mission and outreach, especially to young adults. Afterwards briefly renamed the Westminster Fellowship, Open Doors proved popular. Lawson's particular inspiration was a weekly schedule of distinguished guest speakers from the workaday world. A discussion on "Communism and Christianity" led by Lawson and Bruce Fergusson, the assistant provincial archivist, was one of the highlights of the program for 1947–48.[4] Lawson sought to reach out to youth by engaging their attention and educating them in spite of themselves. The Westminster Fellowship combined socializing with thoughtful discussion of the day's headlines, such as the "Margaret-Townsend crisis" – whether HRH Princess Margaret, the Queen's younger sister, should marry a divorced commoner (she did not).

Lawson also came to Saint David's determined to realize his vision of mission and outreach as evangelism. The bulletin of 26 October 1947 announced, "A canvas of the homes in this area will be made by the people of this church in a few weeks … Every church should serve the area where it is situated. The souls in this area are our responsibility. This is a planned piece of home mission work to gather in the unchurched." The opening of the new hall in October 1951 made possible a more ambitious and varied program. In the autumn of 1951 Lawson brought up the question of work among underprivileged youth in the immediate vicinity of Saint David's. He thought that since the church now had sufficient facilities, some type of weekday program might be instituted.[5] Such was the genesis of the weekly after-school for inner-city children ("our first serious attempt to do a piece of Mission work in the crowded area where our Church stands").[6] By February 1952 the bulletin could report, "Our picture hour and song service for the children of the community held every Wednesday at four is doing quite well. Miss MacCausland [deaconess] is in charge."

The irony of the situation was lost on no one: the richest downtown church sitting cheek by jowl with one of the poorest and most densely populated of downtown neighbourhoods. This Wednesday Afternoon Mission School was inaugurated in cooperation with Acadian (established 1915), the Protestant public school nearest the church. "On Albemarle," writes historian Judith Fingard, "the school catered to the poor children of the slums."[7] In the heyday of Halifax as a garrison town, Albemarle Street (renamed Market in 1917) was the heart of the red-light district.

Demand for a place in the mission school was heavy; beginning with about 70, the school at its height in 1960 served as many as 110 children. The teaching staff was drawn from progressive women in the congregation, chief among them Agnes Leaman, who took over as superintendent after

Deaconess Estelle MacCausland was assigned to extension work in Dartmouth in May 1952. Particularly noteworthy was that the church officer (custodian) provided operational support.[8] The children were fed, entertained, and evangelized. Beginning in 1959, the school sent a group of its enrollees to Synod's summer camp (Camp Geddie) near Merigomish in Pictou County.

The Wednesday Afternoon Mission School continued to thrive until the population base that it served disappeared. In 1962 the school collapsed almost overnight, the victim of changed demographics. In April 1959 the city school board announced that Acadian School would close after the 1960–61 year, when redevelopment of the slums would have moved children to the Mulgrave Park housing estate in the North End.[9] "With the change in the population in the neighbourhood of our church," ran the final report, "the attendance at the Mission School during the winter of 1962 was very small."[10] It did not reopen in the autumn. Some forty years after the school ceased, a former worker in it was recognized and stopped on the street by an "alumnus" to be told how much the experience had meant to this person as a child.[11]

Other than a two-week summer-vacation Bible class conducted by Roberta Shaw, there was no further activity until May 1963. Saint David's hosted a one-day seminar on evangelism and social action led by the secretary of the church's board of that name (established 1945), now part of the Life and Mission Agency.[12] Frank Lawson, ever kicking against the goad, was conspicuous by his absence. His response came the following month, when he preached a five-part series of evening sermons on "Christian witness in a secular society." By Christian witness, Lawson did not mean social action; faith could not be made alive by works. Nor did he mean evangelism as the Board of Evangelism conceived it. Evangelism *was* Christian witness, pure and simple; social action did not enter into it. Evangelism and social action may not have been mutually exclusive, but there was no connection, much less a relationship, between them. It was like mixing apples and oranges. Evangelism *and* social action was a compromise with the secularism of the secular world in which Christian witness had to take place.

THE MACKAY PASTORATE

Lawson's concept of evangelism as social action was different from Session's, and so nothing further could be done until his departure. In 1967 Saint David's joined the Morris Project, a collaborative effort of the

South End churches. Its support group was initially chaired by the director of Christian education, Deaconess Emily Drysdale. This summertime play-school was based at Morris Street School, where some former Acadian pupils had been transferred. Its purpose was to develop "social resources" for the needs of young people in that part of the city. By the spring of 1970 it was providing a "Tot-Lot" for preschoolers, a youth club, and a supervised study centre. Initially, Saint David's people figured prominently, especially elder T.K. Guildford, his daughter Janet, and Shaw's successor, Drysdale. The Morris Project survived for twenty years, on a gradually diminishing scale.[13]

In the autumn of 1968 Saint David's joined an ecumenical consortium of local churches – Roman Catholic, Anglican, and United – which estab-lished Nova Scotia's first group home for boys. Planning began in 1965 when the Children's Aid Society of Halifax asked the local Welfare Council to assess the needs of emotionally disturbed teenagers in the psychiatric hospital. It was recommended that the CAS attempt to establish a "group home," then a new concept intermediate between institutionalization and fostering which has since become a staple of social and community ser-vices. The idea was taken up by the South End churches and especially by St Andrew's United, which had a long tradition of social-welfare outreach. In 1968, to mark the United Nations' International Human Rights Year, St Andrew's established a human rights committee. Such determination to give "visible evidence of respect for human rights" moved well beyond practical Christianity and was a new concept among mainstream Halifax churches. The proposal was brought to a joint meeting of the Session and Trustees of Saint David's in October 1968 and then came before a special congregational meeting as a joint recommendation from both bodies. Saint David's agreed to fund the group home project up to a maximum of $6,000.

The Interchurch Group Home for Boys opened in March 1969. Its overall success resulted from a commitment to meet a specific, identified need that hospitals and conventional family homes could not. Under the terms of the consortium agreement, the churches involved purchased a building on Oxford Street in Halifax (renamed Genesis House in January 1989). The Children's Aid Society managed and operated the home, using it as a treatment centre. The United Way contributed towards operating expenses, while the provincial Department of Public Welfare covered the costs of the residents.[14]

Elder Herbert K. Mosher was among the incorporators, and thereafter two representatives came from among the trustees. Gloria Mader, the final secretary-treasurer, was the longest-serving trustee, while Michael de la Ronde, chair of Trustees at Saint David's, was for several years chair of the board of the home. In 1999 the Children's Aid Society decided to cease operating Genesis House as a group home for youth in care and was replaced on an interim basis by the provincial Department of Community Services. It was almost with a sense of relief that Saint David's responded to an offer from one of the six partners to buy out the others. The deal was finalized in 2004, and Saint David's reclaimed its 10 per cent share on the sale of the facility to St Paul's Home, at five times the original investment.

There was more to mission and outreach than spending money out of doors. In 1969, the same year the Interchurch Group Home for Boys opened, the report of the General Assembly's special committee on life and mission, *Into the 70s in Life and Mission*, was issued. On the cusp of its centenary decade, The Presbyterian Church in Canada was more bastion than beacon; the punctuation mark at the end of the final line of the report said it all: "Planning for mission in the 70s?" In line with the spirit of the LAMP report, Session in February 1969 asked the Christian Education Committee "to do the initial spadework preparatory to establishing a special Committee to study the whole position of the Church in this changing world."[15]

Session's move was provoked, if a little belatedly, by the controversial address given by the Reverend Dr Joseph McClelland, a professor at Presbyterian College, Montreal, at the pre-Assembly congress in June 1967, in which he accused the church of congregationalism and irrelevance. Though McClelland was roundly condemned, Saint David's showed considerable interest when excerpts from McClelland's address ("Blueprint for the Church") appeared in the *Presbyterian Record* and a tape recording of it was played in the church hall after evening service on 23 February 1969. Further stimulus was given on 9 March by the exchange preacher, Wrenfred Bryant, minister of Cornwallis Street (African) Baptist Church and a convinced social activist. His sermon posed the question, "Where is your brother?"

A "resources" committee of Session was duly put in place, but there was uncertainty as to the nature, purpose, and scope of any direct action that might be taken. The initiative did not enjoy the support of the minister or the clerk of Session, and by then, the Lawsonites were a minority in Session. The new special committee was not so much as mentioned in the annual report or the bulletin. For D.B. Mackay and Ralph Kane, Christian education meant training youth to become Christians, not training Christians to become social activists. Kane, and no doubt many others, thought that the church's mission was to evangelize through preaching and worship, and that money was better spent on building congregations. Others thought that social service was a more effective form of evangelism than preaching and worship. It was an old quandary. Those who remembered the Disruption knew perfectly well that behind the church union movement lay the social gospel – practical as opposed to spiritual Christianity.

In February 1970 a twelve-person Encounter team, a panel of experts on social and economic development, came to Halifax to meet with citizen action groups; they included local clergy in their consultations. A Black American team member, the Reverend Lucius Walker Jr, who was both a Baptist minister and a social worker, characterized the clergy's platitudinous response as "a picture of pious irrelevance."[16] City churches in general came in for some very bad press on account of their failure either to acknowledge the need for or to focus on Christian social action. But planning for action was going on behind the scenes.

In March James Hayes, the Roman Catholic archbishop of Halifax, announced the formation of a non-profit ecumenical housing corporation.[17] The slums had relocated from the downtown to the north suburbs, where slum landlords continued to flourish. Among those leading the charge against them was Alderman David MacKeen, a sometime trustee of Saint David's. No sooner had Archbishop Hayes made his announcement than the Reverend A.E. Morrison, superintendent of missions for the Atlantic Synod, published in a Halifax newspaper an "op-ed" scoring the church for being out of touch with the needs of the people and failing to advance beyond "denominational housekeeping."[18] Morrison's fellow progressive A.O. MacLean, minister of Calvin Presbyterian and then moderator of Presbytery, was involved in the discussions that led to the launch of the Interfaith Housing Corporation; but Presbytery itself, in order to participate officially, had first to raise the $1,000 necessary for a share. The IHC was incorporated in January 1971 and for a decade functioned "as a non-profit developer of new housing and as a housing resource group" for low-income families. Saint David's gave to it both a manager – Jim Duke (T.K. Guildford's then son-in-law) – and a director-treasurer – elder Kenneth A. Mader. Another Presbyterian, Howard Jack of Iona Church, was director and president.[19]

"We are living in a changing world," Ralph Kane wrote of the jubilee year, 1975, "and this is affecting not only our secular but also our spiritual life. The Session is aware of this changing pattern and its influence on the work and witness of the Church both at present and in the future."[20] Saint David's had been drifting if not floundering, and the centenary was a not unwelcome distraction. After an entire year spent celebrating the past and ignoring the present, the question – what of the future? – loomed large on the near horizon.

THE PACE PASTORATE AND BEYOND

The advent of John Pace, who had spent the previous six years in social work, seemed to point the way forward. In his pastoral letter of December 1976, Pace suggested that the first step towards playing a constructive role in the world was to build a "caring community" within the walls. Christian social action was not an end in itself and had no credibility if Christians could not be seen to be practising care and loving-kindness among themselves.[21]

It was a theme that Pace reprised throughout the next ten years. Like Lawson before him, he envisaged a large role for Saint David's in Halifax, extending well beyond social service and conventional evangelism to encompass public humanistic education. This was outreach in the broadest sense: the church as good citizen and contributor to the well-being of society at large. If Lawson was a Christian socialist, then Pace was more a believer in Christian social science. For Pace, a student of the Russian existentialist religious philosopher Nicolas Berdyaev,[22] the ultimate purpose of outreach was not to evangelize individuals but to create a Christian society.

Pace set out his fourfold "dream of service" in a sermon entitled "The human enterprise," delivered on New Year's Sunday, 1982, and printed in the annual congregational report for 1981. He dreamed of a church more accessible to seniors, better programs aimed at the Christian family unit, a more diversified ministry to serve community as well as congregation, and an enlightened denominationalism that did not allow Presbyterian tradition to get in the way of Christian witness. Proud as he was to have made up in three years the ground lost in seven, Pace was nevertheless unable to realize his dream of employing a social worker or psychologist to work out of Saint David's. His vision required focused effort as well as money, and it was easier to throw money at social problems than to take direct action with a view to helping to solve them.

The annual congregational meeting in January 1980 saw the establishment of a committee for human rights whose task it was to identify worthwhile causes to support. A year later, three "good works" were approved: the hot-lunch program of Cornwallis Street United Baptist Church – $10,000 over two years; the Emergency Shelter for Adolescent Girls (Children's Aid Society) – $5,000; and Foster Parents' Plan of Canada – $1,104 a year for three years to enable the Church School to "adopt" four children. Three special projects became four in 1982, when $3,000 over three years was committed to the local YMCA to help finance an expansion of its facilities.

An emergency shelter for teenaged girls had existed from 1977 to 1980, and the Children's Aid Society spent the next three years trying to replace it. In August 1983, however, the CAS had to abandon its attempt for want of government funding. Some twenty years later, the Interchurch Group Home would have gone the same way had not one of the church agency partners taken it over when government support was withdrawn. Despite everything, the concept of the church as social agency persisted at Saint David's. A nursing student from Dalhousie University arrived in 1983 to carry out her practicum in community nursing. The arrangement was repeated in 1984.

By the mid-1980s, organized outreach at Saint David's had ceased altogether for lack of interest or resources or both. After 1985, the Kirk Session review does not mention any home missionary endeavour. Session had a local missions committee (afterwards renamed "community outreach"), but there is no evidence of activity. Resources, both human and financial, were fewer, and Saint David's itself too needful and preoccupied with internal matters to mount ambitious programs. It was an age of redistribution and retrenchment, not expansion. Direct social action continued within the women's organizations, as it had always done, and flourished there.

It was not until 2001 that mission project planning on a broad scale resumed. Helen M. Watson, a retired public health nurse and pillar of Saint David's from her youth, died leaving one-third of her $1 million estate to Saint David's to be "used exclusively for local missionary work in Nova Scotia." This bequest led to a number of initiatives, most significantly the opening of "David's Place," a partnership between Saint David's and the Victorian Order of Nurses of Greater Halifax. The VON provides a nurse for three hours a week, while Saint David's contributes facilities and volunteers. This Friday morning program is a wellness clinic in the broadest sense. Each visitor is welcomed without assumptions or prejudgment, addressed by name, and in every way treated with the respect due a fellow child of God. Saint David's volunteers serve the guests and visit with them, while the VON health professional provides basic care and counsel.

Fifty years after the first serious attempt to do mission work in the grimy area where Saint David's stands, once one of the city's worst slums, Presbyterian social action underwent a new birth. Everything else had changed, but the poor were still with us. Late in Frank Lawson's pastorate, after the Wednesday Afternoon Mission School ended, a newish elder with a social conscience had proposed an initiative similar to David's Place, only to have the minister veto it.[23] For Lawson, always skeptical about social action disconnected from evangelism, the imminence of the kingdom of God meant that the poor had the gospel preached to them.

13

Voluntary Organizations

All the non-essential organizations at Saint David's have, in their bewildering variety, contributed to its development as a congregation and its formation as a community. The second issue of its short-lived *Monthly Magazine* (November 1932) featured by way of "Notes on the Societies" a snapshot of current activity of the Ladies Guild, the Badminton Club, the Young People's Society, the Trail Rangers (for young teenaged boys), and the Young Ladies Guild. "The Guild are at present engaged in sewing for the needy, especially for those among whom Miss Lena Fraser is working at the port [of Halifax]. Many who are being deported are without sufficient clothing." It was an age of xenophobia and anti-Communist hysteria in which prospective immigrants from eastern Europe were being turned away as undesirable aliens. Some were even being successfully prosecuted in order to justify their deportation.

THE WOMAN'S MISSIONARY SOCIETY

By far the most prestigious women's organization was also the first to organize. The Woman's Missionary Society auxiliary came into existence a week *before* the congregation and lasted fifty years. The WMS was the oldest women's organization in the church, and in the autumn of 1924 the WMS Eastern Division led the Disruption in the Maritimes Synod. Between the establishment of the provisional continuing synod in October 1924 and the coming into force of the United Church of Canada Act in June 1925, no organization stood in higher esteem among non-uniting minority Presbyterians than the WMS. While the Halifax Presbyterian Church Association was hardly large enough to have its own Women's League,[1] the WMS supported the Halifax PCA financially. It was important for the continuation of the church – especially in areas such as metropolitan Halifax, where there were no continuing congregations and therefore no continuing WMS auxiliaries – that the WMS should organize an auxiliary and a presbyterial as speedily as possible.

Formed on 19 February 1925 by the WMS Eastern Division's president, Mrs L.A. (Mary R.) Moore, the Halifax auxiliary met regularly every month. The first executive had seven vice-presidents, each representing the auxiliary of a "lost" congregation. March saw the organization of a junior WMS auxiliary. Early in July, at a Presbyterian women's conference at Grafton Street Church, a WMS presbyterial was organized representing the former presbyteries of Halifax and Lunenburg-Yarmouth.

In April 1926 the WMS took responsibility for employing the Presbyterian port secretary, Deaconess Lena Fraser, who, as chaplain to immigrants, was the church's official representative at the Ocean Terminals "immigration shed" (Pier 21). The big event of 1926, however, was the WMS Eastern Division's golden jubilee celebration at Saint David's in September. It seemed especially fitting that the WMS, born at St Matthew's in Halifax in 1876, should meet at the home of the new congregation which continued the church in Halifax. The moderator of the General Assembly came down in person to offer the thanks of the whole Church to Presbyterian women of the Maritimes.[2] The WMS Eastern Division convened at Saint David's again in September 1931; five years later the diamond jubilee meeting was held there, as was the seventy-fourth (1950), which saw a woman of Saint David's, Blanche (Redmond) Teasdale, elected president. In September 1966 and again in 1982, the Eastern Division returned to Saint David's for its annual meeting. By then the local auxiliary had expired.

In 1929 a mission band[3] was organized and named in honour of the retiring president of the Eastern Division – the Mary R. Moore Mission Band. By 1943, however, the junior auxiliary had disappeared altogether, and the mission band had been but briefly resurrected. Though the more active Saint David's women were members of both organizations, during the war the Ladies Guild overtook the WMS as the service club of choice ("A small percentage of the women of St David's congregation belong to the Missionary Society").[4] In the autumn of 1947 the WMS junior auxiliary was resurrected. The late Janet Fraser Andrews, in whose memory the new organization was to be named "The Janet Andrews Missionary Group," had been the wife of a former member of Session. The Janet Andrews, which affiliated with the WMS in 1948, operated largely independently of the senior auxiliary, which by the early 1950s was in decline.[5]

Attrition was slowly killing the WMS – senior in more ways than one – and there was not room or need for two missionary auxiliaries. By 1970, when Mary Jane Mackay was president of the Halifax and Lunenburg presbyterial, conventional missionary work both at home and abroad had been supplanted by home helpers, a transition that Mrs Mackay probably supported. In 1976, the Eastern Division's centenary, the Saint David's senior WMS auxiliary formally disbanded. The Janet Andrews, which continued to flourish, became the WMS at Saint David's. In September 1987 the Woman's Missionary Society Eastern Division changed its name to the Atlantic Mission Society (AMS).

By the 1990s the Janet Andrews was suffering the same fate as its predecessor. The ranks were being depleted but not replenished; intergenerational transition was impossible. Saint David's was not big enough to accommodate the AMS, the Ladies Guild, and, from 1981, the Saint David's Auxiliary. By April 2001 the Janet Andrews was unable to fill all the executive positions required in order to be an auxiliary in good standing of the Halifax-Lunenburg presbyterial and so decided to become Home Helpers. The following year its éminence grise, Mary Jane Beattie (formerly Mrs D.B. Mackay), died and in 2003 the Janet Andrews disbanded; seventy-eight years of WMS history at Saint David's came mutely to an end. But the presbyterial that had been founded there carried on.

THE LADIES GUILD

The Women's Working Society, as the Ladies Guild was originally known, came into existence in April 1925, shortly after the Presbyterians took possession of Grafton Street Church. The timing was not coincidental; without dedicated premises, there was little women church workers could do to build the infrastructure of the new congregation. The Ladies Guild began as one women's organization among others and was by no means the *primus inter pares*. Over the years, however, it became the most important voluntary organization in Saint David's. It has also outlasted all the other women's groups, of which, at their peak in the early postwar years, there were as many as five.

Women's working societies began to appear in The Presbyterian Church in Canada after 1897 in order to support both the home mission work of deaconesses and congregational operations, temporal and spiritual alike. Women could not be managers, let alone elders, but they could work in aid of both. Their mandate was as broad as the identified need. From the very beginning, the efforts of the Ladies Guild were directed to both Christian social action and pastoral visitation, on one hand, and operational support to the congregation, on the other. None of the Guild's forty-eight charter members would have come from congregations without women's working societies, and each adult female member or adherent of the new congregation was invited and expected to join the Guild. Being a woman and being there imposed the obligation.

The Guild met weekly, on Monday afternoons, and no defined group within the church set to work sooner or worked harder or more constructively. The Guild began its rise to pre-eminence as early as 1926, when the minister's wife became honorary president, a tradition that survived for seventy years. This was thanks not so much to Mrs Kerr's hosting afternoon teas at the manse as to her participating substantively in the Guild's work by taking the post of treasurer – a tradition that did *not* continue. The name "Women's Guild," in use for a few years, no doubt reflects the influence of Mrs Kerr. The Presbyterian Church in Canada never had a national women's organization, but the Kirk in Scotland did: the Woman's Guild.

The Ladies Guild soon developed and has sustained an enviable reputation for catering for any occasion, whether solemn, such as funerals, or merely social. One afternoon in October 1927, for example, it gave a dinner to the entire congregation. Yet there has been much more to its work than serving tables. The Guild's first constitution, adopted in 1926, provided that 25 per cent of its capital be reserved "for general Church or emergency purposes." The idea for an annual autumn fete (now the Holly Tea and Sale) was successfully tested as early as November 1927. Over the years it became the guild's chief fundraiser.

By the autumn of 1932, as the Depression deepened and the congregation's financial position deteriorated, the chair of the Board was reduced to going cap in hand to a meeting of the Guild, where he was assured that it would raise money for the congregation.[6] In January 1941 the Guild turned over to the Board a large sum to help reduce the mortgage on the church. By October 1942 the mortgage, which at one point stood as high as $53,000, was ready for burning – thanks in no small measure to the Guild's "incessant labours" at debt reduction. Over the years, the Guild has made numerous one-off contributions to defray operating expenses, the largest being $19,500 in 1997 for reconstruction of the driveway. In 1992 the Guild gave $10,000 as the first instalment of an investment fund, the revenue from which was to "be used for the repair and maintenance of the church building proper."[7]

The perception of the Ladies Guild as cash cow led to interest in ex officio representation on the Board. The idea finally came to fruition in 1972, when the Guild treasurer was appointed; it soon lapsed – until 1996, when the Guild gave $11,000 to the Trustees. The following year the president of Guild joined the Trustees, within months was elected an elder, and then served two regular terms as a trustee. The following Guild presidents did likewise.

The Ladies Guild is the only organization at Saint David's, other than the official ones, to have had a continuous existence since 1925. The secret of its longevity was revealed in 1968 by its then secretary, Edith Mosher (afterwards elder): "we are the main working body and fundraising group in the church."[8] In 1984 the Guild, at the instigation of its indefatigable convener of work, Kathleen "Boofie" Chisholm (afterwards elder), became involved in Hope Cottage, a soup kitchen for street people. This has remained the most important but least celebrated of the Guild's outreach programs.

Few of the Guild's activities have been exclusively mission-oriented, and it was the achievement of Boofie Chisholm to broaden the focus of the Guild's direct action: to be to the wide world what it was to Saint David's. Hitherto its outreach had largely consisted of charitable donations to good causes, Saint David's itself being the neediest of all and the principal beneficiary of the Guild's largesse. Chisholm aggressively promoted the Christmas Families initiative, which commenced in 1991 with Chisholm herself as co-coordinator. In 1986 she inaugurated the Lenten chowder luncheons, which have since become the highlight of the Guild's outreach program and a downtown Halifax mid-winter institution.[9]

The chowder luncheons take place each Wednesday noon during the seven weeks of Lent. The recipe is based on the one used by the IODE at its tearoom on Citadel Hill in the 1940s and 1950s. The menu has remained the same since the luncheons began in 1986. It consists of a haddock-based chowder served with a roll and a dessert of homemade gingerbread topped with whipped cream or lemon sauce, followed by tea or coffee. In twenty years the price of admission has doubled from $3.50 to $7.00. Takeout and delivery service are available on request. This event serves hundreds of people each year and is an important fundraiser for the Guild.

The Guild's efforts to recruit younger, single women proved largely unsucessful – for economic reasons. Such women were either in college or had to work for a living and were not available on Monday afternoons, when the Guild used to meet each month. Nevertheless, the Guild enables women of Saint David's to gather in a social setting for fellowship, conversation, and the exchange of ideas. It meets on the first Monday of each month, September through May, in the church hall. Meetings commence with the Lesser Doxology (Gloria Patri) and the Lord's Prayer. A business meeting follows and then a social hour, when tea and light refreshments are served. Occasionally a guest speaker is invited to address the meetings.

The executive consists of a president, first and second vice-presidents, treasurer, recording secretary, and corresponding secretary. There are a number of committee conveners who look after publicity, kitchen, visitation, receptions, and telephone contact with members. The Guild continues to be represented on the Local Council of Women. In 2004 there were thirty on the membership roll, of whom twenty-four took part in all or some of the activities. Most fundraising done by the Guild is for the benefit of Saint David's. Each year money is given directly to the Trustees for use as needed. The Guild donates money to the Church School to fund annual prizes for attendance and for other, incidental needs that may arise. An annual donation is made to Camp Geddie, the synod's youth camp.

Charitable donations also form part of the Guild's outreach work, which focuses especially on non-profit organizations dealing with the needs of disadvantaged women and children. In 2004, for example, nine charitable organizations received financial assistance from the Guild. For two years the Guild assisted a young single mother studying in the School of Dentistry at Dalhousie University by paying for her textbooks and transportation costs. Early in 2005 a special donation was made to the disaster relief fund set up by Presbyterian World Service and Development for the survivors of the tsunami that devastated parts of southeast Asia.

Guild members cater for special events taking place at the church. These include a luncheon for members and adherents attending the annual congregational meeting, luncheons for visiting dignitaries, funerals, and receptions. Two months a year Guild members take their turn serving coffee and pastries to worshippers after service. Formerly, every six weeks the Guild organized and arranged the delivery of stew to Hope Cottage, which depends on local church organizations to supply food for the hot meals served each day to needy people.

A flea market is usually held once a year. Other fundraisers include the preparation of turkey pies for sale. Each year since the 1980s plum puddings have been assemblied for sale. Attractively wrapped in red cellophane, they are enjoyed at Christmas by many local people and circulate as popular gifts all over North America. Since the early 1990s the holiday season has also featured "Christmas Families" – the purchase of gifts and ingredients for Christmas dinner for a set number of disadvantaged families. Though the event is organized and coordinated by the Guild, it is thrown open to the congregation, and many members and adherents enthusiastically take part, "adopting" a Christmas family and buying gifts and wrapping them.

The Holly Tea and Sale, which takes place in November and features a Christmas theme, is the high point of the Guild's year. When it began in

1927, the tea and sale was a socially formal occasion. There was a receiving line, tea was poured from silver tea services, and all who took part dressed in their Sunday best. Most of the women who attended wore fur coats, gloves, and hats to complement their afternoon dresses or suits. Both the dress code and the format have changed with the times; now people wear whatever is comfortable, tea is served from carafes, and the receiving line has long since disappeared. There are still handcrafted knitwear and home baking for sale, however, and a delicious tea complete with sandwiches and sweets is served. New additions are the silent auction, picture gallery, scarf and accessory boutique, and a table at which dried flowers, herbs, and other delectables from the garden of a former Guild president are offered for sale.

The Ladies Guild has always been to some extent a home missionary society, and the range and diversity of its activities and appeal has meant that it was always able to replenish its numbers. It was fortunate not to be saddled with too long and too glorious a history. Even in 1925 the best years of the Woman's Missionary Society, the senior organization, were behind it. Though it survived a self-induced disruption in its own ranks, the WMS was largely irrelevant after 1925. When eldership and ministry were thrown open to women in 1966, the WMS, which had opposed the move, was sidelined. Where the United Church was able to turn its WMS into a national organization (United Church Women), The Presbyterian Church in Canada continued to live in a past where the WMS existed for the purpose of giving Presbyterian churchwomen some useful work to do. The Ladies Guild, on the other hand, has always made a virtue of necessity, changing with circumstances and remaining supremely relevant.

OTHER WOMEN'S ORGANIZATIONS

There have been three other women's organizations at Saint David's: the Evening Circle (ca. 1939), the Friendship Group (1945), and the Saint David's Auxiliary (1981). The origins of the Evening Circle, first known as the Ladies Home Circle, are obscure; neither minutes of its meetings nor annual reports previous to 1943 exist. Its primary purpose was "to contact and become acquainted with ladies who are strangers in our Church."[10] The Evening Circle survived until 1959, along the way giving two stained glass windows to Saint David's.

The Friendship Group, which had an informal beginning in the autumn of 1945, was the Evening Circle for younger women. According to the bulletin of 11 November, the prime mover behind the group was Mrs

Russell Yates Finley, whose husband became an elder in 1946. Its first annual report declared, "We have pledged ourselves to no hard and fast rules, but to help wherever and whenever the need arises in the Church." The Friendship Group made itself useful to other societies and to the congregation at large. For years, it mounted an annual spring variety show. The group survived until December 1994, when neither the president nor the secretary, both long-serving, could be replaced. The disbanding of the Friendship Group was announced at the annual congregational meeting in January 1995, prompting the minister to remark on "the wonderful fellowship which had been a hallmark of this group" for nearly fifty years.

February 1952 saw the establishment of the New Member Group, its main purpose being to introduce young women to each other. "Halifax can be a lonely place; we hope to make it easier for the strangers within our gates to gather in each others' homes, and enjoy each others' company."[11] Quickly expanding its remit into areas subsequently covered by the Saint David's Auxiliary, in December 1954 the New Member Group renamed itself the Junior Guild. The second organization of that name, it, unlike the first, had no connection with the Ladies Guild. Chief among the many interests of the Junior Guild were the Church School and the Sunday morning nursery.

In 1959 the scope of the nursery school program expanded beyond its original function of child-minding to include rudimentary Christian education ("the children are responding very favourably to this innovation"). This initiative, however, tended to encroach on the prerogatives of the Church School, and in 1961 the Junior Guild went into hiatus again, reappearing the following year as the "Evening Guild"; it disbanded in 1964. There was no further activity for seventeen years. In 1981 Betty Hatfield (elder, 1984) came up with the idea that led to the establishment of the Saint David's Auxiliary. Just as the Friendship Group signified intergenerational transition from the Evening Circle, so too did the Saint David's Auxiliary from the Friendship Group. All three organizations in their day served much the same purpose: a constructive alternative to the Ladies Guild for younger single or working women.

The bulletin for 25 October 1981 announced under the heading "Junior Guild" that "this new group" would hold its inaugural meeting in ten days' time. The president of the Ladies Guild attended the organizational meeting on 4 November and reported that this "working and church-oriented group … have the wholehearted support and cooperation of the Guild as we look forward to increased interest and activity."[12] The choice of name was not accidental. The Saint David's Auxiliary was not the "Younger Ladies Guild" but an auxiliary of the whole congregation, a parallel and alternative women's organizaton. Officially established on 3 February 1982, it had as its mandate to "contribute to the well-being of the Church through the promotion of fellowship, and provide special projects and services."

Some special tasks, such as decorating the sanctuary for Christmas, were delegated by the Ladies Guild, though attending to floral arrangements in the chancel remained the exclusive preserve of the Guild. The Auxiliary's inaugural project and greatest achievement, however, was reviving the newsletter, defunct since 1979. *Happenings at Saint David's*, the fourth of the congregation's five newsletters, first appeared late in 1982. It was dedicated to the venerable Mamie Withrow Hutton, superintendent of the Cradle Roll in the Church School since 1944 and, despite advancing years, still teaching in the junior school. *Happenings at Saint David's* became an annual in 1984, but two years later it abruptly ceased publication. There would not be another congregational newsletter for fifteen years.[13]

Where the Evening Circle and the Friendship Group emphasized ministry to the congregation, the Auxiliary focused on outreach to the community. Among its most active members during the early years was the new lay assistant, Judithe Adam, whose friend Claire Thomson was the group's second president. In 1986 the Auxiliary helped to revamp the nursery, adding capacity for infants as well as toddlers. In keeping with Ladies Guild and Evening Circle tradition, in November 1988 the Auxiliary published *Saint David's Cooks*. "This women's group," declared the preface, "is active in several congregational and community outreach projects and undertakes study sessions to develop an awareness of local and world social conditions." In 1991 the Auxiliary offered both a Valentine's Day dinner and an autumn luncheon. The Harvest (Thanksgiving) event did not survive, but in 1994 the Valentine's Day dinner mutated into the Anniversary Sunday luncheon. In November 2001 the Auxiliary celebrated its twentieth anniversary.[14]

Small in numbers by comparison with the Ladies Guild, Saint David's Auxiliary is nevertheless a true "friendship group," focused and cohesive. Though its work has complemented that of the Guild, the spheres are kept strictly separate. Members of the Auxiliary have resisted perceiving themselves, or encouraging others to perceive them, as prospective graduates into the Ladies Guild. As recently as 2004, the Auxiliary had to lay to rest the "undying perception" that the time had come for the Auxiliary to go the way of the WMS, the Evening Circle, and the Friendship Group and be collapsed into the Guild. The Auxiliary's coordinators used the annual congregational report to remind Saint David's that they were happy with keeping their own structure and identity. Saint David's Auxiliary, after all, has never been the "junior guild," and it has already lasted longer than either of the other organizations which bore that name.

MEN OF SAINT DAVID'S — "SERVIMUS"

An embryonic men's club may have existed as early as 1926, and a men's banquet was held in April 1927. In October of that year the secretary of the PCC's General Board of Missions addressed a presbytery-wide men's conference at Saint David's encouraging them to organize. Symbolically at least, men's work may be considered to have begun one evening in February 1929, when the men gave a dinner to some two hundred Presbyterian Church women.[15] Presided over by the chair of the Board, the dinner was a significant exercise in gender role reversal that led by slow degrees to the foundation of the Men's Club nine years later.

There have been a dozen women's organizations at Saint David's to one men's. Women's organizations proliferated because there was nothing else for women to do. Men already held all the responsibility and made all the decisions. Women's organizations existed as mere surrogates for "the Real Thing" – authority. Women's organizations began to decline only after women were declared eligible for election as elders and managers. With the exception of married couples' badminton, adult "coed" organizations were unheard of until the late 1970s. The Men's Club was not a working society like the Ladies Guild, and it would have been risible to style it the "Gentlemen's Guild." Guilds and societies worked; clubs fraternized.

It was not until 1938 that organized men's work at Saint David's began in earnest. "Men of Saint David's" (the club's formal name) was a conscious attempt to replicate the achievement of the Ladies Guild: to make the point that men could actually do something useful like women – other than serving as paramount authority figures. Indeed, the club's motto – *Servimus* ("We serve") – says as much. During its relatively brief existence, the Men's Club was as large, enthusiastic, and active as the Ladies Guild. Its annual lobster suppers ("Ladies Night"), commencing in 1941, were as popular with church and public alike as the Guild's Lenten chowder luncheons would become twenty-five years after the lobster suppers ceased.

Saint David's was in the vanguard of men's work in The Presbyterian Church in Canada. The national committee of Presbyterian Men was established only in 1956, and it was not until 1958 that the national committee recommended the formation of congregational men's auxiliaries. A full twenty years earlier, in September 1938, the Kirk Session of Saint David's approved a Men's Club and left it to the minister to summon an organizational meeting. It was the first Men's Club in the Halifax church area and gave rise to many imitators. Kerr found himself honorary president, just as his wife was of the Ladies Guild.

At a time when strict gender separation or exclusion prevailed in organizational life – the only exception was the Presbyterian Young People's Society – women church workers had to organize in order to do anything at all. Even deaconesses were rarely if ever assigned to congregations, out of fear of crossing the line; the diaconate may have been ministerial, but ministry was still men's work. The Men's Club was generally understood to be the male equivalent of the Ladies Guild, and to the furthest extent possible, it acted as if it were. Its focus, like the Guild's, was part social and part pastoral (in the broad sense).

The onset of the Second World War within a year of its founding, followed by a long pulpit vacancy, curtailed the growth of the Men's Club; not until the late 1940s did it really "take off." During the war, nevertheless, it played "an important part in the social and religious life of the Church," cooperating with and complementing the Ladies Guild and the other women's organizations and really acting as the Saint David's Auxiliary. By 1943 the president of the Men's Club was singling out for special mention "the Sick Visiting Committee, whose visits to the hospital conveying cheer and comfort and extending the hand of fellowship to patients is work that is impossible to evaluate. In this alone, if in nothing else, the group is doing a grand job."[16] In the postwar period the club's sphere of activity expanded to include boys' work. It was responsible for introducing Cubs and Scouts, both of which in their day were extremely popular with children and youth.

At its height in 1950, its twelfth year of operation, the Men's Club was regarded "by many outside of our Church as one of the leading and most successful Men's Clubs in any church in the Maritime Provinces."[17] So proud were the charter members of their creation that, in his silver jubilee history of Saint David's, elder Clifford Torey limited his discussion of organizations to one – the Men's Club. Frank Lawson was a staunch supporter of the Men's Club, and as his pastorate began to wind down, so did it. The club's most enthusiastic members were the founding generation, and as they aged, moved away or died, or simply lost interest, they were not replaced.

A club catering to their fathers did not necessarily appeal to young men coming of age in the early 1960s. Events such as the Maritime Synod Council Conference and Rally ("The program of the Church is the program for the men of the Church"), which Saint David's hosted over a weekend in May 1960, did little to stimulate interest. The descent of the Men's Club was as rapid as its rise. The case for collective action by Presbyterian Men remained unproved. At a time when the laity played no role in worship and elders and trustees – the real men's clubs – had their hands full, the question was moot. At a time when the church was agonizing over the role of women, organizations such as Presbyterian Men looked, and tended to sound, male chauvinistic.

No longer fashionable or perhaps even feasible, by 1960 the Men's Club was on its last legs. That autumn it attempted to disband but was dissuaded by Session, which felt that the club still had "a function to fulfill in the congregation."[18] In 1962 the annual lobster supper – "the gala event of our year" – was not held, and 1963 saw the last one. The silver jubilee of the Men's Club was celebrated on 30 October 1963. By then the secretary, a prominent elder, was brazenly asserting that all male communicants and adherents of Saint David's were deemed to be members of the club, though only sixty-six had formally joined. By 1964, its last full year of operation, club membership was largely confined to elders and trustees, and its activities were "at a low ebb."[19]

The Men's Club had simply outlived its usefulness. Frank Lawson was on the verge of vacating and the Men's Club of expiring. Presbyterian Men disappeared from the church in 1973, the tension inherent in "men's work" between mere socializing by men who happened to be Presbyterians and Christian fellowship unresolved. Men of Saint David's who wished to serve did not need to belong to a men's club in order to do so.

OTHER ORGANIZATIONS

Dating from the autumn of 1986, Ease into Fitness is not only the youngest organization but unique at Saint David's. Neither, strictly speaking, a congregational organization nor specifically aimed at Saint David's women, it has always attracted participation by some of them. From the start, moreover, it has been coordinated by a member of the congregation.

Ease into Fitness is an effective, if unusual, form of outreach. It hearkens back to an earlier time when there was an Athletic Association coordinating the activities of the Badminton Club, Boys' "Q" Club, CGIT basketball team, and Tuxis Squares/Trail Rangers. The association was presided over by a committee consisting of representatives of the member clubs, an elder, and a trustee, and it served as an arbitration panel authorized to deal with any matter brought before it by an athletic organization. The Athletic Association promoted not only sport and recreation but also community formation. Saint David's had a Tennis Club and a Badminton Club and even hockey. The Tennis Club was established in June 1925.[20]

The Badminton Club was reorganized as early as November 1926 and remained a staple of recreational life through and beyond the Second World War. By 1936 there was a Halifax Church Badminton League encompassing Anglican, Baptist, Presbyterian, and United churches. In November 1941 a Ladies Badminton Club was formed. After Frank Lawson's arrival, this became Married Couples Badminton.

The Badminton Club survived until 1960 and then reappeared briefly in 1976. Three years later it took on a new and different form. In October 1979 the bulletin announced that a number of individuals in the church were interested in forming a recreation and social club. The object of this group was to engage in recreational activities such as volleyball, badminton, darts, table tennis, and bridge. The following month the group had acquired the engaging name "Intimate Strangers." It was the lineal successor of an earlier organization with another playfully suggestive moniker. The As You Like It Group ("Have you free time when you would like to enjoy the companionship of other men and women?"), introduced in the autumn of 1973, did not get off the ground.

The philosophy of the Intimate Strangers was that those who worship together might also play together. Enjoying John Pace's personal support, the group flourished for nearly twenty years. Beset by falling numbers, however, in 1998, like the Pace pastorate itself, the group just faded away. From first to last it had been faithful to its vision. But while social interaction helped to "sweeten" Sunday morning worship, the church had long since ceased to be the focus of social life for its members.

YOUNG PEOPLE'S ORGANIZATIONS

Youth work began even before the Presbyterians occupied Grafton Street Church. Canadian Girls in Training (CGIT), a 1915 offshoot of the YWCA well represented in all Protestant churches, began in February 1925 in affiliation with the WMS. By comparison, the boys were later in organizing. Tuxis, founded in 1918 as an offshoot of the YMCA, began in December as a club for boys twelve years and older who attended Sunday school.[21] Soon renamed the Boys' Club, Tuxis was superseded in 1929 by the "Q" Club ("perhaps the most unique organization for young men in the Church today").[22]

The success of CGIT and the "Q" Club gave rise in October 1930 to a congregational Presbyterian Young People's Society (PYPS). Aimed at those on either side of the age of majority, a PYPS had existed as early as November 1925 but had not survived. Despite one false start, the PYPS now took off and thrived for thirty years. In 1931 the young people of Saint David's and Knox Presbyterian hosted the Fourth Presbyterian Young People's Rally for the Presbytery of Halifax and Lunenburg.

By 1933 the PYPS had overtaken the CGIT and the "Q" Club. The Depression was beginning to distract, if not to bite, and there were not enough young people with time on their hands to go round. An attempt to organize Halifax Christian youth, instigated by Saint David's PYPS in November 1933, did not get off the ground.[23] Six years later, however, it bore fruit. As already observed, war is a young man's game, and the outbreak of war in September 1939 gave great impetus to youth work among Reformed churches in Halifax. That November the Christian Youth Federation was formed, with Ralph Kane – already serving as chair of the Local Boys' Work Board – as first vice-president. Its aim was "to enrich, co-ordinate and expand the work of Christian Young People in the Halifax District"; its focus was Christian social action.

The induction of a new minister at Saint David's in September 1945 led to a resurgence of organizational activity. A girls' club ("Explorers") was reintroduced for girls too young for CGIT, while Lawson encouraged the Men's Club to reactivate the Boys' Club. In the autumn of 1947 he tried to rejuvenate the Young People's Society by reorganizing its program and renaming it the "Kirk Club." In October Saint David's hosted the eighth Maritime PYPS conference, an otherwise successful event overshadowed by the sudden illness and death of Robert Johnston, who had preached at Saint David's that weekend.

A staunch and outspoken opponent of colour prejudice, Lawson encouraged the youth of Saint David's to reach out to the Baptist Young People's Union at Cornwallis Street (African Baptist) Church, a courageous step in the Halifax of the late 1940s. He saw such initiatives as complementary to his own Sunday evening sermons on hot topics: a Socratic "corrupting of the youth," so to speak, just as he was trying to goad the congregation and the community at large. The experiment proved a little too daring, however, and in the autumn of 1951 the Kirk Club failed to organize. In the autumn of 1955 Lawson promoted and Session approved the Westminster Fellowship, aimed at young adults, as a Sunday evening alternative to the PYPS. In the autumn of 1958 the WF was renamed the Kirk Club, "a teaching and discussion group" on religious themes for youth and young marrieds.[24] It met before Sunday evening worship, while Open Doors – with an outside guest speaker and a more worldly focus – continued as usual afterwards. The revived Kirk Club did not last.

In May 1957 the PYPS presbyterial was reorganized, and in October Saint David's again hosted the synodical meeting, which 179 delegates from across the Maritimes attended. The years 1957 through 1963 were the zenith of the Saint David's PYPS. The organization had never been larger, busier, or more varied in its program – worship, mission, and social-recreational – or more popular. In October 1963 the PYPS synodical meeting returned to Saint David's for the third and final time.

The arrival of Deaconess Roberta Shaw in 1960 spurred the expansion of youth work. To Cubs and Scouts (1950) and Brownies and Guides (1956), all of which were going strong, she added CGIT and Explorers, which were in abeyance. In 1962 Shaw was vice-president of the PYPS. In the summer of 1963 she served as adult adviser to the three delegates from local Presbyterian congregations who were attending the first North American Reformed and Presbyterian Youth Assembly at Purdue University in Lafayette, Indiana.[25]

By the mid-1960s, however, the day of youth organizations was over. No longer could it be assumed that older teenagers would even attend worship or Church School, let alone be active in voluntary groups. There were also questions of definition. Who were young people – preteens, teenagers, young adults, or all three? The needs and interests of each constituency were different. Ralph Kane – perennially young at heart if no longer in years – remained active in the PYPS even after he married at age thirty-seven; his bride, Caroline Hattie, was the treasurer. Even into the early 1960s at Saint David's, persons as old as twenty-five were members of the PYPS.

At the beginning of the regular autumn program in 1965, an open forum was held on the future of Saint David's PYPS. Since the group had been unsuccessful in attracting younger members of the congregation, and since most of its members were older than the nominal twenty-one-year age limit, it was agreed that the organization should disband. Nevertheless, a need was felt to exist in Saint David's for an organization ministering to young adults in church and city. A resolution was therefore drafted and sent to Session asking that the current PYPS be disbanded and a new organization formed for young adults twenty or older, to be known as Saint David's Young Adults Group. Session approved, and on 9 November 1965 Saint David's PYPS was dissolved in favour of Saint David's Young Adults.[26]

The way was thus cleared for the organization of a redefined PYPS catering to young people who actually were young. The year 1965 saw the emergence of two new groups: the PYPS, for teenagers, and the Young Adult Group, for twenty-somethings. Deaconess Drysdale served as "leader and adviser" of the new-model PYPS and emphasized mission and outreach. Under Drysdale's guidance the PYPS inaugurated the Christmas Families project, which was afterwards taken up by the Ladies Guild and became a staple of the congregation's social-service program.

The Young Adults Group, however, soon expired from lack of interest, and in the autumn of 1966 the PYPS was again reorganized along the lines of its pre-1965 namesake. A new group, Saint David's Teens, meeting for purely social purposes, barely lasted a year. Saint David's was only big enough for one youth organization, if even that. Deaconess Drysdale's termination in the summer of 1967 not only poisoned the atmosphere but also undermined organized youth work. Explorers and CGIT, which had already supplanted Guides and Brownies, disappeared in 1967 and the PYPS in 1968. Cubs persisted until 1973 and Scouts until 1968; revived, they lasted until 1979. Brownies resumed in 1980 but disappeared for good in 1985.

At the annual congregational meeting in February 1969, it fell to the minister's son, a former president, to announce that the Saint David's PYPS was "defunct." The valedictory for Synod's PYPS came during the church's centenary celebration. At the annual conference in Fredericton in October 1974, Ralph Kane, who had served as first president of the Maritimes PYPS (1939–44), was presented with a scroll by seventy young people who turned out for a banquet at which he was guest of honour. It was a fitting, if bittersweet, leave-taking. By 1986, when the PYPS observed its centenary, it was but the shadow of a name at Saint David's.

Despite the end of youth organizations, youth participation in church life continued and even flourished. In 1969 Janet Guildford, daughter of elder T.K. Guildford, was one of two members of Saint David's accompanying the minister to the General Assembly as "young adult observers" (now representatives). However, determined efforts through the 1970s to start a youth group all proved abortive. Serious youth work resumed only after the arrival of the first pastoral assistant in 1980. Its scope expanded greatly under the second, Judithe Adam, during whose sixteen-year ministry many children went from toddlers or preteens to young adults. It was clearly seen that youth work was more effective for being at once narrowly focused and unstructured; event- or project-based and non-traditional. Since the demise of youth organizations, Saint David's has been royally blessed with a small but committed and energetic group of teenagers who have not only become members but also participate actively in worship and work. Several have attended the North American Youth Triennium, successor to the North American Reformed and Presbyterian Youth Assembly, or other youth events sponsored by Synod or the national church.

THE CHURCH SOCIAL

"While a church exists primarily to foster the religious life of its people, it should not be forgotten that a congregation ought also to be a society of friends where a common church membership is a sufficient introduction to each other." Thus said the Kirk Session report for 1931. Since the organization of the congregation, the Presbyterians have attempted to practise what they preached. On Friday evening, 17 April 1925, barely two weeks after moving into Grafton Street Church, elders and trustees ("and their wives") were at home to the members and adherents of the Presbyterian Church, Halifax. It was the first "congregational social." By 1932 a reception catered by the Young Ladies Guild was being held in the hall after evening worship. It was not until November 1937, however, that the newspaper advertisement carried the words "Welcome to Saint David's," and it did not last.

Presbyterians are courteous, not smiley-faced or familiar, and it took years for Saint David's members to recover from the siege mentality of the persecuted and victimized minority. It was their compensation for loss – loss of church home, church building, the familiar worshipping fellowship, of a "united church." The first minister, Colin Kerr, inclined to dourness and hauteur and perhaps also a depressive, never challenged the mindset – he was, after all, a complete stranger himself.

The icebreakers were, in that order, the war and Frank Lawson. The Second World War scarcely over when he arrived, Lawson was not born to the purple, nor was he a veteran of the resistance to church union. He had neither birthright nor baggage. He had also had a good war, coping with the consequences by ignoring them and turning them to his advantage. For him, Christians by definition were above war, even wars in which they were involved. Like Paul, moreover, he saw the pastoral ministry as an apostolate to humanity. When he said that everyone, regardless of creed or denomination, was invited to worship at Saint David's, he meant precisely that; anyone who accepted the invitation should expect to find there the life of the party. Over the twenty years of Lawson's pastorate, the culture and collective psychology of Saint David's changed, though not without resistance. As recently as the late 1960s, for example, there were ushers who acted as traffic directors, gatekeepers, and general resource persons at the disposal of those who were interested in what Saint David's had to offer or who wanted information, help, or advice. They also collected, presented, and counted the offering.

Lawson's efforts declined with his lengthening pastorate. The Sunday evening Open Door/Fellowship Hour disppeared in December 1962, another casualty, perhaps, of the war of attrition between Lawson and some members of Session. The post-worship social hour recommenced on a monthly trial basis in 1973, some four years after evening service ended. No sooner had John Pace been inducted than Sunday morning "coffee hour" became weekly and permanent. Pace believed strongly that one of the ways to build a caring community on which to base outreach was to promote congregational social interaction. In theory, the coffee hour was to acclimatize strangers and newcomers and acculturate new members. Its real purpose has been to ingratiate the regulars and permit a post-worship debriefing. Socializing commences in the hall before worship, adjourns for worship, and then resumes immediately afterwards. As Thomas McCulloch remarked, speaking through his alter ego Mephibosheth Stepsure, Presbyterians could not get into church late enough or out of it fast enough.

By 1929 an annual spring picnic for Church School and congregation at large was being held. By 1933 so was an annual congregational supper; in the late 1970s an unsuccessful attempt was made to revive it. As for mission and outreach, so for congregational socializing: the opening of the hall in the autumn of 1951 held out possibilities for new and varied forms of activity. In the early 1950s Anniversary Sunday was followed by a Monday evening "At Home" given by elders and their wives to the membership. The year 1952 saw the commencement of an annual "Family Party"; it survived at least until 1956. The Church School picnic, which from 1944 onwards had been held at the MacKeen estate ("Maplewood") on the Northwest Arm, became the annual congregational picnic in 1971. It lapsed two years later, but was revived in 1978, only to lapse again in 1984. In his pastoral letter of August 1993 John Pace declared that "we are determined to reactivate the congregational picnic," but too much goodwill had been lost on account of the recent induction of the assistant minister. The event was duly held but did not rate a mention in the Kirk Session review of that difficult year. Held intermittently over the next decade, the congregational social was revived yet again in 2003, thanks to the good offices of elder Elizabeth A. Chard, registrar of Saint Mary's University, who placed at the disposal of Saint David's the former estate of Robert Stanfield, "The Oaks."

In 1978 the Easter Sunday breakfast, first attempted in 1964, was successfully revived. The brainchild of elder Kenneth Mader, it was afterwards carried on by his son and fellow elder, Frank. Autumn 1980 saw the beginning of an annual congregational dinner; unlike the Easter breakfast, it did not catch on. The annual congregational meeting was formerly preceded by a potluck supper, but more recently – the ACM having moved from Wednesday evening to Sunday noon – by a luncheon catered by the Ladies Guild. Like the professional mourner willing to attend the funeral of the unreformed Ebenezer Scrooge provided luncheon was served, church people mix the business of worship with the pleasure of refreshments. Social gatherings are a meaningful form of outreach by and for the congregation – the family of worshippers. They emphasize that worship is by definition communal, a people-centred event; given its very public and "open" nature, worship is itself a form of socialization.

14

Expansion

The failure of the Presbyterians to hold either of the two Halifax congregations – St Andrew's and Park Street – where resistance to church union was strongest meant that expansion into either of those areas would happen sooner rather than later. Northward expansion came first, followed thirty years later by westward. As the Presbyterian population of metropolitan Halifax grew, so too did the psychological distance from Saint David's. But only after the mother church had fully cohered could the process of "deconstructing" it begin and the status quo ante the Disruption start to be restored at least in part. The successor to and replacement for St James, Dartmouth, was to be St Andrew's (1953); the new Bethany, Northwest Arm, was to be Calvin (1958); and the new Knox, Lower Sackville, was to be First Sackville Presbyterian (1975).

PARK STREET REBORN

If the expansion of Presbyterianism through the metropolitan area and beyond was a vicarious continuation of congregations that had existed before the Disruption, then nothing typified it better than expansion in the first instance. This was a mission field growing out of the heart of Saint David's itself. In September 1926 the Kirk Session discussed whether to start a Sunday school in the North End and struck a committee of two elders to study and report. One was Robert A. Guildford; he and his son Robert D. had been pillars of Park Street and successive superintendents of its Sunday school. R.A. Guildford had also been clerk of Session at Park Street, but had retired in 1919 to make way for W.J. Kane, another resisting elder. While he was at Saint David's, Guildford's elder's district comprehended the north suburbs and the entire North End of the city. Few elders could have claimed to be instrumental in the founding of two congregations in as many years.

On Sunday afternoon, 7 November 1926, "the North End Branch of the Presbyterian Sunday School" held its first meeting in the former Baptist Temple, at the corner of North and Gottingen streets; it lay within walking distance of the former Park Street Presbyterian Church, which so many of the pupils and more especially their parents knew well. Deaconess Susan Sylvester, designated by the Woman's Missionary Society, Eastern Division, conducted worship, while R.D. Guildford, superintendent of the Sunday school at Saint David's, preached the sermon. The following Thursday evening Colin Kerr himself conducted the prayer meeting.

The "North End Sunday School," as the annual report of Saint David's described it, was the product of restiveness among the dissenting minority of North End Presbyterians. Saint David's was not another Park Street, though former members of Park Street had loomed large in the resistance to church union. At Saint David's, however, they were simply one group among nine; to make matters worse, St Andrew's, where the vote against the United Church had been strongest, had accordingly inherited most of the offices and most of the influence in the new hybrid super-church. Though the clerk of Session at Saint David's, W.J. Kane, had held the same office at Park Street, he did not join the North End protest movement, nor did the Kirk Session report for 1926 take any notice of it at all. It seems clear that those in command considered the move premature, if not unnecessary and inappropriate, at a time when all the church's efforts and resources should have been focused exclusively on building up Saint David's. But accumulating strains and stresses made clear that the path of least resistance was decentralization. The state of affairs before the Disruption was a recent bittersweet memory, and there is no question that the founders of what was to become Knox Presbyterian saw themselves as another Park Street. In the spring of 1925 Park Street had ceased to exist after eighty-two years. The loss of the congregation to the United Church, followed soon after by its absorption by another unionist congregation (St John's), was deeply felt by the resisters who had worked so hard and sacrificed so much to preserve it. Recreating Park Street was thus a high priority, second only in importance to re-establishing the church itself in Halifax.

Another high priority was ministering to the offshoot. Kerr could not be in two places at once, and so in May 1927 Session procured for him as assistant another "superman from Scotland" – George Duncan's nephew, licentiate Robert Duncan. The first regular Sunday evening service of the North End mission field was held on 19 June and attracted over two hundred worshippers. Duncan proved to be an able preacher and pastor, but the arrangement was as short-lived as it was successful. In September he moved on to Presbyterian College, Montreal, to pursue his theological studies. The North Enders were hoping Duncan would return in the spring, but he did not. Nor is it known what became of him.

Work in the North End almost stopped after Duncan's departure, when Synod's superintendent of missions decided against recommending a successor. Saint David's Session went over his head, however, appealing directly to the secretary of the General Board of Missions, which was putting up the money. The decision was overruled, and funds provided for a further six-month lease of the disused Baptist Temple. In November 1927 some seventy North Enders petitioned Session to become a congregation; Session remitted the request to the Board of Missions. Then in April 1928, days before the General Board's involvement was to end, Session called a meeting of the would-be congregation. So enthusiastic was the response that an organizing committee was struck and services resumed the very next Sunday, 22 April. In June, the North Enders having again petitioned, Presbytery authorized the formation of a congregation – "Halifax North Presbyterian Church." The clerk of Presbytery was appointed interim moderator, and in August a session was constituted.

In spirit and ideology, Halifax's second Presbyterian congregation was more Free than Kirk. Its liberation from Saint David's was something of a protest and dissent from the kirk which Saint David's had quickly become and which Park Street had never been. After two years of Kerr, some in his congregation were ready to vote with their feet. The charter membership of Knox Presbyterian (as it was formally renamed), however, was not by any means drawn entirely from North Enders worshipping at Saint David's. There were still Presbyterians in the North End, perhaps even disgruntled former Presbyterian United Churchers, for whom Saint David's was both a little too "high" and a little too far south. Knox was low-church, so to speak, a product of the evangelical impulse within Presbyterianism's broad church.

CHURCH EXTENSION

In his preliminary study of PCC extension work in the postwar period, Stuart Macdonald identifies three specific phases "for understanding new church development": phase 1 (ca. 1945–ca. 1955): local and entrepreneurial; phase 2 (ca. 1956–63): growing issues and coordination; and phase 3 (1964–76): centralized control, stage 1, and (1976–85): centralized control, stage 2.[1] In relation to the five church development initiatives

in which Saint David's was involved in the forty years following the end of
the Second World War, the first (Dartmouth) belongs to phase 1, the second
(Westmount, Halifax) straddles phases 1 and 2, the third (Woodlawn, Dartmouth)
belongs to phase 2, and the fourth and fifth (Knox Relocation and Lower
Sackville) belong to phase 3, stage 1.

Barely two months into his pastorate, in November 1945, Frank Lawson
was suggesting to Session the desirability of undertaking extension work
elsewhere in the city along the lines of the Sunday school that had led to
Knox Church twenty years earlier.[2] What planted the idea in his mind was
that the United Church had just begun work in the Edgewood-Ardmore-
Westmount District of the West End, which had seen rapid growth during
the war, when residential Halifax was bursting at the seams, and would
experience even more rapid growth in the first postwar decade. Worship
was first held in a public school in May 1946, a congregation (Edgewood
United) was authorized later that year, and in September 1948 a church
building was dedicated.

Lawson was also echoing the sentiment of the Presbyterian Advance for
Christ and Peace Thankoffering, set up by the General Assembly in 1945
to fundraise for extension, among other things. One-quarter of the fund
was to be devoted to church building projects and one-quarter to home
or foreign missions. These two, of course, dovetailed nicely. In April and
May 1946, when the capital campaign was underway, a series of articles
appeared in a Halifax newspaper: "Plan New Church Buildings," "Seek
Funds for Extending Church Work," "Church Asks for Funds to Expand
Work," and "Seek to Raise $2,000,000."[3] Overall, however, the Presbytery
of Halifax and Lunenburg did not respond generously to the General
Assembly's appeal. Saint David's did its part – no doubt because its own
clerk of Session, W.J. Kane, was Presbytery chair for the Advance.

In November 1951 The Presbyterian Church in Canada devoted two
weeks to a Christian Outreach Campaign designed to raise the $1 million
needed "to assist in building new churches and Sunday schools." The
St David's bulletin cover for Sunday, 18 November, featured an aerial view
of Halifax Harbour looking eastward towards Dartmouth. Frank Lawson
probably had more than foreign missions in mind when, in a blistering
sermon delivered 9 December 1951 ("Two men at church"), he excori-
ated the missionary outreach of the Protestant churches.[4] What applied
to foreign missions applied all the more at home, where the need was
felt. The question was not whether new congregations would be planted
but where first – in Halifax, which already had two flourishing Presbyterian churches, though neither suburban, or in Dartmouth, eastward across

Halifax Harbour, where there was none at all. Dartmouth seemed the higher priority.

Such was the momentum that by early October 1953 Lawson, then moderator of Presbytery, initiated the establishment of an Overall Planning (or Church Extension) Committee "to coordinate the work within the Dartmouth-Halifax area."[5] Comprising three ministers in addition to Lawson, nine elders (six, including the convener, from Saint David's), and the Presbytery deaconess, Estelle MacCausland, the committee was chaired by W.J. Kane. In March 1954 the Church Extension Committee became a joint committee of Presbytery and the churches of Halifax-Dartmouth, where all the extension work was taking place. Two months later Presbytery agreed "that the Kirk Session of Saint David's be asked to give the requested oversight to this work."[6] The committee's brochure depicted St Andrew's, Kimberley (British Columbia), nearing completion in 1951. The Church Extension Committee immediately became a standing committee of Presbytery; it survived until April 1958, when it was disbanded and its funds transferred to the Westmount Church Building Fund (Calvin Presbyterian).

Throughout the 1950s, church extension was in the air. There had not been such an upsurge in church-building in Halifax since the 1860s and 1870s. By the end of 1957 a newspaper could claim, "Church building in the Halifax and Dartmouth area during 1957 was big business – to the tune of over two and a half million dollars paid into construction of new churches and other church facilities."[7] The baby boomers and their parents were filling the churches. Despite lacking a weapon in his arsenal remotely comparable with the ucc's Church Extension Board,[8] no one in Presbytery supported church extension more determinedly than W.J. Kane. By 1955 the Saint David's Church Expansion Fund had its own treasurer and financial statement published separately in the annual report. Saint David's tried to shoulder its burden of responsibility, but acting as a congregational development bank would prove a bridge too far, and the financial consequences would reverberate into the 1970s and beyond.

DARTMOUTH REBORN

The Kirk had been planted in Dartmouth in 1827 and had disappeared a century later, in 1925, by which time there were two congregations, St James and Stairs Memorial – three, if one counts Woodside-Imperoyal, the union church, originally a mission field of Stairs.[9] There was no resistance to church union to speak of. Uniting majority Presbyterians were in the ascendant, Stairs Memorial not voting and St James voting 84 per cent in favour of the United Church, of a mere 36 per cent who bothered to vote at all. (The small size of the poll was a far better indicator of the level of support for the United Church than the actual vote. The purpose of voting, after all, was not to join the UCC but to stay out of it.) The remnant of non-uniting Presbyterians from Dartmouth attended Saint David's. Among them was H.D. Creighton, who became elder late in 1926, his district being all of the town.

In the summer of 1951 Frank Lawson reluctantly found himself interim moderator of the vacant rural pastoral charge of Musquodoboit Harbour and Dean. Anxious to keep his summer student assistant, Willis Sayers, in work between Sundays, Lawson hit upon the idea of a survey of Presbyterians in the town of Dartmouth. An intensive assessment was carried out in the north end of Dartmouth, where churchless Presbyterians were thought to be numerous. Lawson, supervising the exercise, was unimpressed with the results and not in favour of proceeding any further.[10] Sayers, however, persisted, informing Presbytery that while there were only three interested Presbyterian families, 119 children would attend a Sunday school if one was started.[11] Lawson may have feared that the chief casualty of Dartmouth extension would be Saint David's. If so, future developments were to prove him wrong. Nor was it the last that Dartmouth would see of Willis Sayers.

Presbytery decided to apply to the WMS, Eastern Division, for a deaconess. "Help for Halifax" declared the Saint David's bulletin of 13 January 1952, alluding to the imminent arrival of Deaconess Estelle MacCausland, who had been appointed to the Halifax area. She was to work in and from Saint David's and devote her time to children's classes and organizations, pastoral visitation, and the like. Other than serving briefly as superintendent of the Wednesday Afternoon Mission School ("City Project"), Deaconess MacCausland was to do no work at Saint David's at all. Her two years in metropolitan Halifax would be claimed entirely by church extension.

The direct involvement of Saint David's in Dartmouth extension began in the spring of 1953 when the Ladies Guild provided money for hymn books and other aids to worship. After a building site was purchased in December 1953, the WMS, Eastern Division, pledged $10,000 security for a loan from the Bank of Nova Scotia to finance church construction. At the Saint David's annual congregational meeting in January 1954, Lawson spoke on the outreach program of the PCC at large and then focused on the needs of the metropolitan area in the immediate future. Dartmouth needed a church, and so did northwest Halifax; $150,000 would be required and could be raised.[12] In January 1955 the annual congregational meeting approved a resolution from the Trustees to pay between $1,000 and $1,500 a year for ten years to Dartmouth against principal and interest on its bank loan. In 1958 the congregation received another $1,000 from the Ladies Guild and gifts totalling $2,700 from Saint David's.

The sod for the new church was turned in June 1955 and the cornerstone laid in September. The name St Andrew's was adopted, a reference to the fact that the first Presbyterian church in Dartmouth had been Kirk and had been named after an apostle, as kirks invariably were. In September the Kirk Session was formally constituted, and on Sunday, 22 January 1956, St Andrew's Presbyterian Church was dedicated by the moderator of the General Assembly. The building, on School Street in central Dartmouth, was designed by draughtsman Herbert A. Hattie, a member and later elder of Saint David's.

By 1964, when the commitment to St Andrew's, which had cost between $10,000 and $15,000, ended, the financial situation of Saint David's was critical. No one saw more clearly than the chair of the Trustees, a successful independent businessman, that yet another "every member visitation" was necessary.[13] Saint David's generous financial support of St Andrew's was indirect compensation for failing to support it through transfer of membership. The habits of twenty-five years were not easily broken; so there would not be a secession from Saint David's as in 1928, when Knox was founded. Dartmouthians at Saint David's did not vote with their feet, as Halifax's North Enders had done; they stayed put.

"THE PRESBYTERIAN CHURCH OF
NORTHWEST HALIFAX"

For over thirty years after the Disruption, there was no Presbyterian presence in the west end of Halifax. Bethany United was flourishing, and a new congregation, Edgewood United (on the northern edge of the new Westmount subdivision), was founded in 1946. Both congregations built new churches, in 1958 and 1955 respectively. Church extension in the fast-growing residential suburbs of Halifax's West End thus became the chief undertaking of Presbytery's new Church Extension Committee. The committee met at Saint David's in November 1953 and appointed its convener, W.J. Kane, chair of a select committee "to investigate the possibilities of beginning a new church in Halifax." In December Halifax and Lunenburg appealed to other presbyteries in the synod for assistance in building a new church in Westmount, where there were as yet no other Protestant churches. The area between Chebucto and Bayers roads in the

West End, formerly home to Halifax's airport, had in the late 1940s become the site of a new veterans' subdivision.[14]

In January 1954 the secretary of the General Board of Missions met with members of Saint David's and Knox to gauge the level of popular support for the initiative. Later that month a building lot in the heart of the Westmount subdivision (on Peter Lowe Avenue) was secured through the efforts of elders Torey and McInnes of Saint David's. In February a joint meeting of Session and Trustees of Saint David's decided to support the building of a new church in the West End. In March Deaconess MacCausland was seconded from Dartmouth to conduct a survey of Presbyterians in the area. By May she had interviewed two hundred families and found twenty to twenty-five interested in forming the nucleus of a church. In October the Trustees recommended that "Saint David's should be willing to finance the salary of a Clergyman or Deaconess for a period of three years so that a congregation might be organized in the Westmount area."[15]

Yet the special congregational meeting held later that month produced no action on the Trustees' proposal. The meeting's small turnout – twenty-eight out of some five hundred – suggested skepticism about its purpose. On the face of it, financially supporting church extension when Saint David's itself was in the red to the tune of over $22,000 looked preposterous. The chair of the Trustees understatedly observed that "there was a general feeling in favour of church extension but ... up to the present no group had come out strongly in favour of doing something." Two mission fields were one too many for Saint David's to support, and since Dartmouth was both relatively more important and much further advanced, it would be the focus of maximum effort.

Though the meeting approved starting up a branch Sunday school under the supervision of Session, by the end of 1954 enthusiasm for the Westmount extension project had lapsed. It is not clear whether the proposed Sunday school ever got off the ground. Deaconess MacCausland was not replaced, and no elder of Saint David's was willing or able to take on the job of catechist. Yet for four years, 1955 through 1958, Saint David's carried on its balance sheet under "liabilities" an average of $1,700 a year for the Westmount Sunday school.

In December 1956 the Reverend A.E. Morrison, the Synod superintendent of missions, resolved to kick-start the process. He summoned to a meeting in Westmount School all those willing to support a Presbyterian church in the West End. The upshot was that by March 1958, eighty-one persons had transferred to the new congregation. The Kirk Session, constituted in November 1958, included elder Eben Morrison of Saint David's. In

December a Presbytery commission, chaired by Lawson and including among its members W.J. Kane, was set up to help the new congregation build a church. In July 1959 Lawson, as acting moderator of Presbytery, turned the first sod, and in December Presbytery approved the name chosen – Calvin Presbyterian Church. The cornerstone was laid in February 1960. Earlier that month Saint David's gifted Calvin $15,000 to help defray the $130,000 cost of its state-of-the-art building; a bank loan was procured to finance the gift. The umbilical cord was never really cut. Some Presbyterians who lived in the West End still found their way to Saint David's, preferring the mother church to any satellite. Indeed, the traffic was two-way. During the Mackay pastorate, for example, Calvin was a refuge when the atmosphere at Saint David's became oppressive. Three elders transferred to Calvin, one of whom became clerk of Session in 1973.

"FULFILMENT OF A DREAM AT BEL AYR PARK"

A thriving suburb on the outskirts of Dartmouth, Woodlawn provided an excellent opportunity for the PCC to grow with the circumambient community.[16] In September 1960 it was reported that St Andrew's was sponsoring a Sunday school in Woodlawn "with a long-range view of establishing a new work there."[17] In April 1963 Presbytery applied unsuccessfully to the General Board of Missions for an ordained missionary to assume responsibility for the work. In 1964, however, Willis Sayers was persuaded to return to Dartmouth after an absence of thirteen years to build a new congregation in outer suburbia. He served until June 1968. Public worship was held for the first time in Penhorn School on 27 September 1964. Within three months there would be a congregation, in eight years a church building.

The same month that worship commenced, Presbytery wrote to Saint David's expressing thanks for services rendered towards the start-up costs of Woodlawn extension: "The Session of St David's … donated the sum of $500 to cover the incidental expenses associated with the beginning of this new work, and also loaned us a pulpit [Bible]. We are grateful for their interest, and for their help in this way." In November, members petitioned Presbytery for a congregation. Presbytery concurred, and on 6 December 1964 the Woodlawn Extension Charge was formally erected. Four assessor-elders were appointed, including the clerk of Session at Saint David's. The mother church gave to the new congregation as its first clerk of Session one its own newest and youngest elders – Stewart Reeves. Woodlawn was also well ahead of its time in appointing two women to the board of managers, a daring step that elsewhere followed, rather than preceded, the election of women as elders.

In February 1965 the name Iona was adopted over the sole objections of Frank Lawson, who had had personal experience of the restored Iona Community. By autumn 1967 Presbytery, led by Donald B. Mackay, was throwing cold water on Iona's plan to incorporate the old-fashioned way and issue bonds and debentures to raise money for land and building fund purposes. Sayers, moderator of Presbytery when the political battle over financing Iona was at its height, could not hold his own against a senior minister of Mackay's experience and prestige. By the spring of 1968 he had had enough and returned to Ontario: "Among many frustrations there had been the difficulty of obtaining land on which to locate a church, and it had been an experience dealing with the changing scene in our Church's activities."[18] The changing scene could be summed up in two words – Donald Mackay. His arrival at Saint David's midway through Sayers's pastorate at Iona disrupted the latter's well-laid plans for the fledgling congregation.

Mackay became interim moderator of Iona and saw to it that Sayers was succeeded by an incisive young protege of his, Peter Alexander McDonald, whose first pastorate it was. Iona resented being unequally yoked to St Andrew's in a pastoral charge and having a neophyte minister more or less foisted on it by Presbytery fiat. McDonald, however, was mature beyond his years and rose effortlessly to the challenge. A master diplomatist, he soon won over Iona, whose minister he remained until 1975, and he put his connection to Saint David's to the best possible use.[19]

After a lengthy search and lengthier negotiations, agreement to purchase a church building site was reached in December 1968. At the behest of Presbytery's Pastoral Oversight Committee (successor to the Church Extension Committee), the site was gifted to Iona chiefly by means of grants from Saint David's and the General Board of Missions. In November 1969 Mackay briefed the Trustees on the history of Saint David's involvement in the project and Iona's prospective transfer of land, expected in about two years. Funds to complete the purchase would then be required. Mackay further reported that the clerk of Session was recommending a gift of $12,000 to help cover the cost.[20] Ralph Kane was speaking not for Session but for Presbytery, which had asked that Saint David's donate $12,000 towards the estimated $29,000 cost of Iona's building site. The Trustees agreed, and in January 1970 the recommendation went before the annual congregational meeting, which approved it. Coincidentally, the projected deficit for that year was $12,000.

At the annual joint meeting of Session and Trustees in January 1971, Mackay introduced a delegation from Iona led by the minister, McDonald, "who wished to speak to the meeting." It was moved and seconded to recommend to the annual congregational meeting a multi-year gift to Iona of up to \$25,000 for building purposes.[21] This recommendation was occurring at a time when there was "a serious decline in givings by the congregation," and the sum had to borrowed from the bank. One voice of fiscal sanity cried in that wilderness: elder Herbert Mosher "pointed out a wide discrepancy between budgeted income and what we should expect from extrapolating past givings."[22] He also objected to entering as a permanent line item a \$13,000 liability to cover commitments such as had been made to Iona. Once again the Ladies Guild rode to the rescue, within the year contributing \$6,000 towards the Saint David's commitment to Iona's land purchase.

KNOX CHURCH RELOCATION

By the late 1950s Knox was faced with the absolute necessity of relocation. Its neighbourhood was a slum, both dangerous and decrepit, and slum clearance was in full flourish. The population was moving north and west, and the church building was not worth salvaging. There was also a nice historical irony: Park Street had once relocated – from the north suburbs (Poplar Grove) to the near North End (Park Street), not far from Knox's original site. In May 1961 the minister, J.J. Edmiston, informed Presbytery that an ideal building site in the far North End was available for a knockdown price.[23] No action was taken other than to revive the Church Extension Committee, which had fallen dormant.[24] It took over a dozen years to realize, but the building site in which Edmiston tried to interest Presbytery would become the second home of Knox Church.

Nothing further had been accomplished by the time Edmiston vacated in May 1963. That autumn Knox acquired as minister someone accustomed to new church development – Randolph D. MacLean (1915–99). Relocation was the task presented to MacLean when he was asked to consider Knox. He accepted appointment as an "ordained missionary" on the understanding that the project was to be completed within two years. Having just come from a year of ministry in Glasgow, MacLean was very interested in inner-city work. He anticipated that the relocation project would be accomplished fairly readily, so that he and his congregation could get on with outreach and social ministry in the North End community. There were many ups and downs, however, Presbytery itself being in two minds about the relocation in view of its cost.[25]

A pronounced evangelical like Knox's other ministers, R.D. MacLean would, unlike them, have an unusually long pastorate of twenty years. He immediately set to work. In 1966 the building site in the far North End, cheek-by-jowl with Grove Church of old, was leased from the City of Halifax.[26] But there was not money enough to secure the sixty-year lease, let alone build the church. In 1971 Saint David's came to the rescue by undertaking to pay up to $2,500 "ground rent" per year for five years to secure the lease until such time as building could commence. It was money that Saint David's could ill afford. By the end of January 1973 the treasurer was reduced to circularizing Session a balance sheet for that month, which meant "that the congregation are not making their contributions in sufficient amounts to pay the day-to-day expenses of the Church, to say nothing of reducing the debt."

Sunday afternoon, 31 March 1974, saw the turning of the first sod for the new Knox Church. Two weeks later the treasurer of Saint David's, in some desperation, wrote to the members and adherents soliciting a substantial increase in weekly givings, which on average had fallen to $530. So critical was the situation that the congregation had had to borrow $3,000 from the bank to cover its overdraft, while a demand loan of some $10,500 was outstanding.

Practices such as these were controversial in the eyes of a few, not just because of the "critical financial state" of Saint David's but also because it was contributing towards the capital cost of building a new church as well as paying for the land on which it was to be built. Like the Iona project, Knox's relocation did not involve moving an old church to a new site or rebuilding on the same site. It concerned a new church on a new site, a large aspiration for a congregation with 131 members at the end of 1970 (Iona had even fewer). For some at Saint David's, the fundamental issue was responsible stewardship of the congregation's constricting resources. For others the issue was tradition: Knox was not just "one of us"; it was part of us.

SACKVILLE REBORN

First Sackville Presbyterian Church highlighted the difficulties of trying to combine denominational expansion with ecumenical cooperation. Knox Presbyterian in Lower Sackville (1890) had been the smaller part of a two-point pastoral charge that went United in 1925.[27] It was not until the late 1960s, when a modern highway connecting the area with Halifax opened, that the Sackvilles (Lower, Middle, and Upper), small and rural, began to grow rapidly and evolve into a thriving bedroom community and metropolitan suburb. Even Donald Mackay made a point by moving in 1971 to a trailer park in Lower Sackville, raising eyebrows if not hackles at Saint David's.

The mission field was inaugurated in September 1973, and public worship began in Sackville High School. For the first year, 1973–74, the mission field was without an ordained missionary, but by September 1974 a minister had appeared in the person of R.K. Anderson, a foreign missionary returned from Japan. Presbytery appointed an assessor session, with A.E. Morrison as interim moderator and Nora Ashworth of Saint David's as interim clerk; Ralph Kane was also a member, as was Murray Alary, a once and future member-elder of Saint David's. The congregation was recognized in January 1975, and a board of managers elected in March. A year later the Kirk Session was formally constituted. In November 1978 the Presbyterians dedicated their sanctuary in the former home of the Rock Church (Pentecostal), the moderator of the General Assembly preaching. At this point Sackville asked for financial assistance in order to buy the property, and Saint David's responded with its customary generosity. The annual congregational meeting in January 1979 accepted a resolution from a joint Session-Trustees committee to pay Sackville $2,000 a year for five years to help reduce the debt. All this was occurring at a time when Saint David's was between major building restoration projects and was already carrying a $10,000 commitment to the Knox College Restoration Project.

KENTVILLE REBORN

Presbyterianism had disappeared from the Annapolis Valley on 10 June 1925. The PCC's only victory was "turning" the Baptist minister in Kentville, David Graham Ross (1878–1955). Ross went on to a busy career as a Presbyterian minister, serving as interim moderator of Saint David's during the long and difficult Kerr-Lawson vacancy. Most Methodist and Presbyterian congregations in the Valley were de facto union churches before 1925.[28] In Wolfville, however, there were enough continuing Presbyterians to establish a congregation in 1929. It was gone by 1937, and by 1955 A.E. Morrison was reporting to Presbytery that there was insufficient interest in the Wolfville and Kentville area "to warrant any further action."[29]

Thirty years later the situation had changed for the better. In the summer of 1989 Presbytery was investigating possible extension work in the King's County area. Presbytery's committee was a Saint David's affair –

the minister, the clerk of Session, and the assistant clerk. A one-day visitation to determine the level of interest was conducted, and volunteers for that purpose were sought from the five metropolitan congregations. The results of the canvass were sufficiently encouraging that Sunday evening, 15 October 1989, saw John Pace and Judithe Adam-Murphy travel to New Minas (between Kentville and Wolfville) to conduct worship. King's Presbyterian Church, New Minas, was officially recognized at a service in the Christian Reformed Church in Kentville in April 1990.

By the late 1990s King's Presbyterian was ready to build a church. Encouraged by P.A. McDonald, then convener of Presbytery's New Minas Fundraising Committee, King's looked hopefully towards Saint David's, which was represented on the committee. It would not be disappointed. In the autumn of 1997 King's approached Saint David's for financial assistance in building a church. Session referred the request to its missions committee for study. As a result, in January 1998 Session decided to recommend to the annual congregational meeting a one-off gift of $25,000 and an interest-free loan of $25,000, repayable whenever. It fell to elder Kenneth Mader, a former treasurer and the convener of Session's committee, to bring the matter before the annual congregational meeting on 28 January.[30]

A motion incorporating the recommendation was duly made, seconded, and carried, though far from unanimously ("The vote on the motion was successful"). Some would have given more; others nothing at all. Generally speaking, there was a sense that an era was ending; that, in relation to church extension, Saint David's would from now on have to do something other than give away or lend money badly needed at home. Such a magnanimous gesture would have been inconceivable but for the impending resignation of the assistant. It was recognized that Adam-Murphy would not be replaced and that the money required to pay her stipend could be put to a different use.

The gift-loan proved increasingly controversial the closer King's Presbyterian got to approving its building plans and turning the first sod. The Saint David's annual congregational meeting in January 1999 adopted a motion to bind King's Presbyterian to commence repayment of the loan in five years, an unreasonable requirement that altered both the letter and the spirit of the original commitment, however ill-advised it may have been when it was made.

TODAY AND TOMORROW

The King's Presbyterian gift-loan was the straw that broke the camel's back. Though the role of Saint David's had to change from providing financial support to supplying infrastructural and moral assistance, it continued to be a promoter and facilitator of new congregations. In March 1993 the minister had met with the moderator of the Korean Presbyterian Church in America, the Canadian counterpart of which was interested in establishing a congregation in Halifax. Asked to provide a home, Saint David's declined; it is unclear why. The venture in any case was short-lived. Ten years later a similar overture would meet with a much more positive response from Saint David's.

In late March 2003 the minister was approached by Korean Presbyterians asking whether Saint David's would be willing to allow them to conduct Korean-language worship services in the church. Agreement was reached in April; in May public worship began, and the Korean Presbyterian Church of Nova Scotia was incorporated with its registered office at 1537 Brunswick Street (the Saint David's church office). By the autumn of 2005 the congregation had affiliated with the PCC Presbytery of Eastern Han-Ca, thus regularizing its status and providing for the arrangement with Saint David's to continue indefinitely.

Shades of the old Saint David's reappeared in 2004, when Session approved a modest grant of $3,000 to Tantallon–St Margarets Bay Extension, lying squarely in the midst of the fast-growing conurban sprawl west of the metropolitan area. Saint David's was continuing to cast its bread upon the waters, but the modus operandi was different. The source of the grant was not operating funds, much less a bank loan, but the Helen M. Watson investment fund, which was to be "used exclusively for local missionary work in Nova Scotia." What better cause than a new congregation in a burgeoning population centre where no Presbyterian church had ever existed? There was and had always been more to the role of Saint David's in Presbytery extension than money. Elders of the church served on the organizing committee for Tantallon–St Margarets Bay, and two members, elder Valerie Macdonald and Carol Dobson, wrote a moving account of the inaugural worship service on 12 September 2004.[31]

Extension is outreach to both church and world. Its purpose in part is to help fellow Presbyterians down on their luck to organize for preaching and public worship. Because it was new at the time of the Disruption, when the continuation of The Presbyterian Church in Canada was assumed to depend on continuing congregations, Saint David's has always seen itself as having a special mission and ministry in relation to church extension ("outreach" in the narrow sense). Though the assistance it rendered was in kind as well as cash, it too often took the form of the latter. Presbyterians within and outside Saint David's expected that the metropolitan cathedral church would do its duty by those would-be or fledgling congregations less privileged than itself. With privilege, or at least pride of place, came responsibility – noblesse oblige. As the chair of the Trustees put it in his annual report for 1975, "The Presbyterian Church of Saint David [is] the key church of Presbyterianism in the Halifax and Dartmouth Metropolitan area."

Though neither the oldest nor the largest congregation, Saint David's was and had always been the most important in Presbytery. Other churches looked to it for financial and moral support. In June 1978 John Pace, then moderator of Presbytery, preached the golden jubilee sermons at Knox Presbyterian. Ironically, the "Historical Sketch" issued for the occasion made little or no reference to the role of Saint David's in launching and sustaining Knox beyond the payment of the ground rent. The Park Street Guildfords were long gone and with them any vestigial memory that Knox was an offspring of Saint David's. Yet from Sunday school in 1926 to mission field to congregation in 1928, Knox Church had been nurtured by Saint David's. Almost from the beginning, denominational expansion was a significant part of congregational development.

$$15$$

Church Property

THE OLD METHODIST BURYING GROUND

The site on which Saint David's stands is far more historic than the church itself. Methodism arrived in Halifax in June 1782, when William Black (afterwards superintendent preacher), the "Apostle of Methodism" in the Maritimes, first preached there. Black settled in Halifax in 1786, and six years later Zoar Chapel was dedicated. The Methodists had a church but no cemetery. In 1793 William Goreham, a devout Wesleyan shopkeeper who a year earlier had stood third on the list of subscribers for the new church, gifted land for a burying ground.[1] The Methodist burying ground remained in use until 1844, when Camp Hill Cemetery opened and all other burying grounds within the city of Halifax were permanently closed for sanitary reasons.

By the end of the 1840s, Zoar was inadequate and needed replacing. Since empty building lots in the old town were scarce and expensive, the trustees decided to rebuild on a site both near and dear that they already owned. Despite scruples about disturbing the saints' rest, the new church was constructed towards the front of the Old Methodist Burying Ground, facing Grafton Street, the graves and gravestones lying mainly to the south and west. Tradition says that the rear of the church covered the bones of "Bishop" Black, who died in September 1834 and whose gravestone "stood for a long time beside the door leading to the minister's vestry."[2] There was a tradition in the early Christian church of building cathedrals over the bones of apostles such as William Black; so the disused denominational cemetery seemed an appropriate site for the "sanctuary successor" to the first church. Grafton Street Wesleyan opened in June 1852. William Goreham lived almost long enough to see it rise on the site he had donated for a burying ground nearly sixty years earlier.

By the autumn of 1925, when the Grafton Street Church property was on the market, concerns were expressed about the fate of the Old Methodist Burying Ground, should the land be sold for commercial use. Its acquisition by the Presbyterians, however, calmed those fears. In 1950 Saint David's decided to build a new hall over the burying ground, directly behind the church. Concerns about the disposition of the gravestones prompted the Board to advertise in the Halifax newspapers. It received only one expression of interest – from Constance Bell, the remains of whose great-great-grandmother, Ann Cross Bell (died 1834), were interred in the Old Methodist Burying Ground. Atop her grave was a fine stone erected by her son, the merchant Hugh Bell, then a trustee of the Methodist Society. The Bell gravestone was removed and afterwards mounted in the vestibule between church and hall, while all thirty-six gravestones were mapped and about half of them laid flat in situ before being covered by the floor of the new building.

THE SECOND GRAFTON
STREET METHODIST CHURCH

"Our holy and our beautiful house, where our fathers praised Thee, is burnt up with fire; and all our pleasant things are laid waste." With these words from Isaiah 64:11, the editor of the *Provincial Wesleyan* began his account of the destruction of the first Grafton Street Church late on a "bitterly cold" Sunday afternoon in February 1868.

The call for tenders for a replacement building was issued on 4 May, and the building contract awarded about a week later. The plans and specifications had been drawn up by David Stirling, a Scottish Kirkman and the province's leading architect; the contractor was to be George Frederick Blaiklock, one of Halifax's master builders.[3] Among Stirling's achievements were the Halifax Club (1862), Keith Hall (1863), the Provincial Building (1864) – now home to the Art Galley of Nova Scotia – the Poor Asylum (1867), and the School for the Blind (1868). In 1866–67 Stirling designed five Halifax churches – Trinity and St Mark's (both Anglican), Northwest Arm and St John's (both Presbyterian), and St Joseph's Roman Catholic in the North End. It was an era of church-building.[4]

Nor was new Grafton Street the only Halifax church then under construction. Kaye Street Wesleyan, dedicated in August 1869, was built in brick in the same style; Stirling probably designed it too. The best known of David Stirling's three surviving Halifax churches is Fort Massey Presbyterian (1871), built in his signature Early Gothic Revival style.

Stirling's creativity – liberated in Fort Massey and the "Gothic dream" of old Westminster Presbyterian, New Glasgow (1876) – was restrained by the prerequisites of Methodist ecclesiastical house style. In Grafton Street we have the happy marriage of "Methodist Chapel" – a vernacular deriving from Early English – and Gothic Revival. According to one architectural historian, Stirling's "churches displayed an archaeologically correct mastery of Gothic concepts and detail, whether in Early English or Decorated Gothic style, or a combination of the two."[5]

Stirling's architectural drawings for new Grafton Street have not survived, but it is clear that, apart from the sloping roof-covered aisles, Grafton Street Methodist was a plainer version of old St Joseph's Roman Catholic Church, destroyed in the Harbour Explosion of 6 December 1917. The east front of the building facing Grafton Street was to be sixteen metres long and the sides twenty-nine metres. (Between design and execution, however, the depth increased by five metres.) The building materials were brick and sandstone.

Construction began almost immediately the tender was awarded, despite a stonemasons' strike in progress. By mid-October 1868 the walls were up and the structure nearly ready for roofing. When completed, the steep pitch roof was said to have been "covered with slates of the very best quality." By May 1869 new Grafton Street was far enough advanced to be used for church meeting purposes. By August it was "rapidly approaching completion." The church was dedicated on 7 November 1869.[6] Like old Zoar several blocks north on Argyle Street, the church faces east.

The imposing facade of Grafton Street Church belies the essential simplicity of the building. Five ornate foliated finials project above the roof-line, four of them capping decorative buttresses. The highest, simulating a spire, complements the large trifenestrated and traceried Gothic window that overlooks the pointed entrance porch with its deep recessed, moulded arch. On either side of the porch and high window are two rows of small lancet windows; the circular moulding of one of them terminates in sculpted stone faces of the brothers Wesley – John and Charles. So striking and deceptive is the Gothicizing facade that it is easy to forget that Grafton Street is not Gothic Revival; it is Methodist Chapel overlaid with Gothic ornament.

The only significant alteration that the church is known to have undergone in its fifty-six-year Methodist occupancy occurred in 1911. At that time choir and organ moved downstairs from the east gallery to the minister's platform at the front. By 1925, when the Presbyterians leased it, the church was not in good shape. The 1911 renovations had been undermined by damage inflicted by the Harbour Explosion of 1917. Nor had the building been properly maintained; the facade and window frames were slathered with paint, apparently in an effort to weatherproof the stonework.[7] A telling "snapshot" of the exterior condition is the specification for outside repairs obtained from a builder in the autumn of 1925, when the Presbyterians were considering whether to purchase.[8] They did not have the $6,500 quoted to spend on repairs, and it would not be until 1978 that a three-year "Restoration Programme" commenced. It was followed by a second in 1991 and a third in 2003.

CHURCH EXTERIOR

The most noticeable feature of the exterior of Saint David's is the magnificent stonework on the facade. One must look up to appreciate the delicacy of the carving in the sandstone pinnacles, which are highly decorative and lend a distinctive touch to an otherwise very severe building, devoid of much ornament. Sandstone is also used in the large windowsills on the north and south walls, at the steps, around the frames of the two small windows on the front, and as caps on the buttresses. Architect Stirling, of course, was the son of a stonemason and once held a commercial interest in a stone quarry.[9] He knew how to use stone and was obviously fond of it.

The side walls, like the early cathedrals of Europe, feature grounded buttresses. These function as effectively attached columns that strengthen the walls between the large window openings. Buttresses allowed the medieval builders to construct ever higher walls with ever larger windows, while reducing the risk of collapse. By the same token, they allowed Stirling to design walls with relatively large windows and at the same time support the very heavy weight of the roof. These stepped buttresses, with sandstone caps ("set offs") to shed water, become thicker towards the base. Unfortunately, over the years the buttresses, straining under the massive roof load, started to spread out at the top. This movement was arrested using tie rods, which stretch across the interior width of the building. At the same time the buttresses were rebuilt, with reinforced concrete replacing the original brick. The sandstone caps were carefully reset, and the new buttresses are the same shape as the original.

The front of the church was built using high-quality red-clay brick with lime mortar; a good portion of it has survived to this day. Large areas (including the pilasters) have been rebuilt using modern brick and Portland cement mortar. The remaining portions of the original brickwork – the flat walls between the pilasters – have very thin mortar joints, thus giving better visual emphasis to the brick. Both the side walls and the back wall were also built with brick, but the brick was stuccoed with a cementitious material ("mastic"). Though stucco has fallen out of favour in view of Halifax's climate, it was a common exterior treatment in 1869, eminently suitable to a building of this sort. Devastating fires in Halifax and other Canadian cities, not to mention the loss of the first church, meant that non-combustible brick was the construction material of choice.

Solid masonry walls exhibit the "cathedral effect." Because of their great mass (compared to thinner wooden walls), they take longer to heat up and cool off. Thus they maintain the interior temperature of the building more stably; they are also structurally sound. It took a huge quantity of brick to build the walls of Saint David's, which range from four to eight bricks thick. Moreover, in order for the building to be weathertight, the outer wythe (layer) of brick must be of such a high quality as to reduce absorption. A lower-quality brick can be used on the outside wythe if it is coated with stucco, a plastery, cement-like material that can be trowelled or brushed on. Though stucco will keep the wall more or less dry by shedding, it also absorbs water. Moisture penetrating the stucco can be carried off as vapour if there is adequate air circulation inside the building, which "breathes" through its exterior walls. Saint David's was built with this air circulation capacity, and there are two passive systems to achieve it. (By the same token, seasonal humidity from within can breathe out.)

The first system is behind the decorative plaster on the inside of the walls. The plaster is formed on spaced wooden laths that are held away from the brick wall by spacers of wood strapping. An air space of two or three centimetres behind the wooden laths enables the plaster to "breathe," thus allowing air to circulate and the masonry wall to dry. To avoid air stagnation, the builder inserted a series of vertical shafts in the exterior walls. These allowed the gravitational movement of air from basement to gallery. The system is still in place, but with one exception does not work properly since the outlets at the top have been blocked. There remains in the baseboard at the northeast corner of the gallery a single cast-iron grating through which one can still feel the air move. Air also moves in the vicinity of the other shafts, despite pieces of wood plugging the vents. This system was an early form of "destratification"; unsightly electric ceiling fans are now used to achieve the same effect.[10]

The stucco eroded from exposure to wind, rain, and sun, but it could be repainted and renewed at reasonable cost about every twenty-five years. As long as inside air circulation was maintained, stucco proved to be a suitable, economical material. Regrettably, in 1978 an inferior coating was applied for this purpose. The first and most noticeable difference was colour: the new product only came in white and could not be tinted. The building had been a buff or tan colour previously, which complemented the sandstone window frames and red brick masonry. A second and far more serious effect was that the new product did not permit the building to breathe. It caused moisture to be trapped inside the wall and resulted in severe degradation of the brick, to the point of structural failure. Remarkably, the material was not removed and replaced; indeed, its application was celebrated.[11] When the origin of the problem could no longer be denied, Saint David's sued the contractor. The action was settled out of court.

Though a striking feature of the exterior, the windows have changed greatly in character since 1869. They are appropriate to the "Decorated" style Stirling chose for the facade: heavy tracery in a geometrical pattern divides the large window area into smaller panels and helps support the large pointed arch. At first they were glazed with a pebbled or striated glass, which allowed for high translucency but limited transparency. It was thus possible to use the building in daytime without artificial light. There was renewed appreciation of the effect of this characteristic in the summer of 2004, when the echo organ in the gallery was dismantled for rebuilding. The great east window was exposed for the first time since 1928, and light streamed into the church virtually unimpeded, significantly brightening the interior.

Nothing is known of the stained glass windows of the later Methodist era, which were all destroyed in the Harbour Explosion of 6 December 1917. The stained glass windows erected inside the post-1917 windows during the Presbyterian era have gradually darkened the interior to its present sombreness. It remains possible, however, to detect a variety of types of glass in the surviving unstained windows installed after the explosion. At that time, glass from Boston, New York, Toronto, and other centres was rushed to Halifax and used as needed. Some windows were carefully restored, while others were hastily reglazed using whatever materials were available. The variety of glass in Saint David's suggests the latter method in some cases. Though a few small operable sections were provided in the stained glass, these appear to be only for condensation control purposes; they allow no access to the operational portions of the original windows. Casement sections in each original window once opened for ventilation, but have been painted shut for many years. The installation of security screens has also aggravated the darkening of the interior. Restoration work in 2005 included removing the south-side window screens, noticeably improving daytime illumination.

Photographic evidence exists that demonstrates the roof was once covered in slate tiles laid in patterns. Appearing as light and dark stripes in the roof, they gave a horizontal layering effect. Similar buildings elsewhere also show patterns within the more lightly coloured layers. The slate tiles were removed in 1950 and replaced by asphalt shingles of uniform colour. Because of the steep slope of the roof, wind uplift is not the problem it would be on lower roofs, and so the shingles lasted a long time. During restoration in 2003 and 2004, fibreglass shingles were laid on new plywood sheathing. This has formed a good base and provided some reinforcement to the roof structure – but at the expense of the roof's ability to breathe.[12]

CHURCH INTERIOR

The only known photograph documenting the interior in the Methodist era antedates the renovations of 1911; it shows the front of the church before choir and organ moved down from the east gallery. Prominently top centre is the chandelier, which appears today almost exactly as it did then. Its bright metallic finish may have faded, but the many suspended glass "shades" remain. Visible in the corners are the hammerbeam arches. These traditional forms date back to the sixteenth century and were popular in many local buildings, among them St Matthew's United Church – a reminiscence, perhaps, of the plans that Stirling had unsuccessfully submitted for new St Matthew's a decade earlier. They appear unchanged to this day.

The west wall front displays plaster carefully patterned to resemble stonework. It appears that the various blocks were painted in at least three different shades or colours, in order to simulate individual stones. Natural light entering through the large windows, which were not darkened by stained glass, emphasize the faux stonework. It is likely that the colour of the walls was very subdued. Paint chips seem to confirm that the walls were painted a warm grey stone colour. The sky blue seen today is a modern embellishment, dating from the Presbyterian era.

The large pointed arch which since 1928 has formed the opening to the chancel is "blind" – just a blank wall. The arch is also patterned to resemble stone, but seems to be one colour. The infill of the arch appears to be finished in a lightly textured material and painted darker than the surrounding walls. In the centre, leading from the vestry, is an elaborate doorway with a steeply pitched and richly embellished wood frame. It is similar to, but much more elaborate than, other doors in the church. It is finished in a dark, glossy varnish, similar to the other woodwork. On either side of the door frame are hymn boards.

Flanking the vestry door are padded benches that extend to each side of the arch. In front of the door is a large decorative pulpit, the only item of ecclesiastical furniture visible. This has Gothic arches set in the front and turned pilasters on the corners, but does not closely follow any of the built-in forms. A platform with treacherous-looking curved side steps projects into the nave and forms a very simple "stage" or dais. Its floor appears to be dark stained wood, some five steps above a lower platform. The lower platform is raised above the main floor level by two steps. It is separated from the nave of the church by a wood communion rail (removed in 1927), supported by brass decorative posts and fronted by a kneeler. The front of the dais is slightly curved and is relieved by a series of pointed arches formed in the lightly coloured wood facade. A small table is placed at the lowest level, possibly for the offering plate. No gate is visible in the communion rail, but one or more of the sections typically would have been hinged to open upwards.

To either side of the platform are facing pews, at right angles to the main pews. They abut the wall at a wood wainscotting, above which appears to be some other material, perhaps fabric or painted plaster. There are small windows on each side of the west wall below the gallery, as well as a large marble memorial plaque – perhaps Bishop Black's, which is now in St Andrew's United Church. The centre aisle is just visible, and the front rows of pews (removed for the building of the chancel) appear the same as those in the church now. They are slightly curved towards the front and feature dividers, which are in fact reinforcements to stiffen the thin backs. The gallery pews extend all the way to the west wall and also terminate in a wood wainscotting.

This "before" photograph more or less represents the building as Stirling designed it – a large, but plain sanctuary that suited Methodist custom. The most significant questions that arise regard access to the building. No doors are visible on the west end, and worshippers had to use either the side doors or the front doors facing Grafton Street. The only other outdoor access was to the furnace room below the platform.[13] What facilities existed were probably limited to the vestry. An 1896 newspaper sketch of the church viewed from the south shows nothing other than the separated schoolhouse, which antedated the church proper by four years.[14]

When, in 1925, the Presbyterians took over Grafton Street Church, it did not meet their needs either physically or liturgically. Nevertheless, the only major structural alteration that the interior has undergone occurred in

1928, when the "business" end of the sanctuary was completely redesigned and rebuilt. By August organ, pulpit, and platform had been swept away. The Gothic arch over and above the platform was unbricked and cut out to full size. What lay behind was converted into a semi-decagonal apse with chancel opening onto a choir. (It was designed by prominent local architect Sydney P. Dumaresq, whose wife was a member of Saint David's.) The apse is dominated by a high rose window, which pierces its broad central section, and the hexagonal panels of which feature stained glass images of the Holy Spirit in the form of an angel, the Four Evangelists, and Saint Paul. (The symbolism is appropriate, given the Presbyterian emphasis on preaching and proclaiming Jesus as the Word of God.) The window was donated by the Frank K. Warren family, Mr Warren being first chair of the Board (1925–28) and a member of the rebuilding advisory committee. The chancel rose window was inspired by the one at St Matthew's United, where the Warrens had been members before the Disruption. That the window was set in the wall about two degrees out of level has tormented some observers, but the anomaly goes unnoticed by most. Behind the chancel were added a minister's study and choir room. Modern washrooms were also installed, and the entrance to the boiler room below was altered.

The chancel is perhaps the most significant and recognizable part of the church, and its design requires some explanation. The minister (Kerr) and the choirmaster (Scott-Hunter), both veterans of the Church of Scotland, can be given much of the credit for the concept behind the design. Beneath the choir and great organ, new space was created, not much wider than corridors. The facing banks of perpendicular pews were replaced by, respectively, the Session room (south) and the Board room (north). The organ console was placed more or less in its present setting, in order to communicate with the various air ducts and pneumatics that ran under the floor and up inside the walls to each organ division. The new walls were panelled to match the organ cases above. The apse and choir would not have been out of place in a Roman Catholic or Anglican church, much less a Scottish kirk. Facing choir stalls, using the pews recovered from the main floor, completed this raised platform, opening on to the chancel, where the communion table was placed.

The lower walls of the chancel are faced with wooden linenfold panelling, topped with a frieze of carved wooden grapes and grain. This attractive material is from a liturgical catalogue, probably selected by the architect in consultation with the rebuilding committee. The upper plastered walls are decorated with gold-painted stencilled images of the Burning Bush, the logo of The Presbyterian Church in Canada from its founding in 1875.

The most precious and most Presbyterian artifact in Saint David's is the black walnut pulpit that once dominated the chancel of old St Andrew's on Tobin Street. Described in 1878 as the finest piece of carved church-work in eastern Canada, the octagonal pulpit, complete with Greek columns, was designed by David Stirling for a kirk much larger than Saint David's. It features in bas-relief the traditional Burning Bush motif of the Church of Scotland, flanked on either side by the saltire, or St Andrew's cross. Salvaged when St Andrew's was abandoned in 1917 and stripped of its furnishings, the pulpit was sold to the Presbyterians along with Grafton Street Church. The pulpit was placed on the liturgical north side of the chancel, which according to high kirk tradition was always deemed to face east. The brass lectern opposite confirmed the Scoto-Catholic emphasis.

The Word proclaimed from the lectern and preached from the pulpit must at all costs be heard. The demise of the central hot-air heating system in 1946 obviated the need for large, open floor registers. The openings were filled and linoleum installed over the aisle floors, followed by carpet. A final carpeting occurred in 1978 and lasted until 2004, when parts of it were removed and a noticeable improvement in the acoustical character of the sanctuary followed.

The hot-air heating system was no doubt less than satisfactory. Air circulation to the balcony would have been limited by the small size of the air shafts (which were not intended solely for heating), and the building would have been uncomfortably cold in winter. While the hot-water system improved comfort, however, it was at the expense of appearance. The long ranks of cast-iron radiators lining the side walls on both levels are not aesthetically pleasing. On closer examination, it seems that they were second-hand and were possibly acquired, together with the boiler, from another building. Folklore has it that they came from the Capitol Theatre (which received a new heating system at the time), courtesy of a trustee who was employed by the contractor.

THE CHURCH HALLS

In April 1865 the Grafton Street Methodist trustees purchased for $1,000 a strip of land north by northwest of the church for a schoolhouse. The 1852 church was bursting at the seams; by February 1865 the schoolroom at the back was not large enough to accommodate the two hundred students and twenty teachers.[15] The new two-storey facility, brick with a slate roof, opened in May 1866, a few months after the formation of the Halifax and Dartmouth Sabbath School Association. Church schools were then undergoing a great revivial. State-of-the-art premises led quickly to the establishment of the Grafton Street Wesleyan Sabbath School Society, which flourished for fifty years.

The "schoolhouse," as it was known throughout its Methodist life, stood near the north property line and some distance from the back door of the church;[16] this location, if not the direction of the wind, helped save it from the conflagration that consumed the church in February 1868. The inconvenience of having to go outdoors to reach the hall, as it came to be known, and its inadequate size, not to mention its unsafe and irremediable condition, were factors in the decision to build anew. Over the twenty-five years of their occupation, the Presbyterians repaired and renewed the hall on several occasions. As recently as the summer of 1946, for example, the eighty-year-old building was enlarged and redecorated – an entire room added to permit storage – and a new oil-burning hot-water heating system installed. Saint David's was preparing to rescue the hall yet again in 1950 when a condition report by a structural engineer made clear that it was beyond reclamation and would have to be abandoned.

Saint David's decided not to throw good money after bad. It remains unclear, however, why the new hall was not built on the site of the old, which the congregation rejected the Session-Trustees' recommendation to sell, despite an offer of $12,000. The answer would seem to lie in the desire to have a hall attached to the church. That effectively limited the choice of building site to the Old Methodist Burying Ground, the larger part of which lay directly behind the church. Closed for eight years before the first church was built, the burying ground seems to have been a minor factor in locating the new hall. Its floor level was established so that it is clear of the burying ground, a concrete slab spanning the graves. Despite intitial concerns about legal liability – there was none – the Presbyterians had no scruples building on the site of the burying ground such as had deterred the Wesleyans from doing so in 1866.

The 1951 hall is a conventional building of its time designed by James N. Boulter, MRAIC, an adherent of Saint David's. Built onto the back of the church, it measures about 17 by 18 metres and dovetails with the 1928 chancel and new vestry. The wood gymnasium floor is built on top of the slab spanning the burying ground and is a bouncy "live floor" suitable for sports such as badminton and basketball. The 5.5-metre-high gymnasium ceiling dominates the central part of the building. The walls are built of 36-centimetre-thick "Speed Tile," a hollow clay masonry unit promoted for its light weight, insulating ability, and suitableness for interior plaster and exterior stucco finish. The exterior was stucco to match the church, with wood windows and a decorative band course (or feature strip) let in to relieve the uniformity of the walls. The high gymnasium roof is built of wood trusses, with insulation above a highly combustible pressed wood fibre-type acoustic ceiling tile. Two large vent stacks on the roof could be opened to exchange the air when heat built up in the room. The wood trusses are supported on clay tile columns, which show as pilasters on the exterior walls.

Ancillary rooms were built around the hall, such as the kitchen and what is now called the lecture room; both of these face south. The layout of the kitchen was exactly as it is today, the only room from 1951 that has not changed its function. Against the north wall in the area now occupied by the stage were two classrooms, while a solid wall faced the hall proper. Along the west side were windows, with sills 2 metres above the floor, similar to a school gymnasium. A small vestibule and cloakroom occupy the area now outside the church office. A portable sectional stage appeared at the north end of the hall. In the area now occupied by the nursery was a Church School office and washrooms, and on the east side, two more small classrooms.

The hall was serviced with gas, which at the time was still generated in Halifax by burning coal at a central plant. Radiator recesses are shown on the 1951 architectural drawings. As the hot-air heating system had been replaced by a hot-water one five years earlier, the hot-water boiler may have been gas-fired for a time. Domestic gas was discontinued in Halifax shortly afterwards, and the boiler converted to oil.

As early as November 1958, the new hall was short on space, particularly for Church School purposes, and building an extension was under consideration. The postwar baby boom resulted in large numbers of school-age children, and the building was already bursting at the seams. Ironically, the hall extension facing Brunswick Street rose on the site of the old hall. It contained four single and two double classrooms, the Church School superintendent's office, a spacious minister's study, and a sitting room, along with more washrooms. Architectural drawings prepared by Duffus Romans and Single were stamped by Henry Romans, with the date 20 December 1961. The building was constructed with solid masonry walls – concrete block on the inside and Lantz Grey range brick on the exterior – a wall construction typical of its time. The walls are insulated with 6 centimetres of batt insulation and finished on the inside with gypsum lath and plaster. Roof and ceiling are of structural steel, while concrete was used for both floors. The existing hot-water heating system was extended from the hall proper, requiring some awkward piping arrangements. Two new fans were added to the existing gravity vent stacks in the hall roof. The electrical system was also modified to accommodate the rebuilding. A typically "efficient" functional structure of the early 1960s, after Le Corbusier, the hall is faced with a light tan brick in panels between vertical window bands.

Because of the slope of the land down from Brunswick Street, the hall extension is built into the hill and the lower floor is well below grade, resulting in a split entry. The door is on the landing between the two floors. A pointed Gothic arch window dominates the south wall, while its upper portion, fronting the minister's study, is glazed with coloured glass. Another pointed arch window with coloured glass highlights the entrance, but is concealed in part by a cantilevered canopy over the double-door entrance. On the south end of the west elevation a mosaic-tile cross, 1.5 metres by 90 centimetres, is set into the brick. This understated symbol is not illuminated and is set some 12 centimetres deep into the wall, thus reducing its visibility.

The Christian Education Centre, as the hall extension was known until 1967, included several renovations to the 1951 hall. Many of the original rooms were subdivided, opened up, or eliminated as part of the rebuilding. The most striking change was the new stage, built in place of two classrooms, with a new raised roof above. This costly addition must have been made with some use such as amateur theatricals in mind; rooms to each side could serve as dressing rooms. No significant repair work was conducted in the hall after the 1962 rebuilding. A small renovation in the area of the kitchen servery took place in the 1970s, resulting in the present appearance. At the same time the custodial officer was given more storage space adjacent to the kitchen.

YESTERDAY, TODAY, AND TOMORROW

A second restoration program in 1991 addressed mostly the interior of the church building. The sanctuary was redecorated, some insulation added to the attic, and the heating control system altered. Fundamental structural and systemic problems, however, were not addressed. By the end of the decade, serious deterioration was evident throughout the complex. Proactive and preventive maintenance was non-existent, and major expenditure in several areas was soon found to be necessary. In 2000 a proposal was made to the board of managers to commission a "Condition Report" – a detailed inquiry by trained architectural and engineering professionals that would review the building and systems, identify shortcomings, and outline the nature and probable cost of repairs, replacements, and other work appropriate or necessary. It would also establish priorities and provide a tentative schedule of work.

Prepared in March 2002 by MacFawn and Rogers Architects Limited, the massive and detailed Condition Report proposed an ambitious program of restoration and renewal. A five-year timetable outlined some $1.5 million worth of work needed. While a number of deficiencies were recognized in the hall, the focus of this third major restoration program has been on the 1869 church proper. In 2003 the south roof was reshingled. Work was completed only days before the arrival of Hurricane Juan on 28 September, and the roof survived without so much as a leak. Remarkably, so did the rest of the building; only a small stone pinnacle was dislodged by the winds. Unfortunately, torrential rains following the hurricane resulted in backed-up drains, and several rooms were flooded. The 2004 program called for reshingling the north roof. In early spring, however, it became apparent that both boiler and oil tanks were about to fail. All were replaced in a major undertaking that saw the installation of a fire-rated boiler room, two new boilers and two new flue liners, a new water heater, and two new oil tanks. The north roof was also reshingled, and a number of smaller internal projects carried out. These included installing a code-compliant fire alarm system.

Antedating 2004's restoration work was the removal of the front two rows of pews, creating more room for children's stories and musical performances, as well as coffins or urns at funerals or memorial services. The decision to acquire a new concert grand piano that year necessitated rebuilding the floor at the foot of the chancel, adding new hardwood, and refinishing existing material. The floor was reinforced from below to support the weight of the piano and to correct sagging resulting from serious deterioration of the joists.

Removal of the deteriorated stucco also proceeded from recommendations made in the Condition Report. The structural engineers diagnosed that most of the underlying brick, sometimes to a depth of two wythes, had failed because of surface spalling and would have to be replaced before a new coating could be applied. In 2005 the west (back) wall was repaired. Once the old coating was removed, the diagnosis was confirmed. When the brick was rebuilt a new – proven – coating was applied, on a mesh of stainless steel, and tinted to match the colour of the stucco that had been sandblasted off in 1978 and replaced with the faulty exterior finish. By the end of 2006 the north wall had been restored, and its stained glass window frameworks rebuilt.

It was also in 2006 that Saint David's was designated a provincial heritage property. The importance of Grafton Street Methodist Church as an architectural artifact and its symbolism to generations of Presbyterians who have worshipped there since 1925 cannot be overstated. The priority is to return it to sound condition. At the same time the function and use of the hall, original and extended, are also under consideration. It represents a large space, minimally utilized and expensive to maintain. Saint David's attitudes towards witness in the community and work and worship in the church will require sustained collective self-examination before an effective and affordable solution that promotes preserving the 1869 heritage building, while at the same time sensitively utilizing the rest of the property, can be found.

Epilogue

The onset of the third Christian millennium coincided with the fourth quarter of Saint David's first century. The congregation found itself in much the same position as The Presbyterian Church in Canada in 1925 – significantly down in its number of active members but determined on renewing its resources and energizing its call to worship and mission.[1] Twenty-first-century Christians are like first-century ones – evangelists for an inconvenient truth that concerns everyone. Presbyterians, for their part, are a minority among Christians, who are in turn a minority among persons of faith. Yet just as congregations, however small or shrinking, enrich the denominational theme with variations, so too denominational themes enrich and diversify the Christian church. Conversely, the extinction or submersion of denominations impoverishes Christian witness, depriving the Church of distinctive traditions in the interest of economies of scale. Regardless of their origins and circumstances, all these denominations are common-purpose and common-value communities. The Christian church is a community of communities, a vast worshipping, witnessing, and evangelizing fellowship.

In a recent sermon the minister of Saint David's called for "radical hospitality" and "passionate worship." Though his four predecessors would have used different language, both they and Saint David's have always striven to practise that preaching. The church's 2002 vision statement affirms the existence of "a worshipping, sharing, welcoming community," aspects of identity formation on which the mission statement elaborates. While prayer may be solitary, worship is a communal undertaking, and one can no more be a committed Christian outside a community of committed Christians, small or large, marginal or mainstream, than outside

Sunday morning public worship. Not for nothing did the 132nd General Assembly of The Presbyterian Church in Canada declare 2006–7 the Year of Sabbath.

Saint David's is a liberal evangelical congregation within a mainstream Protestant church in which evangelical renewal has had a conflicted history.[2] All Christians are "born again," and all Christian churches are evangelical by definition. They preach not to the converted but to the yet-to-be converted and in order to induce conversion. The Church's mission is to proclaim the Gospel. Dillwyn T. Evans, moderator of the 96th (1970) General Assembly, which met at Saint David's, put it thus: "Too many of us speak of Jesus Christ as though he were a dead martyr, for whom we hold memorial services every Sunday. We should be getting across the idea that we are servants of a living Lord. Sunday should be a day to celebrate with joy."[3] Saint David's emphasizes that Christian commitment is a life sentence, not incarcerating but liberating. Freed by knowledge of the truth from sin, ignorance, and death, the Christian is free indeed. In Reginald Bibby's formulation, Saint David's is a quintessential "restless church," well positioned to help realize what Bibby's sociological investigations suggest is an emerging religious renaissance.[4]

Saint David's never was The Presbyterian Church in Canada writ small, an established non-uniting majority congregation that voted to stay out of the coming United Church of Canada in order to continue Presbyterian. Instead it was a new creation. In no other major Canadian centre that was home to a comparable number of congregations was the PCC wiped out as in Halifax. In a sense, the birth of Saint David's was an ironic defeat for the very historic denominationalism it was meant to, and did, subserve. The congregation began life outside and without the sanction of the official church, the better to complicate its evolution by offering more of the same as an alternative. The Presbyterians who united to found Saint David's risked everything for an "underground" church – even congregationalism, the very antithesis of Presbyterian polity.

Comparing the origins of Saint David's with its development, the historian detects evidence of the genetic fallacy: mistaking "the becoming of a thing for the thing which it has become."[5] The persistence of the PCC in spite of itself was an exercise in counterfactual history and in that sense illegitimate. This "counter-evolutionary" event was not meant or expected or deemed possible to happen, but it did. Saint David's contributed to a revolution from below that limited and varied the parent church's future as part of a new enhanced religious family. It was always part of something bigger than itself, even – perhaps especially – when it was not. For that reason it seemed trapped in the moment of its birth. An exigency of circumstance became an immutable tradition.

Saint David's first few months of forced congregationalism – keeping the local church alive during the painful transition from PCC to Presbyterian to PCC – were meant to be strictly temporary and were. But their impact was so profound that in the collective memory they stand as normative self-definition. They are the source of Saint David's superiority complex, a sense of mission to the whole church engendered by the proud memory that for one brief shining moment Saint David's, an outlaw congregation sanctioned only by the law of the land, *was* The Presbyterian Church in Canada in Halifax. The congregation came first and then the church, a polar reversal of due process. The mothers and fathers of Saint David's were overwhelmed by the sheer un-Presbyterian impropriety of what they were doing – defying the church in order to save it from itself.

If the months February through July 1925 were pure climax, then the years following were a very long anticlimax. Getting down to business as an "ordinary" Presbyterian congregation, as if the Disruption had not happened and everything had not changed, proved challenging. Nearly 120 years of history were undone in an instant and the clock turned back to a time when Halifax had only one regular Presbyterian church. Saint David's was not the tenth congregation under the old dispensation but the first under the new. The parts of many converged to form a new whole.

The church collectively is no stronger than its smaller or weaker congregations. According to the 2001 census, The Presbyterian Church in Canada was the religious denomination that reported the sharpest decline in Nova Scotia between 1991 and 2001 – 35.6 per cent. Nationally, Presbyterians fell to the bottom of the top ten Christian churches – 1.4 per cent – after "Protestant, not included elsewhere." The decline provincially was twice that of metropolitan Halifax (17.3 per cent).[6] In 2003 the minister of Saint David's gave an interview to a Halifax newspaper in which he stated that despite The Presbyterian Church in Canada's having reported the sharpest drop in attendance at Sunday worship, he was not discouraged.[7]

Reginald Bibby's trope "remnant resilience in the mainline" (that is, mainstream Protestant churches) applies equally to The Presbyterian Church in Canada as to the Presbyterian Church of Saint David. Just by being there, it has proved how resilient the remnant was – so resilient that even as the official church was passing out of existence, the underground one could summon into being new bodies to continue it. The Presbyterian Church in Canada after 10 June 1925, and new congregations such as Saint

David's in place on that day, fit perfectly the model proposed by Charles Brockwell and Timothy Wengert.[8] Historians of the Christian experience must examine impressionistic or indirect evidence (not just the records) of "subversive" organizations whose history has been lost, hidden, or ignored in the interests of a hegemonic master narrative – in this case the United Church of Canada. Saint David's iconography (pulpit and stained glass windows), liturgy, oral tradition, popular history, and architecture speak volumes about the origins and development of the congregation, as well as the new history of the reborn Presbyterian Church in Canada emerging from the Disruption.

APPENDICES

APPENDIX A

Glossary

BURGHER/ANTI-BURGHER: "Breach" in the Secession Church of Scotland in 1747 over the propriety of taking the civic oath; replicated in Nova Scotia, 1786–1817

DISRUPTION: (1) Schism in the Church of Scotland in 1843 ("Great Disruption"); (2) schism in The Presbyterian Church in Canada in 1925

DISSENTER: (1) A Scottish Presbyterian not of the Kirk; (2) a member of The Presbyterian Church in Canada who opposed or resisted union with the Methodist and Congregational churches in 1925

FREE CHURCH: Withdrawal in 1843 of congregations from the Church of Scotland resulting from the Great Disruption; replicated in Nova Scotia, 1844–60

THE KIRK: The Church of Scotland, as by law established

PRESBYTERIAN: A Dissenter, as opposed to a Kirkman (member of the Kirk)

THE PRESBYTERIAN CHURCH IN CANADA: Union in 1875 of the Canada Presbyterian Church, the Presbyterian Church of Canada in connection with the Church of Scotland, the Presbyterian Church of the Lower Provinces, and the Presbyterian Church of the Maritime Provinces in connection with the Church of Scotland

PRESBYTERIAN CHURCH OF NOVA SCOTIA: Union in 1817 of the Presbytery of Truro (Burgher Seceder) and the Presbytery of Pictou (Anti-Burgher Seceder)

PRESBYTERIAN CHURCH OF THE LOWER PROVINCES OF BRITISH NORTH AMERICA: Union in 1860 of the Presbyterian Church of Nova Scotia with the Free Church in Nova Scotia and Prince Edward Island and, in 1866, in New Brunswick

SECESSION CHURCH/ASSOCIATE SYNOD: Withdrawal of ministers and elders from the Church of Scotland in 1733

UNIONIST: A member of The Presbyterian Church in Canada who supported union with the Methodist and Congregational churches in 1925

UNITED CHURCH OF CANADA: Merger in 1925 of the larger part of The Presbyterian Church in Canada, the Methodist Church of Canada, and the Congregational Union of Canada

The Constitution ("Eight Resolutions")

Resolutions Passed at Organization Meeting of The Presbyterian Church, Halifax, Held on Thursday, 26th February 1925

I.   That we, members and adherents of The Presbyterian Church in Canada, residing at present in the City of Halifax, and vicinity, do hereby resolve to form ourselves into a Congregation to be known as "The Presbyterian Church, Halifax."

II.   As to matters of faith and government, we adopt as our Standard the principles set forth in the book of *Rules and Forms of Procedure*[1] at present in use in The Presbyterian Church in Canada and we declare it to be our intention, after the 10th day of June 1925,[2] to associate ourselves as a Congregation with the continuing Presbyterian Church in Canada, in the meantime remaining an independent Presbyterian Congregation.

III.   We receive and approve and authorize to act as spiritual officers of this Church until the 10th day of June 1925 and as long thereafter as may be deemed necessary by the Congregation, the following previously elected and duly ordained Elders, namely:

W.C. Bauld	W.J. Kane
W.N. Brown	R.D. McCleave
F.W. Christie	H.L. Stewart
A.D. Falconer	Dr John Stewart
R.A. Guildford	[C.L. Torey][3]
R.D. Guildford	H.D. Wallace

and such other elders as may hereafter associate themselves with this Congregation and we authorize and empower these, until otherwise ordered by the Congregation under the convenership of Rev. Frank Baird, or of one of themselves to appoint a Clerk and thereafter have charge of the spiritual interests of the Congregation, including the order of Worship, the Sabbath School, the Service of Praise, the securing of supply for the pulpit and in conjunction with the Board of Trustees, the submitting of a name or names to the Congregation to be voted on as a possible Minister of the Church, reserving nevertheless, to any member of the Church the right to submit a name to be voted on as aforesaid.

IV.   We approve also in accordance with Chapter 178 of the Revised Acts [Statutes] of the Province of Nova Scotia [1923],[4] in terms of which this meeting was duly called, of the election of a Board of Trustees whose duty it shall be to secure contributions for Missions, the payment of the salary of the Minister, and the maintenance and support of the work of the Congregation, and in conjunction with the Elders, after due and full consideration has been given to the matter, to submit to the Church recommendations to be voted on regarding the purchasing, leasing or building of a permanent place of worship for the Congregation. The Trustees, who shall continue in office till their successors are appointed, shall appoint their own Chairman, Secretary and Treasurer and they shall hold in trust for the Congregation all real and personal estate of the Congregation and shall be subject at all times and touching all matters to the instructions of the Congregation.

V.   Meetings of the Congregation may be called by the Elders, the Trustees or on the requisition of ten per cent (10%) of the Communicant members of the Church.

VI.   The Communicant members of the Church shall be those who join it on profession of faith or who bring certificates from other Christian Churches. Adherent members of the Church shall be those of the age of 18 and upwards, who by attendance and registered contribution to the support of the Church identify themselves with the Congregation. These with the Communicant members shall have a vote at all meetings of the Congregation regularly called.

VII.   And finally, we earnestly invoke the Divine blessing upon this our undertaking to form a Congregation of the Church of Christ, and we invite all who are of like mind and spirit to associate themselves with us in this our endeavour to preserve and perpetuate the Church of our fathers in this City and community; and we humbly pray that we who are thus combining for the worship of God and the extension of His Kingdom on the earth, by our devotion to exalted Christian ideals in both doctrine and conduct become such a Church, that, out of it, as out of Zion, the perfection of beauty, God shall shine.

VIII.   Nothing in the foregoing Resolutions shall prevent the members of this Congregation from adding to, or altering, or annulling any of the aforesaid Resolutions on the vote of two-thirds (2/3) of those members present at a Congregational meeting regularly called for that purpose, notice of which, setting forth the purpose of the meeting, having been read at the regular services of the Congregation on the two Sundays preceding such meeting.

APPENDIX C

Elders and Trustees

ELDERS

Note: **Boldface** denotes elders who were trustees.

Adam-Murphy, Judithe, 1984–93; lay/pastoral assistant, 1982–93; ordained minister and inducted assistant, 1993

Alary, Murray W., 1968–71, 1984– ; assistant clerk of Session, 1985–97; clerk of Session, 1997–

Anderson, Norman, 1968–74

Anderson, Robert, 1971–77

Andrews, Thomas Erle, 1929–43; inducted

Archibald, Charles M., 1929–37

Ashworth, Frank R., 1939–50

Ashworth, Nora, 1968–75; first woman elder; first woman commissioner to General Assembly from within Atlantic Synod

Baillie, A.K., 1928–38

Bauld, William C., 1925–52; charter elder

Bell, Joseph Poole, 1960–68

Bell, Norma, 1977–2000

Brown, Gordon, 1997–2002

Brown, William N., 1925–30; charter elder

Caldwell, A. Lloyd, 1960–96

Calkin, Melvin, 1984–

Calkin, Patricia, 1997–

Cameron, George F., 1955–58

Cameron, Hugh, 1984–88

Cameron, John R., 1977–80

Campbell, Alexander, 1959–61
Campbell, David K., 1963–[67?]
Campbell, Jamie S., 1990–
Chard, Elizabeth A., 1968–2007; first woman elder; assistant superintendent of
    Church School, 1969–96; superintendent, 1996–2007
Chisholm, Kathleen Louise ("Boofie"), 1990–2003
Christie, Frederick William, 1925–26; charter elder
Clark, Olive, 1980–
Clarke, Lorne Otis, 1953–64
Clarke, Reginald, 1977–
Cohn, Arthur Raymond, 1977–89
Craig, David, 1990–
Craig (Stewart), Margaret, 1990–
Crawford, William, 1984–88
Creighton, Henry D., 1926–42; "treasurer of budget"
Crowell, Harry E., 1960–96; church officer, 1984–87
Dauphinee, Peter, 1990–99
Davidson, Allan, 1929–31
Davison, John MacN., 1980–2000
Dick, Robert, 1955–70
Donaldson, Frank, 1953–58; inducted
Falconer, Alexander Duncan, 1925–32; charter elder; chair, Board of Elders;
    president, Halifax Presbyterian Church Association
Finley, Russell Yates, 1946–48
Fraser, A. Sinclair, 1939–57
Fraser, Frank, 1963–65
Fraser, Martin Luther, 1948–55; induction
Fyfe, MacPherson, 2004–
Gardiner, Richard, 1990– ; church officer, 1987, 2000–4
Guild, John E., 1955–56
Guild, Robert A., 1980–
Guildford, Frederick Moir, 1926–60
Guildford, Robert Alexander, 1925–28; charter elder
Guildford, Robert Douglas, 1925–47; charter elder
Guildford, Thomas K., 1963–80
Haldane, Vanora, 1997–
Harper, William L., 1946–[ca. 1964]
Hattie, Herbert, 1963–[before 1990]
Hines, Leonard Allan, 1959–70
Holloway, Thomas Edgar, 1946–53, 1963–70

Hunter, Arthur MacWilliam, 1952–87

Kane, Ralph Waterman, 1948–97; clerk of Session, 1960–97; superintendent of Church School, 1944–96

Kane, William John, 1925–60; clerk of Session, 1925–60; charter elder

Kennedy, (the Reverend) Cecil Howard, 1948–69

Kennedy, Elizabeth Catherine, 1971–80

Kennedy, Robert, 1968–69

Knox, Donald, 1977–

Langille, Harry Russell, 1952–67

Luther, John E., 1939–59; "treasurer of budget"

MacAulay (Hatfield), Elizabeth, 1984–96

MacCulloch, Vincent K., 1959–90

MacDonald, Avard Stewart, 1971–95

Macdonald, Valerie, 1997–

MacDonald-Parsons, Shelley, 2004–

Mackay, Davida, 2004–

Mackay, Malcolm B., 1977–

MacKeigan (Tanton), Barbara, 1980–

Macleod, Donald A., 1959–70; treasurer of Presbytery

MacPherson, Colin, 1997–

Mader, Frank, 1997–

Mader, Kenneth A., 1971–

Mahon, Crawford E., 1953–61

Matheson, William, 1990–92

McCleave, Robert David, 1925–26; charter elder

McCleave, Robert Jardine, 1971–2000

McClintock, Fred, 2004– ; inducted

McCurdy, Archibald C., 1960–86

McInnes, Herbert Murray, 1952–67

McLeod, Murdoch Edward, 1952–83; assistant clerk of Session, 1968–83; clerk of Presbytery, 1963–70

Miller, Christine, 1971–2000; secretary of Presbytery, 1970–80; church secretary, [1967?]–87

Miller, George P., 1980–2003

Miller, John Crawford (Jack), 1955–67

Minnikin, Rick, 1997–2000

Mitchell, George MacGregor, 1977–2000

Mitchell, Reginald C., 1939–71

Morrison, Eben Balcom, 1952–58

Morrison, Phyllis, 2004–

Mosher, Edith, 1977–91
Mosher, Herbert K., 1955–76
Mossop, James, 1955–61
Palmeter, Harold Stirling, 1952–80
Palmeter, Ian H.M., 1980–97
Perrin, George, 1968–70
Phippen, Mary, 1980–90
Pryor, Harry Oswald, 1929–37
Purves, A.H. Blair, 1960–80
Reeves, Stewart, 1963–64
Roberts, Johannah, 2004–
Ross, Garry T., 1980–83
Ross, Harry A., 1939–52; communion roll clerk
Seary, J. Ellis, 1971–
Sinclair, C. Hibbert, 1968–70
Sommerville, Anne, 1997–
Stalley, Frank, 1984–2002
Stewart, Herbert Leslie, 1925–53; charter elder
Stewart, John, 1925–33; charter elder
Stokes, Thomas H., 1939–42
Tanton, Roy F., 1959– ; dean of Session
Tate, D.G., 1971; shortest-serving elder – three months
Tattrie, Arthur Daniel, 1948–[before 1990]; inducted
Torey, Clifford Lewis, 1925, 1946–62; inducted
Wallace, Herbert D., 1925–51; charter elder
Wamboldt, John, 2004– ; assistant superintendent of Church School, 2003–
Ward, William, 1990–2000
Wright, Robert W., 1959–[90?]

TRUSTEES

Note: **Boldface** denotes trustees who were elders. Trustee succession list not complete.

Allen, John H., 1978–82
Anderson, A.L., 1958–60
Anderson, Robert, 1968–70; vice-chair, 1969; chair, 1970
Ashworth, Brian, 1978
Ashworth, Dennis, 1975–77
Ashworth, Frank R., 1932–37, 1941–50; vice-chair, 1942–43

Baillie, A.K., 1926–29; treasurer, 1926

Barclay, Victor, 1972–74

Barnhill, Clarence E., 1940–42, 1946–52; secretary, 1942

Barnhill, J.L., 1928–31, 1933–35

Bauld, Henry Gibson, 1925; charter trustee

Bayne, Charles H., 1927–29

Bayne, Walter, 1931–33

Begg, Jean, 1970–72, 1977–79

Bell, Eric A., 1960–65; secretary, 1961–64; chair, 1965

Bell, Joseph Poole, 1957–59; vice-chair, 1957–58

Bell, Lewis A., 1966; elected January, resigned February

Bentley, Margaret, 1986–88

Bishop, Ann, 1985–87

Booth, Wendy, 2003–

Brooker, Shelley, 1999–2000

Brown, Clifford, 1967–69

Brown, Gordon, 1988–95; treasurer, 1988–94

Bruce, Ed, 1994–96

Buchanan, Robin, 1953–55; treasurer, 1953, 1972

Cahill, Barry, 2001–7; vice-chair, 2004; secretary, 2005–7

Caldwell, A. Lloyd, 1955–56, 1958–68; secretary, 1955–56, 1958–60

Calkin, Melvin G., 1973–78; secretary, 1974–75, vice-chair, 1977

Calkin, Patricia, 1997– ; treasurer, 2000– ; first woman treasurer

Cameron, Daniel Alexander, 1926

Cameron, Ernest, 1928–30, 1933–35

Cameron, George, 1936–38, 1942–44

Cameron, Hugh, 1979–81

Cameron, John M., [1950–52?]; secretary, 1952

Cameron, John R., 1975–80

Cameron, Robert Burns, 1957

Campbell, Alex, 1954–56

Campbell, Edward E., 1959–69

Campbell, Jamie S., 1988–93

Campbell, James Wilson, 1946–51

Campbell, Murray, 1962–64

Campbell, Peter, 1983–85

Cann, John H., 1957

Chard, Elizabeth A., 1991–2007; secretary, 1991–2001; chair, 2001–7

Chisholm, John Scott, 1925–28, 1931–42; vice-chair, 1928; chair, 1931–42; charter trustee; longest-serving chair

Chisholm, Kathleen Louise ("Boofie"), 1987–92
Chisholm, Sheldon P., 1960–69
Clarke, Malcolm, 1985–87
Clarke, Mary-Lou, 1992–94
Clarke, Reginald, 1971–74
Cohn, Arthur Raymond, 1970–72
Coley, Thomas A., 1964–66
Coley, Thomas J., 1952–63
Collins, Gerry, 1992–94
Collins, Graham, 1988–90
Coon, Thomas R., 1982–85; vice-chair, 1983–84; chair, 1985
Coté, Richard, 1992–94
Cox, A. William, 2001–3
Crawford, William D., 1980–85
Creighton, Henry D., 1925–26; charter trustee
Crowell, Harry E., 1974–79; vice-chair, 1976
Culp, Howard, 1974–76
Cummings, Alfred Graham, 1925–27; charter trustee
Dauphinee, Peter, 1985–90
Davison, John MacN., 1969–71; vice-chair, 1970; chair, 1971
Davison, Kenneth B., 1967–69
Davison, Peggy, 1998–2000
de la Ronde, Michael, 1990–2001; vice-chair, 1991; chair, 1992–2000
Delugt, Gerard, 1981–83
Dobson, Carol, 1994–97
Donaldson, Frank, 1948–50
Duke, James, 1977–78
Duncan, Greg, 2005–
Dunlop, Douglas, 1987–88
Fergusson, Charles Bruce, 1948, 1972–74
Finley, Russell Yates, 1927–29, 1930–32, 1935–37; treasurer, 1927–32
Francis, Thomas H., 1925; charter trustee
Fraser, A. Sinclair, 1937–39
Freeman, Gerald M., 1958–63; vice-chair, 1961
Frost, Todd, 2004
Fyfe, Mac, 1991–
Gamester, Herbert W., 1952–55; secretary, 1953; treasurer, 1954–55; died in office
Gardiner, George, 1941–46
Gardiner, Richard, 1989–2000
Gashus, Oue K., 1970–72

Kennedy, Robert, 1965–67; chair, 1966–67

King, Donald A., 1925–27, 1929–31; vice-chair, 1925–27; chair, 1929–31 (resigned); charter trustee

Kyle, Alister, 1977–78

Langille, Harry Russell, 1942–47; secretary, 1943–47

Langille, Paul, 1991–93

Lappin, Joseph, 1995–2002

Leaman, Allan Alfred, 1955–62; vice-chair, 1959–61 (resigned)

Liston, Robert, 1995–98

Logan, Don S., 1952–54

Logan, Jotham W., 1928–30, 1932–34

Lusby, Robert, 1971–73

Macaloney, Charles W., 1925–26, 1928–30, 1932–37; charter trustee

Macaulay, Murray A., 1925, 1931–36; charter trustee

MacCulloch, Vincent K., 1950–58, 1959–61, 1971–73, 1975–81, 1983–85; vice-chair, 1978; chair, 1979–80

Macdonald, Alvin F., 1926–27, 1929–31; vice-chair, 1929–31

MacDonald, Avard Stewart, 1966–68, 1974–76, 1989–91

MacDonald, D.J., 1926, 1936–38

MacDonald, Douglas M., 1971–72; vice-chair, 1972

MacDonald, James W., 1969–71

Macdonald, Jeanne, 1992–97

Macdonald, Roderick, 2001–

Macdonald, Valerie, 1981–86; secretary, 1983–86

Macdougall, W.I., 1928–30

Mackay, Davida, 2003–

Mackay, Malcolm B., 1974–76, 1994, 2004– ; vice-chair, 2005–7; chair, 2007–

MacKay, Myron, 1951–53

MacKeen, David, 1963–68; secretary, 1968

MacKeen, Henry Poole, 1925–28, 1930–32, 1936–38; charter trustee

MacKenzie, C.E., 1926–28, 1930–32

MacLean, Neil, 1987–91

MacLean, Sybil, 1975–80

MacLennan, Alex, 1977–82

MacLennan, Carol, 1984–85

MacLeod, Alex, 2001

MacLeod, Allister, 1989–91

Macleod, Donald A., 1949–57, 1967; secretary, 1950–51

MacLeod, Herbert K., 1955–58

MacLeod, John Simon Fraser, 1943–48

MacLeod, R.E., 1930–32; secretary, 1929–32

MacMillan, John C., 1969–70

MacPherson, Colin, 1983–86, 1998–2003; vice-chair, 1999–2003

MacPherson, Hugh, 1993–98; vice-chair, 1994–98

MacQuarrie, Janet, 1974–82

MacRitchie, James J., 1943–51

Mader, Frank, 1993–99; treasurer, 1994–98

Mader, Kenneth A., 1959–71; treasurer, 1959–71

Marshall, Charles A., 1951–54, 1962–67

Marshall, John S., 1983–88; chair, 1986–88

Matheson, William, 1986–88

Maxner, Charles (Chuck), 1999–2001

McAlpine, Linda, 1991–96

McClintock, Fred, 2003–7

McCurdy, Archibald C., 1958–63

McCurdy, Ross, 1983–89

McInnes, Herbert Murray, 1944–59, 1973–81; treasurer, 1944–55, 1972–79

McKay, Angus, 1959–60

McLeod, Arthur J., 1951–56

McLeod, Murdoch Edward, 1941–49; treasurer, 1943–44, vice-chair, 1945; secretary, 1948–49

Miller, Donna, 2005–7

Miller, George P., 1961–68, 1977–85; vice-chair, 1979–80; chair, 1981–82

Miller, Terris, 1972–73

Millie, A.C., 1927–29

Minnikin, Florine, 1981–83

Minnikin, Fred S., 1967–68

Minnikin, Paula, 1995–2000

Minnikin, Rick, 1995–97

Mitchell, George MacGregor (1st), 1925–28, 1929–32, 1941–49; vice-chair, 1932; charter trustee

Mitchell, George M. (2nd), 1935–37, 1951–56; vice-chair, 1952–53; chair, 1954–56

Mitchell, George M. (3rd), 1963–68, 1986–91; secretary, 1965–67, chair, 1968, 1989–91; vice-chair, 1986–88

Mitchell, John R., 1958–60

Mitchell, Reginald C., 1930–36

Moore, Joseph, 1986–93; treasurer, 1986–88 (resigned); vice-chair, 1992–93

Moreira, Judith, 1971–73, 1983; chair, 1972–73; first woman chair

Morrison, Phyllis, 2002–

Mosher, Herbert K., 1937–42, 1954

Mossop, James, 1954–55

Mowatt, A.S., 1942–44

Murray, J. Norman, 1959–61

Myers, Clyde, 1968–70

Palmeter, Diane, 1989–91, 2002

Palmeter, Geoffrey, 1998–2000

Palmeter, Harold Stirling, 1941–49

Palmeter, Ian H.M., 1969–71, 1986–88; secretary, 1969–71

Pasquet, Robert, 1989–92

Pate, David, 1994–2000

Pearo, Lester, 1962–67, 1971–72

Perrin, George, 1970

Phippen, Isabel, 1980–81

Piers, Derek, 1970–72

Priest, J. Ernest, 1950–52, 1956–58, 1964–66; chair, 1957; treasurer, 1958

Pronych, Peter, 1973–75

Purves, A.H. Blair, 1960–62, 1972–80; vice-chair, 1975; chair, 1976–78

Quinn, Edmund R., 1969–71

Quinn, Shirley, 1971

Rive, Desmond, 1982–84

Robb, E.B., 1929–31, 1933–38

Roberts, Johannah, 2003–7

Robertson, John S., 1957–60; chair, 1958–60 (resigned)

Romans, Molly, 1968–70; first woman trustee

Ross, Garry T., 1977–83; secretary, 1978–82

Ross, Harry A., 1934–36

Ross, Hugh, 1933; justice of the Supreme Court

Seary, J. Ellis, 1967–69, 1973, 1976–78, 1986–88; chair, 1969

Sedgewick, Kenneth Middleton, 1945–47

Service, Nigel, 2003–7

Sharp, James, 1976–77

Sherar, Michael, 1989–91, 1999–2001, 2003–5

Slade, Carolyn, 1999–2004

Smart, James, 2001–

Smith, Arthur W., 1973–75; vice-chair, 1973–74

Smith, Aubrey DeWolfe, 1925–27, 1929–31, 1933–35, 1936–38, 1942–50; secretary, 1933–35; charter trustee

Smith, Mary, 1968–71, 1981–86; first woman trustee

Sommerville, Frank, 1986–90; vice-chair, 1989–90

Stairs, James, 1960–61

Stalley, Frank, 1979–84; vice-chair, 1981–82, chair, 1983–84

Stewart, Charles B., 1950–54

Stewart, Chester Bryant, 1978–82

Stewart, Herbert Leslie, 1942–50

Stewart, J.W., 1959–61

Stoddard, Robert H., 1937–45; vice-chair, 1937

Stokes, Thomas E., 1937–42; secretary, 1940

Stuart, Ian M., 1981–82

Sutherland, Guy D., 1953–58; vice-chair, 1954–55

Tadros, Michael, 1974–76

Tanton, Wendy, 1973; elected but did not serve

Taylor, Steven, 1993–2003

Teasdale, Eric, 1960–62, 1964–66, 1973–77; chair, 1961–62, 1974–75

Teasdale, Lorne E., 1929–31, 1935–37

Thatcher, Edward, 1982–83

Thompson, Andrew, 1995–97

Thompson, Sedley Fraser, 1925–28; charter trustee

Torey, Clifford Lewis, 1929–31, 1934–36, 1942–45, 1946–47; chair, 1943–45 (resigned), 1946–47

Tupper, Carl, 1963–68; vice-chair, 1963–68

Turner, Margaret, 1972–76; first Ladies Guild ex officio representative

Vickery, E.J., 1956–58

Wallace, George D., 1926

Wallace, Herbert D., 1935–37, 1941–51; chair, 1948–51; died in office

Wamboldt, John, 1999–

Ward, William, 1992–94

Warren, Frank K., 1925–28; chair, 1925–29; charter trustee

Weedmark, N.J., 1961

White, David, 1984–87

Wichman, Lois, 1987–90; secretary, 1988–90

Wilson, J. Sutherland, 1949–51, 1954–56, 1964–65; vice-chair, 1956

Winsby, Kenneth W., 1948–50, 1958–60, 1962–64; chair, 1963–64

Wood, Dennis T., 1971–73

Wood, Reginald W., 1952–54

Wooster, Percy, 1943–46; vice-chair, 1944, 1946 (resigned); chair, 1945

Wright, Robert W., 1948–56; vice-chair, 1948–51; chair, 1951–53

Yeoman, Robert Forsyth, 1925–27, 1932–34; charter trustee

Yorke, Douglas, 1955–57; secretary, 1957

Bibliographic Essay

This book is based on primary sources, both archival and printed. Chief among the former are the archives of Saint David's, consisting of communion (professing member) rolls and registers of baptism, marriage, and burial; minutes of meetings of the Kirk Session and Trustees (board of managers); Session correspondence (from 1959); annual reports; scrapbooks (from 1925); newsletters (intermittent from 1969 but continuous since 2001); Sunday and special-event bulletins; and minutes and other records of voluntary organizations. In 2003 the papers of the late Ralph W. Kane, clerk of Session, 1960–97, became available. They include papers of his father, William J. Kane, clerk of Session, 1925–60, and have proved a mother lode for historical research.

Church law prohibits access to Kirk Session minutes less than fifty years old, but that restriction pales by comparison with the mishap that befell Saint David's archival records about 1962. Many early and important materials were lost or indiscriminately destroyed: the original minute book of congregational meetings from organization onwards; Board meeting minutes, 1925–27 and 1933–41; correspondence of Session and Board earlier than 1959; several years' worth of annual reports; the communion roll, 1932–52; and records of the Halifax Presbyterian Church Association, excepting only the covenant subscription book. Some much more recent documents have also been lost or destroyed, a case in point being the 1974–75 centenary celebration scrapbook compiled by Joanne Pronych, a member of the congregation's committee for the centenary of The Presbyterian Church in Canada. On short-term loan from the church office, it was presumably not returned by one of the borrowers.

Other important sources include the minutes of both the superseded and continuing Presbyterian Presbytery of Halifax (Halifax and Lunenburg) and the Maritimes (Atlantic) Synod; the monthly *Presbyterian Record,* official organ of The Presbyterian Church in Canada; and the annual *Acts and Proceedings of the General Assembly of The Presbyterian Church in Canada,* both before and after 1925. The original Maritimes Synod weekly, *Presbyterian Witness* (1848–1925), proved indispensable, as did the "Churches" page of Halifax's Saturday afternoon newspapers – the *Mail* and (until 1948) the *Echo/Star.* Two unpublished congregational histories – one from 1950 by Elder Torey and the other from 1975–79 by Elder McCleave – provided inspiration as well as historical context.

Notes

1 Jane Doucet, "Down, but Not Out: A Halifax Church Tries to Catch Its Breath," *Presbyterian Record*, February 2003, 14–17.

2 These concepts derive from the work of Reginald Bibby. See his *Fragmented Gods: The Poverty and Potential of Religion in Canada* (Toronto, 1987); *Unknown Gods: The Ongoing Story of Religion in Canada* (Toronto, 1993); and, more recently, *Restless Gods: The Renaissance of Religion in Canada* (Toronto, 2002).

3 Bedford, Bethany (Armdale), Fort Massey, Park Street, St Andrew's, St James (Dartmouth), St John's, St Matthew's, and Stairs Memorial (Dartmouth).

4 Seceders were those who broke away from the Kirk in 1733 over the right of congregations to call, rather than patrons to settle, ministers. The founder of the Secession, Ebenezer Erskine, is memorialized in Erskine United Church, in Glenholme, Nova Scotia, the oldest Presbyterian congregation in Canada.

5 "This body originated in Scotland through the deposition [in 1761] of the Rev Thomas Gillespie by the General Assembly of the Church of Scotland for refusing to take part in the settlement of an objectionable presentee, and they took their name from its being their avowed object to give 'relief' from the evils of patronage" (George Patterson, "Pioneers of Presbyterianism in the Maritime Provinces of Canada," chap. xx, asterisked footnote, in George Patterson papers, MG 1, vol. 742, NSARM). See also N.R. Needham, "Relief Church," in Nigel M. de S. Cameron, ed., *Dictionary of Scottish Church History and Theology* (Downers Grove, Ill., 1993), 702–3.

6 The Free Church originated in the 1843 secession from the Kirk (the "Great Disruption") on the issue of church-state relations and secular patronage. It arrived in Nova Scotia the same year.

7 Merged in 1925 with St John's.

8 Knox (Halifax), St Andrew's (Dartmouth), Calvin (Halifax), Iona (Dartmouth), First Sackville (Lower Sackville), and Tantallon–St Margaret's.

9 N. Keith Clifford, *The Resistance to Church Union in Canada, 1904–1939* (Vancouver, 1985).

10 Ibid., 154.

11 Nothing comparable to John Alexander Johnston's magisterial dissertation "Factors in the Formation of The Presbyterian Church in Canada, 1875" (PhD thesis, McGill University, 1955) exists for factors in the Disruption of the Presbyterian Church in Canada in 1925.

12 Excellent and characteristic examples of Douglas F. Campbell's work include "A Group, a Network and the Winning of Church Union in Canada: A Case Study in Leadership," *Canadian Review of Sociology and Anthropology* 25 (February 1988): 41–66; "Engaging Third Parties: Canadian Church Unionists and Their Opponents in the Secular Forum," *Journal of Church and State* 33 (winter 1991): 75–94; "Presbyterians and the Canadian Church Union: A Study in Social Stratification, *Papers of the Canadian Society of Presbyterian History*, 1991, 1–32; and "Class, Status and Crisis: Upper-Class Protestants and the Founding of the United Church of Canada," *Journal of Canadian Studies* 29 (autumn 1994): 63–84.

13 N. Keith Clifford, "Church Union and Western Canada," in Dennis L. Butcher et al., eds., *Prairie Spirit: Perspectives on the Heritage of the United Church of Canada in the West* (Winnipeg, 1985), 283–95.

14 Thomas Andrew Stinson, "'A Kind of Question That Raises Feeling': Nova Scotia Presbyterians and the Formation of the United Church of Canada" (MA thesis, Dalhousie University, 1991).

15 James D. Cameron, "The Garden Distressed: Church Union and Dissent on Prince Edward Island, 1904–1947" (PhD thesis, Queen's University, 1989); distilled in "The Garden Distressed: Church Union and Dissent on Prince Edward Island, 1925," *Acadiensis* 21 (spring 1992): 108–31.

16 Kenneth W. Gunn-Walberg, "The Church Union Movement in Manitoba, 1902–1925 – A Cultural Study in the Decline of Denominationalism within the Protestant Ascendancy" (PhD thesis, University of Guelph, 1971).

17 John R. Cameron, "The Story of Church Union of 1925 in the Presbytery of Pictou of the Presbyterian Church in Canada" (BD thesis, Presbyterian College, Montreal, 1969).

18 Donald S. Moore, "Disruption in the Canadian Presbyterian Church" (MTh thesis, Pine Hill Divinity Hall, 1971).

19 Gunn-Walberg, "The Church Union Movement in Manitoba," 318.

20 Frank E. Archibald, "Contribution of the Scottish Church to New Brunswick Presbyterianism from Its Earliest Beginnings until the Time of the

Disruption, and Afterwards, 1784–1852"(PhD thesis, University of Edinburgh, 1933).

21 Eldon Hay, *The Chignecto Covenanters: A Regional History of Reformed Presbyterianism in New Brunswick and Nova Scotia, 1827–1905* (Montreal and Kingston, 1996).

22 Laurie Stanley, *The Well-Watered Garden: The Presbyterian Church in Cape Breton, 1798–1860* (Sydney, NS, 1983).

23 A. Douglas C. Earle, "The Story of Pictou Presbyterianism from Its Beginnings to the Union of 1875" (MDiv thesis, Atlantic School of Theology, 1973).

24 John S. Moir, *Enduring Witness: A History of The Presbyterian Church in Canada,* 3rd ed. rev. (Burlington, Ont., 2004).

25 William Klempa, ed., *The Burning Bush and a Few Acres of Snow: The Presbyterian Contribution to Canadian Life and Culture* (Ottawa, 1994); Charles H.H. Scobie and G.A. Rawlyk, eds., *The Contribution of Presbyterianism to the Maritime Provinces of Canada* (Montreal and Kingston, 1997); and John S. Moir, *Early Presbyterianism in Canada,* ed. Paul Laverdure (Gravelbourg, Sask, 2003).

26 G.A. Rawlyk, ed., *Aspects of the Canadian Evangelical Experience* (Montreal and Kingston, 1997).

27 For the scholarly literature, see John S. Moir, comp., "A Select Bibliography of Early Canadian Presbyterianism," in Moir, *Early Presbyterianism in Canada,* 207–63, and the "Current Bibliography of Canadian Religious History," published in the Canadian Catholic Historical Association's annual *Historical Studies.*

CHAPTER ONE

1 Burkhardt Kiesekamp, "Community and Faith: The Intellectual and Ideological Bases of the Church Union Movement in Victorian Canada" (PhD thesis, University of Toronto, 1974).

2 Based on and adapted from "The Scottish Church Initiative for Union Proposal" (January 2003), section 1.1.

3 There is no proper biography of William Patrick (1852–1911), a major figure in the religious development of Canada in the first decade of the twentieth century. Ironically, he was never received into the ministry of The Presbyterian Church in Canada. Material on Patrick is taken from N. Keith Clifford, *The Resistance to Church Union in Canada, 1904–1939* (Vancouver, 1985), 11–35 passim.

4 Union discussions between the United Free Church and the Church of Scotland began in 1909 and dragged on for nearly twenty years.

5 "The Proposed Union," *Presbyterian Witness*, 9 April 1904; "Halifax Ministers and Laymen also Cape Breton Preachers Are Strongly for Union. Important Action Taken by Representatives of the Presbyterian and Methodist Churches in Halifax at Meeting Held at Residence of A.M. Bell," *Halifax Herald*, 2 April 1904.

6 James G. Greenlee, *Sir Robert Falconer: A Biography* (Toronto, 1988), 95.

7 Ibid., 94.

8 During the 1904 General Assembly, Pollok published in the *Presbyterian Witness* an article in which he set forth his conception of a united church of Canada as a "Catholic Presbyterian church"; see "Church Union," *PW*, 18 June 1904. Before and during the 1910 General Assembly, he published a six-part series of articles on church union in *Presbyterian Witness*, 7 May– 11 June 1910.

9 See, generally, Everett H. Bean, "Frank Baird (1870–1951): Father in the Synod of the Maritime Provinces," in W. Stanford Reid, ed., *Called to Witness: Profiles of Canadian Presbyterians: A Supplement to* Enduring Witness, vol. 2 (Toronto, 1980): 111–17.

10 "Assembly Notes," *Presbyterian Witness*, 19 June 1909. The other was Robert Campbell, senior clerk of the General Assembly. Concerning Sedgwick, see Frank Baird, "Church Leaders of Yesterday III. – Dr Thomas Sedgwick," *Presbyterian Witness*, 20 November 1924. See also Clifford, *The Resistance to Church Union*, 16.

11 For an account of this meeting and what follows, unless otherwise indicated, see Presbyterian Church in Canada, *Acts and Proceedings of the General Assembly … 1910*.

12 "Presbyterian General Assembly Pronounces for Church Union," *Halifax Herald*, 8 June 1910.

13 Clifford, *The Resistance to Church Union*, 47.

14 Ibid., 43.

15 Ibid. (Church "Federation" Association).

16 On this subject generally, see John R. Cameron, "The Story of Church Union of 1925 in the Presbytery of Pictou of The Presbyterian Church in Canada" (BD thesis, Presbyterian College, Montreal, 1969), 31–79.

17 This account and what follows, unless otherwise indicated, are based on the official minutes of annual meetings of the Maritimes Synod of The Presbyterian Church in Canada, UCC MCA.

18 On this subject, see Michael Owen, "Keeping Canada God's Country: Presbyterian Perspectives on Selected Social Issues, 1900–1915" (PhD thesis, University of Toronto, 1984).

19 "Synod Notes," *Presbyterian Witness*, 16 October 1909.

20 "Joint Union Committee Organizes," *Halifax Herald*, 6 October 1923; see generally James D. Cameron, "The Garden Distressed: Church Union and Dissent on Prince Edward Island, 1904–1947" (PhD thesis, Queen's University, 1989), 87–8.

21 "Split in Presbyterian Congregation in Glace Bay," *Morning Chronicle* (Halifax), 14 September 1922. See also D.M. Gillies, *Zigzags of a Cape Breton Clergyman* (Whycocomagh, NS, 1928).

22 Minutes of annual Synod meeting, October 1923 (Saint John), MCA.

23 "Proposed Church Union," *Presbyterian Witness*, 6 January 1906.

24 "Regarding the Proposed Union," *Presbyterian Witness*, 27 January 1906; "The People Hear of Church Union," *Halifax Herald*, 19 January 1906.

25 "Presbytery refrained from passing any opinion on the desirability or non-desirability of union, as they felt that the time had not come for such a step" ("Pictou Presbytery," *Presbyterian Witness*, 16 February 1907).

26 Halifax Presbytery minutes, 17 September, 17 December 1907, MCA. (A remit is "a question addressed to a lower church court from a superior one, for discussion, advice and response"; see John S. Moir, *Handbook for Canadian Presbyterians* [Toronto, 1996], 110.)

27 Halifax Presbytery minutes, 20 December 1910, MCA.

28 It is not known what percentage of the total number of congregations voted. Many did not.

29 Halifax Presbytery minutes, 24 April 1912, MCA. Clifford is mistaken that "details of the voting in individual churches were not recorded" (see *The Resistance to Church Union*, 57).

30 William Orr Mulligan (Bedford) and Robert Johnston (Park Street); the stance of Victor Guest Rae (Stairs Memorial) is not known.

31 Halifax Presbytery minutes, 24 April 1912, MCA.

32 Clifford, *The Resistance to Church Union*, 65–6, 72–3.

33 For an extremely shrewd comparative analysis of the votes from the Presbyterian perspective, see John McKeen, "Church Union Leadership" (letter to the editor), *Presbyterian Witness*, 9 September 1916.

34 Clifford, *The Resistance to Church Union*, 58.

35 Ibid., 95.

36 See ibid., 87–100 passim.

37 "The Presbyterian Call," *Eastern Chronicle* (New Glasgow), 22 September 1916.

38 "Presbyterian Convention," *Presbyterian Witness*, 14 October 1916.

39 After the formation of the regional PCA, McKeen became its treasurer and remained so until his death in December 1924. See, generally, "John McKeen Passed Away in New Glasgow," *Morning Chronicle* (Halifax), 11 December 1924.

40 The executive management committee of the city government; separate
   from the city council.

41 "Presbyterians Organize to Maintain Church of Their Forefathers," *Morning
   Chronicle* (Halifax), 4 October 1916; "Presbyterian Convocation," *Truro Daily
   News*, 4 October 1916.

42 See "Presbyterian Synod Personalities," *Morning Chronicle* (Halifax),
   5 October 1926.

43 "Accept the Challenge" (letter to the editor), *Morning Chronicle* (Halifax),
   15 November 1922. The Presbyterian resistance to church union received
   extensive and favourable coverage in the *Chronicle* because its proprietor,
   Fleming Blanchard McCurdy, a millionaire financier and former federal cabinet minister, was an anti-unionist and prime benefactor of what became the
   Presbyterian Church of Saint David. On the other hand, William H. Dennis,
   proprietor of the *Herald* and *Mail*, was a unionist.

44 Clifford, *The Resistance to Church Union*, 117.

45 This account and what follows, unless otherwise indicated, are based on
   records in the archives of St Andrew's United Church and [G.A. Burbidge
   and M.D. Morrison], *Historical Sketches of St. Andrew's Church, Halifax, N.S.,
   United Church of Canada* (Halifax, 1949), 33–4, 62–4.

46 "Report of Joint Committee on the Proposed Union of Grafton St.,
   St. Andrew's and Robie St. Congregations" (31 May 1920), Vertical File,
   vol. 111, doc. 22, NSARM.

47 See, for example, Bureau of Literature and Information of the Joint
   Committee on Church Union, *The Cry for Another Vote: Reasons Why There Can
   Not and Ought Not to Be Another Vote on Church Union* (Toronto [1923?]). The
   title of this section is taken from Cameron, "The Garden Distressed," ix.

48 See Clifford, *The Resistance to Church Union*, 122–3.

49 "Presbyterian Church Conference," *Evening News* (New Glasgow), 27 May
   1921.

50 "To Maintain Old Church of the Fathers," *Morning Chronicle* (Halifax),
   14 September 1921.

51 "Meeting of Presbyterians Decide to Oppose Unionist Movement to Limit,"
   unidentified newspaper clipping, 2 December 1922, Maritimes PCA scrapbook, Archives of the Synod of the Atlantic Provinces, PCC, Summerside,
   PEI.

52 "Old Church Will Remain in Canada," *Morning Chronicle*, 29 June 1923.

53 Trustees' minute book, 28 August and 27 September 1923, St Matthew's
   United Church records, MG 4, vol. 64, NSARM; "Trustees of St. Matthew's
   Opposed to Church Union," unidentified Halifax newspaper clipping,
   probably from *Morning Chronicle*, in minute book.

54 On this subject generally see Roberta Clare, "The Role of Women in the Preservation of the Presbyterian Church in Canada: 1921–28," in William Klempa, ed., *The Burning Bush and a Few Acres of Snow: The Presbyterian Contribution to Canadian Life and Culture* (Ottawa, 1994), 259–77.

55 "Urged Not to Commit Themselves," *Morning Chronicle* (Halifax), 30 April 1923; full text and signatories.

56 "Upheld the Old Blue Banner," *Morning Chronicle* (Halifax), 13 April 1923.

57 Peter Bush, *Western Challenge: The Presbyterian Church in Canada's Mission on the Prairies and [in the] North, 1885–1925* ([n.p.], 2000), 228–9.

58 This account and what follows, unless otherwise indicated, are based on the published *Journals* of the House of Assembly and Legislative Council and on Halifax daily newspapers. There was no Hansard at the time.

59 "Will Continue Old Church in Canada," *Morning Chronicle* (Halifax), 25 March 1924.

60 "Opposing Sides in Battle Array in Full Dress Debate," *Morning Chronicle* (Halifax), 2 April 1924.

61 Stewart was the eldest son of a former moderator of the Free Church of Nova Scotia, the Reverend Murdoch Stewart, and dean of medicine at Dalhousie University.

62 *Halifax Herald*, 15 April 1924. The text is too extensive to reproduce in its entirety.

63 Until 1928, Nova Scotia had a bicameral legislature; the Legislative Council was the unelected upper house, or senate.

64 In order to clarify matters – and, more importantly, prevent two votes – Nova Scotia in May 1925 amended its United Church of Canada Act to provide that any vote taken under the act of incorporation would stand as *the* vote for the purposes of the provincial act (see *Statutes of Nova Scotia*, 1925, c. 167).

65 The United Church of Canada Act, *Statutes of Nova Scotia*, 1924, c. 122.

CHAPTER TWO

The title of this chapter is taken from the title of chapter 8 of Stuart C. Parker, *Yet Not Consumed: A Short Account of the History and Antecedents of The Presbyterian Church in Canada* (Toronto, 1946).

1 Maritimes Synod minutes, 14 September 1921, MCA; "Church Union Overture Sent to the Assembly on Its Own Merits," *Morning Chronicle* (Halifax), 16 September 1921; N. Keith Clifford, *The Resistance to Church Union in Canada, 1904–1939* (Vancouver, 1985), 119.

2 In September the Woman's Missionary Society, Eastern Division, convened
  in New Glasgow for its annual meeting. At the initiative of its president – a
  resister – the synodical divided into pro- and anti-union organizations, each
  carrying on under the same name. (The Presbyterian WMS is now the
  Atlantic Mission Society; the unionist WMS is the United Church Women.)

3 "'Shoulder to Shoulder': Rallying Cry of the Presbyterian Association,"
  Morning Chronicle (Halifax), 8 October 1924.

4 "Provisional Synod Will Be Formed," *Morning Chronicle* (Halifax), 9 October
  1924.

5 Aside from the official minutes, which are not descriptive, these proceedings
  are covered in detail in several articles beginning on the front page of
  Halifax's *Morning Chronicle,* 9 October 1924. Unless otherwise indicated, this
  account and what follows are derived from that source.

6 "Recommends Vote on Union to Be Taken as Early as Possible," *Morning
  Chronicle* (Halifax), 9 October 1924.

7 The text of all eleven resolutions is given in Synod minutes, as is the
  recorded vote on the fourth of them.

8 For an editorial post-mortem from the "anti" perspective, see Gadfly
  (pseud.), "The Meeting of Synod," *Eastern Chronicle* (New Glasgow),
  24 October 1924.

9 "Synod of the Maritime Provinces," *Presbyterian Witness,* 23 October 1924.

10 "The Synod of the Maritime Provinces," *Eastern Chronicle,* 14 October 1924.

11 The view taken by the Presbyterian Church Association was that the "legal"
   PCC ceased to be Presbyterian on the day on which the United Church of
   Canada Act received royal assent, and that it had thereby forfeited all its
   moral and spiritual authority over its members.

12 "Provisional Synod of Presbyterian Association Held Conference at Truro,"
   Daily News (Truro), 8 April 1925.

13 The J. Gresham Machen archive at Westminster Theological Seminary in
   Philadelphia includes a file containing "protracted correspondence with Rev.
   Robert Johnston, New Glasgow, Nova Scotia regarding summer work in
   Nova Scotia and Prince Edward Island for Princeton Seminary students"
   ("Canada – recruitment of students to work there for the summer").
   On Machen's role, see John S. Moir, *Enduring Witness: A History of The
   Presbyterian Church in Canada,* 3rd ed. rev. (Burlington, Ont., 2004), 226.

14 The others were the Reverend Dr D.J. Fraser, principal of Presbyterian
   College, Montreal; Cyrus MacMillan, chair of the Department of English at
   McGill University; and Stuart Parker, minister of St Andrew's, Toronto.

15 This account and what follows are based on Halifax Presbytery minutes,
   April–May 1924, and Synod minutes, October 1924, MCA.

16 Johnston observed that Presbytery had for years packed its commissioners to the General Assembly with unionists, and that the degree of cooperation between Presbyterians and Methodists had been exaggerated. See Halifax Presbytery minutes, 23 April 1924 ("Charges against Rev. Robert Johnston"), MCA. For a thorough discussion of the matter, see Thomas Andrew Stinson, "'A Kind of Question That Raises Feeling': Nova Scotia Presbyterians and the Formation of the United Church of Canada" (MA thesis, Dalhousie University, 1991), 82–4.

17 Stinson, "'A Kind of Question That Raises Feeling,'" 168–9.

18 They were Frank Baird (Bedford), Donald MacOdrum (St Andrew's, Halifax), and D.B. Marsh (Hamilton, Bermuda).

19 "Happenings in Halifax Presbytery," *Presbyterian Witness*, 12 February 1925.

20 Excerpt from unpublished memoir of Dr Murdoch Morrison, elder of St Andrew's, in M.D. Morrison papers, MG 1, vol. 707, file 4, NSARM.

21 "Opponents of Organic Union Present Their Pleas," *Morning Chronicle* (Halifax), 18 November 1924.

22 "Anti-Unionists Hold Meeting," *Morning Chronicle* (Halifax), 7 November 1924.

23 R.W. Ross, minister of Fort Massey.

24 Ten members in congregations of less than 100, 25 in congregations between 100 and 500, 50 in congregations between 500 and 1,000, and 100 in congregations of over 1,000 members.

25 Unofficial summaries obtained by tabulating results of ballots cast on congregational membership in the United Church showed a majority of over 2,000 against union; see "Church Union Vote," *Morning Chronicle* (Halifax), 23 March 1925.

26 Halifax Presbytery minutes, 22 October 1922, MCA.

27 "Theologues for Church Union," *Morning Chronicle* (Halifax), 11 December 1924.

28 "Union Voting Commences in Local Churches," *Halifax Herald*, 23 December 1924.

29 "Where to Vote on Church Union," *Morning Chronicle* (Halifax), 24 December 1925.

30 "Churches of Halifax All for Union," *Halifax Herald*, 9 January 1925.

31 Stinson, "'A Kind of Question That Raises Feeling,'" 173n33. "Adherents" are non-communicants who support the congregation financially and participate in its life.

32 The main title of Stinson's thesis, "A Kind of Question That Raises Feeling," is taken from MacOdrum's sermon on the subject, delivered on 18 January 1925, in advance of the vote in St Andrew's. According to the minister of Fort Massey, writing a few days later, "St. Andrew's here is in a stew"

(R.W. Ross quoted in Stinson, "'A Kind of Question That Raises Feeling,'" 2; see also "Mr. MacOdrum's Position" (letter to the editor), *Morning Chronicle* [Halifax], 20 January 1925).

33 "No Hope of Unanimity in the Church," *Morning Chronicle* (Halifax), 19 January 1925.

34 Minutes of St Andrew's trustees' and congregational meetings, 1920–25, are missing. This account and what follows are based on Session minutes (mfm at NSARM) and the unpublished memoirs of Murdoch Morrison, leader of the unionists at St Andrew's (see note 20 above).

35 "St. Andrew's by 123 Majority Goes Union," *Morning Chronicle* (Halifax), 11 February 1925.

36 "Jubilee Service on the Eve of Church Union," *Morning Chronicle* (Halifax), 25 May 1925.

37 R.W. Ross, "What Church Union Will Mean for the City of Halifax," *The New Outlook*, 10 June 1925, 37.

38 "Great Assembly Being Planned by Continuing Presbyterians in June," *Morning Chronicle* (Halifax), 23 April 1925.

39 "Strong Church to Continue in the East," *Morning Chronicle* (Halifax), 10 June 1925.

40 Acts 1:1.

41 Moir, *Enduring Witness*, 223.

42 In G.A. Rawlyk, ed., *Aspects of the Canadian Evangelical Experience* (Montreal and Kingston, 1997), 137.

43 David B. Marshall, *Secularizing the Faith: Canadian Protestant Clergy and the Crisis of Belief, 1850–1940* (Toronto, 1992). See especially the introduction, "Secularization and the Writing of Canadian Religious History" (3–24), and the index, s.v. "church union."

44 On this subject generally, see John A. Vissers, "Interpreting the Stuff of History: The Theology and Practice of History in the Presbyterian Tradition in Canada," *Papers of the Canadian Society of Presbyterian History* 16 (1991): 75–99. The term "ecclesiastical historicism" is Kenneth Gunn-Walberg's; see his "The Church Union Movement in Manitoba, 1902–1925 – A Cultural Study in the Decline of Denominationalism within the Protestant Ascendancy" (PhD thesis, University of Guelph, 1971), 166.

45 John S. Moir, *Handbook for Canadian Presbyterians* (Toronto, 1996), 73.

CHAPTER THREE

 1 "Majority in the Ballots 2362 Against," *Morning Chronicle* (Halifax), 14 February 1925. The point, of course, is that only congregations with a

strong non-uniting minority or non-uniting majority voted at all; so the "poll" was heavily weighted against the United Church. Voting congregations were no less deeply divided than the church at large, where at least 782 congregations went United without voting (or rather, voted against voting). Congregations that did not include a vocal non-uniting minority did not, for obvious reasons, vote at all. By 1 May 1925 only 48 per cent of congregations had voted, and Manitoba and New Brunswick could not vote until after 10 June. See, generally, "Summary of Church Union Vote," *Evening Mail* (Halifax), 2 May 1925, and "Presbyterian Vote Record," *Morning Chronicle* (Halifax), 5 June 1926.

2 Unidentified Halifax newspaper clipping, November 1925, PCOSD archives.

3 Bedford, Bethany, Fort Massey, Park Street, St Andrew's, St James (Dartmouth), St John's, St Matthew's, and Stairs Memorial (Dartmouth).

4 "New Presbyterian Church Planned," *Morning Chronicle* (Halifax), 10 January 1925.

5 "New Congregation Assured for City," *Evening Mail* (Halifax), 12 January 1925.

6 *Evening Mail* (Halifax), 17 January 1925. Fred M. Guildford, formerly of Park Street, became an elder of Saint David's in 1926.

7 "Anti-Unionists May Build New Halifax Church," *Halifax Herald*, 19 January 1925.

8 "To Maintain Old Faith and Old Church," *Morning Chronicle* (Halifax), 19 January 1925; "Anti-Unionists May Build New Halifax Church," *Halifax Herald*, 19 January 1925.

9 A twelfth, Clifford Torey, soon recanted and returned to St Andrew's; he afterwards rejoined the Presbyterians and was elected elder of Saint David's in 1946.

10 "Presentation Made to the First Baptist Church," *Morning Chronicle* (Halifax), 18 April 1925.

11 *Revised Statutes of Nova Scotia*, 1923, c. 178.

12 "Organizing a New Church in Stellarton," *Morning Chronicle* (Halifax), 15 January 1925.

13 An indication of how serious a view was afterwards taken of the matter appears in the title page of the early printed annual reports, where from 1928 onwards it was claimed – quite erroneously – that the Presbyterian Church of Saint David was "organised as a congregation of the Presbyterian Church in Canada, January 22nd, 1925." The date may refer to the decision by the executive committee of the Halifax PCA to proceed with organizing a congregation *outside* the official church, a very big step that potentially risked alienating those among the non-uniting minority who were loyal

Churchmen – opposers, even resisters, but not schismatics or in any sense rebels against the official Presbyterian Church in Canada.

14 In the *Morning Chronicle* (Halifax) of 20 February 1925 Baird published a lengthy excoriation of Halifax Presbytery's church union committee and, more especially, its convener, John A. Clark of St Matthew's; see "Mr Baird's Answer."

15 "New Congregation Now Established," unidentified Halifax newspaper clipping, 27 February 1925, PCOSD archives.

16 "New Church Was Formed Last Night," *Morning Chronicle* (Halifax), 27 February 1925.

17 Broadsheet, PCOSD archives.

18 B.W. Russell, KC, to R.F. Yeoman, 24 January 1925; in reply, John Stewart and W.J. Kane to B.W. Russell, KC, 2 March 1925. Unless otherwise indicated, these details and what follows are based on materials in the archives of St Andrew's United Church, Halifax.

19 On this subject, see generally [G.A. Burbidge and M.D. Morrison], *Historical Sketches of St. Andrew's Church, Halifax, N.S., United Church of Canada* (Halifax, 1949), 11–22 and 27–31.

20 "Methodists Will Erect New Church on Robie Street," *Morning Chronicle* (Halifax), 14 January 1925.

21 Kane, McCleave, and Scott Chisholm (a trustee).

22 *Statutes of Nova Scotia,* 1927, c. 139.

23 *Statutes of Nova Scotia,* 1927, c. 141. The unamended section 11 of the act read, "No real property shall be either purchased, sold, conveyed, mortgaged or otherwise disposed of by said trustees until authorized by *a majority of those present* at a regular meeting of the congregation called for the purpose of giving such authority and at which a majority of those entitled to vote at such meetings of the congregation are present" (italics added). The amendment also provided for voting by proxy as well as in person.

24 "Census Shows 81 [*sic:* 80.1] Per Cent Are for Union," *Morning Chronicle* (Halifax), 23 December 1924. These were the results of a straw poll of the ministers.

25 This section and what follows, unless otherwise indicated, are based on the multipart file "Church letters from Jan 18/25 to Dec 31/26 [*sic:* 25] re supply for sabbath days prospective pastors and all letters concerning the congregation / W.J. Kane session clerk and treasurer," PCOSD archives.

26 See, for example, "A Scottish Welcome," *Morning Chronicle* (Halifax), 4 July 1925.

27 "Presbyterian Church Functions on Mainland of Nova Scotia Again," *Eastern Chronicle* (New Glasgow), 3 July 1925.

28 "On all sides I hear that Mrs. Campbell's conversations with certain other ladies whom I will not mention probably did more than anything else to prompt his refusal" (R. Johnston to W.J. Kane, 29 August 1925, PCOSD archives).

29 "Presbytery of Pictou, N.S.," *Presbyterian Record* (Montreal), September 1925, 264.

30 "Maritime Synod Goes On with Work of Rebuilding Old Presbyterian Church," *Morning Chronicle* (Halifax), 7 October 1925.

31 Presbyterian Church in Canada, *Acts and Proceedings of the Fifty-Second General Assembly … 1926*, 127.

32 "White, John," in Nigel M. de S. Cameron, ed., *Dictionary of Scottish Church History and Theology* (Downers Grove, Ill., 1993), 866.

33 In 1922 the "new minimum stipend" for ministers was $1,800 (see *Presbyterian Witness*, 12 October 1922). Both Johnston and Baird had declined calls from continuing congregations in Ontario offering twice that amount. Johnston pointed out to Kane that while Halifax could offer as large a stipend as was necessary to attract the right man, it could under no circumstances go beyond $5,000.

34 See generally "The Presbyterian Manse," *Morning Chronicle* (Halifax), 11 March 1926.

35 MacGlashen to R.J. Wilson, 11 January 1926, IC/CU/PCC box 8, file 181, United Church of Canada/Victoria University Archives, Toronto.

36 "The Rev. Colin MacKay Kerr," *Evening Mail* (Halifax), 21 January 1926.

37 Reminiscence by Baird's son Hamilton, who was present, noted on the transmittal list of his father's papers (Frank Baird papers, Presbyterian Church in Canada Archives and Records Office, Toronto).

38 "Eloquent Welcome to New Scotland and to the Canadian Church," *Morning Chronicle* (Halifax), 23 January 1926.

39 "Notable Progress Made by Auld Kirk Last Year," *Morning Chronicle* (Halifax), 28 January 1926.

40 This account and what follows, unless otherwise indicated, are drawn from the scrapbook of Halifax daily newspaper clippings kept between 1925 and 1928 by W.J. Kane, now in PCOSD archives (mfm at NSARM).

41 Presbyterian Church in Canada, Presbytery of Pictou, minutes, 29 April 1926 (mfm at NSARM).

42 "Formation of a New Presbytery," *Morning Chronicle* (Halifax), 7 October 1926.

CHAPTER FOUR

1 "Presbyterians Celebrated Their Second Anniversary," *Morning Chronicle* (Halifax), 17 January 1927.

2 "Rev. Colin McKay Kerr First Sermons in the Presbyterian Church," *Evening Mail* (Halifax), 25 January 1926.

3 Unidentified Halifax newspaper clipping, March 1926, W.J. Kane scrapbook, PCOSD archives (mfm at NSARM).

4 His PhD was from the Lutheran University of Jena.

5 "Message from Old Scotland to New Scotland," *Morning Chronicle* (Halifax), 4 February 1926.

6 Robert J. McCleave, "The Presbyterian Church of Saint David of Halifax, Nova Scotia" (unpubl. ms., 1974), 15H, PCOSD archives. The sermon concerned was "Modern thought and religion – The philosophy of Einstein and Eddington," delivered at the evening service on 2 February 1930. The following month Kerr used the fourth chapter of the Confession ("Of Creation") as the basis for a scholarly sermon on the theory of evolution.

7 Report of the Kirk Session, 1926, PCOSD archives.

8 "Not Reckoned in Terms of 'the Market,'" *Evening Mail* (Halifax), 20 June 1933.

9 Concordat (1929) between the Holy See and the Kingdom of Italy.

10 *Halifax Mail,* 16 July 1932, "Churches" page.

11 Sermons with titles such as the following do not inspire confidence in their accessibility: "The discipline of thought," "Fatalism," "Cynicism," "Predestination," "Spiritual invalids," "The making of a sceptic," "The story of the church in Scotland" (series), "The religious views of the poet Burns," "The poetry of Robert Burns and its relation to the religion of its time," "Problems of the Resurrection" (evening series), "Immortality" (evening series), "Modern civilization and Christianity," "Modern thinkers and Christianity – Lord Haldane," "Modern light on Old Testament history," "The need of spiritual vision," "The analyst and religion," "The invisible universe," "Health and religion" (shades of Christian Science?), "The failure of modernism," "Spiritual blindness," "The reasonableness and necessity for the Incarnation," "Predestination and the nations," "The need for a vision of God," and "What is truth?"

12 This last topic may, indeed, have had a very serious purpose; a minister had been deposed by Presbytery for committing adultery.

13 *Evening Mail* (Halifax), 12 April 1930, 31 January 1931, 22 April 1933, and 20 February 1937.

14 "To Give Lecture Series on What the Church Believes," *Halifax Mail*, 10 February 1934.

15 Now merged in the World Alliance of Reformed Churches, of which both the PCC and the UCC are members. The World Presbyterian Alliance was founded in 1875 and first convened in Edinburgh in 1877.

16 The others were English, German, and Bengali. Kerr would also have known Latin and Greek and probably Hebrew.

17 PCOSD, Session meeting, minutes, 21 March 1934 (mfm at NSARM).

18 "Reveals How Gracious Is New Queen," unidentified Halifax newspaper clipping, 14 December 1936, PCOSD archives.

19 "'Saint Columba' Is Recommended as Church Name," *Halifax Daily Star*, 4 February 1929.

20 St Columba's was the name of the Highlanders' church in Glasgow, where Gaelic was the language of divine service, as well as of the Church of Scotland chapel in Pont Street, London, where Field Marshal Sir Douglas Haig had been a member and elder; see "Paid Tribute to Late Earl Haig," *Halifax Daily Star*, 13 February 1928.

21 "David I of Scotland," in Nigel M. de S. Cameron, ed., *Dictionary of Scottish Church History and Theology* (Downers Grove, Ill., 1993), 233.

22 Concerning the status of King David, see David McRoberts, "Scotland's Sole Canonized Saint," *Saint Peter's College Magazine*, June 1949, 28n.

23 "Debates at Assembly Are Heated" (unidentified Halifax newspaper clipping, 7 June 1927, W.J. Kane scrapbook, PCOSD archives [mfm at NSARM]).

24 Unidentified Halifax newspaper clipping, 18 January 1930, PCOSD archives.

25 "Chimes from the Belfry," *Halifax Chronicle*, 6 August 1932; reprinted in *Presbyterian Record* 57 (October 1932): 299–300.

26 "Session Report," 17 January 1934, PCOSD archives.

27 The second was Kerr's successor, Frank Lawson, who served in 1959–60. Saint David's hosted Synod in 1926 and 1935, but would not do so again until 1949.

28 "Neglect not the gift that is in thee, which was given thee by prophecy, with the laying on of the hands of the presbytery."

29 Then, as now, the Book of Forms makes clear that the board of managers and the congregational meeting are at all times subject to the authority of Session and Presbytery. Boards of managers and congregational meetings were unknown to the Kirk in Scotland; they were strictly a Seceder and Free Church phenomenon. Even in Canada they appeared only in Kirk churches with Congregational or Seceder roots, such as St Matthew's and St Andrew's in Halifax.

30 "Plan Service of Witness," *Halifax Mail,* 15 April 1944.

31 "Clerics Adopt Program for Aid to Enlisted Men," *Halifax Herald,* 3 October 1939.

32 Presbytery of Halifax and Lunenburg, minutes, 5 May 1942 (mfm at NSARM).

33 "St David's Church Damaged by Blaze," *Halifax Mail,* 9 May 1942.

34 "St David's Church Marks Special Events with Special Services," *Halifax Mail,* 5 October 1942.

35 "Missionary Parley Held," *Daily Star* (Halifax), 27 October 1942.

36 PCOSD, annual congregational meeting, minutes, 28 January 1942 (mfm at NSARM).

37 PCOSD, Trustees' meeting, minutes, 11 January 1943 (mfm at NSARM).

38 C.M. Kerr to Presbyterian Church of Saint David, 24 September 1943, PCOSD archives.

39 Presbyterian Church of Saint David, *Nineteenth Annual Report, 1943* (Halifax, 1944), 13–14.

40 No minutes of any of these meetings survive.

41 Carleton Stanley, character for C.M. Kerr, 16 November 1943, Stanley Papers, UA2-163, file B-61, DUA.

42 Both Clifford Torey, chair of the Board, and H.L. Stewart, a charter elder, had been elders of St Andrew's, and both had opposed the call to Kerr, Torey so determinedly that he returned for a few years to St Andrew's United.

43 Kane to Robert Johnston, 7 March 1944, PCOSD archives.

44 "Resigns Post at St David's," *Daily Star* (Halifax), 14 March 1944.

45 "Clergy Honour Rev. C.M. Kerr," *Halifax Herald,* 1 April 1944.

46 C.M Kerr to Carleton Stanley, 21 April 1945, Stanley Papers, UA2-163, file B-69, DUA.

47 Presbyterian Church in Canada, *Acts and Proceedings of the Ninety-Second General Assembly* (Toronto, 1966), 593.

CHAPTER FIVE

1 W.J. Kane to Frank Baird, 13 March 1944. This account and what follows, unless otherwise indicated, are from the 1944–45 vacancy committee records (chair's personal file), PCOSD archives. They were carefully preserved by the clerk of Session after the collapse of the vacancy committee in April 1945. No other records of the long search for a successor to Kerr survive.

2 PCOSD, Session meeting, minutes, 6 May 1945 (mfm at NSARM); neither Lawson's letter nor Session's reply is extant.

3 The main attraction of Canada, Ontario, and London was Ray Lawson (1886–1980), a distant cousin and influential businessman who became lieutenant-governor of Ontario while Lawson was minister of Saint David's. The Lawson family were benefactors of the University of Western Ontario. In 1934, the year after Lawson graduated, the Lawson Memorial Library opened. See, generally, J.R.W. Gwynne-Timothy, *Western's First Century* (London, Ont., 1978), 825, s.v. "Lawson."

4 Francis Lawson, application for admission, 26 June 1933, Alumni records, Union Theological Seminary Archives, New York.

5 Information from Laurence DeWolfe and Kate Lawson (daughter).

6 "St David's Minister Inducted," *Halifax Mail*, 8 September 1945.

7 "St David's Celebrates Anniversary," *Mail-Star* (Halifax), 19 November 1955.

8 Information from the Reverend Dr John R. Cameron.

9 "Red-faced, not Red-minded" (unidentified Toronto newspaper clipping, ca. 4 May 1945); see also "Must Heed Achievements of Russia – Presbyterians," "The Church Examines Communism," "A Church Synod Declares Itself," "Soviet May Shape Future Religion, Clergymen Told," "It Is the Hand of the Synod, but Not the Voice of Presbyterianism," "Is Synod's Face Red," and "Has the Kirk Reversed Itself?" (all in Frank Lawson papers, privately held).

10 "Committee Didn't Approve Cleric's Report to Synod: Remarks on Communism Were Not in Text, but Said Merely 'After-Thought,'" unidentified Toronto newspaper clipping, 1945, ibid.

11 "Says Millions Of Minds Poisoned," unidentified Halifax newspaper clipping, 1946, ibid.

12 "Church Can Learn from Communism Says Pastor," *Halifax Chronicle-Herald*, 6 February 1951.

13 PCOSD, Trustees' meeting, minutes, 9 September 1948 (mfm at NSARM).

14 PCOSD, twenty-first annual report, 1945, 8.

15 "Progressive Spirit at Saint David's," *Halifax Mail*, 31 August 1946.

16 Frank Lawson, "Where Did Our Children Miss Out in Religion?" *Christian World Pulpit* (London), 26 January 1956, 30.

17 On this subject generally, see the minutes of the Presbytery of Halifax and Lunenburg (mfm at NSARM); the Rockwood trial case file (in the custody of the clerk of Presbytery); Perry F. Rockwood, *Triumph in God: The Life Story of Radio Pastor, Perry F. Rockwood* (Halifax, 1976); "Divisive Doctrine," *Time*, 17 March 1947; and Brian Currie, "The Voice that Pleads and Threatens," *4th Estate* (Halifax), 6 October 1976. See also David R. Elliott, "Perry F.

Rockwood: The 'Lone Ranger' Syndrome," in Canadian Society of Presbyterian History, *Papers 2003*, 17–33. See the same author's "Knowing No Borders: Canadian Contributions to American Fundamentalism," in George A. Rawlyk and Mark A. Noll, eds., *Amazing Grace: Evangelicalism in Australia, Britain, Canada, and the United States* (Montreal and Kingston, 1994), 372–3.

18 "Fitting Celebration Is Planned by St. David's," unidentified Halifax newspaper clipping, January 1950, PCOSD archives.

19 "Presbyterian Anniversary," *Mail-Star* (Halifax), 10 June 1950. See, generally, Presbyterian Church in Canada, *Addresses – from the Pre-Assembly Congress of 1950 – and the 76th General Assembly* (Toronto, 1950). This was the first pre-Assembly congress since the Disruption.

20 A professor in Dalhousie Law School from 1952 to 1959, the Honourable Lorne O. Clarke, QC, was chief justice of Nova Scotia from 1985 to 1998. He was probably the youngest elder in the church at the time of his election in 1953, and he was also unofficial leader of men's work in the presbytery.

21 See MacLennan's preface to the republication of the essay as "Help Though Mine Unbelief" in *Cross-Country* (Toronto, 1949), 132. See also Elspeth Cameron, *Hugh MacLennan: A Writer's Life* (Toronto, 1983), 219–20, and Elspeth Cameron, ed., *The Other Side of Hugh MacLennan: Selected Essays Old and New* (Toronto, 1978), 15.

22 *Halifax Mail*, 7 March 1950.

23 *Mail-Star* (Halifax), 28 November 1959.

24 *Mail-Star* (Halifax), 19 November 1960. Lawson's last contribution to "The Clergy Comments" was "Christianity Has No Choice … My Brother or My Enemy," *Mail-Star* (Halifax), 14 November 1964.

25 Lawson, "Our Churches Have Failed Us," *Star* (Montreal), September 1960, 16.

26 "Seven Sermons on Preparation for Matrimony," *Mail-Star* (Halifax), 13 January 1962. Lawson did not even shy away from the question of birth control, which was not openly discussed in polite society.

27 "A Man with a Mission," *Mail-Star* (Halifax), 28 January 1961.

28 "New Evangelism Promotes Response from All Levels," *Mail-Star* (Halifax), 23 September 1961.

29 "Home Prayers Crusade Plan Interest Grows," *Mail-Star* (Halifax), 11 April 1964.

30 "The Differences," *Presbyterian Record*, June 1964, 3.

31 PCOSD, annual report, 1963, 1.

32 PCOSD, 40th annual congregational meeting, minutes, 27 January 1965 (mfm at NSARM).

33 PCOSD, 38th annual congregational meeting, minutes, 30 January 1963
    (mfm at NSARM).
34 PCOSD, 40th annual congregational meeting, minutes, 27 January 1965
    (mfm at NSARM).
35 Eyewitness private information.
36 Presbytery of Halifax and Lunenburg meeting, minutes, 9 September 1965
    (mfm at NSARM).
37 PCOSD, annual report, 1971, 30.
38 Confidential information.
39 Kane to Rev. and Dr Lawson, [after 14 September 1965], PCOSD archives.
40 PCOSD, joint meeting of Session and Board, minutes, 15 November 1965,
    PCOSD archives.
41 "Large Congregation Told: Jesus the Realist Did Not Condone Sin yet Public
    Opinion Is Loaded with Sentiment," *Evening News* (New Glasgow),
    11 January 1971.
42 "Bible View," *Mail-Star* (Halifax), 8 May 1976.
43 Morning sermon, 9 July 1961.

CHAPTER SIX

 1 McCleave, who scored a decisive victory over the Liberal incumbent, was
    elected an elder in 1971.
 2 The signed call to Dr Mackay is extant and in 2003 was donated to the
    PCOSD archives by his son, elder M.B. Mackay.
 3 This section and what follows are based on a biographical sketch of his
    father by M.B. Mackay and the official minute of the Presbytery of Halifax
    and Lunenburg on the occasion of D.B. Mackay's retirement, 17 June 1975.
 4 Information from Mary Harvey (née Mackay).
 5 "Presbyterian Synod Rejects Invitation," *Chronicle-Herald* (Halifax), 8 October
    1965.
 6 "Key '73 Projects Begin in Metro Area," *Mail-Star* (Halifax), 2 December
    1972. See, generally, John S. Moir, *Enduring Witness: A History of The
    Presbyterian Church in Canada*, 3rd ed. rev. (Burlington, Ont., 2004), 274–5.
 7 "Open Pulpits to Fight Discrimination – Schiff," *Mail-Star* (Halifax),
    12 March 1969.
 8 "Noted Presbyterian to Speak at Anglican Church," *Mail-Star* (Halifax),
    10 May 1969.
 9 "Presbyterians Plan Assembly," *Mail-Star* (Halifax), 7 March 1970.
10 "Presbyterianism in Halifax," *Presbyterian Record*, June 1970, 3.

11 PCOSD, Trustees' meeting, minutes, 9 February 1970 (mfm at NSARM).

12 John S. Moir, *Handbook for Canadian Presbyterians* (Toronto, 1996), 112; see also Moir, *Enduring Witness*, 268–9, and "Delegates to Study Findings of Church Analysis Report," *Chronicle-Herald* (Halifax), 10 June 1970. The Ross Report's full title was *Ministry of The Presbyterian Church in Canada: Report on a Program of Research and Development for The Presbyterian Church in Canada relating to Pastoral and Other Ministries in the Changing Context of The Presbyterian Church in Canada / Conducted by P.S. Ross & Partners in Cooperation with the Committee on Recruitment and Vocation of The Presbyterian Church in Canada.*

13 "Denies Church Is 'Stuffy,'" *Mail-Star* (Halifax), 16 May 1970.

14 "Large South End Churches Struggle with 'New' Realities of Poverty, Transience," *Mail-Star* (Halifax), 20 April 1974.

15 PCOSD bulletin, 7 April 1974.

16 "Presbyterians in Canada Mark Centennial in 1974," *Mail-Star* (Halifax), 1 June 1974.

17 "Centennial Celebration Off to a Fine Start," *News from the Presbyterian Church of Saint David* 8 (spring 1974): 1.

18 "A Call for Reconciliation: Open Letter …," *Presbyterian Record*, June 1975, 2.

19 Mackay thus missed the visit in August of the moderator of the Church of Scotland, Dr George Reid. Just how much had changed in the nine years since the previous visit by the moderator of the Church of Scotland is clear in that Reid could be in Halifax without visiting or preaching in any of the local Presbyterian churches. Halifax newspapers paid more attention to his presence than the Presbytery of Halifax and Lunenburg did.

20 Quoted in Donald B. Mackay alumni file, Princeton Theological Seminary archives.

21 "'A Great Venture in Faith,'" *Mail-Star* (Halifax), 7 June 1975.

22 Five years earlier, Lawson made the same point differently – by word and sacrament according to Celtic tradition: "It is not an attempt to recover the dead past, but to reclaim the substance of great worship as practised by simple, eager and fervent people in the first flowerings of the Christian mission"; see "Recall Tradition of First Church Worship Custom," *Mail-Star* (Halifax), 2 May 1964.

23 Matthew 2:16–18.

24 In November 1970, when Mackay replaced him as moderator, McDonald succeeded Murdoch McLeod as clerk. In November 1974 he became president of the Halifax-Dartmouth Council of Churches. McDonald went on serve as interim moderator of Saint David's during the next two vacancies and conducted Mackay's memorial service in 1984. In 2003–4 he was

moderator of the General Assembly, the first Halifax minister since the Disruption to reach that pinnacle.

25 PCOSD, 60th annual congregational meeting, minutes, 23 January 1985.

CHAPTER SEVEN

1 The Mackays paid a return visit in November 1978, but Dr Mackay did not conduct the service or preach.

2 Bob McCleave, "Moves from Business to the Pulpit after Challenge from Newspaper Editor," *News from the Presbyterian Church of Saint David* 14 (spring-summer 1976).

3 Ibid.

4 John Pace, *A Banner, a Dream and a Drum: Sermons from a Nova Scotia Pulpit* (Halifax, 1986), 5.

5 Paraphrasing Duncan McDowall, *Quick to the Frontier: Canada's Royal Bank – A History* (Toronto, 1993), 317.

6 John Pace quoted in McCleave, "Moves from Business to the Pulpit." For a fuller account, see "One Question Changed a Man's Life," *Hamilton Spectator*, 23 May 1964.

7 Pace, *A Banner, a Dream and a Drum*, ix.

8 Thomas Melville Bailey, ed., *Wee Kirks and Stately Steeples: A History of the Presbytery of Hamilton ... 1800–1990* (Burlington, Ont., 1990), 51.

9 John S. Moir, *Enduring Witness: A History of the Prebyterian Church in Canada*, 3rd ed. rev. (Burlington, Ont., 2004), 267.

10 Pace's text was 1 John 3:2 ("We know that when he shall appear, we shall be like him"), and the title of his sermon, "Jesus Christ – *the first man*."

11 *News from the Presbyterian Church of Saint David* 14 (spring-summer 1976).

12 "Chaplains Active on Campus," *Mail-Star* (Halifax), 9 September 1972.

13 PCOSD bulletin, 31 October 1976. In January 1978 the university newspaper gave Pace a front-page feature: "The Chaplaincy: 'Solid Ground Amid the Chaos of Campus Life,'" Saint Mary's University, *Times*, 31 January 1978.

14 "Churches: Decline Seen as 'Asset to Ecumenism,'" *Mail-Star* (Halifax), 4 August 1982 (interview with John Pace).

15 The newsletter ceased publication in 1979. Revived in 1982, it lasted for three years. Despite an unsuccessful attempt to revive it in 1997, the newsletter was not seen again until 2001.

16 *Mail-Star* (Halifax), 8 December 1979.

17 "Pews Packed for Queen's Silver Jubilee Service," *Mail-Star* (Halifax), 21 May 1977.

18 Esmond Bulter, secretary to the governor general, to McCleave, 19 January 1977, PCOSD archives.

19 "To Mark Queen's Accession," *Mail-Star* (Halifax), 14 May 1977.

20 "Crown Canada's 'Fertile Centre,'" *Mail-Star* (Halifax), 1 September 1978.

21 P.E. Trudeau to John Pace, 29 September 1978, PCOSD archives.

22 PCOSD, joint meeting of Session and Board, minutes, 9 January 1978 (mfm at NSARM).

23 Information from the Reverend E.M. Iona MacLean.

24 Unless otherwise indicated, this account and what follows are based on information received from the Reverend Amy E.H. Campbell.

25 PCOSD, Trustees' meeting, minutes, 2 March 1980 (mfm at NSARM).

26 "Proposed Job Description for Pastoral Assistant" [1979], PCOSD archives. One of the duties was revealingly described: "Supply the pulpit during minister's absence for study leaves, vacations, anniversaries, etc. To be investigated further."

27 "Pastoral Assistant Joins Church," *Mail-Star* (Halifax), 27 September 1980.

28 Presbytery of Halifax and Lunenburg meeting, minutes, 24 June 1982 (mfm at NSARM). It was not until 1991 that diaconal ministers were recognized as full equals and given a vote in Session and Presbytery.

29 Information from the Reverend E.M. Iona MacLean.

30 PCOSD, annual report, 1983, 4.

31 Ralph W. Kane to Evelyn van Beek, 10 October 1984, PCOSD archives.

32 Pace, *A Banner, a Dream and a Drum*, title page.

33 It soon looked as if a younger contemporary of Catherine Calkin's would follow in her footsteps. In the spring of 1992 Laura Alary, daughter of the assistant clerk of Session, was received by Presbytery as a student candidate for ministry. Graduating MDiv from Knox College in 1996, she was afterwards licensed but did not proceed to ordination, instead entering academic life.

34 Calkin went to Avonton, a pastoral charge in small-town Ontario, where in 2007 she remains the minister.

35 PCOSD, Board meeting, minutes, 9 April 1992 (mfm at NSARM).

36 Pace to Kirk Session, 18 August 1992, PCOSD archives.

37 *Frank* 136 (10 February 1993), 17. See also "John, Judithe and the Laying On of hands," *Frank* 134 (2 February 1993). Pace was understandably very upset by these unkind cuts, and the source of the inside information was threatened with litigation if found out. No further articles appeared.

38 It was also ironic. As long ago as 1982, Pace had moved in Presbytery that its management committee bring forward guidelines for congregations when

they were dealing with the retirement of their minister; the motion was defeated (Presbytery of Halifax and Lunenburg meeting, minutes, 20 April 1982 [mfm at NSARM]).

39 Jane Johnson was inducted to Iona, Dartmouth, in December 1987. She afterwards seceded to the United Church.

40 PCOSD, annual report, 1993, 12.

41 At the time of his death, Palmeter was associate chief justice of the Supreme Court of Nova Scotia.

42 *Atlantic Canada Frank*, 4 November 1997, 15.

CHAPTER EIGHT

1 On Farris's career at Knox, see Brian J. Fraser, *Church, College, and Clergy: A History of Theological Education at Knox College, Toronto, 1844–1994* (Montreal and Kingston, 1995).

2 This account and what follows are based on confidential information and records of the search committee.

3 This section was contributed by the Reverend Dr D. Laurence DeWolfe.

4 A nineteenth-century secession from the Reformed Protestant Dutch Church, which arrived in Canada via the United States and whose Canadian numbers were significantly augmented by postwar emigration from the Netherlands. The Halifax congregation, founded in 1958, was well established by the time DeWolfe arrived. For its history, see its website at http://www.allnationscrc.org/who/history.html.

5 Session was already considering a proposal to hire a full-time assistant minister, but nothing came of it until 1980.

6 In 1981 the General Assembly, responding to overtures received in 1979, 1980, and 1981, appointed a special task force on "Liberty of Conscience in the Ordination of Women." The first woman minister in the Atlantic Synod had been ordained at Saint David's in May 1977.

7 PCOSD, 74th annual congregational meeting, minutes, 31 January 1999.

8 As a tribute to their minister's achievement, several members of the congregation contributed to a fund that allowed both DeWolfe and his wife to attend the graduation ceremony.

9 Stewards by Design did not train the team in a systematic stewardship program, though it did include an introduction to one such program, which the stewardship task force had considered and rejected.

10 The Stewards by Design team adapted the text from a document produced for a Presbyterian church in Guelph, Ontario.

CHAPTER NINE

1 *Revised Statutes of Nova Scotia*, 1927, c. 178.

2 The rationale for the decision is unknown. The minutes of the joint management committee were placed in the now lost congregation meeting minute book.

3 *Statutes of Nova Scotia*, 1925, c. 133.

4 *Seventh Census of Canada, 1931*, vol. 1, *Summary* (Ottawa, 1936), 239.

5 PCA membership roll, opened November 1924 (mfm at NSARM). The number on the original states 504, but the names have been miscounted.

6 "Ordained into the Eldership," *Halifax Chronicle*, 14 January 1929.

7 Thomas Erle Andrews, a Quebecer who came to Halifax about 1927.

8 Paraphrasing PCOSD, annual report, 1963, 32.

9 PCOSD, special congregational meeting, minutes, 3 December 1967 (mfm at NSARM).

10 Years later, when Chard was in the midst of a divorce, Kane suggested that she take a leave of absence from Session. She declined, pointing out that divorced male elders were not expected to do so (private information).

11 Email from Dr Elizabeth A. Chard, 14 September 2004.

12 PCOSD, annual report, 1958, 4.

13 PCOSD, Trustees' meeting, minutes, 20 October 1970 (mfm at NSARM).

14 Based on "Responsibilities of Ruling Elders" (The Elders Institute, ©1991).

15 *Presbyterian Witness*, October 1940, 4.

16 PCOSD, first annual report, 1925, 25.

17 "Rendering Fine Service to Youth of Community," *Evening Mail* (Halifax), 28 April 1928.

18 "Ordinarily a list of the names of children baptized in a congregation, but some time after World War I the name was extended to child care service provided during the worship period" (John S. Moir, *Handbook for Canadian Presbyterians* [Toronto, 1996], 38).

19 When Armagh was new, in the spring of 1956, Lawson saw to it that an appeal for support appeared in the bulletin.

20 "Deaconess Appointed to St David's Congregation," *Mail-Star* (Halifax), 25 June 1960.

21 Unless otherwise indicated, these pages are based on Roberta (Shaw) Pocklington, "St David's Presbyterian Church – June 1960 – October 1963" (unpubl. ms., 2003).

22 "Roberta Shaw," *Mail-Star* (Halifax), 18 March 1961.

23 PCOSD, annual report, 1962, 11.

24 "New Christian Education Centre Opens" and "Saint David's New Education Centre Opens," *Mail-Star* (Halifax), 13 October and 17 November 1962.

25 PCOSD, annual report, 1963, 11.

26 PCOSD, Trustees' meeting, minutes, 19 June 1967 (mfm at NSARM).

27 PCOSD, annual report, 1975, 10.

28 Confidential information.

CHAPTER TEN

1 On this subject generally, see Thomas Harding, *Presbyterian, Methodist and Congregational Worship in Canada Prior to 1925* (Toronto, 1994), 9–51.

2 For the very Scottish Presbyterian background to this question, see W.D. Maxwell, *History of Worship in the Church of Scotland* (London, 1955) and *Outline of Christian Worship* (Oxford, 1936). Maxwell, who relied heavily on the "Euchomachia" of Nova Scotian Kirk minister George Washington Sprott, claimed in all things to be building on both the practices of Calvin and the outline of worship set out in the Westminster Directory of Public Worship.

3 PCOSD, Session meeting, minutes, 22 January 1926 (mfm at NSARM).

4 PCOSD, annual report, 1926, 11.

5 PCOSD, Session meeting, minutes, 19 November 1928 (mfm at NSARM).

6 "Symbolic exclusion of all unworthy persons from the Lord's table at the time of the Lord's Supper by requiring that communicants previously obtain by examination a communion token which was a 'ticket of admission' to the sacramental table" (John S. Moir, *Handbook for Canadian Presbyterians* [Toronto, 1996], 51). The expression "fencing of the table" refers back to the practice of building an actual fence around the aggregation of long tables where communion was dispensed at outdoor services in the Highlands and in the early days of Highland immigration to British North America. The communion token was handed in at a gate in the fence.

7 This mission was counterpoint to the annual ecumenical Good Friday afternoon service at J. Wesley Smith Memorial United (formerly United), in which Presbyterians as a rule did not participate. Its identification with the United Church and, worse, with church union (it began in 1925) made the service unacceptable among Presbyterians.

8 "Presbyterians to Sponsor Spiritual Mission Here," *Mail-Star* (Halifax), 29 March 1958.

9 "Church Revives Ancient Custom," *Mail-Star* (Halifax), 3 March 1962; "Recall Tradition of First Church Worship Custom," *Mail-Star* (Halifax), 2 May 1964.

10 Indeed, it was a standing joke in the Mackay family that wherever "DB" went, he found himself presiding over the end of evening service. When yet another family ceased to attend, he could be heard muttering, "Now the Joneses have got a TV" (information from elder M.B. Mackay).

11 "Calendar," in *Oxford Dictionary of the Christian Church*, ed. F.L. Cross, 3rd ed., ed. E.A. Livingstone (New York, 1997), 264.

12 The communion service, of course, was superadded. New Year's Sunday evening communion service a few days later proceeded as usual.

13 This section was contributed by the Reverend Dr D. Laurence DeWolfe.

CHAPTER ELEVEN

1 See "Was Halifax Businessman, Choirmaster," *Chronicle-Herald* (Halifax), 22 February 1965.

2 "To Hold Classes," *Daily Star* (Halifax), 26 May 1928.

3 "Musicians Score Triumph," *Daily Star* (Halifax), 26 April 1928.

4 "Organ Recital Great Success," *Evening Mail* (Halifax), 28 December 1928.

5 "Gives Farewell Organ Recital," *Daily Star* (Halifax), 23 May 1945.

6 "Musician of Marked Ability," *Halifax Mail*, 25 February 1939.

7 "Oratorio Acclaimed Exceptional Treat," *Mail* (Halifax), 31 March 1933. Thirteen years later, as organist and choirmaster herself, Fowler would reprise *Elijah*; see "Choir Marks Anniversary," *Daily Star* (Halifax), 4 February 1946.

8 "Ladies Musical Club," *Daily Star* (Halifax), 17 February 1934.

9 Information from Kathryn (MacIntosh) Schwartz.

10 On Hamer's twenty-two years at Mount Allison, see John G. Reid, *Mount Allison University*, vol. 2, *1914–1963* (Toronto, 1984), passim.

11 This account and what follows are based on material in the Harold Hamer Papers, Mount Allison University Archives, Sackville, NB, accession 9902.

12 "Service of Music to Be Held Sunday," *Mail-Star* (Halifax), 12 November 1949.

13 "Professor Harold Hamer Retires as Organist," *Mail-Star* (Halifax), 4 May 1961.

14 Hamer to Mackay, 8 July 1970, PCOSD archives.

15 See, generally, "Thinks Future Bright for Church Organ Music Here," *Halifax Mail-Star*, 15 November 1952.

16 Scott-Hunter to J.E. Ledoux (Casavant representative), 20 April 1928, Casavant Frères corporate archive, St-Hyacinthe, Que.

17 Paraphrasing "Presbyterian Church," *Evening Mail* (Halifax), 29 September 1928.

18 "Fine New Organ Was Used for First Time," *Daily Star* (Halifax),
    17 December 1928.

19 "Extensive Changes Made in Chancel of Historic Church," *Daily Star*
    (Halifax), 22 December 1928.

20 "Organ Recital Great Success," *Evening Mail* (Halifax), 28 December 1928.

21 PCOSD, Trustees' meeting, minutes, 15 November 1965 (mfm at NSARM).

22 Hill, Norman and Beard, *The Organ in the Presbyterian Church of Saint David /
    Halifax, Nova Scotia* [1968], 3.

23 PCOSD, 4th annual report, 1928, 39.

24 PCOSD, 29th annual report, 1953, 19.

25 Confidential information.

26 PCOSD, 76th annual report, 2000, 36.

27 "Audrey Farnell to Be Guest Soloist," *Mail* (Halifax), 14 September 1946.

28 "Amherst Girl Is Soloist," *Daily Star* (Halifax), 16 September 1946.

29 Information from Doris (Mrs Leonard) Mayoh.

30 "Enjoyable Recital Is Presented," *Mail-Star* (Halifax), 15 March 1951.

31 "Oratorio by Massed Choirs of Halifax Churches Wins Praise," *Daily Star*
    (Halifax), 11 April 1934; "Warm Praise Accorded Choirs for Oratorio," *Mail*
    (Halifax), 12 April 1934.

32 "Choral Society Performs before Capacity Audience," *Mail-Star* (Halifax),
    19 December 1952.

33 Donald B. Mackay to MacLean, 24 June 1970, Ross Nelson MacLean papers
    (privately held).

CHAPTER TWELVE

1 "Dr Kerr Heard in Second of Sermon Series," *Daily Star* (Halifax),
   11 February 1935.

2 PCOSD, 19th annual report, 1943, 25.

3 Isobel McLean to Laurence DeWolfe, 13 February 2003, PCOSD archives.

4 PCOSD, annual report, 1948.

5 PCOSD, Session meeting, minutes, 13 November 1951 (mfm at NSARM).

6 "Open Church Day-School," *Mail-Star* (Halifax), 9 October 1954; see also
   "Mission Unlimited," *Presbyterian Record*, May 1960, 10–11.

7 In Shelagh MacKenzie, ed., *Halifax Street Names: An Illustrated Guide* (Halifax,
   2002), 96.

8 Frank Lawson reflected on the school in one of his published sermons:
   "Where Did Our Children Miss Out in Religion?" *Christian World Pulpit*
   (London), 26 January 1956, 29–30.

9 "Acadian School Out after 1960," *Mail-Star* (Halifax), 14 April 1953.

10 PCOSD, annual report, 1962, 13.

11 Confidential information. The tradition continues: by the 1990s, one of the three destinations to which the Church School was forwarding its "mission" offerings was the Ward 5 Tenants' Hot Meal Program – Mulgrave Park.

12 "Presbyterian Church Plan for Christian Social Action," *Mail-Star* (Halifax), 25 May 1963.

13 For a critique of the Morris Project, see "Where a Community Project Has Gone Astray," *4th Estate* (Halifax), 12 June 1969.

14 This account is based on the CAS Halifax brochure "The Group Home … a Community Project."

15 PCOSD, Christian Education Committee meeting, minutes, 12 March 1969.

16 "No Answers from Churches," *Mail-Star* (Halifax), 28 February 1970. Walker was founding director of the Interreligious Foundation for Community Organization.

17 "Church Answers the Call of the Homeless," *Mail-Star* (Halifax), 21 March 1970.

18 "A Matter of Opinion: The Local Congregation May Be Obsolete," *Mail-Star* (Halifax), 21 March 1970.

19 See, generally, Janet Guildford, "Churches Provide Interfaith Housing in Halifax," *Presbyterian Record*, December 1976, 14–15.

20 PCOSD, annual report, 1975, 2.

21 PCOSD, annual report, 1976, 1.

22 PCOSD, annual report, 1977, 1–2.

23 Information from T.K. Guildford (elder, 1963).

CHAPTER THIRTEEN

1 On this subject generally, see Roberta Clare, "The Role of Women in the Preservation of The Presbyterian Church in Canada, 1921–28," in William Klempa, ed., *The Burning Bush and a Few Acres of Snow: The Presbyterian Contribution to Canadian Life and Culture* (Ottawa, 1994), 259–77.

2 "Women's Work Saved Presbyterian Church," *Morning Chronicle* (Halifax), 23 September 1926.

3 See John S. Moir, *Handbook for Canadian Presbyterians* (Toronto, 1996), 85.

4 PCOSD, 19th annual report, 1943, 30.

5 PCOSD, annual report, 1953, 16.

6 PCOSD, Trustees' meeting, minutes, 27 October 1932 (mfm at NSARM).

7 Kathleen Chisholm to Gordon Brown, 9 March 1992, PCOSD archives.

8 PCOSD, 44th annual report, 1968, 20.

9   See "Church of St David Volunteers as Hardy as the Lent Lunch Chowder,"
    Mail-Star (Halifax), 23 February 1994.

10 PCOSD, 19th annual report, 1943, 27.

11 PCOSD bulletin, 9 March 1952.

12 PCOSD, annual report, 1981, 22.

13 A snapshot of Auxiliary activity appears in the executive circular opening
    the 1985–86 season: SDA president and vice-president to women of Saint
    David's, 28 August 1985.

14 See president's retrospective in PCOSD, annual report, 2001, 25.

15 Unidentified Halifax newspaper clipping [26 February 1929?], W.J. Kane
    scrapbook, PCOSD archives.

16 PCOSD, 19th annual report, 1943, 23.

17 PCOSD Men's Club, "Annual Lobster Supper, 3 May 1950" (brochure).

18 Clerk of Session to A.D. Smith (secretary), 12 October 1960, PCOSD
    archives.

19 PCOSD, annual report, 1964, 20.

20 "Presbyterians Form Tennis Club," *Evening Mail* (Halifax), 20 June 1925.

21 "New Tuxis Group Is Formed in City" (undated Halifax newspaper
    clipping), in PYPS scrapbook, PCOSD archives.

22 PCOSD, 5th annual report, 1929, 41.

23 "Protestant Young People to Gather," *Daily Star* (Halifax), 22 November
    1933.

24 "New Kirk Club at St David's," *Mail-Star* (Halifax), 18 October 1958.

25 "Purdue University Conference," *Mail-Star* (Halifax), 13 July 1963; see also
    Pocklington, "St David's Presbyterian Church and North American Youth
    Assembly on Ecumenicity," *Mail-Star* (Halifax), 13 July 1963.

26 Paraphrasing PCOSD, annual report, 1965, 23.

CHAPTER FOURTEEN

1   Stuart Macdonald, "The Presbyterian Church in Canada and Extension
    Work, 1945–1985: Initial Findings," *Papers of the Canadian Society of
    Presbyterian History*, 2003, 48.

2   PCOSD, Session, minutes, 19 November 1945 (mfm at NSARM).

3   *Daily Star* (Halifax), 20 April, 25 May, 8 June, 22 June 1946.

4   "Says Smug Self-Interest a Blight on the Church," *Chronicle-Herald* (Halifax),
    10 December 1951.

5   Halifax and Lunenburg Presbytery, minutes, 7 October 1953 (mfm at
    NSARM).

6 Ibid., 11 May 1954.

7 "Millions Poured into New Church Building Program," *Mail-Star* (Halifax), 28 December 1957.

8 "To Form New Extension Board," *Mail-Star* (Halifax), 11 September 1954.

9 On this subject generally, see Harry Chapman, ed., *Mustard Seeds: The Journey of Dartmouth Churches* (Dartmouth, 1999).

10 Information from Rev. J.J. Edmiston, then clerk of Presbytery and afterwards interim moderator of Dartmouth.

11 Halifax and Lunenburg Presbytery, minutes, 11 September 1951 (mfm at NSARM).

12 PCOSD, annual report, 1953, 3.

13 PCOSD, annual report, 1964, 4.

14 See generally Dorothy J. Bell, "The Dream and the Reality: A History of Calvin Presbyterian Church, 1953–1979" (unpubl. ms., 1981).

15 PCOSD, annual report, 1953, 2.

16 The title of this section comes from the *Mail-Star* (Halifax), 10 April 1976.

17 Halifax and Lunenburg Presbytery, minutes, 13 September 1960 (mfm at NSARM). See also generally Chapman, *Mustard Seeds*, 83–4.

18 Halifax and Lunenburg Presbytery, minutes, 14 May 1968 (mfm at NSARM).

19 Over the years P.A. McDonald became a leading and highly influential figure in Presbytery and Synod, succeeding Saint David's Murdoch McLeod as clerk of Presbytery in 1970 and crowning his achievement in 2003 with election as moderator of the General Assembly.

20 PCOSD, Trustees' meeting, minutes, 3 November 1969 (mfm at NSARM).

21 Ibid., 14 January 1971. The same meeting decided that $8,500 be budgeted each year to cover the amortization of gifts to the local congregations over a period of five years.

22 PCOSD, annual report, 1971, 30.

23 Halifax and Lunenburg Presbytery, minutes, 17 May 1961 (mfm at NSARM).

24 In 1964 Presbytery decided to have the post of convener of church extension included in the committee on home missions (ibid., 12 May 1964).

25 Information from Rev. Iona MacLean.

26 "Roads to Be Shut as Church Goes Up," *Mail-Star* (Halifax), 31 March 1967.

27 Robert Paton Harvey, *Historic Sackville* (Halifax: Nimbus Publishing 2002), 91–2.

28 "Church Union at Wolfville," *Morning Chronicle* (Halifax), [ca. 6 November 1922].

29 Halifax and Lunenburg Presbytery, minutes, 27 January 1955 (mfm at NSARM).

30 PCOSD, 74th annual report, 1998, 8.

31 Available at http://hfxlnbg.pccatlantic.ca/tantallon/index_Page883.htm.

CHAPTER FIFTEEN

1 Halifax County Deeds, book 30, page 77 (mfm at NSARM). A further gift was made in 1798.

2 [G.A. Burbidge and M.D. Morrison], *Historical Sketches of St Andrew's Church, Halifax N.S., United Church of Canada* (Halifax, 1949), 11. It is now affixed to the Black family monument in Camp Hill Cemetery.

3 See, generally, Robert Tuck, *Churches of Nova Scotia* (Toronto, 2004), 65–70 ("The Stirling Churches: Neo-Gothic Debutantes").

4 "Yet Another Church," *Reporter* (Halifax), 30 May 1865.

5 Robert Tuck, *Gothic Dreams: The Life and Times of a Canadian Architect, William Critchlow Harris, 1854–1913* (Toronto, 1978), 18, 20.

6 For a detailed account, see "The New Wesleyan Church," *British Colonist* (Halifax), 9 November 1869.

7 "Remodelling of Old Grafton St Church Will Reveal Hidden Beauty," unidentified Halifax newspaper clipping, 2 December 1928, congregational scrapbook, PCOSD archives.

8 Enclosed in Lang to Warren, 2 December 1925, PCOSD archives.

9 See, generally, Susan Buggey and Garry D. Shutlak, "Stirling, David," in *Dictionary of Canadian Biography*, vol. 11, *1881 to 1890* (Toronto, 1982): 856–7.

10 The passive system was plugged off when a hot-water heating system was installed in the building. It was later found, of course, that there was stratification, with all the hot air collecting at the ceiling, and so the electric fans were installed in the 1970s.

   Because the plaster is not airtight, sound waves are able to travel through it. Some of the sound bounces off, but some penetrates through to the brick behind and is reflected back through the plaster and into the room. Some of the sound is absorbed by the wood lath and strapping, but a significant amount is reflected back into the church. This effect gives the building its acoustical character. The very slight difference in time between the reflection of the first sound from the plaster and the second wave from the brick gives the room a more lively feel. Various suggestions about insulating the exterior walls would result in the complete loss of this effect and result in an acoustically "dead" room.

11 "Special Treatment Given," unidentified Halifax newspaper clipping, June 1978, congregational scrapbook, PCOSD archives.

12 The longevity of shingles depends to a degree on their ability to cool from beneath in relation to air circulation in the attic.

13 There are traces of the old steps visible in the basement, under the present kitchen.

14 "The Romance of Early Methodism in Nova Scotia," *Halifax Herald*, 27 June 1896.

15 "Wesleyan Sabbath School," *Evening Reporter* (Halifax), 4 February 1865.

16 The door, now with glazed window, still stands at the head of the stairs behind the chancel leading from church to hall.

EPILOGUE

1 See generally Mark A. Noll, *What Happened to Christian Canada?* (Vancouver, 2007), and the sources cited in the notes to that publication.

2 On this subject generally, see Kevin Quast and John Vissers, eds., *Essays in Canadian Evangelical Renewal: Essays in Honour of Ian S. Rennie* (Markham, Ont., 1996), and, more recently, A. Donald MacLeod, *W. Stanford Reid: An Evangelical Calvinist in the Academy* (Montreal and Kingston, 2004). For the pre-Disruption PCC and the role of evangelicalism in the church union movement, see David W.R. Plaxton, "A Whole Gospel for a Whole Nation: The Cultures of Tradition and Change in the United Church of Canada and Its Antecedents, 1900–1950" (PhD thesis, Queen's University, 1997).

3 "New Presbyterian Moderator: 'Gospel Is Alternative to Despair,'" *Mail-Star* (Halifax), 13 June 1970.

4 Reginald W. Bibby, *Restless Churches: How Canada's Churches Can Contribute to the Emerging Religious Renaissance* (Toronto, 2004), 181.

5 David Hackett Fischer, *Historians' Fallacies: Toward a Logic of Historical Thought* (New York, 1970).

6 See http://www12.statcan.ca/english/census01/Products/Analytic/companion/rel/ns.cfm; and "Religions in Canada," available at http://www12.statcan.ca/english/census01/products/highlight/religion/Page/Halifax. For an overview of the 1991 evidence, see Reginald W. Bibby's research note: "Canada's Mythical Religious Mosaic: Some Census Findings," *Journal for the Scientific Study of Religion* 39 (June 2000): 235–9. Bibby's argument, afterwards confirmed by 2001 census evidence, is that the decline of historic denominationalism – Christian and Protestant alike – does not reflect the decline of Christianity. See also Bibby's *Restless Gods: The Renaissance of Religion in Canada* (Toronto, 2002).

7 "Disappearing Presbyterians," *Mail-Star* (Halifax), 11 October 2003.

8 Charles W. Brockwell Jr and Timothy J. Wengert, "Christian History in Ecumenical Perspective: Principles of Historiography," *Fides et Historia* 24 (1992): 40–53. See also Wengert and Brockwell, eds., *Telling the Churches' Stories: Ecumenical Perspectives on Writing Christian History* (Grand Rapids, Mich., 1995); and Peter Bush, "Consulting the Amateurs: What Academic Church Historians Can Learn from Congregational Historians," Canadian Society of Church History, *Historical Papers*, 2005, 111–29, and the sources cited there.

APPENDIX B

1 That is, the third (1902) edition of the Book of Forms.
2 The date on which Parliament's United Church of Canada Act came into force.
3 By July 1925 Clifford Torey had changed his mind and reverted to being an elder of St Andrew's United. He rejoined Saint David's in 1928 but was not elected elder until 1946.
4 Religious Congregations and Societies Act.

Index

Page numbers in italics refer to illustrations.